Emporialism

Emporialism

Department Store Fictions
and the
Politics of the Mediterranean

AMR KAMAL

Cover Credit: Ville de Paris, Bibliothèque Forney. Used with permission.

Published by State University of New York Press, Albany

© 2024 State University of New York

All rights reserved

Printed in the United States of America

No part of this book may be used or reproduced in any manner whatsoever without written permission. No part of this book may be stored in a retrieval system or transmitted in any form or by any means including electronic, electrostatic, magnetic tape, mechanical, photocopying, recording, or otherwise without the prior permission in writing of the publisher.

Links to third-party websites are provided as a convenience and for informational purposes only. They do not constitute an endorsement or an approval of any of the products, services, or opinions of the organization, companies, or individuals. SUNY Press bears no responsibility for the accuracy, legality, or content of a URL, the external website, or for that of subsequent websites.

For information, contact State University of New York Press, Albany, NY

www.sunypress.edu

Library of Congress Cataloging-in-Publication Data

Names: Kamal, Amr, 1976– author.
Title: Emporialism : department store fictions and the politics of the Mediterranean / Amr Kamal.
Description: Albany : State University of New York Press, 2024. | Includes bibliographical references and index.
Identifiers: LCCN 2024003652 | ISBN 9781438499475 (hardcover) | ISBN 9781438499482 (ebook) | ISBN 9781438499468 (paperback)
Subjects: LCSH: French literature—History and criticism. | Egyptian literature—History and criticism. | Department stores in literature. | Consumption (Economics) in literature. | Imperialism in literature. | Department stores—France—History. | Department stores—Egypt—History. | National characteristics, French in literature. | National characteristics, Egyptian in literature. | Literature and society—Mediterranean Region. | LCGFT: Literary criticism.
Classification: LCC PQ145.1.D36 K36 2024 | DDC 843/.90991822—dc23/eng/20240525
LC record available at https://lccn.loc.gov/2024003652

For my parents

Contents

List of Illustrations	ix
Notes on Translation and Transliteration	xiii
Acknowledgments	xv
Introduction	1
1 Emporialism in the Footsteps of Empire	27
2 Emporialism at the Crossroads of Empires	75
3 An Empire of Values: The Emporium in Zola's *Au Bonheur des dames*	107
4 Modeling Empire: Emporialism and Transnational Feminism	149
5 Jacqueline Kahanoff's *Jacob's Ladder*: Between Emporialism and Levantinism	187
6 Neo-Emporialism and the Politics of Memory	237
Notes	275
Works Cited	303
Index	339

Illustrations

1.1	Advertisement for rugs, Maison à la Place Clichy, 1898	21
1.2	"The Queen of Printemps," Printemps catalogue, 1910	22
1.3	Catalogue cover, Le Bon Marché, 1913	23
1.4	Catalogue cover, La Samaritaine, 1932	23
1.5	Catalogue cover, La Samaritaine, 1938	23
1.6	Catalogue cover, Printemps, 1939	23
1.7	Passage du Caire, Paris	24
1.8	Poster of Wanamaker's exhibition on Napoleon, circa 1900	24
1.9	A phalanstery, Charles Fourier	24
1.10	"Two Creators: One Work," La Samaritaine, 1929	24
1.11	Harem, catalogue Le Bon Marché, front cover, 1873	25
1.12	Trade caravans, catalogue Le Bon Marché, back cover, 1873	25
1.13	Rug collection, Gerôme's trip to Egypt, "L'Orient offert par les Grands Magasins du Bon Marché," catalogue Le Bon Marché, 1913	25
1.14	Dress style "Armenian," catalogue Le Bon Marché, 1878	26
1.15	Dress style "Muslim," catalogue Le Bon Marché, 1878	26
1.16	Interior hall, Le Bon Marché, 1904	26

x | Illustrations

1.17	Workshop at Le Bon Marché, 1904	26
2.1	Caricature of Ferdinand de Lesseps parting the Isthmus of Suez	69
2.2	"Egypt Carrying Light to Asia," Auguste Bartholdi	69
2.3	Interior hall of Galeries Lafayette, 1914	69
2.4	Interior hall of Sednaoui, 2023	69
2.5	Omar Effendi department store, exterior, 2013	70
2.6	Le Bon Marché Succursale de Vichy, exterior, catalogue Le Bon Marché, circa 1925	70
2.7	Calendar, Grand Magasin Paschal and Cie, 1895	70
2.8	Prince Farouk opposite a toy advertisement, Le Bon Marché, 1929	71
2.9	"This dress is incomplete," cartoon, *al-Lata'if al-Musawwara*, 1922	71
2.10	Women in public spaces, cartoon, *al-Lata'if al-Musawwara*, 1917	71
2.11	"Cairo the Gay City on the Nile as It Is Today," cartoon, *al-Lata'if al-Musawwara*, 1919	72
2.12	"The progress of fashion over half a century," *Rose al-Yusef*, 1927	72
2.13	"Yesterday and Tomorrow," cartoon, *al-Lata'if al-Musawwara*, 1919	72
2.14	Sednaoui bilingual catalogue, front cover, Winter 1927/28	72
2.15	Sednaoui bilingual catalogue, inside cover, Winter 1928/29	72
2.16	Egyptian humor, *Images*, 1929	73
2.17	"L'Été chez Sednaoui," advertisement, Sednaoui, *La Femme nouvelle*, Summer 1950	74
3.1	Exterior of Le Bon Marché, catalogue Nouveautés Hiver 1879–1880	106

3.2	Inside map of *Au Bonheur des dames*, drawn by Zola	106
3.3	Street map for *Au Bonheur des dames*, drawn by Zola	106
4.1	Magazine cover, *L'Egyptienne*, 1932	146
4.2	Nahdat Misr, *Egypt's Awakening*, Mahmud Mukhtar, *L'Egyptienne*, June 1928	146
4.3	A play at a kermess, *L'Egyptienne*, March 1927	146
4.4	A play at a kermess, performers in costumes, *L'Egyptienne*, March 1927	147
4.5	Avril de Saint Croix pensive at her desk	147
4.6	Juliette Adam pensive at her desk, *L'Egyptienne*, February 1925	147
4.7	Huda Shaarawi pensive at her desk	147
4.8	Huda Shaarawi, standing portrait, *L'Egyptienne*, June 1926	148
4.9	Julie Siegfried, standing portrait	148
4.10	Kamala Nehru, *L'Egyptienne*, July 1932	148
4.11	Jehan d'Ivray, *L'Egyptienne*, March–April 1928	148
4.12	Ehsan al-Koussi, *L'Egyptienne*, May 1929	148
4.13	Madame Rouchdi Pacha, *L'Egyptienne*, March 1926	148
6.1	Advertisement, Chemla Frères, *L'Egyptienne*, February 1927	235
6.2	Façade Bazar Hotel de Ville Paris, 2022	235
6.3	Map of Alexandria, 1905	236

Notes on Translation and Transliteration

I have followed the system of transliteration used by the *International Journal of Middle East Studies*. In a few cases, I deviated from this system to respect the variations and nuances particular to the languages or dialects of the documents. For instance, the Egyptian letter *jim* has been rendered into a G if necessary. I used accepted English spellings for well-known place names and people, such as "Zaki," "Qasim Amin," "Cairo," and "Suez." For the reader's convenience, I transcribed "Shaʿrawi," as "Shaarawi." When quoting a text, I respected the spelling of names given by the authors, especially in the notes, where the text is provided in the original language. For instance, names like "Shaarawi" or "Nabarawi" could be found written as Charaoui or Nabaraoui in French texts. A name like "Cicurel" could be found transcribed as "Sikourel" depending on the original language of the document or the translator's preference.

All translations, unless otherwise indicated, are my own. Any modifications or clarifications needed were added in brackets.

Acknowledgments

Writing from the Emporium

Few years ago, I would not have imagined that I would make the final edits of this manuscript at the Graduate Center in New York, formerly known as the Altman department store. Somehow the narrative of this book remains entwined with that of an emporium, in this case one that tells another story—that of New York City.

This book, spanning four continents, bears the voices of many individuals I met along this journey. First, I am thankful to my family for their constant support. I was equally lucky to have an exceptional dissertation committee at the University of Michigan, Ann Arbor: Michèle Hannoosh, Anton Shammas, Carol Bardenstein, Jarrod Hayes, Frieda Ekotto, and Mona Domosh. Their generous support as scholars, advisers, and colleagues directed me along the way. I am truly indebted to Michèle Hannoosh for all her support and feedback over the years.

I thank Todd Shepard, to whom I owe the title of the book, and Vanessa Valdés, who believed in this project. Nancy Reynolds, Samuel Weber, Beth Baron, Bettina Lerner, Maxime Blanchard, Ammiel Alcalay, and the late R. Sharia Taleghani generously provided insightful and thorough comments during the manuscript workshop at the Graduate Center. Sania Lanfranchi Sharawi imparted her memories and knowledge of Huda Shaarawi's journey. Deborah A. Starr shared her invaluable collection of Jacqueline Kahanoff's writings. I also thank Frédéric Lagrange, Franck Mermier, Delphine Pagès El-Karoui, Alessandro Guetta, Méropi Anastassiadou, Dina al-Kassem, Kathryn Babayan, Mary D. Lewis, Kader Konuk, Artemis Leontis, Yopie Prins, Daniel Herwitz, Ruth Tsoffar, and Karla Mallette.

I am grateful to Patrick Tonks for his patient and rigorous editing of the initial manuscript. I cannot forget my colleagues, friends, and students who helped throughout the project. Christophe Bertossi, Emma Chub, Claire Dauge-Roth, Tamara Maatouk, Mariam Elhaies, Ahmed el-Ghoul, Zeinab Zohny, Malak Kamal, Maria Hadjipolicarpou, Nikolas Kakkoufa, Maysa Khedr, Efrat Bloom, Başak Çandar, Christopher Meade, Olga Greco, Amin Moghadam, Vincent Sallé, Marwa Sharafeldin, Ramon Stern, Corine Tachtiris, Joseph Viscomi, Ido Amnon, Genevieve Creedon, Shannon Winston, Maayan Eitan, William Gertz Runyan, Rostom Mesli, and William Stroebel.

Support for this project was provided by a PSC-CUNY Award, jointly funded by the Professional Staff Congress and the City University of New York. This work would not have been possible without the generous support of the Institute for the Humanities, the Center for European Studies, and the Institute for Women and Gender at the University of Michigan, Ann Arbor; the Lurcy Foundation; the Paris Program in Critical Theory, CERMOM, CUNY Faculty Forum Publication Workshop; the Rifkind Center at the City College of New York; and the Department of Comparative Literature, as well as the Middle East and Middle East American Center, at the Graduate Center.

Finally, I am thankful for the numerous archives and archivists who helped me complete this project: Shahira al-Sawi, Marie-Delphine Martellière, Françoise Meyniel, Maha Abdel Moneim, Ola Essam, and Tine Lavent. The Centre d'Études Alexandrines, Bibliothèque Forney; Bibliothèque Nationale de France; La Ville de Paris; Musée Bartholdi; Emili Vilà Museum; the archives of Galeries Lafayette in Paris; Dar al-Kutub; the Women and Memory Forum in Cairo; the Netherlands-Flemish Institute in Cairo; and the Rare Books and Special Collections at the American University in Cairo.

Parts of the introduction, chapter 5, and chapter 6 were previously published as an article under the title "Ghostly Labor: Ethnic-Classism in the Levantine Prism of Jacqueline Kahanoff's *Jacob's Ladder*," *International Journal of Middle East Studies*, vol. 49, no. 2 (2017): 255–75.

Introduction

Describing a toy department store, French poet Charles Baudelaire writes: "There is in a [toy] department store an extraordinary gaiety that makes it preferable to any beautiful bourgeois apartment. Doesn't one find in it an entire life made in miniature, even more colorful, cleaned, and polished? One can see gardens, theatres, beautiful outfits, eyes like diamond, cheeks ignited by makeup, charming lace, cars, stables, drunkards, charlatans, bankers, comedians, clowns . . . kitchens and entire well-disciplined armies with the cavalry and artillery."[1] For Baudelaire, the toy department store represents a cosmology: an entire world in miniature along with its respective "morale," or value regimes. The store comprises miniature spaces (gardens and theaters) as well as figurines reflecting the diverse human geography of the city. The shelves display a plethora of social types who embody different moral and ethical values: drunkards, bankers, comedians, and soldiers. In comparing the store to a cityscape and a bourgeois apartment, Baudelaire underscores the hybrid nature of the department store. The emporium collapses the distance between the private and public spheres, between the household and the marketplace, between the market and the city, and finally between the market, the theater, and the larger empire. In his description, the store features as a space of excess—"more colorful and brilliant than life itself."[2] For him, such exaggerated theatricality is a quintessential and euphoric element of modernity. Baudelaire alludes to this fact in *The Painter of Modern Life*, where he also characterizes modernity as being "livelier than life itself."[3] By reiterating (almost verbatim) the sentence in both texts, Baudelaire draws attention to the avid aspirations of modernity and, by extension, the modern department store, which aims to simulate and contain a utopian plenitude and material abundance. More so, by mirroring the empire with its miniature "well-disciplined armies" and populations, the emporium merges its own commercial utopianism with the expansionist imaginary of imperialism. The emporium echoes the imperial promise of an ideal world by exhibiting, controlling, and cataloguing people and things.

This book examines the phenomenon of emporialism, or the convergence between the spaces and imaginaries of empires and emporia in the context of a modern Mediterranean divided among the British, French, and Ottoman empires. By "emporia," I refer to department stores as part of a commercial network that emerged during the second half of the nineteenth century in synchrony with late imperialism. My study focuses on nineteenth-century French and Egyptian department stores after the Suez Canal project to show that empire and its commercial heterotopia, emporia, are two sides of the same coin. As I argue, born simultaneously, the modern empire and the emporium articulate the ambition of expansion and appropriation, of rearranging the world order into new hierarchies of gender, races, classes, and objects. Emporialism was most often organized around the celebration, or the rejection, of a phantasmatic colonial—typically Orientalist—fantasy.

The book explores emporialism as a set of phenomenological experiences, discursive and social praxes, and mechanisms of control and negotiations of agency, stemming from the intersection of modernity, colonialism, and mass consumption. I aim to show the regimes of value, social praxes, class, race, and gender relations that these embody, expose, and reimagine. Emporialism operates on various scales at once, with one hand fashioning global connections and another fashioning the subject's body, aspirations, and intimate desires. In the Franco-Egyptian context, department stores were part of multivalent social and political connections. They participated in the construction of Mediterranean and national memory as well as other interrelated factors, such as French and Egyptian national identity and the image of the middle class in France and Egypt from the nineteenth century to the present.

In what follows, I pursue an analysis of the space of emporia, their iconographic and literary representations, and their relation to empire across the Mediterranean. My study focuses on the major department stores in Paris, Cairo, and Alexandria, which frequently featured in advertisement, fictions, biographies, and sometimes movies. These include Le Bon Marché, Printemps, La Samaritaine, Galeries Lafayette, and Bazar de l'Hôtel de Ville from France. The list of stores also includes Cicurel, Sednaoui, Chemla, and

Omar Effendi from Egypt. To analyze the cultural context and narratives surrounding these emporia, I draw on secondary texts and evidence from the stores and their literary and visual representations. I concentrate on the major literary works that refer to department stores in French, Arabic, English, and sometimes Hebrew. I consult various primary archival materials related to the emporium—such as caricatures, catalogues, and advertisements from the nineteenth and early twentieth centuries—all of which reveal the early iconography of emporialism. The first two chapters contextualize the phenomenon of emporialism in France and Egypt through print media and biographies. The subsequent chapters offer a literary analysis of French and Egyptian fictional and autobiographical texts on department stores. I examine writers from Egypt, France, and Israel/Palestine—Émile Zola (chapter 3), Huda Shaarawi (chapter 4), Jacqueline Kahanoff (chapter 5), Latifa al-Zayyat, Out-el-Kouloub, Paula Jacques, Ilios Yannakakis, Robert Solé, and Ronit Matalon, and others (chapter 6)—for whom emporialism serves to interrogate personal, communitarian, and national identity.

Emporialism encompasses the dynamics of consumer culture spanning the late stage of imperialism up to decolonization (1850–1960): an epoch that paved the way for the global present. Emporialism melded the objectives and discourse of the colonial civilizing mission with those of industrial and commercial utopianism. Because of their expansive network across the world, nineteenth-century department stores existed and mediated between several political, economic, and social regimes of value. In his study of Marx's *Capital*, David Harvey uses the term "value regimes" to denote the regional geographical and geopolitical variations that permit the global flow of capital from one place to another. He underscores primarily the differential costs of labor on which the circulation of capital depends (Harvey *Marx*, 151–74). I extend the notion of "value regimes" to encompass not only the costs of production and consumption, which enable the flow of capital, but also the social, civic, political, scientific, and moral regimes, or systems of values, which the strategies of emporialism introduced, modified, or displaced to establish the shared ethos and character of a proto-global middle class. I follow in the footsteps of Arjun Appadurai to explore the multivalence of value regimes as "moral and cosmological" frameworks "within which commoditization is restricted and hedged" (Appadurai 25). I examine how the cosmos of the stores and their celebrated memory (cosmographies) reflect, reinforce, alter, or contest larger social practices and political regimes of values. In this case, *value regimes* refers to larger political systems and ideologies and to the various aspects of economic and cultural capital, such as questions of taste, aesthetics, and academic influence, as Pierre Bourdieu (*Distinction*) points out in his studies of cultural and symbolic capital. They also include questions of the imaginary, memory, writing, and modes of reading. All of these shape the process of social and cultural formation.

In *The Communist Manifesto*, Marx and Engels expose the multilateral connections between literature, consumerism, cosmopolitanism, and imperialism, which I seek to analyze:

> The bourgeoisie has through its exploitation of the world-market given a cosmopolitan character to production and consumption in every country... In place of the old wants, satisfied by the productions of the country, we find new wants, requiring for their satisfaction the products of distant lands and climes. In place of the old local and national seclusion and self-sufficiency, we have intercourse in every direction, universal inter-dependence of nations. And as in material, so also in intellectual production. The intellectual creations of individual nations become common property... *and from the numerous national and local literatures, there arises world literature.* It compels all nations, on pain of extinction, to adopt the bourgeois mode of production; it compels them to introduce what it calls civilisation into their midst, i.e., to become bourgeois themselves. In one word, it creates a world after its own image. (64–65; emphasis added)

In its shaping of tastes and needs, capitalism produces simultaneously new spaces of consumption and a common imaginary leading to the rise of a "world literature," shaped by market forces (77). In that sense, literature cannot be reduced to a historical document or an aesthetic product. As Saree Makdisi argues, the birth of modern literary genres should be examined as part and parcel of the development of capitalism and imperialism.[4] Such controversial and intimate complicity between capitalism and literature remains at the heart of debates in literary studies, as I elaborate later. The nineteenth-century emporium and its later rendition in fiction and various media lie at the crux of this connection. Literature, films, and myths representing the department store embody the emporium's ethos and aesthetics. This relationship is not unilateral, however. Projecting at once the images of a bourgeois household, a marketplace, a nation-state, and empire, the site of the emporium and its representations have the potential to expose and problematize the interplay of all these elements that shaped our present.

Nineteenth-century department stores present a paradox in relation to value. Although department stores were some of the first establishments to introduce fixed and clearly displayed prices, they were sites in which several social and economic values confronted each other. For consumers, entering the nineteenth-century department store entailed a complex encounter and negotiation with various value regimes beyond the price label of the displayed product. It involved reorienting the sensorial experience and redefining spatial practices, class, race, gender relations, aesthetics, national identity, and communal belonging. Through its efforts to popularize an ideal taste and promote mass consumption, the emporium documented and participated in a moment of violence in the creation of national, social, cultural, and gender distinctions. Upholding the ethos of emporialism, the department store fostered a multicultural social model born at the intersection of different economic, social, and political currents sustained and negotiated inside and outside the store. In his work on cosmopolitanism, Elijah Anderson designates the marketplace as one of the spaces that produces a cosmopolitan canopy and the social conditions, allowing for a pluralist lifestyle and diverse encounters under the rubric of economic exchange. In conversation with this concept, I use the word *agora-cosmopolitanism* to highlight the civic lesson imparted by emporialism. This modern form of market cosmopolitanism, which required the temporary suppression of conflicts for finalizing sales transactions, was partially informed by industrial utopianism. As the following chapters show, in practice, agora-cosmopolitanism often challenged the ethos of emporialism.

In fact, the history of cosmopolitanism as a civic model has a long historical connection to the marketplace, going back to the teachings of Diogenes (404–323 BCE) and the Cynic tradition. Diogenes himself set his place at the heart of the agora (the market), as a strategic site from which he underscored his disdain for material goods (Nussbaum, *Cosmopolitan* 67). When asked where he was from, Diogenes replied "Κοσμοπολίτης' ἔφη" [I am a citizen of the world] (Laertius 65). For him, cosmopolitanism meant to belong everywhere with no attributable origins. In her assessment of this moment, Martha Nussbaum explains that Diogenes's positionality "suggests . . . the possibility of a politics, or a moral approach to politics, that focuses on the humanity we share rather than the marks of local origin, status, class, and gender that divide us. It is a first step . . . [toward] Kant's vision of a cosmopolitan politics that will join all humanity under laws given not by convention and class but by free moral choice" (*Cosmopolitan* 1–2). For the Cynics, cosmopolitanism, Nussbaum argues, was understood as a form of conscious "exile" ("Kant" 11). What remains intriguing in this anecdote is the entwined and intimate connection between capitalism and cosmopolitanism. From its initial conception at the marketplace, cosmopolitanism takes on one of the main attributes of capital, that of claiming no origins. Akin to the cosmopolitan Diogenes, who made the marketplace his makeshift residence, the ideal of capital is to remain in permanent circulation and displacement. "Utopian" and constantly in translation—in the dual sense of the word as movement and creative reiteration in various forms—capital paradoxically belongs everywhere and nowhere at once (Venuti 469, 485). Diogenes's words mark the double aspect of cosmopolitanism and the constant tension between consumption, the market, and civic society. In another moment, Diogenes suggests that an able person who could participate in the body politic is one who could travel freely, ironically, just like capital does.

As the rhetoric of the modern marketplace, emporialism encompasses these multivalent meanings of cosmopolitanism. Modern imperialism as a capitalist venture relied on mass consumption and the creation of new markets. Nineteenth-century department stores translated the worldview of imperialism, along with its perpetual promise of adventure and acquisition, into the quotidian phenomenological experience of shopping at the center of imperial and colonial metropolises. The emporium manipulated the economies of scale and iconographies of consumption by adapting its image to various levels and maps, ranging from the individual to the global.[5] In so doing, the emporium mirrored and tightened its grasp over the shopper's body, the spaces of the household, the city, the nation-state, and the empire. Nineteenth-century department stores existed at the crux of multiple overlapping and competing political, economic, and social "value regimes": colonial and postcolonial, traditional and modern, imperial/colonial and postcolonial. Emporialism translated the cosmos and hierarchies of empire into a set of social, spatial, and discursive praxes articulated through the emporium's urban settings, decoration, promotional materials, marketing campaigns, and business management. In this context, the multiscalar power of the emporium can be gauged as a space of entrapment and empowerment simultaneously. As Neil Smith suggests, "scale can be constructed as a means of constraint and exclusion, a means of imposing identity, but a politics of scale can also become a weapon of expansion and inclusion, a means of enlarging identities" ("Homeless/Global" 114).

By monitoring the gates of social inclusion and exclusion, emporialism prepared the stage for the creation of what is currently known as global middle-class culture. In his study of the English middle class, Simon Gunn posits: "Arguably the real myth of the middle class is not so much its invention as a product of political discourse, as the idea of its immaculate conception, emerging sui generis in late-eighteenth century England and developing in splendid isolation within the confines of the nation-state to stand as the exemplar of a modern society and modern polity for the rest of the world" (70).[6] Gunn demystifies the origins of the middle class, attributing it instead to a set of material conditions and transnational relations. By the same token, the department store, one of the key institutions for shaping the middle class around the world, did not emerge "sui generis . . . in splendid isolation within the confines of the nation-state" (70). Rather, the stores were an outcome of the enmeshment of local and global circumstances, as well as constant transnational exchange, which gave form to this institution, its workers, and its customers. As Bruno Latour affirms, the myth of modernity relies on a double gesture, a simultaneous process of "conjoined" birth and dissimulation of ambiguous origins (13). Modernity hinges on an artificial caesura that frames the modern moment as unique and pure, distinct from a hybrid complex past. But such is the story of the middle class, the emporium, and the modern Mediterranean.

To understand this web of transnational connections in the Mediterranean context, I take a significantly long timeframe to trace how the spaces and the imaginary of these sites, along with the discursive practices around them, evolved across different epochs and spaces. The narrative spans French and British control of the Suez Canal and its nationalization after Egyptian independence (1859–1956). The urban and commercial geographies I examine begin with a Mediterranean project envisioned by French philosopher and utopian Claude Henri de Saint-Simon (1760–1825), who sought to unite the entire sea via a network of trade and transport (*Oeuvres complètes*). Although department stores were not a calculated factor in the official French project, they became cogs in the larger commercial network connecting the various modern urban centers. Saint-Simonianism started as a utopian industrialist ideology claiming to establish social justice and abolish differences through collaborative large-scale projects. His followers, mainly entrepreneurs and engineers who rose to rank in the French government during the Second Empire (1852–1870), translated their worldview into a series of commercial and urban plans, including the Haussmannization of Paris, the universal exhibitions, and a Mediterranean project, centering on the construction of the Suez Canal. The nationalization of the canal in 1956, four years after Egyptian independence, could be considered another turning political and imaginary point in the history of emporialism. In the Egyptian context, the postcolonial moment often entwined the nationalization of the canal with the subsequent nationalization of business enterprises, including department stores. It also marked the departure of the various Mediterranean communities from Egypt.

French and Egyptian department stores present a complex and multilayered example reflecting the phenomenon of emporialism. They expose a Mediterranean web of relations that exceeds the limits of the nation-state: transnational, interimperial, transregional, and translocal. They shed light on the various intermediary agents that exist in these regimes of values. Social connections established in and around the department stores complicate the typical dialectics of the Marxist teleological framework of class struggle or the postcolonial binary of colonizer and colonized. In France, the stores drew inspiration from the aesthetics of the Oriental bazaar and stood for the exotic and the decadent. On the other side of the sea, Egypt was situated at the crux of three empires at once: Ottoman, British, and French. In contrast to their Parisian counterparts, Egyptian emporia stressed their strong affinity with French culture. Yet most of the Egyptian *grands magasins*, established between the 1880s and 1930s, were not French businesses; they were mainly built by Jewish and Levantine immigrants who spoke French, held European passports, and hired Francophone Egyptian, Syrian, Lebanese, Italian, and Greek employees. The stores sought to emulate Parisian sites, and customers and employees communicated in French, in an Arabic-speaking country simultaneously ruled by the Ottomans and the British. The stores were showcased as French, but they represented a much richer Mediterranean cultural and human geography that exceeded French culture. Ironically, these stores outdid their authentic French competitors in Egypt, such as Galeries Lafayette, Printemps, and Le Bon Marché.

To capture the role of nineteenth-century French and Egyptian department stores in the larger context of the Mediterranean history, I rely on a multiplanar reading. By *multiplanar reading*, I mean a multidimensional investigation that attends to the various meanings of the physical space of the department store and its subsequent representation, uses, and receptions in literature and visual culture. Just as the context and significance of the stores are not fixed across time and space, neither are the dynamics of emporialism. I aim to contextualize how the actual department stores and their subsequent renditions in literature are enmeshed in a complex set of overlapping intersecting and intersectional maps. These maps are constantly evolving. They produce and actively engage with a multitude of value regimes across times and contexts. Each situation deserves to be examined as part of an interconnected but different plane of analysis relative to the value regimes with which it negotiates, that is, the discursive and power currents in which the emporia and their fictive representations are entangled.

Emporialism as Schemata of Urban Memory

Despite—perhaps because of—their current decline as shopping spaces, department stores are still the object of writing and rewriting of memory. For many French and Egyptian writers, they come to embody an imperial or colonial past along with its formative racial, gender, and social relations. As I argue, department stores in literature cross the threshold from being a marketplace or a social space to develop their own mythology in literature and cinema. In the Mediterranean Franco-Egyptian context, the intertwined discourse of empire and emporia make the site of the department store a rich literary motif for probing the different factors underlying national identity, cosmopolitanism, and social relations. By creating their own literary renditions, what I call cosmographies of the department store, several authors used the department store to document the history of their nations or that of the Mediterranean basin divided among three empires. I use the word *cosmography* to describe how authors reconstruct that worldview in their writings. These writings reveal the ambiguity of emporialism as a mechanism of power, whereby empire and emporia are set as competing images: reflecting and denouncing each other.

Looking at the cosmos created by the department stores (cosmologies) and their cosmographies (writers' renditions) unpacks the underlying connections between the emporium and its later literary representations across time. The various texts in the book center on the memory of consumption, in contrast to actual practices of consumption. They reveal how the memory of consumption operates as an independent cultural product to be consumed by readers at large, wherein memory of consumption reenters the political economy as a fetishized good with proper values and meanings. Circulating as cultural capital, it builds its own set of intersectional connections and relations. Precisely, memory of consumption serves as a superstructure to reorder social relations of production through the theme of a nostalgic return to a bygone past mediated by material culture and consumerism. The narratives and anecdotes about the emporium complicate our notions of material culture, which for a long time were perceived along the binary of gift versus commodity. However, the narratives do not fit either category. Yet they play a central role in the process of economic transaction and the consolidation of social networks (Myers 5–8).[7]

Despite the passage of time, to a certain extent modern shopping still relies on emporialism: namely, the colonial desire for discovery and pursuit of unexpected bargains, as well as the consumers' aptitude for scanning, classifying, and locating objects. Such an imaginary remains relatively operative in contemporary global culture, beyond the context of department stores. Consider the name of the world's largest shopping websites. Amazon (Jeff Bezos intended to call his company Cadabra) and AliBaba, the virtual equivalent of nineteenth-century emporia, still keep faint traces of an allotopic (other places) imperialist imaginary. The former evokes the unruly colonial jungle, the latter *The Thousand and One Nights*. Both names conjure the image of the European explorer. Both reiterate an imperialist panoptic worldview, paired with the ambition to locate and access the fortunes of distant lands, all with a click of a button.[8]

Examining nineteenth-century emporialism excavates the roots of the social connections and histories that emporialism, and later globalism, sought to suppress or produce. Although emporialism thrived in the nineteenth-century emporium, it still operates on several levels in present-day social relations. Creating an interior setting that maintains an illusion of being out of time and place, topographies of consumption represent the tip of an iceberg towering over a set of convoluted and multilayered social maps fraught with desire and tension. The simple act of uttering the name of a department store automatically activates a set of ethnic, class, and gender images strongly associated with its commercial brand and targeted clientele. Each name signals a distinctive network of relations: Barneys (New York elite), Le Bon Marché (French urban elite), Walmart (American working class), Target (American Millennials), Tati (ethnic working class and migrants in France), Galeries Lafayette (tourists), Monoprix (French post–World War II generation and now Millennials), Cicurel (Egyptian colonial elites), or Omar Effendi (Egyptian bureaucrats and later socialist Egypt's working class).

Contemporary French culture still harbors many idiomatic expressions: remnants of emporialism and its Orientalist, intersectional allotopic, "allochronic" cross-Mediterranean, commercial imaginary.[9] To give two examples: the expression "Je ne suis pas [un] marchand de tapis" [I am not a carpet seller] implies that the speaker is not a haggler, in other words an

Oriental, but a man with a European work ethic, a man of his word. "C'est le bazar!" [This is a bazaar!] portrays a state of loss of control and disorder. Both expressions bring back the specter of the phantasmatic imperial past of the department store—with its expansive ethnographic classifications and obsession with order and control—onto the current map of existing social and economic relations. They highlight two opposing regimes of value. They effect an imaginary divide between an idealized European work ethos and an inferior Oriental counterpart. To lose control is to devolve into an Oriental or primitive state of being, just like Zola's Paris under the impact of the *grand magasin* (see chapter 3). Perhaps the most interesting expression that encapsulates contemporary French urban and cultural geography is "l'arabe du coin," which refers to convenience stores located on nearly every street corner in Paris, often managed by Arab immigrants: ubiquitous shops, almost invisible, but always available for last-minute and after-hours errands. These shops have become part of what Ulrich Beck calls the "banal cosmopolitanism" of the marketplace: a form of passive multicultural coexistence that is not guided or motivated by an intentional questioning of civic relations. It is more of a social veneer, a "cosmopolitanization," than an ethical cosmopolitanism (1–14; 40–47).[10]

By the same token, just like the department store and its Others, the contemporary imaginary is still haunted by the racial imaginary of emporialism, whereby the images of certain professions and commercial systems are reified into clichés of race, gender, or sexuality: the nail salon worker, the dry cleaner, the doctor, the lawyer, the hair stylist, the restaurant chef, or the fashion designer. These examples trigger automatic racialized and gendered images crafted by emporialism, which become central to shaping actual economic and social relations. They are products of an intersectional slippage, or a gendered pairing of ethnicity and class: a process I call *ethno-classism*. They are cemented together not only by a repertoire of visual references and narratives but also by the original material conditions that made some of these networks possible in the first place: a situation that blurs the boundaries between the real and imaginary, where stereotypes about certain ethnic groups paradoxically limit their access to certain economic fields and facilitate their success in specific professions. In such conditions, embracing the stereotype and integrating via emporialism becomes a form of survival: a partial tactical empowerment out of an economic and social necessity. This is one of the many ways the imaginary translates into relations of production. In using the term *ethno-classism*, I seek to explore this gender, class, and racial dynamic in relation to broader economic and social factors, stressing in particular the role of the working class and its representation in the construction of a cosmopolitan and elitist image. Moreover, I seek to move beyond the binary scope of metropole and colony to account for the interplay of several imperial and cultural spheres of influence and for the conscious role of individuals in this process.

To examine the significance of emporialism playing over various scales and maps, I would like to rethink the history of the department store as part of a double schema: urban and memory. By *urban schema*, I mean an institution that came to symbolize modernity and was reproduced around the world for that purpose. In using the term *memory schema*, I rely on Astrid Erll's definition of the term, in which she posits that the recollection of any event refers to a chain of "narratives, images and myths circulating in a memory culture." This imaginary produces a schema, or an initial imaginary and an organizing structure, for the subsequent reconfiguration of this memory in addition to that of similar events (Erll 110–11). Precisely in exploring the memory of the emporium, I examine the connection between the production and circulation of these schemata and that of capital. Emile Zola's novel *Au bonheur des dames* (1883) is a case in point. Zola's depiction of the department store became a schema, or prototype, for subsequent references to the emporium. These include literary and media productions around the world, academic scholarship across disciplines, accounts of collective memory, and even the store's setting itself. For instance, in 2022, Le Bon Marché sponsored an immersive theatrical performance of Zola's novel inside the store.[11] The stores and their literary and theatrical representations operate in different contexts. Each work, or its interpretation, encompasses its own regime of values and engenders new meanings to the emporium.

The field of translation studies could shed light on the dynamics between the production and practice of space and the development of literature across empires. Recent works by Shaden Tageldin, Rebecca Johnson, Maya I. Kesrouany, and Samah Selim reassess the role of translation and adaptation of European literature in Egypt and the Levant in the late nineteenth and early twentieth centuries. Such translations, or "mistranslations," did not merely copy a Western European repertoire of literatures and ideas; rather, they represented a new regime of values that constructed its own version of modernity (Johnson 2). I want to rethink the spread of symbolic sites of capital and modernity in the same manner: as a process of translation, adaptation, or mistranslation, of both the semiotics of space and capital, which constructed its unique language of modernity in every locale. In fact, the circulation and manifestation of modern capital embody the various meanings of the word *translation*, denoting a movement from one place to another and a transformation. Thinking of department stores as urban schemata of modernity allows one to examine the emporium as a space in translation situated at the intersection of imperialism, urban planning, architecture, financial and cultural capital, literature, and memory.[12] My aim is not to produce a structural, undifferentiated reading of these spaces as the symptomatic progress of capital around the world, nor as a colonial/postcolonial consequence around the Mediterranean basin. Instead, I aim to look at these spaces and their related representations as part of a complex dynamic: a multidimensional assemblage, in a process of rhizomatic, multidirectional, intersectional formation, that produces its own rhetoric and grammar of spatial relations and modernity. Department stores are a consumerist, capitalist, nineteenth-century phenomenon that relies on exogenous and endogenous socioeconomic and cultural resources and conditions. Urban sites of modernity accrue an initial symbolic meaning through their aggregate reconstruction as a map that activates other global, "borrowed" memories of empire. On the other hand, they produce unique social praxes and meaning once immersed in a specific local context. Architectural design and the production of space do not operate in a vacuum; they never begin on a blank slate. As a system of signs, architecture and urban planning are part of a chain of signification. They rely on and produce a cache of meanings, images, and memories that are activated, deferred, or modified through their reiteration. They activate the tensions and conditions underlying the civics of hospitality and cosmopolitanism that undergird the relation between self and Other, guests and hosts, or in a national context between citizens, residents, migrants, and visitors.[13] Memory in architecture and planning is part of a multilayered and multipronged process that involves a confrontation between the various histories of the design and those of the locale, each with its own set of meanings and practices.

In tracing the history of empire and emporialism, I seek to situate the Middle East as a key player in shaping world culture. I aim to challenge the persistent anachronistic orientalist epistemological lens that constructs an imaginary narrative of the region as trying to catch up with modernity by mimicking a progressive Europe.[14] To give an example, the notion of diversity in nineteenth-century Middle Eastern cultures was far more complex than its European counterpart. It brought to the forefront many questions pertinent to the contemporary discussions of cosmopolitanism. Nevertheless, seen from the Eurocentric lens of the era, which took nationalism and eugenics as a yardstick for progress, this multicultural lifestyle was deemed a prenationalist backward phase. This does not imply that this practice was exemplary. It also had its challenges, injustices, and shortcomings in the way it integrated the individual into the body politic.[15] However, the thriving of *vernacular cosmopolitanism* in the region reveals that in many cases the conditions in the Middle East anticipate the various challenges that would later face Europe, rather than the other way around (Werbner).

The map of the Mediterranean basin or that of the Middle East occupies several overlapping planes at once. Each requires a multidirectional and intersectional analysis that attunes to its complexity.[16] It is simultaneously a map of the Arab world; the Ottoman Empire; the French, Italian, and British colonies; and emerging nation-states. This map keeps on changing, affected by migrations and different political currents, which in turn changes how the Mediterranean is remembered and presented. For instance, the population movement around the Mediterranean during the early twentieth century is a complex, multidimensional situation in relation to several regimes of value. Traced on the map, the trajectory of migrants from Tunisia, Greece, or Turkey to Alexandria appears to be a short, straight line. However, the complex legal system, and the conditions of extraterritoriality to which they were subjected, mark a convoluted web of routes that went through many imperial centers—Paris, London, Istanbul, and Cairo—before reaching the migrant's final destination (which could be just few hours away from their point of departure).[17] The stark contrast between geographical proximity and legal meandering opens a space of action or even survival, as was often the case for colonial subjects, through which they could acquire job opportunities, education, or other rights. As Ann Laura Stoler and Frederick Cooper argue in the broader context of empire: "Social taxonomies allowed for specifics form of violence at specific times. How a person was labeled could determine that a certain category of person could be killed or raped with impunity, but not others. It could open or close down the possibilities for marriage, housing, education, or pensions. At the same time, the criteria used to determine who belonged underscored the permeability of boundaries (6). I see the colonial map of the Middle East, as Will Hanley suggests, as a domain of "overlapping sovereignties" and "multilevel citizenship." As he argues, Ottoman Egypt offers an example of the complex construction of political and cultural allegiances and belonging. For lack of adequate language, these connections fall outside the purview of a Eurocentric nationalist framework, since "actors and institutions in such systems often employ singular identities to present themselves in imperial administrations, social science research, and litigation" (90–91). In that context, I approach the late nineteenth and early twentieth centuries as the early manifestation of a modern "global Middle East" (Kozma, Schayegh, and Wishnitzer 1–8).

The complex and interconnected history of the Mediterranean teaches us that the dynamics of culture formation call for a multiplanar and multiscalar reading that allows us to investigate how a text dialogues with other literatures and contexts and operates in various "value regimes" whose social and economic effects vary accordingly by mediating among local and regional systems and wider imperial, proto-global, or global ones. To imagine that process, consider a text not simply as a two-dimensional plane but as part of a rhizomatic structure. Like coordinates in a geometric graph, a text continuously intersects with many planes at once. The planes of interaction multiply across time and contexts. Here the discourse of emporialism, the space of department stores, and subsequent literary narratives intersect and dialogue with other texts and social and historical contexts across time, with their own value regimes that engage in a process of constant resignification. The same could be seen with texts, artworks, or other items of material culture. This kind of reading draws on Deleuze and Guattari's strategy to prioritize connections and assemblages in contrast to fixed spaces.

In embarking on such a reading, I do not aim to reduce language and literature to an economic equation but to think how the impact of language and literature is manifold and might be mobilized in various ways across time and space. The regimes of value include that of academics and writers and their role in shaping Mediterranean memory. As writers, critics, and readers, our linguistic choices and theoretical frameworks still resonate in social and economic relations. Whether our objective is to engage with or resist specific modes of writing and readings, we establish different value regimes that add to and complicate these relations.

In *Fous du Caire*, Mercedes Volait proposes "une histoire croisée" of the Mediterranean, specifically of Franco-Egyptian relations (29).[18] By referring to a multiplanar reading, I adopt this viewpoint. At the same time, I aim to expand this analysis to encompass a multiplicity of maps on which this history developed beyond the duality of exchange. These maps reflect the complex dynamics of race, class, and gender. To give an example, in her assessment of feminist geographies, Linda McDowell underscores the importance of considering the plurality of feminism by evaluating the intersectional connections between feminism and the various power dynamics shaped by race and class. In an early work, she quotes the following words by Griselda Pollock: "Feminism is not for gender what Marxism is for class, and postcolonial theory for race. First, there is a range of feminisms, in varying alliances with all the analyses of what oppresses women" (Pollock 3–4, qtd. in McDowell, *Gender, Identity* 10; McDowell, *Working Bodies* 64–75; Spivak "Three Women"; Simonsen; LeFebvre). To be more precise, neither race nor class is homogeneous or singular. Our modern notions and representations of race, gender, and class relations, which remain in flux, developed synchronically and symbiotically in the age of imperialism. None of these concepts emerged separately within the safe confines of a disciplinary petri dish in the laboratories of Marxist, gender, or postcolonial studies. Gender, class, and race are mutually constructive and always relational. For this reason, it is important to think of these factors, or as McDowell calls them, "the traditional axes of difference," as constructing several maps or planes simultaneously, each with its own field of power (*Working Bodies* 68). In considering them as separate elements, we undermine the multidimensional or multiscalar power structure in which they are enmeshed. As McDowell asserts, time and space are key factors in the assessment of intersectionality and its dynamic of power (*Working Bodies* 64; McCann and Kim 25; Crenshaw; Simonsen). I hope that a multiplanar reading draws our attention to the limitations and blind spots marked by academic boundaries and their regimes of analysis.

The same principle applies to the field of Mediterranean studies. To parse through the different meaning of emporialism as a spatial practice and a literary memory in the Mediterranean, I look at these spaces and their related representations as part of a complex dynamic. In each new location, the department store is enmeshed in a new regime of values, which casts a different light on the space itself and emporialism as a discursive and social praxis. Beyond the rhetoric of emporialism, the department store and the various narratives spun around it produce different, sometimes competing meanings, each with a recalibration of civic, race, class, and gender relations. Drawing on Mikhail Bakhtin's theory of the novel, Eve Troutt Powell invites us to attune to the "heteroglossic" aspect of a notion like race in the Middle East. By *heteroglossia*, she refers to the various subvariations and contextual meanings of this term that are irreducible to their typical imperial classifications (*Different Shade* 18). Bakhtin draws attention to the "problem of internal differentiation, the stratification characteristic of any national language" (*Dialogic Imagination* 67). Similarly, in my analysis of citizenship, race, class, and gender, I hope to attend to the polyglossic and heteroglossic manifestations of these concepts, especially in the context of three empires, where subjects negotiate among various languages, linguistic registers, and regimes of values. Treating the aforementioned terms as "words with a loophole" or "words with a sideward glance," I seek to examine the multiple pathways, discourses, and connections they generate across time and space (Holquist xxi). As Ella Shohat suggests;

> To place gender and sexuality studies, American and ethnic studies, and area and postcolonial studies in critical dialogue, in sum, would require a multichronotopic form of analysis, particularly in terms of the ways space is imagined and knowledge is mapped within academic institutional practices. It would ask us to place the often-ghettoized histories, geographies, and discourses in politically and epistemologically synergetic relations. It would require showing how variegated pasts and presents, "locals" and "globals" parallel and intersect, overlap and contradict, while also analogizing and allegorizing one another. (*Taboo Memories* 14)

In pursuing a multiplanar reading, then, I aim to steer away from the two limited competing currents that still dominate the representation of the Mediterranean: one a totalizing clichéd image, the other its fragmented nationalist counterpart. The situation is best summarized by terms coined by Michael Herzfeld and Ian Morris: "Mediterraneanism" (Herzfeld, "Practical Mediterraneanism" 67) and "Mediterraneanization" (Morris 33). On one extreme, the Mediterranean is treated as a unified undifferentiated space, while on the other, the sea is rendered as a set of global networks. In many cases, the attempt to reconstruct a totalizing image comes at the expense of effacing local specificity or marginalizing the complex lives around the basin, once filtered through the postcolonial or Marxist lens.[19]

By the same token, the field of world literature is caught between similar tensions that frame Mediterranean studies: between a totalized image and a fragmented one, between neo-Marxism, postcolonialism, and globalization. World literature, just like Mediterranean studies, is strongly connected to the history and dynamics of globalization. As Marx and Engels anticipated about the complicit connection between the future of capitalism and literature, advocates of world literature continuously grapple with the challenge of constructing a unified corpus of texts that opens up to express a universal cosmopolitan human experience without erasing difference. In depicting world literature, David Damrosch explains that "world literature has often been seen in one or more of three ways: as an established body of classics, as an evolving canon of masterpieces, or as multiple windows on the world" (15). Such a depiction automatically raises many challenges: How can we produce world literature without reenacting the same imperial and capitalist violence of the civilizing mission and its legacy of appropriation and normativization? How could we create world literature in contrast to "worlding literature," to use Gayatri Chakravorty Spivak's insightful critique of Martin Heidegger's term? The former involves a multilateral conversation, one that does not erase difference. The latter enacts a situation where academics and readers inadvertently reconstruct the playful imperialist fantasies and cultural hierarchies of the universal exhibitions (*Critique* 114–15).[20] In this case, texts are gleaned, translated, and ventriloquized via a hegemonic language only to conform to existing value regimes: namely, the ethos of a West European or American middle class. Literature, like other disciplines, has inherited its own share of nineteenth-century imperialism. This question is especially relevant when treating a space like the nineteenth-century emporium, which relied on translating world cultures into profitable clichés.

In *Against World Literature*, Emily Apter invites us to break away from a Euro-American-centric and capitalist lens by retracing a literary journey of the untranslatable, namely, that which perhaps temporarily resists annexation and appropriation in a globalized context (178). Dialoguing with Spivak's notion of worlding in the contemporary context of urban studies, Ananya Roy and Aihwa Ong suggest an alternative approach to "worlding." For the authors, "worlding" should focus on the way different actors respond to a matrix of impending challenges, without the necessity to reinscribe their decisions into a teleological narrative of resistance (11).

My project of a multiplanar reading draws on literature and urban studies. A multiplanar reading aims to reconsider literature as part of several irreducible maps, each with regimes of value irreducible to one another. By *multifocal* and *multiscalar*, I mean an alternation between the microscopic and the macroscopic that attunes to the resignification of each element and, by extension, the way it produces a different meaning from one plane to another. A multiplanar reading traces the process of reiteration and subsequent deferral of meaning a text or an image (or any other sign) produces, which fails to translate from one context to the other. While acknowledging larger homogenizing forces that contribute to the many currents shaping our reading reception and circulation of literature and culture, a multiplanar reading works to avoid a deterministic teleology by looking at intersections and dialogues, and finally deferring to the irreconcilability of the maps.

The goal is to reach beyond the Bakhtinian dialogic framework focusing primarily on intertextuality or intertextual connections (Bakhtin, *Dialogic*). A multiplanar and multidirectional approach seeks to capture a multidimensional process of signification, as the text or the object of study occupies and confronts several geographic, social, political, linguistic, and other value regimes implicit inside and outside the text, such as the circumstances of production, consumption, and circulation (contexts, frames of references, and power structures). As we expose these various regimes, we work to overcome a two-dimensional reading of history and social relations produced by intersectional slippage and erasure or an anachronistic representation of spaces and groups based on racial, class, and gender differences. In this case, a multiplanar reading evaluates the different agents and actors without eclipsing the different ideological currents and the paradoxical economic or political positions in which they are enmeshed.

Multivalent texts, iconographies, and artworks are constantly producing and negotiating with a multitude of value regimes, expressed by the impending tension between close reading and other forms of interpretation, between parsing the semiotic and semantic coordinates of a sign (a text, a sentence, a word, or a picture) and reading the book through its social, historical, and political coordinates. A multiplanar reading allows for a close reading of a text, while acknowledging the instability of reading and the other possibilities a text creates. Each approach functions in several regimes of values, shaped by the many academic disciplines and constraints in which they are interpreted. Multiplanar reading aims to avoid a hierarchy of narratives guided by the already deeply entrenched classifications that divide the Mediterranean and the Middle East, shaped by the history of empires or contemporary Mediterranean politics of North/South, or First World/Third World. Images and relations around the sea do not exist in a vacuum. Class relations, as well as American, European, and Arab scholarly circles, establish their own regimes of values and provide the material and imaginary resources and options available for academics and writers.

A multiplanar reading does not seek to distill or crystalize a set of variable elements into a homogeneous digestible narrative. It pulverizes rather than synthesizes, expands rather than scales down. To capture a glimpse of the complexities of the world we live in, it follows certain threads for investigation and allows others to fray and come apart at the seams. To open a space for intervention and interpretation by other scholars and readers, it pursues rhizomatic trails that crisscross and delimit the text, or the object of inquiry, through a series of intersectional territorializations and deterritorializations. In this framework, I opt for the term *plane* versus *territory* to draw attention to the simultaneous, coeval, multidimensional, and continuous process of the construction of meaning, beyond the possible illusion of a horizontal (primarily diachronic) rhizomatic progression. Each plane represents value regimes in which individuals, texts, or objects of art exist and with which they negotiate. Each element pertains and engages continuously with new value regimes, which in turn inform other planes.

A multiplanar reading seeks to overcome unilateral interpretations that erase differences by foregrounding the untranslatable and closely observing the slippage in the chain of signified that consequently re-creates meanings. In so doing, it acknowledges that the different stories of the Mediterranean are not only multiple realities around the sea but paradoxically a product of continuum and necessary for the circulation of capital. Different imaginaries, fictional and nonfictional, including academic inquiries, also embody what Peter Szendy calls the "numismatic" quality of capital. Like capital, these elements are widely recognizable and exchangeable. They are in constant motion and partake in creating and shaping the different regimes of values around the sea (Szendy 7). Just as various people navigate the numerous paths across and around the Mediterranean, the sea itself, captured in images and narratives, circulates among people. This simultaneous multilateral movement creates cross-Mediterranean social bonds, shapes civic relations, and influences desires and needs. It multiplies and consolidates imaginaries, as well as views and practices of labor, class, gender, and race.

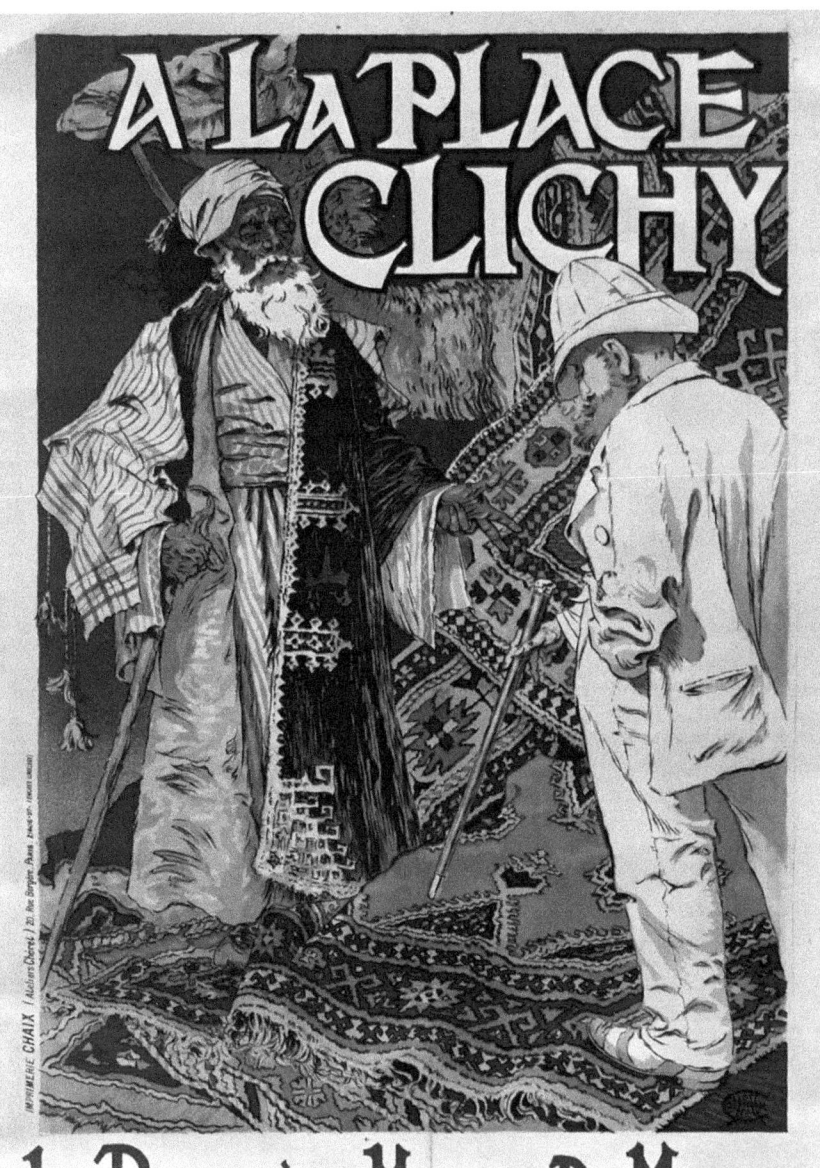

Figure 1.1. Advertisement for rugs, Maison à la Place Clichy. 1898. *Source*: Bibliothèque Nationale de France. Public domain. Used with permission.

Figure 1.2. "The Queen of Printemps," Printemps catalogue, 1910. *Source*: Ville de Paris, Bibliothèque Forney. Public domain. Used with permission.

Figure 1.3. Catalogue cover, Le Bon Marché, 1913. *Source*: Ville de Paris, Bibliothèque Forney. Public domain. Used with permission.

Figure 1.4. Catalogue cover, La Samaritaine, 1932. *Source*: Ville de Paris, Bibliothèque Forney. Public domain. Used with permission.

Figure 1.5. Catalogue cover, La Samaritaine, 1938. *Source*: Ville de Paris, Bibliothèque Forney. Public domain. Used with permission.

Figure 1.6. Catalogue cover, Printemps, 1939. *Source*: Ville de Paris, Bibliothèque Forney. Public domain. Used with permission.

Figure 1.7. Photograph, passage du Caire, Paris. *Source*: Photo by author.

Figure 1.8. Poster of Wanamaker's exhibition on Napoleon, circa 1900. *Source*: Ville de Paris, Bibliothèque Forney. Public domain. Used with permission.

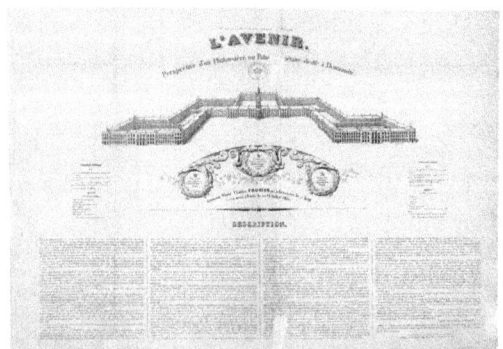

Figure 1.9. A phalanstery, by Charles Fourier, L'Avenir. *Source*: Bibliothèque Nationale de France. Public domain. Used with permission.

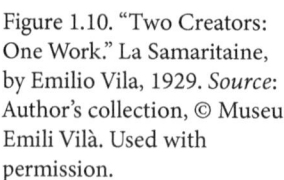

Figure 1.10. "Two Creators: One Work." La Samaritaine, by Emilio Vila, 1929. *Source*: Author's collection, © Museu Emili Vilà. Used with permission.

Figure 1.11. Harem, catalogue Le Bon Marché, front cover 1873. *Source*: Bibliothèque Nationale de France. Public domain. Used with permission.

Figure 1.12. Trade caravans, catalogue Le Bon Marché, back cover, 1873. *Source*: Bibliothèque Nationale de France. Public domain. Used with permission.

Figure 1.13. Rug collection, Gerôme's trip to Egypt. Catalogue Le Bon Marché, "L'Orient offert par les Grands Magasins du Bon Marché," 1913. *Source*: Ville de Paris, Bibliothèque Forney. Public domain. Used with permission.

Figure 1.14. Dress style "Armenian." Catalogue Le Bon Marché, 1878. *Source*: Bibliothèque Nationale de France. Public domain. Used with permission.

Figure 1.15. Dress style "Muslim," Catalogue Le Bon Marché, 1878. *Source*: Bibliothèque Nationale de France. Public domain. Used with permission.

Figure 1.16. Interior hall, Le Bon Marché, Historique des magasins du Bon Marché, 1904, 20. *Source*: Ville de Paris, Bibliothèque Forney. Public domain. Used with permission.

Figure 1.17. Workshop at Le Bon Marché. Historique des magasins du Bon Marché, 1904, 32. *Source*: Ville de Paris, Bibliothèque Forney. Public domain. Used with permission.

Chapter 1

Emporialism in the Footsteps of Empire

Ahmad Zaki and the Department Store

During his visit to the Universal Exhibition in Paris in 1900, Egyptian man of letters Ahmad Zaki Pacha stopped to contemplate the pavilion of the Ottoman Empire: a place, he declared, "where one finds himself at home and among his people. A refined palace that models Islamic Oriental architecture in the best manner" (*al-Dunya* 143).[1] Standing in the pavilion's reception area, Zaki wondered with pride at the sumptuous space decked with luxurious furniture, lavish rugs, and kilims from the ceiling to the floor. Unfortunately, this awe changed to bitterness once he noticed a price tag on a chair. To his great disappointment, Zaki realized that the pavilion was nothing more than an exhibit put together by the Parisian emporium A la Place Clichy! The Orient and Zaki's home empire were on sale by the grand emporium (143–46).[2]

Collaborating with the universal exhibition, the department store created a theatrical setting, a sort of a living tableau, to offer a sensorial experience of the Ottoman Empire. The store achieved this effect by mixing and matching the material cultures attributed to the region. Attempting to fathom this situation, Zaki made a thorough examination of the pavilion, only to realize that all the items were indeed owned by the department store. "What an unfulfilled moment of happiness!" he exclaimed. Not only was "the place where one finds himself at home" exhibited for sale, it was also a fake one produced by Europeans and Rūmīs (Greeks).[3] His description echoes other French visitors who likewise noticed the "vile" prices of European imitations and the absence of Ottoman producers, which left the display and promotion of Turkish goods, especially rugs, at the control of two French department stores (Delbeuf 3–9; Uslu). Finally, Zaki left the pavilion and resumed his journey across the exhibition grounds. He had to use a city guide published and distributed by another department store, Le Bon Marché (Zaki, *al-Dunya* 198).[4]

What Zaki encountered at the pavilion could not be solely interpreted as an expression of imperialism. The overall experience was carefully designed and charted by the emporium. The emporium monitored his senses and guided his steps across the exhibition. Zaki observed firsthand the affinity between empires and emporia: He saw his homeland and the Ottoman Empire defined, mapped, and re-created by the department store. Blending the imaginaries of empire and commerce by means of commodities, the emporium constructed a fantasized cosmopolitan world, meant to be later dismantled and sold piecemeal to consumers. Along with imperialism, Zaki witnessed the emergence of the emporium as an active transnational economic and cultural player. His era could be best described as the age of emporialism.

In this chapter, I examine the phenomenon of emporialism by reconstructing the historical context of French department stores and their iconographic representations in a selection of promotional materials, such as advertisements, guides, and catalogues. As I argue, emporialism embodied the complicity between imperialism and the emporium. Emporialism translated the modern experience of shopping into an exaggerated imperialist East-West dialectic, "more colored and brilliant than life itself," in Baudelaire's words, when he described Parisian modernity and the department store.[5] In this phenomenon, Orientalism occupied a vital place. This trend continued strongly till the interwar period.

Emporialism was not strictly a French phenomenon either. In fact, Zaki encountered a similar worldview at the English emporium. At an English department store, Zaki learned a remarkable lesson on Foucauldian biopower, namely, the role of the store in classifying, shaping, and controlling the bodies of customers and workers.[6] In a previous trip to London in 1892, he gave an account of the Whitely department store as an example of the many emporia available in the city. William Whitely, who began as a peddler, established a major department store that employed about "five thousand salesgirls." Zaki lost his way among the aisles while listing the endless products on display. The "warehouses" (*al-makhāzin*, or *magasins*) encompassed the world within their walls. The stores encompassed an entire cosmos placed on display for its customers. They contained all types of materials: jewelry and precious stones, metals and woods, and every kind of flora and fauna, plants, fresh and dry food, and "land, sea, and air animals" (Zaki, *al-Safar* 136). The stores cast their dominion over all aspects of human life. They mastered the world and the body. They had everything that a person might need "from the cradle to the grave." They catered to people from "every class," "the royalty and the military, the army, and the navy" (136). There were "clothing for the body, the head, the hands, and the feet ... internal and external." It was even said that Whitely imported an elephant for a client (136–38). After this thorough report, Zaki commented, "one should not be surprised then that the [English] people resorted to the *necessity of colonizing* [*isti'mār*] and strove to procure gold to their country from every province on earth, until their city became the world's market" (137–38; emphasis added). In Zaki's mind, the violence of imperialism and the emporium were already connected and justified to a certain extent. Nonetheless, he did not miss the artificial and illusionary aspect of this consumer utopia. He underscored the stark difference between the wealth of the emporium and the dire poverty on the streets of London. For Zaki, beyond the paradisical milieu of the department store, London was a city of extremes. He concluded his account on the English emporium by quoting a verse from Shelley: "Hell is a city, much like London" (139).

An Industrial Utopia

Zaki's life and experience, however, did not fit the megalomaniac mercantile cliché set at the universal exhibitions and the imagined geography constructed by the semiotics of emporialism. His connection to the world and to modernity could not be reduced to an encounter between a progressive productive West and an indolent, archaic, but artisanal East, whose industry and lifestyle only acquired meaning through the taste of the European consumer. As an elite colonial subject, Zaki Pacha's lifestyle would be perceived as more of an imitation than an authentic cosmopolitan experience (see chapter 2). Zaki was an active agent who assessed matters consciously and methodically. During his trip to London in 1892, he participated in the International Congress for Orientalists, where the members discussed the "value of Orientalist studies in commerce" (Cordier 418). In his writings, he followed the thorough methodology of Orientalists, placing the various European nations he visited under careful study, to inform his Arab audience. Zaki prided himself on providing a detailed account of France and the exhibition, which he buttressed with numbers and statistics. Directing the Orientalist lens toward Europe and turning Orientalism into *Occidentalism* might not have been an intentional part of the exhibition's organizers' plan (Volait, "Ahmad Zaki" 21).[7] This does not necessarily imply that Zaki was critical of eurocentrism and its structure of knowledge. In fact, he was more concerned with the absence of Ottoman industrialists than with the role of the department store or the exhibition in promoting Orientalist clichés. To a certain extent, he embraced a positivist Western European vision of progress and tried to make sense of a contradictory world, at once interconnected via networks of trade and transports and meticulously carved into races, classes, genders, producers and consumers, nation-states, empires, colonies, and protectorates.

Like many imperial subjects, Zaki navigated and crafted his own space among the myriad categories and classifications that made his world. He was a Francophone Egyptian man of letters who spoke French, Arabic, English, Italian, and Spanish. Zaki did not see himself as a French subject but, like many members of the Egyptian bourgeoisie, preferred French to English, since it was not the language of his colonizer (Reynolds, *A City Consumed* 14–15; Wahba 74–79). He was born in Alexandria in 1867 to a Moroccan father and an Egyptian (or possibly a Kurdish) mother (Volait, "Ahmad Zaki" 21–27). As an Egyptian, he paradoxically inhabited an empire and a colony at once. He was subject of both Ottoman and British rule when Egypt, also a semi-autonomous state with a royal family of Ottoman-Albanian origins, claimed its own colonial venture in Sudan. At the exhibition, he highly praised the Egyptian pavilion (*al-Dunya* 77, 94–101). Even so, professing his pride of his nation-state did not prevent him from proclaiming the Ottoman Empire as his larger homeland. His connection to imperialism was equally complex. As an Arab subject of Moroccan origins, Zaki visited the pavilions of the North African colonies under French control (77). In contrast to the territories of the Maghreb, Egypt did not constitute a French colony. France was a satellite empire: one that annexed the Egyptian territory via cultural and linguistic ties. Because of the Suez Canal project (1858–1869) and the long history of Franco-Egyptian exchange dating as far back as Napoleon's expedition (1798–1801), French universal ideals and language had a constant presence, to the extent that French functioned as a lingua franca among the upper classes, the literati, and the various foreign minorities. Although Egypt and other Arabo-Muslim regions were under British and French control, Zaki had mixed views of imperialism. In other writings, he expressed nostalgia for the bygone Arab presence in Spain. He had studied Spanish and visited the vestiges of Muslim Andalusia. Finally, his identification with other cultures and regions extended beyond the limits of faith, Arab identity, or a shared Ottoman heritage (*al-Safar* 335–96). At the exhibition, he hailed the quality of the Japanese pavilion, which made the "Orient shine proudly before the Western nations" (*al-Dunya* 112).

In sum, Zaki perceived himself as an upper-class Egyptian, Arab, Muslim, Ottoman, Oriental, and an enlightened Orientalist who participated in founding the Arab Oriental Association in 1922. He was a citizen of multiple empires, a colonial subject, and an active conservationist of Islamic and Arab heritage (Volait, "Ahmad Zaki" 21–22; Zaki, *al-Dunya* 210–15). Most important, Zaki's impression of the exhibition did not ultimately fulfill the organizers' main objective of exalting French superiority over its rivals. In addition to applying the methods of Orientalism to the study of France, he admired the pavilion of the German Empire (*al-Dunya* 189–221).[8] This would not have pleased the Frenchmen, since Germany had annexed the region of Alsace-Lorraine in 1870; nor would it have impressed the British, his actual colonizers. Zaki praised Germany's great interest in conserving Arab and Muslim heritage.

Interestingly, the French nation did not fit this reductive picture either. At the turn of the century, France faced several political and social challenges. Beyond the debacle of the German occupation and the fall of the Second Empire in 1870, the state faced significant divides between city and country, workers and bourgeoisie, leftists, socialists, anarchists, democrats, royalists, seculars, and supporters of the Church.[9] In this context, in addition to manufacturing consumer goods, the French regime aspired to produce a homogeneous national culture that could turn workers and "peasants into Frenchmen" through a large-scale educational program and a centralized network of industry and commerce.[10] The most telling sight that reflected this situation is that of exhibition visitors on the moving sidewalk who resembled "goods on a conveyer belt" (Friedberg 85; Szendy 145; see also Papayanis 129–68). France was in the process of manufacturing goods and modern citizens, and both were on display by the emporium and the exhibition. Walter Benjamin described the universal exhibitions as "places of pilgrimage to the commodity fetish," a space in which the worker occupies center stage briefly as a client (7). Indeed, the worker took center stage not only as an active agent but also as a commodity fetish in his own right. At the exhibition, France—modern Paris, its workers, and its peasants—was the raw material of a modern nation to be manufactured and showcased. Just as the Egyptians saw a simulacrum of their nation and ruling empires carefully reenacted at the 1900 exhibition, the French visitors encountered a model of old Paris.[11] The miniature city, set up to contrast with modern Paris, served as a chronotope, a temporal and spatial marker, to clearly delineate the break between the nation's troubled past and an aspirational progressive present (Bakhtin, *Dialogic Imagination* 84).

Such a French utopian worldview, however, was as precarious as the façades of the universal exhibitions that Zaki admired. Despite the emporium's effort to showcase France as a model empire of sciences and rational order, they failed to deliver an immaculate image to the public.[12] For instance, Le Bon Marché frequently celebrated the image of the French Empire before and during the exhibition. In 1897, three years before the exhibition, the store produced a map detailing the French colonies (Le Bon Marché, *Carte des colonies*). Ironically, the same emporium helped debunk the myth of the grand empire. Leafing through the visitors' guide distributed by Le Bon Marché, Zaki learned that the booklet was produced by a German company. The store had no choice but to negotiate with a rival empire since France did not have similar technology for binding books (Zaki, *al-Dunya* 198–99). The flawless image of the French empire marketed by the store was built at the expense of national pride. Zaki saw the failure of the network of transport across the exhibition's grounds. He noted the frequent accidents on the moving sidewalk constructed to facilitate the movement between the pavilions (123–31). He learned about the collapse of the pedestrian bridge, which connected the Celestial Globe to the exhibition grounds, leading to the death of several visitors (53–55).

For Zaki, the emporium and the exhibition portrayed a mixed image of success and failure, strength and vulnerability. Indeed, both sites, the emporium and the exhibition grounds, strove to uphold a broader national narrative of progress. They emerged during Second Empire France, in tandem with an industrial utopian project that reached to Zaki's homeland. This vision was spearheaded by the disciples of philosopher Henri de Saint-Simon (1760–1825), who gained prominent positions after the coup by Napoleon III. They envisioned an extensive network of trade, communication, and transport, aiming to rectify France's social tensions and position the nation as a leader of Europe and the sea. In his writings, Saint-Simon claimed that "if the philosophy of the past century was revolutionary, that of the nineteenth century should be organizational" (3:158).[13] The Saint-Simonians presented social justice in a form of a consumer utopian spectacle led by entrepreneurs and industrialists. The French organizational ideology of that era shifted from the philosophy of *alignement* [alignment] to the philosophy of *percement* [cutting through, or piercing] (Pinon, "Une nouvelle géométrie" 83 and "Percée" 91; Mead, *Making Modern Paris* 204). In contrast to the more conservative urban plan during the July Monarchy (1830–1848), the Haussmannian project swept everything on its way to open urban space and construct its vision of an interconnected metropolis. On the international front, this strategy extended to encompass the reorganization of Zaki's own nation-state, the Egyptian territory, and the larger Mediterranean through the construction of the Suez Canal. The project aimed to create a network of trade and transport uniting the sea, with Paris at the center. The Saint-Simonians viewed their capital as a "nodal point within a global network of cities" (Papayanis 129). In their imagined map, they strove to turn the Mediterranean into a French *mare nostrum*: a modern marketplace, produced by collaborative projects, bridging East and West. In the words of Michel Chevalier, councilor to emperor Napoleon III, the sea would become a large "forum," a "nuptial bed," uniting the Orient and the Occident ("*Le Globe* 5 février 1832," 116 and "*Le Globe* 12 février 1832," 117).

The French emporium became a central cog in this new world. The first department store, Le Bon Marché, began its expansion in 1869, the same year as the inauguration of the canal. The store served as a prototype for its subsequent global counterparts. As the canal dominated the trade routes from Europe to Asia, it reduced the travel time from Europe to India to approximately one month (Barak 22–26). In the following decades, department stores mushroomed in various urban centers around the world—Paris, London, Chicago, New York, Berlin, Cairo, Alexandria, Algiers, Tunis, Beirut, Aleppo, Baghdad, Istanbul, Tokyo, Shanghai, Hong Kong, Buenos Aires, Rome, Milan, and Budapest. For some stores, the Suez Canal was a symbolic Greenwich line to map and classify department stores around the world. For instance, Japanese department store Mitsukoshi was described as "'the largest store east of Suez,' and incomparable to anything else 'east of Suez'" (Moeran 155). To a great extent, the large-scale operation and the survival of these commercial giants relied significantly on the canal's fast and constant supply of merchandise, necessary to satisfy the endless whims of the masses. In sum, Zaki's homeland was part and parcel of the Saint-Simonian imaginary and the discourse of emporialism, in France and elsewhere.

Iconography of Emporialism

By the turn of the century, when Zaki visited Paris, emporialism was no longer a novel phenomenon. It had already become part of the Parisian quotidian. Two years before the exhibition, in 1898, the same department store mentioned by Zaki, À la Place Clichy, published a polychromatic promotional poster for its new collection of Oriental rugs (fig. 1.1).[14] The poster was designed by Eugène-Samuel Grasset for the famous ateliers Chéret. The themes echoed many publications distributed by French department stores to advertise their yearly rug sales. These posters replicated the rhetoric of emporialism. They reiterated the power dynamics of empire by highlighting Orientalist aesthetics.

The poster stressed the French cliché of the bargaining Oriental carpet seller negotiating prices with his customer. A statuesque bearded old man of undefined Eastern origins, dressed in traditional garb, stands opposite a European explorer in safari clothes, whose attire recalls that of Orientalist adventurers and military officers. The European man asserts his dominance by placing his cane and one foot over the rug, suggesting that the rug serves as a metonym for the Orient: a site of battle, a colonial conquest displaced onto the competitive commercial negotiation between men, the colonizer and colonized. The negotiation takes place among male patriarchs in a distant frontier land, away from the domestic realm, although the household might have been the starting point where the rug was manufactured and its endpoint in Europe, where it is to be consumed. Colonial working women, the producers of the rug, and their European bourgeois counterparts, the intended consumers, are absent from the picture.

The relatively larger representation of the salesman and the camel behind him evoke a potential danger faced by the buyer, who tries to assert his dominance by stepping onto the rug. Acting as a middleman, he shields future clients from similar confrontations by intervening on their behalf. The cropped image from the right directs the viewers and aligns them partially with the European gaze, giving a frontal view of the seller. The men's eyes do not meet. The posture of the seller's body, rendered in a slightly larger scale, stands in parallel with the body of his opponent. Both men hold canes replicating their bodies' parallel alignment. The phallic canes suggest a masculine power struggle. Notably, each cane is made of different material, belying each man's origin, social status, and connection to modern industry. The seller carries what could have been a tree branch (a biblical reference to the staff of Moses?), and the buyer holds a finely crafted ivory-topped cane with a metal tip, which he uses to point to the rug, evoking an army officer studying a map of the battlefield.

In a typical Orientalist gesture, a rug (the coveted commodity) splits the picture diagonally, symbolically dividing and mediating between two worlds, two imagined temporalities and geographies, two regimes of economic and social values—a European one and its Oriental counterpart. As Maxime Rodinson suggests: "In the nineteenth century, [the Oriental] became something quite separate, sealed off in his own specificity, yet worthy of a kind of grudging admiration. This is the origin of the *homo islamicus*, a notion widely accepted even today" (60).[15] As mentioned in the introduction, the French popular expression "I am not a carpet seller" implies that the speaker is a man of his word, living by the tenets of European work ethic, in contrast to an Oriental, unpredictable lifestyle. Nineteenth-century emporia celebrated the modern sales policies of fixed price tags, which eliminated the need for bargaining associated mainly with Oriental bazaars. In that sense, the figure of the Eastern carpet seller crystallized as the emporium's other. The poster suggests that the question of difference in value exceeds the parameters of the price tags attached to the merchandise. Europe, and its commerce, are modern, institutionalized, regulated, masculine, assertive, and steadfast. In contrast, the Orient is weak, ancient, inconsistent, and duplicitous. The habitual body language of each trader is remarkably different. The body, according to Pierre Bourdieu, translates one's position in the social world. One's posture and gestures would be deciphered by the viewer as an "embodiment" (incorporation) of social "values" and a system of individual differentiation, reflecting "an entire code of honor" (Bourdieu, *Outline* 291 and *Distinction* 466). The Oriental man, as expected by the European spectator, uses hand gestures to assert himself and close the deal, only to make him look more dubious in the eyes of the viewers. In contrast, the European man maintains the typical bourgeois physical equanimity: a walled facial expression and a self-restrained body posture, with his hands in his pockets.

In addition to promoting its rug collection, the poster markets a romanticized code of conduct among strangers, one that is modeled after the relation between merchants and customers. This mercantile sociability could be best described as agora-cosmopolitanism. Precisely, the framed scene foregrounds the economic transaction as a token experience of cosmopolitanism, between seller and buyer, the latter understood as the heteronormative masculine European by default. Agora-cosmopolitanism consists of this fleeting moment of marketplace civility captured in the image, when political and social conflicts are momentarily subdued under the banner of free-market exchange. This experience of agora-cosmopolitanism is set at the contact zone between the European public sphere—"masculine, secular and rational"—and its antithesis (Habermas 17). As the rug passes from one realm to another, it will be bestowed with new economic and aesthetic coefficients, leading toward its final integration into the cosmos of the European bourgeoisie, where it will be given a new value and will become part of a normative aesthetics and class ethos. These newly acquired values later trickle down to the masses across empires and colonies and back to the Orient.

The Pygmalion Fantasy of Emporialism

If emporialism cast the Orientalist adventure of acquisition as a predominantly masculine enterprise, the consumption and representation of empire is conversely feminine. In the realm of emporialism, the department store and the middle-class woman became symbolic allies. Within the national borders, emporialism promoted another, gendered, ethno-classist, erotic, myth. In parallel with the colonial erotic fantasy of possession and control emerged the Pygmalion masculine fantasy of creating the ideal bourgeois woman.[16] For instance, a 1910 commercial catalogue from Printemps depicts a bourgeois woman as the queen of the store (fig. 1.2). The poster features a giant woman being served by an equally exaggerated miniaturized group of multiethnic sale agents who barely reach up to her knee. In the background behind the woman, one can see a gigantic department store. Through the manipulation of scale, the poster parallels the woman's body with the department store in the background, alluding to the complicity between the store and women. In return for her patronage, the emporium places the empire at the feet of the bourgeois woman. The scale of the woman is analogous to that of the empire and the emporium. The sunrise strikingly evokes the distant Orient, shipped as it were to the warehouses of the department store to shine later over the sky of Paris. She presides over Lilliputian subjects who assist her in securing her social position. She is expected to take the leadership of her miniature empire. If the male industrialist is the organizer and leader of the modern society, the bourgeois woman is his counterpart in the marketplace. She is both maternal and entrepreneurial. She organizes and manages the process of consumption. As a consumer and domesticator of empire, she rearranges the map of empire into a modern, middle-class, domestic utopia. The bourgeois woman rules the national territory and the colonies. European workers and colonial subjects are lumped together into a single indistinguishable group under her command.[17] Like the European trader featured in the poster from Place de Clichy (fig. 1.1), Printemps's client shows her authority by placing one foot over an Oriental rug, held for her by a dark-skinned, half-bowing man dressed in a stereotypical Eastern or Turkish attire. Her other foot is offered to a female European worker who humbly and diligently shines her shoes.

The image directs the viewer's attention to the optics of industrialism by focusing on the collaborative labor carried out by the different agents of the emporium. The poster reads: "Printemps has dedicated itself to the woman. It is for the purpose of adorning her, making her beautiful and pleasing her that thousands of artists, artisans, and employees gathered at Printemps to happily lavish upon her their concern, their labor, and their good grace." The *grand magasin* establishes the bourgeois woman as the collective "oeuvre" of emporialism, crafted by the conjoined efforts of the empire and the emporium. Her body overlaps with the maps of the store, the city, the nation, and the larger empire. Her white European bourgeois image and body are the proud product of emporialism and its labor force, that is, the multitude of colonial subjects and various members of the working class. She, in turn, would serve as a true model and subject for the imperial civilizing mission.

As a model citizen, the image of the European bourgeois woman and body project the aggregate map of a parceled empire produced through the collective work of its colonial subjects and national workers. She comes to represent the whole trade network. To use Peter Gurney's words describing imperial commerce, the bourgeois woman "constituted the lifeblood of the imperial system, binding the savage and the civilized together in a larger quasi-religious endeavour" (104). Consuming the empire, the middle-class Parisian woman becomes herself at the scale of the empire she represents. Her role as consumer of imperial goods and producer of a harmonious imperial image is reflected in her wardrobe, make-up, and household.

Most important, the bourgeois woman's domesticating project executed through consumerism reenacts the mechanisms of racial and class classification and control of empire, a process I call ethno-classism. Examining the history of consumerism in the British Empire, Ann McClintock sheds light on a social paradigm that justifies the control of marginalized groups by means of the civilizing mission. This imperialist model draws on the metaphor of the household, consisting of an imagined universal "family of man" in which the British middle class presides over a hierarchized list of minorities and subgroups distinguished by race and class. Most often, the difference between subgroups from the metropole and colonial subjects is expressed through an ambiguous representation where racial distinctions are evoked to express class difference. In this process, the "domestic space became racialized and colonial space became domesticated." McClintock coined the term "commodity racism" to explain in particular the role of consumption and the "cult of domesticity" in shaping the representation of race and class in the British Empire (*Imperial Leather* 33–36, 52–54). I use the phrase *gendered ethno-classism* to refer to the active consolidation of class status through the manipulation of racial and gendered representation. Ethno-classism constructs an imagined universal hierarchy of race and class, with European bourgeoisie, whiteness, and cosmopolitanism at the high end of the social and ethnic ladder and working-class colonial subjects at the bottom (McClintock, *Imperial Leather* 36). Through the racialization of labor, members of the working class are reduced to Orientalized characters or faceless locals expunged from a Eurocentric bourgeois portrait. Moreover, social ascension and descent precipitate modifications to racial representation; those in the ascent are depicted as being physically and morally close to the European white bourgeoisie, whereas those in the descent are presented in exaggerated and racialized ethnic caricature. Ethno-classism is a manifold act, a covert shift along the binary of race and class that, occurring simultaneously in both colony and metropole, affirms European bourgeois domination. On one hand, it proletarizes colonial subjects, rendering them part of a monolithic group regardless of their background; on the other hand, it racializes the metropolitan labor force by conflating its image with that of colonial subjects. This dual process ignites the imperial fantasy/nightmare of control over the metropole and the margins that is articulated through the civilizing mission, which promises social ascension and economic advancement to both groups. These groups' integration of European bourgeois culture is represented as a form of racial evolution.[18]

The European bourgeois woman featured in figure 1.2 serves as a model for an interimperial civilizing mission, articulated through consumerism and gendered ethno-classism. Her body is the linchpin that holds together the various scales and territories in which the emporium operates: the citizen's body, the household, the city, the nation, and the empire. The middle-class woman bridges the gap between the space of the bourgeois living room and the extensive ambitious reach of imperialism. Her body is the site of reproduction of the bourgeois family unit and that of consumption. The union of metropolis and colony relies on her body, consumer habits, and taste. Interceding between the colonial venture and the emporium, the body of the bourgeois woman brings to life the phantasmatic body politic of the harmonious empire.

Typical of emporialism, the iconography of the Queen of Printemps exposes an ambivalent message. The picture marks the emporium as a space of leisure of the bourgeois woman and imperial panic simultaneously. The image shows a gigantic, Gulliver-like female customer, whose stature dominates the landscape and parallels the large store in the background. The sun rising from the east, piercing a heavily overcast gray horizon, creates an equally promising and foreboding background, a reminder of horror movies. Depicted as a giant, the woman equally becomes an anomaly, an out-of-control horror figure who dominates and threatens French public space and its established order. While the giant woman claims her position as the queen of the store, she could also crush her subjects under her feet. Under the ominous skies stands a gargantuan middle-class European woman, consuming the empire. The power relations between the empire and its favorite female subject are ambiguous, leading the spectator to wonder whether the bourgeois woman is truly at the behest of the empire or the empire comes to acknowledge its servitude to her. Beneath the harmonious capitalist image of an abundant utopia hides its negative counterpart, in which the queen of the department store represents the paranoia of destruction and chaos: putatively, the other side of the coin of the archetypal image of mother nature. If mother nature is the producer of cornucopia, the archetypal customer of emporia is the consumer of industrial utopia. In *The Monstruous-Feminine*, Barbara Creed draws our attention to the masculinist and misogynist anxiety implied in that image, wherein the female body is constructed as an abject: "at times, the horrific nature of the monstrous-feminine results from the merging of all aspects of the maternal figure into one—the horrifying image of woman as archaic mother, phallic woman, castrated body and castrating parent represented as a single figure within the horror film" (27) (Kristeva). This ambivalent stance unconsciously hints at the accusations against French women during that era of ruining the national craftsmanship by allying with the department store and adopting its fashions and taste (Tiersten, *Marianne in the Market* 79–80).

Most important, the image of the giant woman reverses an earlier bourgeois discourse of containment and excess. The uncanny schizophrenic dissonance between her affected feminine gestures, conforming perfectly to bourgeois decorum, and her ominous scale exposes the nightmarish side to the fantasy of emporialism. Whereas her posture and smile adhere to the rules of bourgeois etiquette and control, her gigantic figure stepping over a crowd conveys the opposite dreaded image, which that decorum was meant to control. The image of a giant bourgeois woman represents a paradox of what it meant to be bourgeois. In this image, what should have been a performance of bourgeois civility turns into a performative act that deconstructs what it originally purported to establish. As David Harvey puts it:

> Bourgeois women became not only managers and governors of the household but also took on the role of creators of order, particularly a spatial and temporal order, within the interior space of the household ... The discipline was simultaneously an expression of capitalist rationality and a kind of structured and controlled response to the perceived disorder and uncontrolled passions that reigned not only in the streets but also in the marketplace. This outer space of excessive stimulation and passion was supposed to be closed to them. "A contained woman, contained in a corset, contained in a house, was an orderly kind of woman." (*Paris* 190)

If an industrial and consumer utopia sought to contain and regulate different social factions by means of a commodity spectacle, the image suggests that the ideal of a "contained" woman in charge of organizing the spoils of empire within the idyllic confines of the middle-class household has come to an end. In Bourdieu's terms, the poster shows a female customer whose "hexis" (her "embodiment" of bourgeois restrained manners) conflicts with the scale of her body, and by extension her habitus (her social situation based on her acquired economic and cultural capital, which differentiates her from other classes) (McDowell, *Gender* 40–41; Bourdieu, *Distinction* 169–74). Explaining similar large-scale representations of women in horror films, Creed explains: "Confronted by the sight of the monstrous, the viewing subject is put into crisis—boundaries, designed to keep the abject at bay, threaten to disintegrate, collapse" (29). As a horror figure, the giant bourgeois woman operates in similar manner. As Susan Stewart argues:

> With the development of the bourgeoisie, the marketplace, and the life of towns, we see the gigantic, as part of the grotesque, split into sacred and secular aspects. The gigantic is appropriated by the state and its institutions and put on parade with great seriousness, not as a representative of the material life of the body, but as a symbol of the abstract social formations making up life in the city. On the other hand, the gigantic continues its secular life in the submerged world of the carnival grotesque. (81)

In this context, the manipulation of the various scales of representations, inexhaustible production and consumption, became the expression of a rising bourgeoisie. The giant bourgeois woman stands at the crossroads of these two worlds with opposite values and aesthetics, bringing them together once again. As the sacred and the civic, she is the keeper of social order. Akin to the carnival grotesque, she hints toward material abundance and destruction, most importantly the suspension of rules and class hierarchies (Bakhtin, *Rabelais* 89). Consuming the labor of empire, the queen of the emporium also acquires the ominous quality of the workers and colonial subjects, namely, their potential to occupy public space and disrupt order. The picture of a giant woman surrounded by workers and colonial subjects brings into one place the specter of the various contending populations, which the industrial utopia sought to neutralize by domesticating the empire. Throughout the century, gendered and racialized visions of chaos emanated from both the metropolis and the colonies. To give a few examples, on the colonial front, a romanticized ideal of governance gave way to the dreadful reality of imperialism. In the 1840s, the prospect of a Saint-Simonian civilizing mission was already failing in Algeria, leading to the justification of further violence (Abi-Mershed 71–95; Agulhon, *Republican Experiment* 31–32). The situation was not better within French national borders, where gendered images of social unrest persisted in public memory. Writing in 1877, in his description of anarchy during the revolution, Hippolyte Taine brings to the forefront the memory of riotous women during the revolution: "Laundresses, beggars, shoeless women, hired rough female market-vendors picked up few days prior. Such is the first nucleus, and it keeps on growing; since the group incorporates the women which they encounter, doorwomen, seamstresses, cleaning maids, and even bourgeois women" (*Les Origines* 154).[19] These images remained vivid in the French imaginary, especially with the frequency of popular insurrections throughout the century. In 1871, by the end of the Second Empire, members of the working class protested against their dire living conditions aggravated by the Franco-Prussian War. As Kristin Ross indicates, the Commune represented an antihierarchical "spatial event" centered on establishing the "right to the city" (*Emergence* 4–5). The body of the working-class woman became symbolic of the uprising. In this discourse, the imaginary of a disorderly "savage" working class frequently overlapped with that of colonial subjects (149). The image of the giant patroness embodies this multitude of gendered, racial, and social intersectional memories.

The Sons and Daughters of Emporialism

The iconography and rhetoric of emporialism extended to address every member of the modern bourgeois family. Just as promotional materials for adults stressed a divided world between East and West, modern versus primitive, so did posters and catalogues that addressed children. Catalogues produced at the cusp of two world wars (1913 and 1932) reaffirm the long-celebrated discourse of emporialism. In the catalogues, the emporia produce ever-changing dioramas with malleable borders and protean racial, ethnic, class, and gender relations, which either defy or conform benevolently to the rules of empire. The world with its landmarks, its hierarchies of racialized colonial subjects, and its flora and fauna garnered from the corners of the empire are rendered into inanimate toys, into dolls and other puppets, brought into the household for the entertainment of the white Western European child. A catalogue cover from Le Bon Marché (fig. 1.3) features two European boys dressed in military uniform and flying a plane brandishing the French flag. The two child soldiers pursue two Arab children on horseback. In terms of design, the poster effects a diagonal split, between the European subject on one side and *homo islamicus* on the other (Rodinson 60). The same divide is also found in the Place Clichy's rug poster from 1898. In the top right, the French white boys wielding an airplane represent a superior modern European race. By occupying the skies, the boys take over a divine quality of omnipotence and control. Down below on land, viewers can see two exaggeratedly dark-skinned Arab boys of nondescript origin, dressed in traditional Oriental garb. They bear the sign of the crescent on their turbans, alluding to their faith. The children belong to two diametrically opposed worlds. The Arab boys have stolen the European boys' toys. The Muslim child on the left carries under his arms a white, blond doll, evoking the psychosexual paranoia of white slaves in the harem (see Devereux). The Arab children attempt to escape the European might coming from heaven. Hunted by the French aviators, they leave behind them a trail of dust and toys in the air, recalling the destructions and losses of World War I.

A poster produced by La Samaritaine in 1932, features a smiling white bourgeois blonde girl holding the hand of an African man wearing a fez (fig. 1.4). The girl leads the way forward toward the viewer, toward the metropolis. The sight of animals and colonial subjects together recalls the universal exhibitions and the ethnological exhibits constructed at the imperial metropolis to satisfy the curiosity of the European public.[20] The bourgeois girl in this image is symbolically the daughter of the bourgeois woman from the 1910 Printemps catalogue. Like her mother, the adult bourgeois woman, she recognizes her place in the empire and learns to take charge of the imperial civilizing mission, through the imaginative role-play evoked by emporialism. In the background lies a tropical savage land and a Cambodian temple. A man dressed in a safari suit looks outward at the opposite direction to the girl. He carries a rifle and rides a camel, guarding and controlling the frontiers between the primitive lands and the organized domestic bourgeois realm of the empire.

In 1938, as Europe edged closer toward World War II, La Samaritaine published another promotional catalogue for children's toys (fig. 1.5). The catalogue cover inadvertently blurs the lines between the utopian consumer spectacle and the dystopian end of civilization. The image features a group of children on a boat during sunset near a small island decked with toys. Remarkably, the poster exposes the anxieties of a nation faced with an escalating military conflict. Upon a second look, the observer might wonder whether the island represents a fantastical haven or a heap of discarded consumer goods marking the end of times: bicycles, cars, trains, musical instruments, all gathered into a mountain topped by a giant clown and surrounded by airplanes. The assemblage evokes a pile of rubbish attracting a swarm of flies. In the context of the mounting tension on the European continent, the children waving frantically on the boat give the impression of being the sole survivors of a wartime disaster. Meanwhile, the sun sets on the horizon, signaling the fall of civilization and the end of the industrialist consumer utopia celebrated earlier.

In some cases, the representations in advertisements attempted to suture the various wounds of a dying empire. A Printemps catalogue from February 1939 promoting rugs also brings the specter of an impending war (fig. 1.6). The picture evokes a fortress or a bunker, the kind frequently seen in war images and films of World War II. The salesroom is painted in a dark green color with a map of the Middle East in the background, like a military operation room. The image presents a collection of mechanically manufactured rugs produced in France. The rugs' sandy and ochre palettes recall the distant Eastern deserts at the heart of the store. This time, however, the East is manufactured on French soil by modern machines. Behind the rugs stand three miniature salesclerks. A white Western European man mediates and commands the encounter between an exotic or belligerent East made up of a matrix of races dressed in local costumes. At the center is a European man in a business suit, rendered in sharp, modernist, geometric lines. On each side stands a salesclerk or carpet seller, each with a different skin tone and native Eastern attire with flowing whimsical and puffy fabrics. The different treatment of the attire creates a distinction between a rational European man and his extravagant, primitive, exotic others. The one on the left resembles a pilgrim to Mecca, the other a Turkish man from the provinces. The catalogue cover suggests that a white French man is in control, mediating between the two Oriental men. Through a panorama of ethnic types, the poster set the paradigms of agora-cosmopolitanism by re-creating the nineteenth-century family of man, built around an echelon of races presided over by a Western European merchant. Behind the men, the rugs are organized into piles almost recalling trenches in a battlefield. In contrast to the deteriorating European situation at that time, the image of a minutely organized Oriental space under the direction of a European man provides a sense of security and control. In this context, emporialism mastered and manipulated a flexible geography of scale with mutable borderlands and frontiers that sometimes collapsed the distance between France and the East while mostly keeping their neighboring imperial rival, Germany, securely at bay. In this case, the secure grasp over the Orient relieved the anxiety of powerlessness before another European empire.

A few years later, the end of empires began. The world of emporialism featured in the catalogue covers and posters, presented sometimes as the European man's realm, at other times as the bourgeois woman's household or the bourgeois child's playground, slowly dissipated along with the Ottoman pavilion that Zaki visited.

The Rise of Emporialism

By the early twentieth century, the iconography of emporialism and the image of the department store as a modern commercial institution began to crystalize in the urban imaginary.[21] In her studies of department stores, Meredith Clausen underscores the rise of the department store as an identifiable architectural monument, a building type, whose iconographic traits were adapted from an already established and recognizable language of architecture ("Department Stores"). These elements are borrowed from bazaars, arcades, world fairs, churches, theaters, and train stations. In fact, the department store was more than an iconographic monument. The various emporia around the world shared common features and strategies, productive of the urban changes of the time and the swift circulation of information and ideas. The stores were a by-product of both global and local factors. Through their setting and promotional strategies, emporia established a cosmos with its set of sensorial experiences. They created new desires and needs and retrained their public, both customers and penniless window shoppers, how to view, listen, touch, taste, and consume the world. They taught the public how to code—and decode—race, class, and gender using the visible markers of a rapidly changing fashion, as well as a large influx of consumer goods summoned from distant corners of empire.

In general, what came to be defined as a department store consisted of a multilevel building with large open spaces and a wide atrium allowing for a calculated display of merchandise. Usually stores were located close to transport networks (trains, tramways, buses, and subways). This proximity drew customers from distant suburbs, the provinces, and even neighboring countries. It also brought inexpensive labor from the countryside or the city's outskirts. Akin to the arcades, bazaars, and the universal exhibitions, department stores invested in the visual experience of shopping and the containment and regulation of crowds. Department stores created a condensed space of shopping by bringing a wide variety of products under one roof and single management. The stores' interiors were organized into various specialized departments attended by a large number (sometimes hundreds) of salesclerks of both sexes. They wore uniforms and answered to the head of the department. The department chiefs relayed to a higher chain of command, leading up to the store manager or owner.

In their effort to amplify their progressive status, department stores were the first to adopt the latest technologies, such as gas lighting, already used in the arcades, and later electricity. Stores used innovative methods of interdepartmental communications, such as pneumatic tubes, elevators, and escalators. The owners often hired nationally or even internationally renowned architects who used the latest building technology to impress their middle-class clientele. Many of these architects participated in the design of world fairs and major national monuments. Stores incorporated iron as a building material, emulating the industrialized pavilions in world fairs, train stations, and the Parisian central food market of Les Halles designed by Victor Baltard.[22] This industrialist modern aspect became an iconic feature. The architects, however, had to exercise moderation in their imagination and techniques. Although they sought to highlight their modern and progressive image, nineteenth-century department stores distanced themselves from obscure or avant-garde elements that could shock a conservative public. Before adopting a more modernist design with rectilinear architectural lines after the 1930s, early stores often had a corner rotunda topped with a dome. They incorporated gothic, neoclassical, or Renaissance motifs, easily decipherable by their customers as signs of luxury, femininity, and opulence.

The stores adopted innovative sales strategies, though most often they mirrored their predecessors or other competitors. They enforced fixed prices, eliminated the need for bargaining, and offered a wide array of merchandise suitable for various social strata. The clear pricing served a double purpose. One the one hand, price labels lured customers in and away from boutiques. One the other hand, this unified system represented an efficient business solution, since bargaining would slow down the stores' centralized operations and require individual control for each salesclerk. The stores cut costs by hiring purchasing agents who negotiated directly with manufacturers and producers around the world. They built their own workshops, especially for ready-made garments. Emporia spent unprecedentedly large fortunes on advertising and promotional material, which gave them the upper hand in newspapers and magazines. They also operated their own departments for distributing catalogues and for the receipt and delivery of sales orders worldwide.

Department stores offered an experience that straddled the boundaries between the local and the global. The impact of their setting and intensive promotional campaigns surpassed the effect of the temporary exotic displays at an exhibition. In contrast to the museum or the postcards frequently exchanged during the nineteenth century, emporia brought into the middle-class household a material part of the colonies (Mathur 109–32). Inversely, in the Middle East, Asia, and the Americas, they brought a part of Europe. Egyptian department stores, for instance, modeled their spaces after the architectural design of their Parisian counterparts. Wanamaker department store in New York created a life-size replica of rue de la Paix—the same place where Émile Zola located his famous fictional *grand magasin* (Le Blond 477; Hendrickson 78; Marrey 52). The Japanese store Mitsukoshi in Tokyo adorned one of its façades with lions, evoking Trafalgar Square in London (Moeran 155).

Whereas shopping at the boutique was governed by the interaction between the customer and the salesclerk across the counter, the visit to the open space of the department store involved a matrix of encounters among a multitude of shoppers, the store's employees, and the openly showcased products. The stores mastered the theatrical art of staging insofar as they made both their merchandise and customers part of the display. Each department included mobile display boxes, which could be rearranged for special events and sales, allowing for a creative and flexible staging of merchandise. Department stores inherited the custom of window setting from boutiques and arcades and applied it on a greater scale (Walsh 46–72). They extended the glass panes to cover the entire circumference of the first floor of their buildings. The windows blurred the distinction between the inside and outside. Some stores placed inexpensive goods outside the store to lure customers in. The use of mannequins and lighting helped revolutionize the art of window display. In their setting, the stores closely mimicked the life of the bourgeoisie. In their windows and their catalogues, stores fashioned elaborate tableaux portraying quotidian life. In a few rare cases, they resorted to more elaborate marketing ruses to boost their prestige. They paid regular people to dress in bourgeois attire and pretend to be shopping (Hahn 161). The projection of a bourgeois image aimed to appease the clients' anxiety and model a bourgeois lifestyle for clients, catalogue readers, and window shoppers.

Borrowing further from theaters and opera houses, stores included a large atrium leading to a central staircase. Like the loges of a theater, the different levels overlooked the central hall. The store's interior offered a panoramic view of the building to satisfy and exploit clients' desire for voyeurism. This design crafted various vantage points from which the rising bourgeoisie could exhibit and foreground their image as an ascending class. The affinity with the theatrical was not limited to the emporium's internal setting. Stores were strategically located in proximity to modern spaces of entertainment, such as cafés, theaters, passages, museums, and cinemas. This did not prevent the stores from emulating these venues and incorporating their functions into their internal space. Stores created their own reading rooms, cafés, and child care centers. They organized concerts and set up exhibitions, galleries, and museums.

Emporialism: Fifty Shades of Orientalism

Although the emporium promoted a highly stratified world under the firm rule of imperialism, it operated in a dynamic and interconnected system, which in turn exposed the fragility and porosity of empire. Notably, the word *emporium* holds the traces of this permeable quality.[23] The word *emporium* comes from *emporion* in classical Greek, implying a place where merchants gather. However, the suffix "per" signifies to travel, to cross over, from which comes the image of the traveling merchant or peddler. Another related word is *peirein*, to pass through; from the same suffix is derived the words *porous* and *porosity* (Hendrickson 7).[24] Both words, *per* and *peirein*, reflect central aspects of the emporium. The first hints toward its social origins, since many department store owners around the world began as peddlers, shopkeepers, or salesclerks who ambitiously expanded their dominion by annexing the neighboring buildings. The second one exposes its malleability and porous quality, or its ability to absorb various regimes and lifestyle into its operation system. Whereas emporialism took its cues from the rhetoric of empire, it was also concocted of eclectic elements. Since its rise, the emporium expanded by mirroring and integrating the qualities of its commercial predecessors and competitors and the various social functions of surrounding urban spaces. In fact, most of the characteristic features associated with the emporium predated its establishment. The department store's innovative aspect involved bringing these retail strategies in one space and adapting them to large-scale operations.

Among the various theatrical displays crafted by French department stores, Orientalism took center stage. Since its inception, the French emporium was known as a *grand magasin* or a bazaar. If the word *bazaar* recalls the covered marketplaces in Egypt, Turkey, or Syria, the word *magasin* does not escape that image either. The name *magasin* also derives from Arabic *makhzan* or warehouse, whereby *grand magasin* implies the big warehouse. Aside from the actual origins of their names, early French emporia intentionally invested in associating their image with the fantasy of Eastern material culture. In *The Arcades Project*, Benjamin notices the early department stores' excessive effort to emulate the bazaar through their theatrical use of rugs and fabrics (48).

Long before the emergence of the department store, the imaginary of consumption and the Orient were already intertwined in the mind of the French public. The emporium only absorbed this imaginary into its setting. Similarly staged Orientalist fantasies could even be seen two centuries before the rise of the emporium. In 1669, during his visit to the court of Louis XIV, the emissary of Sultan Mehmed IV, Soliman Moustapha Raca, introduced coffee to the nobility.[25] Like the Ottoman pavilion at the universal exhibition 200 years later, the residence of the Ottoman convoy was remodeled with an "Oriental" flair. Chairs were replaced by large floor cushions. Sumptuous rugs and rich damascene fabrics embroidered with gold completed the setting. Members of the court sat cross-legged, while being served coffee by enslaved black servants (LeTailleur 45). Creating an immersive sensorial experience with Oriental decor and racialized "Oriental types," Raca's pavilion brought the Ottoman Empire into the court of Versailles while framing the act of drinking coffee as a vicarious experience and consumption of the East.

Gradually, cafés emerged on the Left Bank of Paris and on the *grands boulevards*. In its early moments, the coffee shop experience was strongly influenced by the Middle Eastern imaginary. In the eighteenth century, waiters serving coffee in Paris, regardless of their origins, would be dressed in Oriental attire (Fosca 15).[26] Orientalist aesthetics was not limited to the enjoyment of the upper classes; rather, it existed in various social milieux. Some venues, like Café Frascati on Boulevard Montmartre, or the Café Turc on Boulevard du Temple, were designed in Orientalist fashion. While the former catered to a diverse clientele, the latter was mostly frequented by Parisians from the working class (Letailleur 72; Hahn 53).[27]

In the same era and from the same royal court emerged another pillar of the French commercial imaginary: *The Thousand and One Nights*. The first translation of *The Nights* into French, by Antoine Galland, based on an Egyptian manuscript, made its appearance in France between 1704 and 1717. In response to his readers' demands for more stories, Galland indicated that he collaborated with a Syrian priest, currently understood to be Hanna Diyab, who visited the court of Louis XIV (al-Musawi 135–36; see Diyab). This exchange produced three of the most popular stories, all focused on Eastern material wealth: *Aladdin*, *Ali Baba*, and *Sinbad the Sailor*. As early as the eighteenth century, the *Nights* became part of the repertoire of imperial "useful knowledge" needed for the expansion of trade in the East (al-Musawi 28). The translations and illustrated versions served as fodder for the public imagination: a popular handbook for material culture and luxury. As al-Musawi puts it: "*The Nights* has its supply of invention, ruses, and claims to automation. The magic carpet, the flying horse, and open sesame or trapdoors are among just a few of the devices Scheherazade's tales offer as gateways of the mundane, but its sumptuousness becomes also a yardstick to measure wealth" (28–29).[28] For instance, the Mardrus translation of 1899, Mia Gerhardt points out, had more similarities with Parisian "boulevard literature" from the turn of the century than with the actual context and aesthetics of the *Nights* (Gerhardt 103–4, cited by al-Musawi 139). The *Nights* brought to the French masses a mercantile and consumerist discourse that revealed more about the European ambition of acquisition and escapism than about its original Arabic context. The *Nights*' language and iconography, later exploited by the department store, provided a widely recognizable visual reference and a common vocabulary for creating a popular promotional campaign. Annexed to the early language of advertising and marketing, the *Nights* participated in transforming an imagined community of readers to a community of consumers.[29] By the mid-nineteenth century, the imagery of the *Nights* and that of the Orient became a common reference and decorative choice for the commercial spectacle. Trendy boutiques and cafés on the *grands boulevards* were often likened to the fantastical aspect of the *Nights* (Hahn 61; Paul 50).

From Egypt to France to Egypt Again

Within this Orientalist aesthetic framework, Egypt's geography remained the fodder of a vivid commercial imaginary and modern practice of space. A key iconographic Orientalist element of emporialism came from the passages, that is, the shopping arcades, the immediate precursors of the department stores. At a short distance from the *grands boulevards* stands the oldest covered arcade in Paris. The passage du Caire—decorated as it is with distinctive ancient Egyptian motifs—attests to the early entwinement of empire and emporium. The modern fantasy of shopping was thus articulated in the language of the first French imperialist propaganda, that of the Egyptian expedition (fig. 1.7). The passage du Caire represents one of the early urban landmarks connecting the first French empire and consumerism. The passage was constructed in 1799 just after Napoleon's return from his expedition in Egypt (Andia 14; Moncan, *Les passages couverts* 47).[30] Upon his return from Egypt, Napoleon Bonaparte renamed a cluster of streets, currently located in Paris's second *arrondissement*, after Egyptian sites: le Caire, Alexandrie, Aboukir, Dammiette, and Nil (Hillairet 258–59). In so doing, Napoleon inscribed his first imperial venture on the urban memory of modern France. Before the heyday of the universal exhibitions framed the world as a series of tableaux with renditions of Cairene streets and ancient Egyptian temples, Napoleon's re-creation of Egypt's map in Paris planted the seed of a modern Orientalist and consumerist heterotopia at the heart of the French metropolis. The passage du Caire does not solely copy the aesthetics and discourse of Egyptomania during France's First Empire (1804–1815); rather, it appropriates and annexes the map of Egypt to that of the French metropolis, allowing Parisian shoppers a vicarious experience of Napoleon's colonial venture in the Orient. The passage was built on the old site of the Filles-Dieu Convent (Hillairet 259). It adjoined and came to replace a part of the "cour des miracles," where the city's homeless and criminals took shelter. Through this urban reconstruction and modernization, then, Napoleon executed a symbolic civilizing mission projected onto his miniaturized version of Egypt. The target of this mission in this case were the marginalized groups of the city. The first passage harbored several print shops, a striking reminder of the printing press that Napoleon had introduced in Egypt as a token of modernization, in his quest to revive the glory of the bygone ancient Egyptian empire.[31]

The passage du Caire, however, failed to offer the public the Orientalist fantasy the visitors longed for. The writer Amédëe Kermel visited the passage, only to be disappointed by his experience. Kermel expresses his disillusionment of the passage, which conveyed neither the splendor of Bonaparte's empire, nor that of the Orient. For Kermel, the passage had nothing "of the riches of Egypt, nor its perfumes, nor its children, nor the grandeur of its monuments" (68).[32] In a way, his reaction recalls the typical "disenchantment" of French writers during their trips to Egypt, outlined by Edward Said. As Said argues, this aesthetic positioning became part and parcel of a wider orientalist discourse (Said, *Orientalism* 100–102). The subsequent passages, however, built across the city offered numerous entertainment possibilities, and a promiscuous setting. Their panoramas, vaudeville theaters, boutiques, and constant influx of international visitors provided to their public the phantasmagorical illusion that the passage du Caire lacked.[33] The overall propaganda of the First Empire consciously overlapped its image with that of ancient Egypt by means of public parades for Egyptian artifacts and the creation of a distinctive decorative design of furniture, still known as the "empire" style, to embody the spirit of the era (Mansel, *Paris between Empires*). The new furniture design copied ancient Egyptian motifs and adorned the court and the houses of the affluent classes. Benjamin indicates that even French material culture of the era was strongly influenced by the Egyptian mission: "In 1798 and 1799, the Egyptian campaign lent frightful importance to the fashion for shawls. Some generals in the expeditionary army, taking advantage of the proximity of India, sent home shawls of cashmere to their wives. . . . From then on, the disease that might be called cashmere fever took on significant proportions" (55). Just as Napoleon drew the Orient onto the urban map of Paris, Empress Josephine, renowned for her elegant way of wrapping the shawl, became the imperial face and the body for this new trend—the role model for the domestication of Egyptian material culture—and by extension the domestication of the Orient (Couvreur 247).[34] Nonetheless, as Benjamin's words indicate, consumerism took on the ambivalent attributes of the Orient. Consumerism was a symbol of empowerment and distinction, but it was also a source of contamination—a fever, a feminine domain—that exposed an uncontrollable desire that challenged European rational order. The Orient occupied bourgeois spaces, in the guise of furniture, and wrapped around the bodies of French women in forms of shawls. The Orient was both colonizer and colonized, a subjected land and a dreaded enemy. As material culture, the Orient was simultaneously consumed by France and consuming it, by turning it into a domesticated "feminized" colony through consumerism.

The complicity between Napoleon's empire and the emporium extended beyond the borders of France. It resurfaced in the imaginary of department stores across the Atlantic. For instance, emporium mogul Frank Woolworth often compared himself proudly to Napoleon Bonaparte, insofar as he created a replica of the emperor's lodgings in his office and his master bedroom (Hendrickson 121). In another case, in the early 1900s, Wanamaker department store organized a special exhibition on the life of France's first emperor (fig. 1.8). When Wanamaker annexed the neighboring A.T. Stewart's Iron Palace in 1896, the store, in tandem with the imperialist positivist imaginary of expansion, connected the buildings by what they dubbed "the bridge of progress" (Hendrickson 79).

From the Napoleon I to Napoleon III: Eclectic Emporialism

During the Second Empire, the first department store in France coincided with the inauguration of the Suez Canal, another French commercial project that relied on controlling and reorganizing Egyptian geography, under the reign of Napoleon III (see chapter 2). Le Bon Marché, originally founded in 1834, expanded from a small boutique for drapery to a *grand magasin* in 1869 under the ownership of Aristide Boucicaut (Miller 19–27; Clausen, *Frantz Jourdain* 197–99).[35] To a certain extent, Le Bon Marché is credited with setting the standards and the stage for other enterprises of the same type and scale.[36] Some other stores' owners in Paris worked first at Le Bon Marché and modeled their institutions on it. They also borrowed from Boucicaut's administrative and commercial strategies and management philosophy. Over the years, many department stores emerged in Paris, but only a few remain operating today. The most important for the scope of this study, besides Le Bon Marché, are La Samaritaine, Magasin du Louvre, Bazar de l'Hotel de Ville, Printemps, and Galeries Lafayette. In their representation and operation, emporia mirrored the eclectic politics of the

Second Empire. In his description of Napoleon III and his ruling regime, Alain Plessis states: "In the economic and social spheres, it would be vain to try to classify the emperor, to make him the disciple of any given school. He appears in turn as a man influenced by English liberals, as a 'Saint-Simonian,' Caesar, or at times as a socialist. He was above all an eclectic who borrowed from every doctrine whatever in his view could better the lot of the people" (11). Plessis's description of the emperor could also apply to the history of emporia and its owners. Emporia espoused the imperial military imaginary of control to that of social and commercial utopianism. The emporium was a site of an eclectic utopianism and autocratic control under the command of a dynasty of entrepreneurs who became, like their stores, household names. The rise of the *grand magasin* signaled a turning point in urban commercial geography. Since 1815, bourgeois buildings designated the ground floor for commercial spaces (Hahn 34). The *grand magasin* reversed that relationship by taking over entire buildings, while simultaneously calling itself *maison* and *magasin*.[37] The store associated its design and iconography with the emblems and missions of the Second Empire, precisely that of French industrialist utopianism exemplified in the universal exhibitions. For instance, Boucicaut assigned Jean-Alexandre Planchet, Louis Charles Boileau, and finally Gustave Eiffel to design the interior (Clausen, *Frantz Jourdain* 198). Stressing its connection to the city, Le Bon Marché provided maps of Paris for visitors of the exhibitions and tourists in general, where the store was featured as a Parisian landmark.[38] The same promotional strategies were copied by other department stores. Furthermore, to align the expansion and the outreach of the emporium with that of the empire, the stores produced a map of France and its colonies (Au Bon Marché, *Carte des colonies françaises*).

In 1872, Ernest Cognacq married Louise Jay from the Bon Marché and expanded his boutique, La Samaritaine, into a large department store. Much like the Boucicauts, the Cognacqs adhered to a paternalistic social utopian philosophy, strongly informed by Saint-Simonianism, where the entrepreneurial couple actively engaged in the education and formation of his workers. The Cognacqs paid special attention to the role of architecture in conveying the image of their enterprise. In 1883, Ernest Cognacq hired Franz Jourdain to expand his store. Cognacq and Jourdain envisioned a commercial establishment that reflected the emporium's social mission. Jourdain translated Cognacq's social utopianism into architecture. For the first time, Jourdain integrated art and crafts into the design. The building was a true collaborative "oeuvre" among artisans in the Saint-Simonian sense, an artwork that sought to bring art to the public beyond the store's clients. Jourdain created an elaborately decorative and polychromatic façade evoking eastern and southern Mediterranean architecture. Initially, the building's colorful palette, its bare iron structure, and the profusion of undulant flora and fauna motifs shocked the bourgeoisie (Clausen, *Frantz Jourdain* 255–59). For a long time, the store adopted a paternalist socialist agenda which treated the business enterprise as a household that looked after its workers, by offering various economic and cultural services and benefits. This centralized top-down welfare system did not necessarily identify with a wider workers' movement. Managers still resisted union demands and refused to hire employees who received training in institutions for professional training. They preferred employees to be inculcated with the "house" culture (Chessel 287; Badel 299–302).

Later department stores reflected similar social and commercial patterns. In 1855, Auguste Chauchard, a salesclerk at Au Pauvre Diable, in partnership with Auguste Hériot from La Ville de Paris and Charles Eugène, established Le Grand Magasin du Louvre. In 1856, Xavier Ruel founded Bazar de l'Hotel de Ville. In 1865, Jules Jaluzot, the head clerk of the silk department at Le Bon Marché, opened Printemps. After the destruction of Printemps in 1882, Jaluzot assigned Paul Sédille to rebuild the store, and he integrated wrought iron into the design (Caracalla 50). In 1912, Théophile Bader and Alphonse Kahn inaugurated the youngest of the *grand magasins*, Galeries Lafayette. Printemps's and Lafayette's proximity to the *grands boulevards* and their location near three train stations guaranteed a constant flow of customers, both residents and foreigners—England, Germany, and Spain (Van Zanten, *Building Paris* 18). The stores created a symbiotic relation with the boulevards, attracting peddlers and visitors from the cafés, theaters, arcades, and various entertainment spots. Married bourgeois women who saw the passages as outdated and feared to be seen on the *grands boulevards* alone made the emporium their destination of choice for shopping (Giffard 144, 285–93; Gaston-Breton 10–14). On the other hand, the emporia brought to the area hundreds of salesclerks and shopgirls, who lived close to the stores and spent their evenings on the boulevards. During that era, the numbers of salesclerks (*calicots*) reached up to 30,000 (Le Blond 479). Galeries Lafayette stressed its Oriental decoration. In 1919, when Bader assigned architect Ferdinand Chanut to design his new store, Galeries Lafayette, he specifically asked for an Oriental setting that would stimulate the fantasy of the shoppers (Gaston-Breton 33). The new shop extended over 18,000 square meters, on five levels, with a distinctive neo-Byzantine cupola. The initial wall colors and lighting were intentionally selected to give a golden glow that would evoke an Oriental bazaar (Gaston-Breton 34).

Following in the footsteps of empire, French department stores expanded across its territories, spreading its tentacles beyond national borders, either via founding stores and showrooms or by mail order. In 1874, Printemps expanded its activities in Germany, Alsace-Lorraine, Denmark, Russia, Romania, and Norway. Using the service of the Orient Express train, the store delivered its merchandise to the Balkans and Turkey (Caracalla 40). Similarly, Le Bon Marché opened branches in Vichy, Toulouse, Algiers, Buenos Aires, Cairo (Burckhardt 10) and Galeries Lafayette in Cairo, Alexandria, Algiers, Tunis, Meknes, Casablanca, Rabat, Tangiers, and Aleppo (Gaston-Breton 42–47). Celebrating its wide reach, Le Bon Marché produced a large promotional leaflet featuring its Parisian store at the center flanked by a picture of the Cairene branch on the right and the Algerian branch on the left. The leaflet portrayed the store's dominion over both sides of the Arab world, Mashriq and Maghreb, with Paris at the center of this commercial network (Le Bon Marché, *Succurscale d'Algerie*).

Emporialism and Cultural Imperialism: The Rise of the Saint-Simonian-Fourierist Phalanstery

The emporium did not draw its power solely from reiterating the optics of empire. Its activities simultaneously re-created the imagined geography of empire and deployed a strategy of "cultural imperialism." As Marion Young puts it, cultural imperialism enabled "the particular experience and perspective of privileged groups to parade as universal" (10). In this sense, emporialism relied on its potential to operate on several scales simultaneously. Stores were often dubbed "combat units" commanding "an army of salesclerks" (Garrigues 23–25, qtd. in Nord 63). These terms reflected the sheer number of individuals who worked at these organizations and their social and visual impact in the cityscape. By 1911, the twelve major establishments commanded 11,000 individuals, 900 people per store, in contrast to small boutiques who had fewer than 10 employees (Nord 63). Much like the eclectic spirit of the Second Empire, the stores' representation and mission embodied an eclectic utopianism, which I argue gave it the ideological and organizational configuration of a hybrid social utopian space, a *Saint-Simonian-Fourierist phalanx*. On one hand, writers like Zola and other nineteenth-century media depicted the stores as a phalanstery (Nord 65). Notably, in the context of the era, the words *phalanstery* and *phalanx* carry double connotations, that of a military unit and that of the utopian social unit conceived by Charles Fourier. For Fourier, the phalanstery represented an oversized monument, a reminder of the shopping arcades and military bases. The phalanstery is a monumental residential unit for a sustainable cooperative egalitarian community. For instance, an illustration by Fourier shows a phalanstery designed for 1,620 residents, with a part called "street galleries" (fig. 1.9). The site comprises residential apartments and work and cultural spaces, such as workshops, agricultural fields, meeting rooms, and libraries (Fourier, "An Architectural Innovation" 241–45; Benjamin 15–17).[39]

In addition to being constructed as a social utopian unit, the *grand magasin* took on the aspects of the Saint-Simonian network and industrial utopia. The stores were often described as a machine and an octopus whose tentacles reached everywhere (Nord 65, 82). The stores' missions amalgamated the views of early guild traditions, Fourierism, and Saint-Simonianism (Sewell 48).[40] Like Fourier's phalanstery, the emporium advertised itself as a colossal building, a self-enclosed and sustainable utopia, harboring hundreds (if not thousands) of employees. It contained dormitories, refectories, reading spaces, music rooms, and classes. Each emporium presented itself as one large family presided over by an entrepreneurial couple with the store as their oeuvre or life work (Miller 143–44).[41] For instance, Le Bon Marché was run as a household by Aristide Boucicaut and his wife, Marguerite Guérin, who were described as a "laborious" couple; Guérin was the "daughter of the people (Le Bon Marché, *Historique des magasins* 6; Miller 110–11). The image of a presiding entrepreneurial couple brings back the long history of French guilds and *compagnonnage* in France, as far back as the twelfth century, but it was also a signature characteristic of a Saint-Simonian utopianism built around the hierarchal dominion of an industrialist couple who take charge of their employees.[42] Upon his death in 1877, Boucicaut left a considerable business empire with 3,500 employees and thirty departments (Gaston-Breton 12). Madame Boucicaut leagued the store's shares among the managers and the employees (Miller 116–17). Similarly, the workers at La Samaritaine called their manager-patriarch, Ernest Cognacq, "Père Laborem," or Father Labor (Jarry 77). This symbolic structure echoes the guild tradition (*campagnonnage*) and the hierarchal Saint-Simonian community, ruled by a "Father" and "Mother," a priest and priestess. From the Saint-Simonian tradition, the department store took its flair for the spectacle and its expansionism as a part of an interconnected global network. Typical to the Saint-Simonian mission, stores also sponsored the education and the welfare of their employees by providing language classes, music lessons, spaces of entertainment, and mutual funds (Giffard 214–29).[43] An advertisement from 1929 promoted La Samaritaine as a household managed by a husband and wife: Monsieur and Madame Cognacq celebrate their social commitment to their enterprise (fig. 1.10). In its graphic representation, it reveals its hybrid quality as a social utopian space mirroring the ideology of the Second Empire, a Saint-Simonian-Fourierist phalanstery. A massive social structure, bringing under one roof various groups and social classes, plugged into an interconnected web of trade networks.

Educating the Empire

True to its characterization as a hybrid "Saint-Simonian-Fourierist phalanstery," the internal operation of the store and its promotional material executed a civilizing mission aiming to domesticate the empire through commercial utopianism. In its quotidian activities, the department store occupied a protean position as urban space and a disciplinary educational institution that enjoyed an unprecedented grip over the habitus of the modern European subject (the body, the members of the household: husband, wife, and children), the city, the nation-state, the empire, and economic and cultural capital. In its mission to domesticate the empire and educate its citizens, the rhetoric of emporialism presented the emporium as a site of metaphoric battle, between Orient and Occident and between spiritualism and materialism, in which the consumer featured paradoxically as a subject and an object, under the draconian rule of consumerism. Many of the stores' promotional campaigns centered on activating the narratives surrounding the process and fantasies of acquiring the Oriental rug. Emporialism established authorship precisely by means exploiting the epistemological and ontological frameworks of Orientalism. The stores established their authority as experts in Oriental goods by mobilizing and producing colonial and Orientalist knowledge. For instance, several catalogues from Le Bon Marché spanning many decades describe the store's agents as explorers who, despite great challenges, were able to bring back authentic Oriental artifacts to the French public. The catalogue from 1878 advertises the yearly Oriental salon that took place in the fall season (23 September). The pictures appeal to French Orientalist fantasies by providing viewers

58 | Emporialism

with a panoramic vista of the East and an insider's peek into the private space of the harem.

The catalogue's front cover, framed to look like decorative pieces of Orientalist art, shows a painting of a harem set against Moresque architecture (fig. 1.11). The portrayed harem shares a similar floor plan with the setting of the department store, where clients standing in the upper balconies could also enjoy a bird's-eye view of the lobby. The textile hanging from the staircase, featuring the shop owner's name, conflates the space of the harem with that of the store, almost as if the harem belonged to the store's owner. Interestingly, the women depicted are fully covered and not nude odalisques, perhaps because the catalogue's reach specifically targeted bourgeois households. The catalogue reflects what Said describes as the nineteenth-century ethos and aesthetics of the middle-class, "embourgeoisement" with its censored measures for sexuality (Said, *Orientalism* 190). Unlike the typical erotic subjects featured in Orientalist paintings, the catalogues reframe Orientalism as a playful leisurely fantasy devoid of any colonial violence.

Whereas the front cover features the private space of the harem, the back cover of the same catalogue displays a panoramic exterior with desolate ancient ruins (fig. 1.12). At the center of the picture, a caravan of camels heavily laden with goods guarded by Europeans moves toward a fleet of ships, waiting on the distant shore. The image is framed by two ancient statues: an Assyrian man on the right and an Egyptian woman on the left. Lumping together ancient Egypt, Assyria, and Babylon, the catalogue offers a totalizing map of the Middle East as an accumulation of monuments and artifacts. The idea is reinforced by the ruins of a temple on the hill. The presence of armed European men (merchants, explorers, department store purchasing agents) brings to the forefront the different forms of colonial intervention in the East, with its potential of violence.

In addition to imagery, the store's promotional materials rely on a plethora of narratives, anecdotes, and biographies of renowned Orientalists, painters, diorama and battle illustrators, army officers, explorers, and writers to buttress their position as experts in Oriental artifacts. The catalogues from Le Bon Marché, like other stores, constantly associate their rugs with the imperial ambition to study, manage, and control the Orient. Such trends lasted for several decades. For instance, the catalogues of 1910, 1911, 1912, 1913, and 1914 refer to various Orientalist artists and explorers to promote their annual Oriental salon.[44] The catalogue cover from 1910 is decorated as a hand-painted page from an Arabic manuscript, probably the opening page of the Quran. On the cover is the title: "The Orient by Alberto Pasini *offered by* les grands magasins du Bon Marché" (emphasis added). In its mission of promoting rugs, the emporium's marketing strategy depended primarily on an Orientalist machinery of authentication made possible by the "referential power" of a set of Orientalist texts, documents, and artworks (Said, *Orientalism* 20). The circulation of capital, that is, the stores' revenues and merchandise, went hand in hand with the parallel trajectory of Orientalist studies. The emporium's expertise and pedigree rested on the exploitation of a body of knowledge produced by a variety of agents, painters, explorers, army officers, writers, and translators. The Orientalist narrative accompanying the pictures, endorsed with a stamp of the store's owner's name (Boucicaut), confirmed the authenticity of the merchandise and, by association, established his authority over the region. The department store owner took on the task of an Orientalist who "must locate himself vis-à-vis the Orient" by means of genealogy of knowledge and chain of references to be able to finally speak on behalf of (or in this case to sell products from) the Orient (Said, *Orientalism* 20). Linking their operation to that of traders, explorers, archeologists, sociologists, artists, and colonizers, the emporium established their purchase personnel as agents of the empire and the emporium, both insiders and outsiders to the Orient. The emporium and its catalogues became part of the structured body of knowledge defining the Orient and the other corners of the empire. The catalogues exhibited and studied the colonies just as they were "framed by the classroom, the criminal court, the prison, the illustrated manual" (Said, *Orientalism* 41).

Through Orientalist material culture, emporialism transformed the bourgeois home into, as Benjamin suggests, "a theatre of the world" (19), a situation where the phantasmagoria of empire separated the public space of work and the private domain of the bourgeois household. The rug linked the extensive realm of empire to the domestic confines of the bourgeois salon. Its geometric shape anchored and structured the bourgeois space and highlighted its opulence. Treading on the rug communicated and reinforced the imaginary of imperialism and its exploits. To give an example: in 1913, Le Bon Marché published its yearly furniture catalogue, titled "The Orient offered by Le Bon Marché." In its layout, the catalogue exhibits one rug opposite an Orientalist tableau (fig. 1.13). It creates a metonymic relation between the marketed product, the rugs, and the referred space. Through this strategic positioning, the department store overlapped the ambitions and imaginaries of imperialism with household consumption. Acquiring a rug served as a vicarious colonial venture, whereby buyers symbolically possessed a piece of the territory.

Nevertheless, in popularizing the colonial venture by means of consumerism, the rhetoric of emporialism strictly guards the borders between Eastern and Western material culture. Like many other publications from the same store, the layout of the catalogue stresses an aesthetic dichotomy between East and West. Whereas the first part of the catalogue displays Oriental artifacts, especially rugs, accompanied by Orientalist narratives and art, the second part shifts the focus from the Orient to France to exhibit a set of distinctively French-style furniture—Louis XV, Louis XVI, and Empire—which should adorn the bourgeois household. The latter part of the catalogue serves as a national history lesson on French decor for the bourgeois woman.

This assertive imperialist worldview is not devoid of tensions. In the background of this narrative of control surfaces an ambivalent image exposing the fear of engulfment by a modern consumerist culture and, by extension, that of an unruly metaphorical Orient. For instance, the catalogue from 1913 includes a posthumous essay by the famous illustrator of battles Édouard Detaille, which strikingly takes a literary naturalist fatalistic perception, "The tyranny of objects on our habits, on the order and course of our intimate thoughts, is stronger than what we imagine" (Le Bon Marché, "Aux visiteurs" 20).[45] Detaille's anxious words turn the consumer utopia upside down, revealing the reversal between subject and object, collectors and collections, wherein the world of merchandise establishes its imperious dominion over the French citizens in their pursuit of a harmonious household reflecting the magnificence of empire.

Emporialism's promotion of a balanced mélange of East and West attuned with the politics of empire. Annexing the Orient to the bourgeois interior represented a broader ideology that symbolically sutured the social and political wounds of a fragmented empire. Orientalist interior decor became part of the eclectic worldview that mirrored the policies of the Belle Époque—a mélange of social utopianism, liberalism, and even imperial despotism—at a time when the social, urban, and political fabric of the nation was tearing apart (Plessis 11). As an aesthetic bringing east and west together, eclecticism aimed to achieve "harmony" in the household's decor (Lasc 25; Havard 243). In his interior design guide, Henry Havard quotes architect Viollet-le-Duc's words: "A certain harmonious relationship can be established between people and objects, which endows dwellings with a character, like a soul."[46] Viollet-le-Duc's words remarkably echo and even aspire to correct the tyranny of objects depicted by Detaille in the emporium catalogue. Viollet-le-Duc probably alludes to an architectural aesthetic of empathy, in which a space mirrors its inhabitants and conforms to the way they inhabit a space. His words suggest that by reordering and mastering the semiotics of Eastern and Western material culture, one can overcome the tyranny of empire and emporium. To an extent, the mélange of Orient and Occident strikingly resembles the Saint-Simonian organizational project of the Second Empire and its vision of a harmonious Mediterranean system, purporting to end a mythological lifetime battle by uniting East and West.[47]

This notion reflected an overarching national trend beyond the confines of bourgeois households. Eclecticism served to navigate the various partisan currents in the nation, which presented more immediate threats on the social and national levels. On the urban level, for public monuments, especially churches, eclecticism functioned as an apolitical iconographic aesthetic that reconciled the taste of seculars and Catholics (Mead, *Making Modern Paris* 129). Haussmann's urban project replaced familiar spaces with a monotonous sober design that did not give free rein to an emerging bourgeois class to express its dominion over the cityscape. The endless uniform façades acted, in Siegfried Giedion's words, as "a kind of wardrobe into which all the disorder can be crammed," behind which lay building clusters with uneven parceled spaces (675). Eclecticism fulfilled the needs of a rising bourgeoisie who rose to power after the revolution. In contrast to nobility from the ancien régime, the bourgeoisie did not inherit châteaux decked with period furniture demonstrating their aristocratic lineage or their refined taste. Breaking away from a monotonous exterior and a fragmented body politic, bourgeois houses opened onto colorful interiors that carefully produced a perfected and ordered portrait of the empire (Van Zanten, *Building Paris* 41).[48] Eclecticism marked bourgeois status by reconstructing through material culture a history to which they never belonged. As Susan Stewart argues, "collections replace origins with classification, thereby making temporality a spatial and material phenomenon" (154). Mixing the Orient and Occident, namely, French furniture and Oriental decorative pieces, the bourgeoisie connected themselves at once to the empire's past and present. The acquisition and ordering of furniture served to appropriate the prestige of the old regime and the contemporary treasures of the colonies.

Inside the house, Oriental settings projected the typical attributes of the Orient: static, atemporal, and chaotic, subject to rational European control. Rugs conveyed luxury but also absorbed and muted the noise from servants' movements around the house (Havard 427). Orientalism came to fill a lacuna in the house, bridging the gap between tradition and modernity. Designer manuals conceptualized Oriental decor to be "ahistoric"

(Lasc 28). They recommended its aesthetic for rooms whose functions do not tie to French old customs, such as the boudoir and the smoking room (Havard 460–61). Notably, these rooms came to acquire a character that was projected onto the Orient. The boudoir was a space designed to shelter the mistress of the house and contain her mood changes. The smoking room was a masculine domain associated with adventure, fantasy, idleness, and indulgence. These rooms established a persona by embodying an Orientalist cliché: the first a feminine irrationality, the second the masculine bravado of imperialism and an Oriental languid lifestyle associated with "waterpipes" and "clouds of smoke" (Havard 460).

The use of Oriental iconography in the interior was part and parcel of a wider national strategy outside the household. Napoleon's Egyptomania and military campaign, expressed in the passage du Caire, served to build a fictional lineage by filling the lacunae between the history of empires (Egyptian, Roman, and Greek) and that of the nascent French empire. Similarly, in 1833–1836, King Louis Philippe asked his architect Jacques Hittorff to place the Luxor obelisk at the Concorde Square. The king explains his decision to Comte de Rambuteau, the prefect of Paris preceding Baron Haussmann: "I have another reason for placing the obelisk in the center [of the square] is that it will not recall any political event and it is therefore sure to remain, otherwise you might someday see there an expiatory monument or a statue of liberty" (Rambuteau as qtd. in Mead, *Making Modern Paris* 82; Rambuteau 389; Schneider 1:386).[49] For Louis Philippe, Egyptian iconography helped erase the violent history of the revolution and the memory of guillotine, as well as obliterate the prospect of a new republic. A few decades later, during the Third Republic, France's further expansion in the Orient came to fill another political vacuum and compensate for the loss of Alsace-Lorraine to Germany (Mayeur and Reberioux 94–100). Much like the Orient inside the household, representations of the East in public space served to reconstruct French history and project a sense of continuum by bridging the various episodes that shattered the nation. Although deemed the substance of fantasy and escapism, the Orient was a symbolic connective node that operated synchronically and diachronically, mending the fractures in French territory and history.

Orientalism and Bourgeois Women's Bodies

Whereas the furniture catalogues clearly marked the lines where orientalism begins and ends in the household, stores projected similar dialectic boundaries on the bodies of the middle-class and working-class women. In 1869, the same year as the inauguration of the Suez Canal, the summer catalogue from Le Bon Marché promoted new dress styles called *arménienne* and *musulmane* (figs. 1.14 and 1.15).[50] The catalogue includes several ethnic and French provincial references. Through fashion, women come to embody the imperial fantasy of the Universal Exhibition and its *tableaux vivants* as a playful masquerade and proof of imperial appropriation. As Bonnie Smith argues, exaggerated feminine fashion projected an image of plenitude while simultaneously eclipsing the bourgeois woman's body under its profuse details (77–84). An Orientalist fashion confines the body of the bourgeois woman within the realm of a whimsy, mercurial, and infantilized Orient, away from the masculine and rational domain of the public sphere and body politic whose access was restricted to her male counterpart. Ironically, it was also Orientalist fashion, inspired by the Far East, that liberated the bourgeois woman's body from the draconian rule of the corset (Hoganson 86).

If emporialism attempted to exile bourgeois women into the fantasyland of Orientalist cultural camouflage, it guarded working-class women within the secure confines and control of French propriety. Women workers were subject to a civilizing mission crafting them into model citizens of the nation and empire by purging any traits of non-European cultures. For employees, the department store morphed into a symbolic household of the nation, and it executed a strict patriarchal program of containment, discipline, and order. A catalogue published by Le Bon Marché in 1904 shows two scenes from the store. The first represents the store's vestibule full of bourgeois customers, the other the workers' workshop. Each site represents a different world within the same store: the first one bourgeois, festive, theatrical, free flowing, including men and women (fig. 1.16); the other strictly controlled and rigid (fig. 1.17). The image from the store's workshop portrays female department store employees dressed in their somber black uniform, their hair carefully tied in tight buns. Their outfit and behavior recall girls' uniforms of that era's Catholic boarding schools (*pensionnnat*) (B. Smith 168–71). The workers prepare samples to be sent by mail to households across France and around the world. Except for one male worker wielding the machine for cutting the samples, men are absent from the space. Drawing on the rhetoric of the civilizing mission, the emporium fashioned itself as a model successful urban colony where workers, especially women, were subjected to the measures of French bourgeois discipline and control. The illustration appeals to the centralizing spirit of the Third Republic, with its desire to secure a uniform national culture across provincial and class differences. The geometric perspective and the presence of the several supervisors conveys an image of control to counter the widespread cliché of the unruly working-class woman, remnant of the Commune. Taking work as its central theme, the image aims to discredit the perception of the department store as a site of chaos, promiscuity, and transgression. The craftsman depicted alone inside a circle in the lower left corner of the photo stresses a strict division of labor by gender. Men take charge of technical operations and machines while women occupy the secondary role of assistants. The imbalance between the number of men and women assures masculine anxiety. Even if the store would seem dominated by women's presence, it remains under the secure grasp of men insofar as it takes only one man to lead an entire army of docile women. The shop-girls—referred to as *demoiselles*, sit demurely in the confinement of a clean industrial space: a model of hygiene and order (Giffard 89).[51] The strictly monitored workshop occupies the other side of the spectrum from the leisurely, oversized queen of the emporium who monopolizes public space. The photo highlights the workers' grounded position, contained and content in the boundaries of their national, gender, and class roles. Typically, French nineteenth-century emporia exercised significant control over their workers' mobility since they included dormitories for women and workers from the provinces, who spent most of their time between the hostel and the store. By laying claim to the body of the working woman, the stores appeased middle-class anxieties concerning promiscuity and the transgression of class barriers.

A closer inspection reveals that the moral panic translated into the strict theatrical control of bourgeois women, female workers, and colonial Others reflected a general masculine fear of losing control over modern urban and civic space. Indeed, the *grands magasins* helped render women (both workers and customers) more visible in public spaces. For the refined bourgeois woman, however, the emporium was a sign of *déclassement* (loss of social status). Upper-class women often avoided being seen shopping in the department store. According to women vendors from that era, elite women pretended to be shopping for their maids (Giffard 272; Tiersten, *Marianne in the Market* 78). Bourgeois shoplifters constituted another riddle, since they defied the distinction between the social classes, established by sociologists and moralists, who could not simply associate crime with the working classes as they had typically done. Kleptomania was at once a sign of bourgeois women's inability to repress their desire and "a rapacious action traditionally associated with masculinity" (Dubuisson 13; Giffard 120–51;

MagShamhráin 72). As Rachel MagShamhráin has convincingly argued, bourgeois women's tireless demand for suffrage came hand in hand with their disenfranchisement by means of their association with kleptomania and promiscuity, as well as the accusation of jeopardizing the reputation of the bourgeois household due to their frenzied shopping habits in the emporium. Much like the image of the gigantic ominous female shopper, the bourgeois woman was feared to outgrow her prescribed gendered national role and become a full citizen (MagShamhráin 63–91; fig. 1.2).[52]

For female workers, the stores were one of the few domains available outside domestic and sex work. Nevertheless, most women worked in the domestic sphere (Moses 29, 176–77). It was only later, during World War I, that women occupied more positions in the stores, leading to a subsequent competition for wages (McBride 638).[53] Moreover, though sexual promiscuity was the main argument against the department store, sexual liaisons and sex work had always been part of the domestic sphere and Parisian urban public spaces. In 1880, half of the children born out of wedlock in Paris belonged to female domestic workers (Moses 30). Commercial spaces, as early as the Galeries de Bois of the Palais Royal, built in 1781–86 on the property of the future King Louis Philippe, was infamous for gambling, prostitution, and same-sex relations (Moncan, *Les passages couverts* 23; Canac 69; Sibalis). The passages (arcades) across Paris and the *grands boulevards* were also sites for the same activities, to the extent that there were several epithets to describe the various types of prostitutes who frequented the passages (Moncan, *Les passages couverts* 61–74). Compared with these spaces, the constantly surveilled emporium should not have been a source of moral panic. The department stores heralded a new perception and practice of space different from that of the boulevards and the passages during the first half of the nineteenth century. Walter Benjamin argues that the rise of panoramic literature in the first half of the nineteenth century set the stage for the emergence of the *flâneur*, or the leisurely walker, as a social type who sees the city as a landscape (5–6; Hahn 51–56; D'Souza and McDonough).[54] As Vanessa Schwartz explains, "The *flâneur* is not so much a person as *flânerie* is a positionality of power—one through which the spectator assumes the position of being able to be part of the spectacle and yet command it at the same time" (10). By the mid-nineteenth century, the *grands boulevards* were exaggeratingly described by Parisians as the "center of the universe" and the heart of Parisian civilized life. As Alfred de Musset once put it, beyond the passages and the *grands boulevards* lie "the great indies" (Schwartz 19; Moncan, *Les passages couverts* 64; Hahn 131; Goffette

33–42). The linear geography of the boulevards and the passages offered a sense of control to the pedestrian, who could cover their surface in short time. Commenting on the *flâneur*'s pseudo sense of empowerment, Musset's quip was that it only takes a hundred steps to find the entire universe (Musset 281, qtd. in Moncan, *Les passages couverts* 64). To give another example, in his portrait of the city in *Le Diable à Paris*, Balzac presents the *grands boulevards* to his public like as a panoramic tableau going from West to East. He comfortably reads the urban space like an open book ("Histoire et physiologies" 164–67). *Flâneurs*, or leisurely walkers, enjoyed the chaotic and carnivalesque aspect of urban life, in which they could disappear amid a rowdy crowd. For Baudelaire, *flânerie* was a transcendent aesthetic experience. As Michèle Hannoosh suggests, "the modern city [presented] the *flâneur* ... with an image of ... his status as subject and object, implicated in the same urban experience he seems to control" (Hannoosh, *Baudelaire and Caricature* 4). *Flânerie* was a practice of space that derived its power by making the individual at once invisible and the center of things.

This situation began to change with the Second Empire. Paris, which was once built at the scale of the *flâneur*, shifted scale with Haussmann's urban plan to prioritize the circulation of traffic (Giedion 673–74).[55] By the Third Republic, the landscape of the boulevard had evolved from an easily readable panorama into a chaotic space lacking an organizing structure, mostly due to intense commercial activity and advertising (Hahn 131). The perceptual changes stemmed also from the transformation of the city's urban plan, I argue. Similarly, the emporium alienated the *flâneur* and his worldview. In addition to manipulative commercial display, the stores morphed the panorama of the boulevards into a panopticon, which indulged customers' voyeuristic habits while ensuring their visibility by hundreds of employees, including security personnel. The pseudo-panoramic vistas of the stores neither provided the advantage of invisibility nor the euphoria of transcending crowds and space altogether. Instead, they trapped the *flâneur* into the webs of its commercial utopia. Contrary to the fantasy of the anonymous *flâneur*, the stores' vendors devised a plethora of classifications that placed customers under the microscope, akin to colonial subjects under study. The categories encompassed clients' nationalities, taste, shopping behavior, social class, relationship patterns, and even fetishes (Giffard 108–18, 189–204).[56] Benjamin rightfully observes that the emporium was the "last promenade of the *flâneur*" (895). Not only did it place the male *flâneur* in a feminized space, it subjected him to the scrutiny and control of the working class.

For all these reasons, department stores became the rich fabric of a modern urban intersectional mythology: a favorite topic in literature, caricatures, vaudeville plays, musicals, and later cinema. Some of the many themes that fascinated the public were the presence of women in the public sphere, the promiscuous reputation of the stores, and the utopian spectacle of merchandise. All of this served to construct a worldview from the perspective of the female bourgeois shopper and that of her counterpart from the petty bourgeoisie, the shopgirl.[57] Most often the fall of the former was correlated with the rise of the latter. This imaginary world was beset with hysteria, kleptomania, prostitution, and illusions of rapid social ascension and wealth. In addition to the clichés of the fooled husband and besotted male shopper, the emporium's mythology included other masculine elements. Stories were spun around the image of the jack-of-all-trades salesclerk, pejoratively called *calicot* in French (Le Blond 479–80).[58] On the other hand, the trajectory of the emporia's owners from rags to riches and their industrious character provided fodder for a capitalist narrative of success. The fact that a significant number of stores around the world were consumed by fire and eventually rebuilt in a more progressive design made them seem like phoenixes rising from the ashes. All of these aspects enforced the myth of the department store as a monument of modernity that breaks away from a traditional rigid past: a symbol of social ascension and transgression, pragmatism, success, progress, creativity, and survival.

Conclusion

The rhetoric of emporialism worked to mirror the ambition of the empire. At the same time, emporialism strove to appease and camouflage the French elements of moral panic by building in its promotional material a neat world divided along the lines of race, class, and gender, as well as Orient and Occident. Exploring the reductive theatricality characteristic of the emporium and the universal exhibitions, Timothy Mitchell perceives the imperialist drive to render the world into a picture as an attempt to domesticate space by imposing a European notion of control and rational order (*Colonising Egypt* 10–28). The emporium, however, also born in the second half of the nineteenth century, was not part of a top-down imperial project, aiming to rewrite world history by fixing it into a picture. It was a commercial venture whose creators mostly came from humble backgrounds: ambitious salesclerks and shopkeepers who transformed their small shops into gigantic marketplaces over the years. For all its efforts to accentuate imperial progress and hierarchies of power—with coordinates of race, class, and gender—the polarized world depicted in the emporia's posters did not constitute a binary one constrained by the limits of subject and object, colonizer and colonized, empire and colony. The values of agora-cosmopolitanism failed to capture and refused to validate other complex experiences of cross-cultural relations and diversity from the other side of the Mediterranean. This fact could easily be seen in the case of colonial subjects like Ahmad Zaki. Zaki's life experience reflected a different version of cosmopolitanism that neither resonated with the folkloric *tableaux vivants* of the fairgrounds nor matched the celebrated agora-cosmopolitan moment marketed by the posters. In contrast to the promotional material of the department stores and the pavilions on the exhibition grounds, the world of Zaki was, just like an actual emporium, highly porous and entangled. Back in Zaki's homeland, on the other side of the Mediterranean, emporialism told another story.

Figure 2.1. Caricature, Ferdinand de Lesseps parting the Isthmus of Suez, by Etienne Carjat. *Le Boulevard*, 1862. *Source*: © Bibliothèque Nationale de France. Public domain. Used with permission.

Figure 2.2. "Egypt Carrying Light to Asia," Auguste Bartholdi. *Source*: Musée Bartholdi, Colmar. Photograph © C. Kempf. Used with permission.

Figure 2.3. Photograph, interior hall at Galeries Lafayette, 1914. *Source*: © Galeries Lafayette Archives, Paris. Used with permission.

Figure 2.4. Photograph, interior hall of Sednaoui, 2023. *Source*: Photo by author.

Figure 2.5. Omar Effendi department store, exterior, Cairo, 2013. *Source*: Photo by author.

Figure 2.6. Le Bon Marché Succursale de Vichy, exterior, catalogue Le Bon Marché, circa 1925. *Source*: Ville de Paris, Bibliothèque Forney. Public domain. Used with permission.

Figure 2.7. Calendar, Grand Magasin Paschal and Cie, 1895. *Source*: Ville de Paris, Bibliothèque Forney. Public domain. Used with permission.

Figure 2.8. Photo of Prince Farouk opposite to a toy advertisement, Le Bon Marché, January 1929. *Source*: Centre d'Etudes Alexandrines. Public domain. Used with permission.

Figure 2.9. "This dress is incomplete," cartoon, *al-Lata'if al-Musawwara*, 3 April 1922, 16. *Source*: Dar al-Kutub. Public domain.

Figure 2.10. Women in public spaces, *al-Lata'if al-Musawwara*, 19 March 1917. *Source*: Dar al-Kutub. Public domain.

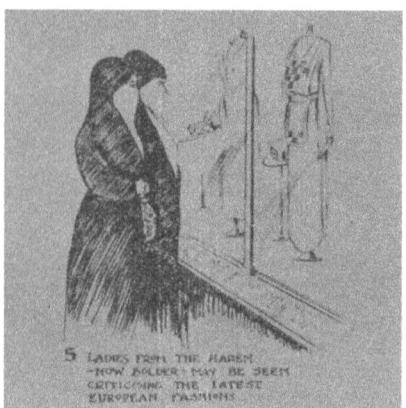

Figure 2.11. "Cairo the Gay City on the Nile as It Is Today," cartoon, *al-Lata'if al-Musawwara*, 13 October 1919. *Source*: Dar al-Kutub. Public domain.

Figure 2.12. "The progress of fashion over half a century," *Rose al-Yusef*, 13 January 1927. *Source*: The Women and Memory Forum, Cairo (WMF). Public domain.

Figure 2.13. "Yesterday and Tomorrow," *al-Lata'if al-Musawwara*, 21 July 1919. *Source*: Harvard University. Public domain.

Figure 2.14. Sednaoui bilingual catalogue, front cover, Winter 1927/28. *Source*: Ville de Paris, Bibliothèque Forney. Public domain. Used with permission.

Figure 2.15. Sednaoui bilingual catalogue, inside cover, Winter 1928/1929. *Source*: Ville de Paris, Bibliothèque Forney. Public domain. Used with permission.

Figure 2.16. Egyptian humor, *Images*, 22 December 1929, 30. *Source*: Centre d'Etudes Alexandrines. Public domain. Used with permission.

Figure 2.17. L'Été chez Sednaoui, Summer at Sednaoui, advertisement, Sednaoui, *La Femme nouvelle*, Summer 1950. *Source*: Centre d'Etudes Alexandrines. Public domain. Used with permission.

Chapter 2

Emporialism at the Crossroads of Empires

By the turn of the century, when Zaki visited the 1900 Universal Exhibition in Paris, the Saint-Simonian commercial utopia had already reached the Egyptian territory, paving the way for the rise of the emporium. Egypt's department stores emerged at the crossroads of three empires: the Ottoman, the French, and the British. These overlapping political and cultural maps required a different rhetoric of emporialism that went beyond the Saint-Simonian binaries of East and West. For instance, when the Parisian *grands magasins* Le Bon Marché, Printemps, Galeries Lafayette, and the Louvre opened branches and distribution offices in Egypt, they were neither the sole department stores in the country nor the only enterprises marketing themselves as French spaces. Their local rivals, Chemla, Sednaoui, Cicurel, Benzion, Orosdi-Back, Gattegno, Hannaux, and Chalon, also framed themselves as French culture hubs. Most of the owners of these French-style businesses hailed from different cultural backgrounds and immigrated from the distant corners of the Ottoman Empire. By the 1930s, the actual *grands magasins* from Paris closed their doors, due to the interwar economic crisis, while their Egyptian competitors survived (Reynolds, *Commodity Communities* 83). In this chapter, I examine the phenomenon of emporialism in Egypt by reconstructing the historical context of the department stores and their iconographic representation in print media, including newspapers, magazines, and catalogues. As I argue, emporialism is not a static phenomenon. It is rather a variegated and multilateral discourse that reflects the power dynamics and tensions between the various competing imperial, national, and social regimes. In the Egyptian context, emporialism attuned to the intricate web of relations that shaped the Mediterranean since the inauguration of the Suez Canal.

A Saint-Simonian Network of Trade and Transport

The industrial utopia, which Zaki saw at the universal exhibition, was the by-product of a utopian journey crisscrossing the Mediterranean, from France, to Egypt, and back to France. The imaginary of the Egyptian emporium bears the marks of that adventure. In 1833, disciples of Henri de Saint-Simon crossed to the other shore of the Mediterranean after failing to sway the French public to their modern social industrialist utopia. After the prohibition of their movement, some members escaped to Egypt during what they dubbed "l'année de la Mère" [the year of the Mother] (Levallois and Régnier 113). Inspired by Napoleon Bonaparte, they traveled to Egypt hoping to find a female messiah, *la Mère* [the Mother] who would join the group leader Barthélemy-Prosper Enfantin, *le Père* [the Father]. The Saint-Simonians called themselves "les compagnons de la femme" [the companions of the woman]. Their egalitarian dream unfolded as a mystical erotic Orientalist feminist quest that should bring equality between Orient and Occident, men and women. This spiritual aspiration was paired with a modern economic project: a new commercial utopia productive of the union between a masculine industrial West and a femininized spiritual East, connected by the Suez Canal. They sought to proselytize their worldview by promoting the Suez Canal project to Egypt's ruler, Mehmet Ali. By 1834, the plague claimed the life of many Saint-Simonians. Survivors returned to France with valuable experience that influenced their country's urban and colonial map during the Second Empire, including Paris's Haussmannization project and the universal exhibitions, which Zaki attended (Levallois and Régnier 103–11; Abi-Mershed 32; Charlety 223–36).[1]

The construction of the canal was realized thirty-six years later by Ferdinand de Lesseps during Second Empire France, when many Saint-Simonians rose in rank in the French government. In 1862, the Saint-Simonian journal *Le Boulevard* parodied Lesseps's success in securing the project (fig. 2.1). Lesseps's caricature reflects the ambivalent and conflicting elements of a utopian geography that Egyptian emporia had to embody. The journal depicts an oversized Lesseps dressed in an animal hide with a large club while straddling the Isthmus of Suez. Legs apart, Lesseps stands like a human bridge connecting East and West, letting European ships pass between his feet.

Lesseps's exaggeratedly large body, his moustache, and his large club express a masculine dominance over a feminized territory, metonymically expressed by the large-bosomed sphinx located on the right side of the parted land. The imagery of a parted isthmus enforces the idea of a sexualized Orient yielding to a masculine Occident exemplified by Lesseps's bravado. The caricature amplifies Michel Chevalier's Saint-Simonian Orientalist imagery, in which the Mediterranean network of trade and transport is simultaneously depicted as a nuptial bed uniting the Orient and the Occident. A member of the group, Émile Barrault, saw Egypt as the site where through their actions, the world would witness their "virility" (Musso, *Saint-Simon* 115).[2] Lesseps's Mediterranean venture represents the advent of the long-aspired eroticized encounter of East and West to end all battles. The French expression "percer le canal" [piercing, or penetrating, the canal] echoes the violent yet romanticized gendered imaginary. At the same time, the caricature reverberates with the Saint-Simonian ideology of *percement* [cutting through] characteristic of George-Eugène Haussmann's urban project, which eliminated everything standing in its way to create a wide network of transport connecting the city (Mead, *Making Modern Paris* 204; Pinon, "Une nouvelle géométrie" 83 and "Percée, tracée" 91) The humorous drawing inadvertently reverses the Saint-Simonian discourse, exposing the underlying anxieties of European control over Middle Eastern and African territories. The depiction of the French entrepreneur in animal hide suggests a fear of contamination, and Lesseps "degenerates" into a primitive man while attempting to reorder Egyptian space by separating its territory from the African continent (implied by the miniature crocodile and the bird on top left).[3]

In the context of this Saint-Simonian imagery, Lesseps's virility finds its mirror-gendered counterpart in the mystified Egyptian woman who undergoes the civilizing Saint-Simonian mission. Her body stands for both a woman messiah and the Egyptian territory. This image is best exemplified in the statue designed by French sculptor Frédéric Auguste Bartholdi for the inaugural ceremony of the canal. Bartholdi's statue represents an Egyptian peasant, a sort of a Marianne figure, holding a beacon (fig. 2.2). The statue, titled "Egypt Carrying Light to Asia," was to be placed at the entrance of the canal. The project was eventually refused by the viceroy. After further modifications, Bartholdi reworked his design and sold it as the Statue of Liberty (Gregory, *Geographical Imaginations* 329; Bräutigam).[4] The Egyptian female peasant was already part of the Saint-Simonian imaginary. In 1834, describing the Egyptian rural woman, the *fellaha*, to her readers, feminist and Saint-Simonian Suzanne Voilquin reiterates the French fascination with this figure: "She is the woman of the people par excellence; she clings to the soil with all her fibers. Her children are the most vivacious. They resist better misery, the lack of hygiene, and all the deleterious ills that attacks and cause the child of the foreigner to disappear, even that of the rich Turk" (289).[5] Voilquin's words sketch to her readers the outlines that later resurfaced in Bartholdi's design and echoed the future nationalist image of Egypt (see chapter 4). Clearly Voilquin had no effect on the design, but her words reveal the persistence and popularity of this imaginary. For Voilquin, the Egyptian peasant is autochthonous, authentic, and eternal. She draws her strength from the Egyptian soil. Standing up and carrying her children over her shoulders, she strikes the viewer with her "biblical" poise (*sa préstance biblique*) (290). Her wretched children are the fittest, and they outlive the foreigner and the rich.

The statue aligns the Enlightenment values of the French Republic with the Saint-Simonian Mediterranean network of trade and transport. "Egypt Carrying Light to Asia" represents the Egyptian nation in the image of a native woman who has successfully undergone the French civilizing mission and whose voice is appropriated to become the spokesperson of French Enlightenment in a European hierarchy of races and cultures, in which Asia becomes the subject of another French subject, Egypt. Derek Gregory suggests that this artwork stands for a Saint-Simonian Orientalist imaginary "to justify domination of an irrational Orient by railroads, canals and commerce, in the name of a superior Enlightenment" (*Geographical Imaginations* 330). Yet what is striking about this image is that through this Orientalist fantasy of an Egyptian Marianne, the French nation takes the form of a native Egyptian woman. The statue becomes an ambiguous moment of national masquerade in which the empire disguises itself as a colonial subject, where "France" dresses up as "Egypt," who dresses up as woman. In this overlapping and exchange of gendered images and histories, the French empire affirms its impact, and perhaps its dependence, on the region. By evoking the nationalist iconography of Marianne, the sculptor concocts a dominant image in Egyptian nationalism, in which Egypt exists as a transcendental national entity that has persisted and survived across the ages. Interestingly, after being rejected by the *khedive*, a modified design of Bartholdi's statue made its way to the United States, where it acquired a new context and became the Statue of Liberty, an iconic symbol of the American dream (Bräutigam 82–85).

Like Bartholdi's statue, Egyptians were figuratively expected to follow the reverse path of Lesseps. The inauguration ceremony for the canal meant to confirm this new image. The ceremony bore all the iconographic elements of the Saint-Simonian utopia present in the cartoon. It was minutely designed to celebrate the union of two divided worlds, East and West (Solé, "L'inauguration"). Akin to the encounter between Lesseps and Barthold's Egypt, the union of Orient and Occident expressed the interplay of several masquerades involving ambiguous, racialized, gendered fantasies. Egypt's Viceroy Ismail, ruler of Egypt and Sudan, affirmed his new status as European. He declared: "My country is no longer in Africa; we are now part of Europe. It is therefore natural for us to abandon our former ways and to adopt a new system adapted to our social conditions" (Mansfield 11). Commemorating the event, Giuseppe Verdi wrote a new opera, *Aida*, celebrating the glorious history of ancient Egyptian imperialism and marking the rest of the continent as a site of doom (Said, *Culture and Imperialism* 111–12; Gitre 38). The opera and the opera house consisted of a Mediterranean collaboration. While Verdi wrote the music, Auguste Mariette, the French Director of the Antiquities Service in Egypt, provided the storyline, which reframed Egyptian history through a Eurocentric lens that valorized ancient Egyptian history and distanced it from its African context (Gitre 17–18). At the same time, the Egyptian territory was gradually detaching itself from the Ottoman Empire. In 1858, Arabic became the official language (Hamamsy 85). By 1867, Ismail had received from the Ottoman Porte the title of *khedive*, a position that granted him autonomous rule of the Egyptian province (Raymond 308).[6]

The *khedive*'s interpellation, which mostly concerned the upper strata of Egyptian society, dictated a change in their subject positions vis-à-vis their geography and history. This new context hints at a dilemma of representation for Egyptians. The residents of Egypt had become not only "'people without history'... but also 'people without geography'... human beings whose relationship to their own land is denied... through a discourse which... separates people from place, and effaces the speaking self" (Gregory, *Geographical Imaginations* 131).[7] In this framework, serving a strategic role in the European economy ushered Egypt into modern history away from an inert, "primitive," prenational African territory. As Egypt became part of the trajectory of international capital, its territory was symbolically sutured to the northern side of the Mediterranean.

The Rise of the Emporium: An Eclectic Emporialism

It is this particular geography that Egyptian emporia sought to navigate. Department store owners in Egypt maneuvered a convoluted cultural and political web straddling several continents. They confronted an imagined geography of overlapping and conflicting maps, drafted by social utopians, imperialists, and nationalists. The new emporia tried to reconstruct the new imagined geography of the Suez Canal while navigating an eclectic imperial utopia.

Most of the stores, in Egypt, such as Tiring, Chemla, and Cicurel, and Sednaoui, were founded by families who moved to the country as part of the internal migration common in the Ottoman Empire and who had connections across the Mediterranean (Kupferschmidt, "Who Needed" 175). In contrast to France, where only the owners of Galeries Lafayette were Jewish, the majority of the famous stores in Egypt were founded by Jewish families. The Egyptian emporia developed as part of the urban commercial fabric, as small boutiques intermixed with traditional and European-styled businesses (Reynolds, *City Consumed* 23–46). They emerged primarily in the Muski area, the Haussmannized part of Cairo (Raymond 311; Abu-Lughod 107–10).[8] Eventually they reached their large-scale operation by steering between the local and global.[9] They integrated most of the strategies followed by department stores worldwide while adapting to the surrounding conditions. Aligning with a local culture capital, they distanced themselves from the Orientalist French consumer fantasy. They avoided the word *bazaar*, opting for *magasin* or *maison* (household). In early Arabic promotional material, the stores were dubbed *al-Makhāzin al-kubra*, after the word *magasin*, which is ironically of an Arabic origin, meaning large warehouses (see chapter 1, note 2).

Among the many department stores that appeared in the Muski quarter was the Tiring store owned by Austrians Victor, Gustav, and Konrad Tiring. The brothers started in Istanbul in 1842 and expanded their business across the region with stores in Salonika and Beirut. The Tirings inaugurated their Cairo store in 1865. Another Austrian citizen, Salomon Stein, founded Stein Oriental Goods Store, which began operation between 1865 and 1867 in Ataba Square in Cairo and between 1875 and 1879 in Alexandria (Kupferschmidt, "Who Needed" 176). Stein stores catered to local and foreign clientele and delivered their merchandise in Egypt and Sudan. The store had branches in Alexandria, Mansura, Tanta, Minya, Asyut, Istanbul, Salonika, and Vienna. The Tiring store, with its famous cupola and Atlas carrying the globe, located across from the old opera house, still dominates the Muski cityscape. The statue of Atlas representing world commerce marks a particularly Germanic iconographic commercial element: one that could be seen to evoke the globe on top of the Tietz Department Store in

Berlin (Whitaker 102). The statue gives insight into the diverse architectural iconography that made the Cairene cityscape not limited to French nor British influences.

Whereas the Tirings originated in Istanbul, The Chemla brothers began as peddlers of olive oil in Monastir and eventually established a shop in Tunis (Shohet, tape 1; Reynolds, *Commodity Communities* 58). This was the first store carrying their name. Like their Cairene competitors (Dar Bakhoush and Le Magasin General), the Chemlas began in Tunis as part of the urban local fabric in the popular commercial district of Bab Suika and then moved next to the *grands magasins* in the French area of the town, by Avenue Jules Ferry, currently known as Currently Avenue Habib Bourguiba (Shohet, tape 1 14). Au Petit Louvre was built on two levels and copied the insignia and the iconography of the Parisian store).

In 1907, the Chemla brothers closed their store in Tunis to open a new *grand magasin* on rue Boulac in Cairo (Avenue Fouad). The Chemlas relocated to Egypt in a group counting more than 200 people between family members and employees (Shohet, tape 1 50). The political climate in the Chemlas' homeland was not very different from its Egyptian counterpart. Both were semi-autonomous Ottoman territories. Whereas Tunisia was under French protection, Egypt was under British protection. As French protégés, and like various entrepreneurs and residents in Egypt, they benefited from extraterritorial diplomatic accords between Europe and the Ottoman Porte. In this context, *extraterritoriality* refers to a legal situation and a phenomenon where Ottoman subjects became protégés of French and British empires by means of travel documents, passports, or, in this case, business registration papers (Stein 2–3). The capitulation agreement provided taxation and juridical privileges to holders of European travel documents in the Ottoman Empire, who were considered under the protection of their respective nation or empire of allegiance (Starr and Somekh, "Editor's Introduction" xv).[10] As Jewish Tunisians, the Chemlas held French passports. The younger children acquired a French education, while the older generation spoke Judeo-Tunisian and Arabic.

In Egypt, the Chemlas ascended the social ladder, mixing with the various communities. From the beginning, they had to master Egypt's cultural and human geography. Upon their arrival at the port, the family was received at the customs by an officer of Tunisian origins. Yvonne Shohet (née Chemla), the daughter of one of the store founders, mentions that she learned the word *Ashkenazi* for the first time when she moved to Cairo and met migrants from Eastern Europe (Shohet, tape 2 34). During that era, the population of Cairo increased from 374,000 in 1882 to 1,312,000 in 1937. In 1927, out of more than a million Cairenes, only 614,000 were born in Cairo (Raymond 311). New residents came from Greece, Italy, France, Britain, Sweden, and Belgium. They belonged to different social classes and backgrounds (Abu-Lughod 115).

When the Chemlas moved from Tunis to Cairo to open their emporium, parts of the city were already Haussmannized. The viceroy ordered the building of new neighborhoods, parks, and an opera house after Haussmann's urban design. Whereas the original objective was to emulate the French urban plan, the actual city built as it was by Italian, French, Egyptian, Levantine, and other European architects embodied a broader Mediterranean aesthetic.[11] In an interview from 1964, Yvonne Shohet (née Chemla), recalls upon her arrival in Egypt reading the details of the Suez Canal inauguration in *La Bourse Egyptienne*. She precisely remembers Ismail's declaration separating Egypt from its African milieu and claiming his nation as a part of Europe (Shohet, tape 2 17). The Chemlas strove to perfect this aspired image belonging to the northern shore of the Mediterranean. Their store was built in a luxurious European style and adorned with gilded Louis XVI columns. The store recruited some of their staff from France. The Chemlas earned the Legion d'honneur from France for promoting French businesses in Egypt. Ironically, the family did not originate from Paris. They were working-class Arab Jews (Mizrahi) from Tunis.

Whereas the Chemlas moved from west of the Ottoman Empire and the Arab world (the Maghreb), the Sednaouis, another entrepreneurial family, came from east of the Arab world (the Mashriq). In 1913, the Sednaouis inaugurated their *grand magasin*. The owners were Greek Catholic Levantines from Sednaya, Syria. Salim and Samʿān Sednaoui moved from Damascus to Cairo, where they worked in the Muski district. The Sednaouis boasted of their new store's architecture, designed by French architect George Parcq (Moustapha 125), which resembled the Parisian *grands magasins*, such as Galeries Lafayette (figs. 2.3 and 2.4). The Sednaouis had Egyptian citizenship by the 1940s (Reynolds, *City Consumed* 60–61).

The owners of the most luxurious emporium in Egypt, the Cicurel family, came from even further east. Moreno Cicurel migrated from Izmir to Cairo, when both cities were still part of the Ottoman Empire. He moved to Egypt in 1870. He was attracted by the country's economic potential (Cicurel 48–49). Like many department store owners, Cicurel began as a salesclerk in another *grand magasin*, Hannaux, until he bought the business in 1887. After operating a successful shop in Muski, Cicurel decided to open a department store on the western side of town in 1909, on Fuad Street opposite the Chemlas. The store employed eighty workers. Cicurel left the store to his sons, Solomon, Yusuf, and Salvator, who transformed it into a large empire with branches all over Egypt. Cicurel's was considered the most prestigious shop catering to the elite. The store sought to capture a larger share of the market by opening other stores for the less affluent classes: Oreco and Trémode, a more modest chain, are akin to Printemps's Prisunic and Lafayette's Monoprix. Although the Cicurels were Francophone, the family held Egyptian citizenship and actively participated in Egyptian social and economic life. Solomon Cicurel was the head of the Jewish Egyptian community. The Cicurels were founding members of Egypt's National Bank, Bank Misr, and they created the Association for Department Stores and Wholesalers (Reynolds, *City Consumed* 57–58; Cicurel 48).

Another entrepreneur, Adolf Orosdi, the founder of the Orosdi-Back department stores, came from Hungary. After the Hungarian revolt of 1848, Orosdi converted to Islam and became an Ottoman subject. He later rebranded his stores as Omar Effendi, after a Turkish bazaar. The first Omar Effendi store was founded in Cairo in 1856 in the Muski area as part of a large network across the Mediterranean region and the Balkans, including Salonica, Izmir, Bucharest, Aleppo, Beirut, Tunis, Varna, Adana, Samsun, Baghdad, Casablanca, Fez, and Meknes (Kupferschmidt, *European Department Stores* 178). Like the other enterprises, a new store with a distinctive cupola and French architecture opened in 1905 on the western side of the city, occupying the corner of Abdel-Aziz and Rushdi Streets (Kupferschmidt, "Who Needed" 178) (fig. 2.5). The store strikingly resembles Le Bon Marché department store in Vichy, France (fig. 2.6).

Despite the insistence on the French image, Egypt's human and cultural geography was far more complex than that of France. Most often, this heterogeneity presented a challenge for the European eye. To give an example, in her novel *Les Porteuses de Torches* (1923), Saint-Simonian French writer Jehan d'Ivray draws a portrait of Egypt's diverse culture divided among three empires, which did not fit the narrow concept of European nationalism. In the novel, a French baron, seated at the terrace of the famous Mena House hotel overlooking the pyramid plateau, tries to explain to a female friend the dissonance between the vista of the pyramid before them and the multicultural character of the society she encounters on the terrace:

> Egypt, you see, is simply an African land, Turkish in name, English in law; we find Egyptians who speak Arabic, hotels where German chefs

cook French meals, served by Swiss waiters, Neapolitan gypsies playing Russian tunes, Wallach women passing as Parisians, and Spanish Jews who say they are English. Only the English of all types are steadfast, and they prove it by the manner they manage people and things here. Only they are kings, because they know how to be practical.[12]

For the speakers, the hotel terrace marks the disconnection between an imagined Oriental landscape and the actual lived space. What is most striking in the baron's description, however, is not the artificiality lamented by his friend or even what he claims to be the accurate rendition of Egyptian society. The baron's statement struggles to reconcile the French Orientalist image of Egypt with his actual urban experience. The multicultural society that the baron and his friend have encountered is not based in any specific national identity, language, or culture. Above all, it cannot be logically connected to the vista of the pyramids. The multicultural aspect of the Mena House hotel, like Egypt itself, renders all these categories questionable and performative to the extent that looking at the pyramids from that comfortable cosmopolitan terrace disturbs the creation of a timeless authentic Egyptian tableau.

The baron's view does not differ much from the Evelyn Baring, Earl of Cromer's understanding of Egyptian society. The British consul general in Egypt quotes Lord Milner's description of Egypt as "a land of paradox." Cairo is a mismatched combination of "old ruin and modern café, [a] dying Mecca and a still-born Rue de Rivoli" (Cromer 127). Egypt is neither an old nation in ruin nor a modern French state. For Baring, the population of Egypt reflects that hybrid space, where "half-breeds of every description, and pure-blooded Europeans pass by in procession" (128). Lord Cromer struggles to make sense of the 1897 population census, which expresses this diverse population. For him, the inhabitants of Egypt do not reflect any homogeneous features or cultural character that tie them to a specific national identity. Walking in the streets of Paris, London, or Berlin, he says, one can find "nine out of ten of the people with whom he meets bear on their faces evidence, more or less palpable, that they are Englishmen, Frenchmen, or Germans" (127). He asks: "Who, in fact, is a true Egyptian?" (128).

In today's context, the same diversity would be celebrated as a reflection of modern cosmopolitan European urban living; for Lord Cromer and the fictive baron ventriloquized by d'Ivray, the mélange of cultures in Egypt, expressed in its residents' disparate clothing styles, customs, and professions, could only be considered a hybrid anomaly in need of correction. From a nineteenth-century British and French perspective, Egypto-Ottoman cosmopolitanism, prior to its adoption of a capitalist consumerist lifestyle, represented a queer scene: at the very least a form of racial regression.[13] This view persisted and even gained more traction with the fall of the Ottoman Empire. In the Turkey of the 1920s, around the same time that d'Ivray was writing her novel, Kemalist policies reframed the Turkish national image by means of a spatial-temporal binary. Whereas the Ottoman Empire belonged to the East, the modern republic was part of the West. In this new context, Levantine cosmopolitan culture, its customs and sartorial traditions, were an unwanted mélange that bore the traces of an unwanted past, a contamination of the modern nation (Szurek 320).[14]

Egyptian emporia mirrored the variegated images of all these empires along with their conflicts. The various regional and national European and Arabic languages and dialects composed the soundscape of daily Egyptian life. Promotional materials and catalogues were published in several languages (Reynolds, *Commodity Communities* 66). The emporium's soundscape echoed the outside milieu; switching from one language to another, the staff and customers navigated the plethora of cultures that made up the Ottoman-Egyptian, Francophone, British Mediterranean colony (Reynolds, *Commodity Communities* 180). As Nancy Reynolds puts it: "Code switching between Arabic and French (or other European languages) resonated with a more fundamental aspect of Egyptian linguistic structure, the heteroglossic nature of classical and colloquial Arabic, in which speakers pitched linguistic registers as a form of power and status" (*Commodity Communities* 67). Employees brought inside the stores the sounds, memories, and tensions of their regions. Linguistic registers across sales counters reflected the dynamics of emporialism at work in the daily life of workers and clients. They marked the overlapping and difference between formal, Levantine, Syrian, Iraqi, and Tunisian Arabic; between southern and northern Italian; between Parisian, provincial, and Levantine French; and between urban and provincial Greek. Store owners hired a diverse pool of multilingual employees who could communicate with and attract a diverse clientele. Stores like Cicurel and Chemla celebrated Jewish, Christian, and Muslim holidays with their staff. They prepared promotional campaigns for each holiday. Similarly, the household of the owners echoed the store's polyglossia (Cicurel 17) (see chapter 5).

Mastering a multi-imperial rhetoric of emporialism was not without conflicts. During the interwar period, the emporium became a battlefield for imperial rivalry. With the end of Ottoman suzerainty over Egypt,

Austrian and German proprieties were sequestered by the British. Austrian stores Stein and Tiring were under severe pressure from the British authority and were forced to procure a special license to continue their operation. Interestingly, Francophilia opened the door for devising extraterritorial strategies necessary for operating in the overlapping dominions of empires. The owner of the Stein stores registered his business in London, but to no avail. His stores were later acquired by the British chain Morums. In contrast, the Austrian-owned chain Omar Effendi was able to overcome most hardships since its owners registered the stores as a French company (Kupferschmidt, *European Department Stores* 34). During World War I, the store increasingly hired personnel with French passports to establish a French image that placed it beyond the grasp of British authority (Kupferschmidt, "Who Needed" 179–80). In this case, switching allegiance to the French empire offered more than prestige; it became a strategy of survival. Even under these pressures, the rhetoric of emporialism remained fluid as it maneuvered the overlapping cosmos of empires and nation-states. Whereas the official business documents proved the store's allegiance to the French empire, promotional campaigns took the opposite direction by celebrating Egyptian nationalism. Omar Effendi increased investment in Arabic advertising to target the emerging generation of urban bureaucrats who received a European-style education, the *efendiyya*.[15] The store, for instance, prided itself on promoting the fez, which was dropped in Turkey but remained symbolic of the Egyptian national attire. The store's name further enhanced the connection between the emporium and this growing urban population (Kupferschmidt, *European Department Stores* 44).

Intersectional Emporialism: In Search of the Bourgeois Egyptian Woman

In its attempt to mirror imperial and national imaginaries, emporialism wielded the balance between Egyptian culture and Francophilia, between a European gendered discourse and iconography of consumption and its counterpart in Ottoman Egypt. Emporialism thereby reflected the transformation of private and public spheres. It documented and manipulated the axes of race, gender, and class to reconstruct a modern Egypto-Ottoman regime of values that drew from (without simply copying) its European counterpart. In such a process, the image of the modern Egyptian bourgeois woman was the by-product of a gendered ethno-class matrix of relations, which pit the Egyptian woman against the bodies of Egyptian, African, and European Others, especially those pertaining to the working class.

In many advertisements, the stores followed the iconographic patterns of their French and European counterparts, by featuring a large-scale rendition of their building occupying the cityscape, a representation that echoed the discourse of imperial dominance (refer to figs. 3.1. and 6.1) (see M. Russell 62–64). In contrast to the European situation, one central element in the ads remained missing: the image of the bourgeois Egyptian woman. In France, as in most European department stores, the bourgeois woman was the favorite subject of emporialism. Her gendered body represented the complicity of empire and emporium (see chapter 1). By gendering the empire, emporialism laid claim to the imperial white bourgeois domestication project: the civilizing mission whose tentacles stretched from the bourgeois living room to the distant corners of the colonies. The body of the French bourgeois woman paralleled that of the emporium and mediated between all these spaces and geographies. As the patroness of the store and the household, the bourgeois woman was the domesticator of the nation and the greater empire through consumption. Whereas in France the bourgeois woman and the emporium were close allies, the same ties could not be quickly forged in Egypt. Purchasing the family's needs, including clothing for the female members of the household, was the task of the patriarch or was conducted via the intermediary of ambulant sellers. In Egypt, shopping in department stores was subject to constant debates among men and women. Some women praised this new lifestyle, whereas others vowed never to step into these modern spaces, which brought together people from various backgrounds and social classes (Baron, "Unveiling" 372–75; M. Russell 38–47).[16]

This situation suggests a crisis in representation in the discourse of emporialism, one that required the construction of a national gendered body to serve as a linchpin bringing together all the maps in which the stores operated and their various scales: the household, the store, the city, the nation, and the empire. Egyptian emporia were not immediately considered the dominion of women. More so, the images of middle-class women in the media and popular culture did not crystallize simultaneously. For Egyptian men, the emerging *efendiyya* class represented the modern urban educated male. They wore European suits paired with a fez. They developed a look and a lifestyle distinct from that of their parents. As Lucie Ryzova argues, the *effendi* did not have a female counterpart. Such absence could be noticed in literature and later in cinema, where either the *effendi* is matched with someone from a traditional background (*bint el-balad*) or, challenging his station, he aspires to win the heart of an upper-class woman (15). In common Egyptian parlance, the word *baladi*, meaning at once local, native, national, or popular, also referred to someone lacking refinement and taste (Reynolds, *City Consumed* 16; Abu-Lughod 191). The colloquial word for traditional woman, meaning literally daughter of the nation or daughter of the city, betrays the dissonance between an old notion of belonging and a modernist national project articulated through European fashion and consumerism. In a sense, the traditional *bint el-balad* conflicted with the iconography of emporialism that sought to conflate the body of the bourgeois woman with that of the nation and the city (see chapter 1).

In the absence of a clear representational image of the bourgeois family, stores developed different ways to bind their premises with national and imperial territories. In some cases, the body of the sovereign king became the commercial model that brought these scaled spaces together. In 1895, *grands magasins* Paschal and Cie printed its promotional calendar in Paris, placing at the center the image of the Egyptian sovereign, Sultan Abbas Helmi II (fig. 2.7). Le Bon Marché targeted the French expatriate community and participated in annual parades and events. On 14 July 1923, the windows were decorated with the French flag, the figure of Marianne, and the words "Vive la France, liberté, égalité, fraternité." The store also boasted a connection to the royal family by adding the royal insignia to its advertisement (Reynolds, *Commodity Communities* 83).[17] For instance, in the Francophone Egyptian magazine *Images* (22 December 1929, 28–29), Le Bon Marché's places its advertisement for toys opposite the photo of the young Prince Farouk, who eventually became the king of Egypt (fig. 2.8). In this case, the emporium forges its alliance with the nation and empire by marketing the Europeanized "Ottoman" bodies of the male members of the royal family. The image of the sultan in a military uniform and that of the prince reflect the different maps in which the stores operated: the empire and the household. This positioning was not a new phenomenon; rather, it dovetailed with an already existing Egypto-Ottoman tradition. The parallelism between the royal household and the citizen's household was already in place since the reign of Ismail, wherein the royal household, its structure, and setting served as a model unit for the larger nation (M. Russell 11–29). On the one hand, this strategy filled a representational vacuum caused by the absence of a clear image of the middle-class woman and her family. On the other hand, it contributed to its emergence and consolidation. The absence of a gendered and domesticated image of the bourgeois household is ironically very salient in Le Bon Marché's advertisement discussed above. The magazine places an ambiguously gendered photo of the prince against an advertisement for dolls set around the dining table like in a tea party. This miniature representation of the bourgeois household represents a typical gendered message that inculcated a middle-class ethos of domesticity by conditioning young girls to become future bourgeois mothers.[18]

Like the ambiguous photo of the prince, advertisements manipulated a fluid language that could speak to both genders. Some promotions featured a generic image of the *efendiyya*. Stores like Printemps placed Arabic advertisements in *Anis al-Jalis*, the first journal directed by a woman, Alexandra Avierino. The store's advertisement from October 1907 proposes home delivery for Muslim customers.[19] Other advertisements forged an alliance with the city by placing a large-scale sketch of the building as the focus of the picture. As Mona Russell argues, a distinctively gendered promotional language began to appear in Egyptian media during the interwar period. For instance, the magazine *al-Lata'if al-Musawwara* includes an advertisement by the Chemla department store addressing women directly (M. Russell 62). In fact, I add, this same Chemla advertisement crosses many gender boundaries at once. In addition to containing a direct message for women, the advertisement invites women to visit the store.[20] This rhetoric marks a shift in commercial discourse wherein the store emphasizes both women's agency and mobility. Typically, ads would call on women to "ask" or "order" merchandise, implying that their husbands would take charge of the purchase process on their behalf (M. Russell 61–62).

In France, stores such as Printemps presented the model bourgeois woman as a Saint-Simonian female ideal: a Pygmalion dream (refer to fig. 1.2). In the Egyptian context, the actual independence project took on this Pygmalion metaphor in which a gendered nation would be the outcome of the collective labor of male politicians.[21] For instance, on 3 April 1922, *al-Lata'if al-Musawwara* published a caricature in which the Egyptian nation appears as an elegant woman with European features being fitted for a fashionable gown by various famous Egyptian politicians (fig. 2.9). As in the French advertisement the "Queen of Printemps" (refer to fig. 1.2), the politicians kneel before this young woman to serve her and complete her fashionable look. In the French catalogue, the Queen of Printemps assisted by the emporium's multiethnic employees reflected the image of the French empire. In the Arabic cartoon, the female customers represent a modern Egyptian nation, an ideal in the making, whose crafters responded to the whims and desire of a demanding ruling woman. The dress bears the words "independence," while the woman says to her helpers, "this dress is incomplete." The woman complains that the dress is still missing a part and that she wants another style. The caption answers that this beautiful lady should be patient for the moment; later she can rule as she likes. The cartoon was published in the context of the negotiation for Egyptian independence and the drafting of Egypt's first constitution after the 1919 revolution. The customer's words allude to the unfinished national project, since the British Empire remained the de facto ruler of the country.

By the 1920s, several Arabic journals, such as *al-Lata'if al-Musawwara* and *Misr al-Haditha*, published the latest fashion trends. *Misr al-Haditha* reprinted models from the Francophone magazine *Le Chic oriental*, wherein the sketched models wear a short transparent veil (*yashmak*) over the face. The cartoon also reveals the emergence of an idealized picture of a modern Egyptian woman: fashionable, yet modest and veiled. The appearance of this image coincided with the increasing mobility and debates over the place of bourgeois woman in society. Conversely, although *al-Lata'if al-Musawwara* relied on the ad revenue from department stores and displayed the latest fashions, the journal constantly criticized Egyptian women's competition over public space, as well as their love for fashion and shopping. Women dressed in a less conservative manner were shown as a source of corruption for pedestrians and a dangerous distraction for drivers.[22] A cartoon in *al-Lata'if al-Musawwara* from 1917 expresses dismay at Egyptian women's increasing presence alongside men in movie theaters, public transport, and shops (most likely department stores, given the large crowds seen in the cartoon) (fig. 2.10). On 13 October 1919, the journal reprinted an English cartoon displaying British impressions of Cairo. The cartoon shows the British perspective of the city, which focuses on two veiled women "from the harem" admiring the latest fashion in window shops (fig. 2.11). The image contrasts the bodies of the Egyptian women with that of elegantly clad mannequins on the other side of the windowpane. The transparent glass pane separating the onlookers from the mannequins features as both a physical and symbolic barrier between the bourgeois Egyptian women and her aspirations for a European-styled freedom. The cartoon also portrays the windowpane as a mirror that projects the hidden desire of Egyptian women, suggesting that Egyptian women from the upper classes live a divided existence. While their bodies are trapped inside the Ottoman veils, the mannequins reflect the women's secret yearning for change.

In the same vein of criticism, other caricatures attempted to predict the future look of Egyptian women. A caricature from *al-Lata'if al-Musawwara* in 1919 features the image of a modern European-styled woman imprisoned inside the body of her larger robust traditional counterpart (fig. 2.13).²³ The cartoon is presented in the gist of a "quo vadis" the modern Egyptian woman, or where are we going from here? The drawing predicts the look of the granddaughters of the 1919 generation, based on the trending fashions among young urban women gradually shortening their veils. The commentator addresses women directly and urges them not to overlook this matter, which is leading to the frustration and surprise of men. As Russell suggests, the caricature shows the veiled woman of yesterday as robust and strong, while the Europeanized one of tomorrow is skinny and sickly (40). The image of the modern woman trapped inside the body of her strong, free-moving veiled matriarch contradicts the actual situation of the era. The cartoon synchronizes with the first anticolonial demonstrations in which women actively participated. The 1919 demonstrations are a key gendered iconic and iconographic moment in Egyptian history, when women were frequently photographed in the streets to document their role in the national movement (Baron, *Egypt as a Woman* 107–34). Although, the caricature praises the traditional woman, it exposes a masculine fear that the European-styled woman contained within would eventually be born and claim more prominence in public space. In contrast to the traditional woman in the caricature, her modern counterpart transgresses boundaries by looking directly and flirtatiously at the readers. Holding an umbrella, a phallic object, she occupies a space between the masculine and the feminine. The cartoon camouflages its anxiety by means of reverse embodiment, or a reversal of the respective habitus of the two women, to use Bourdieu's term. Through the manipulation of scale, the traditional woman is given attributes typically associated with the modern European woman. She enjoys mobility, prestige, and visibility. In comparison, the cartoon bestows the actual social situation of the traditional woman on her modern granddaughter, suggesting that the European-styled woman would have less claim over public space and less social respect.

In 1921, the magazine *Al-Kashkul al-Musawwar* published a caricature titled "the new woman." The drawing presents two young Egyptian women from the middle (or more likely upper) class sitting on the beach. The two friends wear traditional black clothing and cover their face with a *yashmak*. They wear fashionable European shoes, carry umbrellas, and have a modern skinny look. The caption reads: "Can we bear children?"²⁴ In this context, the cartoon associates modernity with women's presence in public spaces and the emulation of European material culture. The women have slightly European features and are located on the seashore, probably in Alexandria: a liminal space between national and European cultures. The viewer can also see the setting sun, which sends the message of national decline and perhaps alludes to the Occident. The cartoon suggests that by abandoning the Egypto-Ottoman tradition of seclusion and veiling, Egyptian women would eventually fail to compete with their European bourgeois counterparts as mothers and citizens.

In 1923, Egyptian feminist Huda Shaarawi made a symbolic gesture of taking off the facial veil in public (see chapter 4). The question of dress, however, remained a vital topic well beyond this moment. A few years later, in 1927, the Arabic magazine *Rose al-Yusef* discussed the question of unveiling by imagining Egyptian women's fashion across the ages, from 1900 to 1950. The drawing shows three women walking in public observed by three respective male onlookers. Each woman and her male counterpart belong to a different decade, 1900, 1927, and 1950 (fig. 2.12). As time passes, the dresses and the veils get shorter. The cartoon draws heavily on commercial culture, in particular that of the emporium. For instance, the caption indicating the year (1900, 1927, 1950) is attached to the women's bodies in a manner recalling price tags affixed to mannequins at department stores. The cartoon also suggests a simultaneous change of the representation of men and women. For instance, the man and woman from the 1900s feature as conservative stately figures. The woman holds an umbrella hidden behind her back. The man from 1927 features as a slim dandy, while the woman wears a shorter dress, walks briskly, and carries a small umbrella around her wrist. Finally, as we get to 1950, the male onlooker is presented as a bodyless horned devil, or rather a cuckold man, watching an unveiled woman with a mini dress. The woman is almost running, the tip of her high heel shoes crosses over the cartoon frame, hinting toward the transgression of her prescribed gender role. She also carries a small open umbrella positioned to look like a semi-erect penis. As time passes and dresses get shorter, the male figures in the cartoon are gradually emasculated. Not only do they remain stagnate, but their bodies dissipate. Meanwhile, their female counterparts adopt a dynamic masculine gait and energy. As they infringe on men's territory, they acquire a visible phallus, alluding to their rising power. The cartoon affirms a general masculine moral panic.[25] Most important, the cartoon was published in a magazine owned, and named after, a woman, which asserts the increasing presence of women in public space and the various forms of unveiling that were taking place. As Beth Baron suggests, "Egyptian women unveiled metaphorically over the course of decades when they put their pens to paper and published their ideas" ("Unveiling" 382–83). If we place figs. 2.13 and 2.12 together and read them as a collage from right to left, like an Arabic text, the caricatures tell the story of the birth of a contemporary European-styled urban Egyptian woman and the anxieties surrounding her emergence across time.

An Intersectional Embodiment

By the late 1920s, the feared modern woman came to life. She was neither sickly nor meek. Instead, she commanded unprecedented attention in the public sphere. Most important, she was a close ally with the emporium and embodied its emporialist worldview. Like her European counterpart, the modern bourgeois consumer was the proud Pygmalion fantasy of the emporium. Her body and household were fashioned by the emporium. The bilingual winter catalogue of *grand magasin* Sednaoui, printed and designed in Paris in 1927, offers a glimpse of this modern woman (fig. 2.14, refer to book cover). The cover presents a grander-than-life modern bourgeois woman with European features, a slim silhouette, elegant clothes, and fashionable short hair. The woman on the Sednaoui catalogue holds a small model of the store. The latest fashion items dangle from the store resting in her palms. The clothes float in the air like Chagall's figures over the Parisian landscape. This time they hover over Cairo. The woman could be French or Egyptian, marking a closer step toward the creation of a global bourgeoisie. Notably, this is not the only representation portrayed in the media or even in Sednaoui advertisements. Other promotional materials, such as the Arabic advertisement for the same store in *al-Lata'if al-Musawwara* on 29 March 1915, reflect the diversity in Egyptian society and the wide lifestyle variations ranging from traditional to European (M. Russell 62). Nevertheless, this representation of a European-styled Egyptian is not unique: other catalogues by Egyptian department stores, such as that of Cicurel, promoted a similar look (Reynolds, *A City Consumed* 66).

Typical to the discourse of emporialism, the emporium ties the image of the bourgeois woman with the store and the maps with which it operates. The giant model looks at Sednaoui's signature branch, designed by George Parcq, which occupies the bottom center against a blue background reaching up to the horizon. The French design of the catalogues betrays a lack of grasp of the Cairene cityscape. In the picture from the catalogue cover, the Sednaoui store is framed by two Islamic monuments, which appear to be Muhammad Ali's mosque in Cairo. In this case, the posture situates the store within an imagined French geography of the Orient, where Egypt's position swerves between the status of a nation and an Ottoman colony. This image situates Egypt in the Mediterranean and emphasizes the Franco-Egyptian connections. The blue color in the picture gives the impression of the Mediterranean Sea reaching up to the European shore. Just beneath the woman stands a minuscule building or a boat. The image of the boat and the sea connecting the shores brings to the forefront the Saint-Simonian Mediterranean commercial utopianism of the interconnected sea, merging East and West.

The iconography of a woman holding a miniature department store is not a novel representation. In fact, similar postures can be seen in other advertisements around the world. Between 1910 and 1912, advertisements with images of women embodying their respective cities and holding miniature models of a department store appeared in Paris, London, and Tokyo. These publications stress the complicity between the city, the store, and the bourgeois woman. They hint that both models, the miniature emporium and the bourgeois woman, occupy the same position. They embody their city and their nation. In contrast, the woman on the Sednaoui catalogue is matched with an entire commercial Mediterranean cosmos.[26]

The catalogue constructs and translates this new look to the modern woman by offering its Egyptian clientele a detailed description of the latest Parisian fashions in French and Arabic. The rest of the catalogue makes an equal effort to shape the various aspects of the bourgeois life. All of the models in the catalogue look European. The inside cover of the catalogue and that of the following year 1928–29) show sketches of the same modern woman in public spaces: in restaurants, with female friends at the opera house, or going with her elegant and athletic European-looking partner to a soirée (fig. 2.15). Extending advice toward bourgeois children, the store recommends that little girls wear miniature styles that resemble their mothers' dresses. The young girls in the catalogues would be the future Egyptian bourgeois women and mothers of tomorrow: in other words, the future allies of the emporium.

These Sednaoui catalogues contrast with the promotional material discussed earlier. The catalogues shift attention from the bodies of the royal patriarch and his sons to that of the bourgeois woman and her daughter. In addition, the store expands its dominion over the bourgeois household by advertising its furniture department on the back cover, featuring the latest Art Deco styles. The store boasts its fine atelier and Parisian decorator, who could be commissioned to design the interior of villas and apartments for Sednaoui's clients. The language of the catalogues is obviously polyglossic, like the territory it represents. The language navigates the distance between French and Egyptian cultures. The text imports French vocabulary of fashion and colors into Arabic. For instance, the text uses the word *médoc*—originally referring to the color of French wine—or a term such as *manteau* instead of the classical Arabic equivalent *moṭaf* or the Egyptian *balto* (derived from the Italian or Greek *paltó*). The use of *manteau* could indicate a Levantine influence, since that term is often used in Syrian and Lebanese dialects. Sometimes the Arabic text differs slightly from the French to negotiate European and Egyptian cultural capitals and the respective notions of elegance and prestige. Whereas the French text reads "even *the most difficult and elegant female customer* (cliente) could find what she needs at the store" (emphasis added), the Arabic version replaces the first words of the sentence with "our clients," which is also gender-neutral language. In addition to (mis)translating etiquettes, fashion, and language, the catalogue mediates between systems of beliefs. In contrast to the French version, the Arabic text concludes with a religious expression "we rely on God" (*ʿAla Allah al-itikāl*).

Upon a second observation, the Sednaoui 1927–28 catalogue cover image reveals another ambivalent message. The giant woman strikingly resembles the unborn woman of tomorrow from the *al-Lata'if al-Musawwara*. Her face has slightly masculine traits. Her modernity and desire for consumerism give her a masculine aspect. Like her French counterpart, the Queen of Printemps (refer to fig. 1.2), the woman is rendered in an exaggerated scale, giving her an ominous character. Both images depict Gulliver-like figures sketched against a miniature cityscape and its corresponding Lilliputian populations. The contrast between the gigantic woman and the small world surrounding her accentuates the symbolic meaning associated with miniature drawings: what Susan Stewart describes as "the transcendence of the upper classes, the reduction of labor to the toylike, and the reification of interiority" (75). The bodies of both bourgeois women reach up to the sky. They mediate between heaven and Earth, between the city and the emporium, as well as between the empire and its provinces and colonies.

In her analysis of the gendered body and social space, Linda McDowell argues that men are often presented as "existence in space and women are insignificance" (*Gender* 41). The image discussed above reverses the hierarchal relation between genders and by extension their connection to the public sphere. Stewart posits that whereas large-scale objects or the gigantic is culturally associated with the infinite, the natural, and that which is beyond human power, the miniature stands for the opposite. It is a utopian domesticized and controlled space. In that sense, the advertisements of the body of the modern bourgeois woman holding the miniature model marks the connections between natural chaos and civilization, between society and utopia. They present us with both extremes: the desire of containment and suppression and the anxiety of losing control of public and civic lives, as also seen in figs 2.12 and 2.13.

In the Sednaoui catalogue cover, just as in the Printemps advertisement, the woman's feminine facial expression and her hand placed over her dress, both signs of bourgeois restraint and propriety, contrast with her threatening scale that renders her out of control. She is both the center of attention and a monstrous presence threatening to crush the nation. She dominates the city, if not the entire world. She commands the landscape and both shores of the sea. Her posture projects an omnipotent divine presence. She amuses herself by lifting a department store off the ground, while looking down at the other *magasin* and the microscopic people standing before its gates. The city's residents at the bottom of the image look like insignificant ants. That modern and global bourgeois woman embodies the antithesis of Jürgen Habermas's public sphere: "the masculine, secular, and rational" (17). The fact that that model takes the attribute of mother nature, or even the divine, places her outside the limits of the public secular sphere. In Sednaoui's catalogue, the bourgeois woman, situated between the mosque and the store, also intercedes between the sacred and the secular.

The fact that the emporium's promotional materials were designed in France raises the question whether this image only existed on the pages of department stores' catalogues. Nonetheless, the modern European-like bourgeois woman, with her connection to the emporium, was becoming widespread in Arabic media and popular culture. The following *taqtūqa* [song] by Saleh Abdel Hay from the same year as the second Sednaoui catalogue, 1929, depicts a similarly European-styled woman dressed in the latest fashions:[27]

> She is just out of the shell / and already raising hell. / What could I say: what a youngster! / What was hidden is now revealed. / She's strutting without a face veil [*bīsha*], winking left and right. / She thinks she's

better than the rest of us / She walks as if on eggshells. A tight cape molds her body, and her hair cut "à la garçonne."²⁸ / Seduction is part of her character / whoever loves her will lose his mind. / Daily from an early hour, she heads to Chemla and then the Bon Marché. Ahh! / Dancing has to be every night, Tango and Charleston / Whatever I say or repeat! (Lagrange, *Musiciens* 671–72, 732)²⁹

Saleh Abdel Hay's *taqtūqa* describes an Egyptian woman who has managed to create a new relation to the city and her body. Like the models in the Sednaoui catalogue, the modern girl bemoaned by the singer walks freely in the streets, face unveiled. She wears tight clothes and a short masculine hairstyle "à la garçonne." The new flirtatious woman manages to invert gender roles and challenges the narrator's masculinity and control of space. He finds himself incapable of courting her or following her lifestyle. The modern Egyptian woman is certainly a consumer well informed of the latest international trends. She spends her morning at Parisian and Egyptian department stores and the evening in nightclubs and cabarets, dancing the tango and the Charleston. Lagrange argues that the various clear references to Bon Marché and Chemla in songs indicates that by the 1920s, the *grands magasins*, including the French ones, had become part of Egyptian popular culture, marking a shift in lifestyle and consumption patterns. He adds, one of the comic aspects of the song is that it does not describe an elite woman but someone who tries to transgress social barriers by emulating the upper classes. Most likely, she belongs to the working class, hence the reference to her style of facial veil that she is supposed to wear, the *bīsha* (Lagrange, "Women" 234–36). The song also conflates the image of the female pedestrian with that of the sex worker, especially considering that this type of song was specifically played in cabarets and brothels.

As Abdel Hay's song suggests, department stores occupied a space shared by sex workers, hailing from the various corners of the French and Ottoman empires.³⁰ In her novel *Ramza*, Out-el-Kouloub mentions the different locations of early department stores in the Europeanized quarters in Cairo, such as al-Azbakiyya and Wagh al-Birka. These neighborhoods were also known for prostitution until the 1950s (Hammad and Biancani 236; Kozma, *Policing Egyptian Women* 82–85). Sex work in these Western-style quarters catered to a growing population and a changing lifestyle metamorphosed by modern urban infrastructure and street lighting (Hammad and Biancani 243). The nightlife in these neighborhoods acquired widespread fame to the extent that they become the subject of a new literary genre: one that came to be known as Wagh al-Birka literature (Hammad and Biancani 236). Describing European prostitution at Wagh al-Birka, or Azbakiyya, Russell Pasha, head of the Cairo police writes:

> [The area] was populated with European women of all breeds and races other than British, who were not allowed by their consular authority to practice this licensed trade in Egypt. Most of the women were of the third class category for whom Marseille had no further use, and who would eventually be passed on to the Bombay or the Far-East markets, but they were still Europeans and not yet fallen so low as to live in the one-room shacks of the Wasʼa which had always been the quarter for purely native prostitution of the lower class. (R. Pasha 180, qtd. in Biancani, "*Let Down*" 97)

The glamorous quarters of the department store are haunted by a marginalized Mediterranean history: that of multiethnic sex workers who came from the different parts around the sea, from places as far as Marseille (Biancani, "*Let Down*" 141–59; Kozma, *Global Women* 89–92). As Biancani points out: "At the imperial level, the existence of a large number of European working-class women being extensively exchanged and trafficked posed serious problems for the legitimization of the racial hierarchy the imperial ethos was based on. The very existence of these 'white subalterns' was highly problematical for the supporters of the imperial enterprise, in that it clearly challenged dominant notions of colonial moral and racial superiority" ("*Let Down*" 104).

Whereas the European discourse was mobilized by the anxiety of "white slavery," the Egyptian discourse stressed the devastating moral impact of British imperialism (Biancani, "*Let Down*" 103; Tucker 153–55). The Egyptian Feminist Union joined efforts with various groups, including Muslim clerics and British feminists. The control of marginal sexualities and social groups consolidated a modern image for the middle and upper classes. By denouncing prostitution, feminists foregrounded Egyptian bourgeois women as guardians of morality and the nation's protectors from colonial influence. The first governmental regulation and legalization of prostitution took place in 1882 and came to be associated with the British army, which sought to protect its soldiers from disease. To complicate matters, the interwar period witnessed the emergence on the public stage of European women from the working class who occupied the opposite end of the spectrum. On the one hand appeared the European governesses and domestic workers caring for bourgeois children. The British, French, German, Swiss, Greek, and Slovene servants and governesses symbolized modern imperial disciplinary codes of conduct (Hamamsy 142; Biancani "Gender"). On the other hand appeared the figure of the European sex worker, who became the center of feminist bourgeois discourse of morality and colonial resistance (Kozma, *Policing* 82). Both fled the poverty and the devastation of the war, looking for better opportunities, and both could be seen at al-Azbakiyya garden. The dissolution of Ottoman social codes required reconfiguring the optics of distinction in public space to separate upper-class women from everyone else who does not have the same pedigree, including European women from the working classes. The body of the European working-class woman, then, served as another intersectional axis of negotiation of imperial, national, and social power. Both the governess and the sex worker became the site of imperial and colonial competition for the domestication of empire (see chapter 5). Whereas the sex worker exposed a violent imaginary of the empire and the emporium, the governess reinforced their celebrated propaganda: the civilizing mission centering on domestic bourgeois propriety.

In this context, the image of the modern European-styled Egyptian woman featured in the Sednaoui catalogue and the *taqtūqa* is not simply a foreign import. Like her European bourgeois counterpart, she is the final product of an intersectional imperialism and emporialism: an intricate matrix of gender, class, and racial relations implicated in consumer culture. Notions of race, class, and gender are productive of a multiscalar and multiplanar dynamic, constantly readapting to fit into new economic, social, and political models and their respective market forces. As Linda McDowell posits, "like skin 'colour', whiteness is a socially constructed marker, the meaning of which is also socially variable across time and space. Whiteness too should be understood 'as ensembles of local phenomena complexly embedded in socioeconomic, sociocultural, and psychic interrelations.' Thus whiteness is a historically specific and variable social formation, a process rather than a categorical attribute, shaped within a racialized problematic" (*Redundant Masculinities* 14; Franckenberg 1, cited by McDowell). In 1929, the same year as the Sednaoui catalogue and the *taqtūqa*, the Egyptian Francophone magazine *Images* published a one-page patchwork of Egyptian cartoons gleaned from Arabic media.[31] The whole page could be analyzed visually as a collage: a representation of the intersectional relations that produced the finalized image of the modern Egyptian bourgeois woman, by means of a gendered ethno-classist matrix of relations (fig. 2.16).

To add to McDowell's and Franckenberg's words, the collage reveals a complex interimperial and intercolonial dynamic that challenges the common binary of empire and colony, or other geographical categories, that of local, regional, and global. The collage overlapped, reconciled, and rearranged the variegated local (urban, rural), national, imperial (French, English, Ottoman), and cultural, (Egyptian, Arab, European, Ottoman) concepts of race, gender, and class into a modern colonial grid of social relations. This intersectional imaginary constructed by mass media worked in tandem with a scientific academic discourse, research practices, and knowledge production, especially in the fields of human sciences (El Shakry).[32]

The layout could be read clockwise or counterclockwise, starting from white bourgeois European woman featured at the top of the page, passing by her Egyptian counterparts, both bourgeois and working class, and ending with the black female servants, or the other way around. The title of the page is framed with the happy faces of a racialized Egyptian man and a woman; their exaggerated plump faces and fat lips suggest they are peasants. The top-center caricature features a European bourgeois woman on a camel, which places her at the top of a hierarchy of race and class. In the same image, her companion, a European man, sits below her on a donkey, a suggestive way to mock him as an effeminate person lacking strong character, while the virile coachman is ogling the European woman. The male tourist asks: "Are there beautiful sights?" The coachman answers: "oh yes very beautiful sights."

Below that caricature, the first image from the left column shows a modern bourgeois Egyptian woman driving a car. The caption reads: "A wise recommendation for the sake of saving lives from women's driving: Every car driven by woman should be preceded by a jockey who announces, 'watch on your right, watch on your left, or the lady will knock you dead.'" In this cartoon, Egyptian modernity is reflected via the body of an upper-class, European-like woman who adopts the latest fashions and technology. Her look contrasts with a racialized image of a black servant (perhaps from southern Egypt or Sudan, Egypt's former colony). The image of the servant brings to mind the upper-class Ottoman tradition of eunuchs who chaperoned women during their errands in public spaces. In this context, the image reverses a long aristocratic tradition, in which vulnerable upper-class women were expected to walk behind the household eunuch, who ensures their safety in public. In this caricature, the servant switches roles from protecting the aristocratic woman to protecting the passersby from her.

The racialized image of the servant recalls the Egyptian viceroy's stance during the inauguration of the Suez Canal: to associate modernity with a separation from, and an imperial claim of guardianship over, the African continent. Various cartoons of the era reiterate an imagined geography: one that has kept Africa at bay. The cartoons stress the racialized bourgeois representation featuring Egypt as a modern fashionable woman, whose complexion contrasts with her primitive, darker-skinned, Sudanese sister (Baron, *Egypt as a Woman* 72–74). In the *Images* cartoons, the bourgeois woman's status is further emphasized by the content of the caricature placed on the opposite side, which presents three female black servants (perhaps formerly enslaved women) who, like "primitive natives," dance while happily polishing the kitchenware.[33]

The caricatures at the center of the left column effect a comparison between the modern urban bourgeois Egyptian and her peasant counterpart. The bourgeois woman is dressed in equestrian clothes and smokes a cigarette. Her car is parked in the background, suggesting her modernity and free mobility. The peasant, with darker complexion and rough primitive traits, confuses the other woman for a man trying to talk to her. She naively pulls her dress to cover her face (an allusion to an old Egyptian proverb). The caricature aims to ridicule what came to be the masculine attributes of this modern bourgeois Egyptian woman, precisely because she adopts a role reserved for men: by occupying public space, smoking, and wielding European technology and fashion. As Homa Hoodfar argues, the act of veiling and unveiling communicates various messages about the wearer, but also about the sexuality of the onlookers. Unveiling before a man suggests that the man is emasculated (107). Here, in contrast, as the peasant places the veil over her head, she strips the modern bourgeois woman of her social prestige and womanhood. The carton implies the queerness of the bourgeois Egyptian woman whose adoption of a modern European role has cost her femininity and the social status associated with a traditional gender image.

The next two caricatures, at the bottom of the page, represent working-class women. In the first one, a man reports to a passerby that a woman has been crushed under the tram. The man answers: "she is lucky the tram was not full." The next caricature features a police officer dispersing the crowd, saying: "nothing here is happening, a man is beating his wife, like yesterday, today, and every day." The first image criticizes gender relations through a classist view of the Egyptian masses, suggesting that the working-class Egyptian male has normalized gender violence. The working-class woman, the main subject of both caricatures, is absent from the pictures. She is either crushed by modern life or by her own husband. In contrast to her bourgeois counterpart, who freely drives the automobile, the poor urban woman succumbs under the weight of a draconian patriarchal tradition. Nevertheless, the fate of working-class men is not very different from that of their female counterparts. The caricature at the center of the right column shows a peasant crossing the railroad in front of a train, while complaining that the train never stops out of respect to let him pass. The picture hints at the dominance of a new European temporality and a cold automated society that, like the minutely scheduled train, stops for no one. The caricature implies that men and women from poor classes are victims of a modern world whose new codes they ignore.

The final caricature, at the top of the right column, features three black servants. This cartoon closes the circle. The placement and content of the caricature, opposite the European-styled bourgeois Egyptian woman and right under that of the European woman, exposes the working-class (or formerly enslaved) black woman as the opposite side of the coin: an erased history of an imperial construction of class, race, and gender. This message is further emphasized, albeit inadvertently, via the caption stating that "we discovered that it seems that the origin of the Charleston dance was the kitchenware washers." Ironically, while the caricature aims to mock a newfangled dancing trend, it reconstructs an erased history of global bourgeois modernity by placing the working-class African woman (servant and formerly enslaved) at the center and genesis of an imperial modernity that constantly excluded her. Notably, the Charleston was an African American dance whose history goes back to slavery, later adopted by white Europeans and Americans (Emery 223–36).

Department store advertisements and media representation constantly reflected the changes in contemporary political and social debates. Decades later, in the 1940s, although shopping became a popular activity among middle- and upper-class women, it remained a source of male social embarrassment. In her speech at the American University in Cairo in 1941, titled "The Problem of the Egyptian Family," Egyptian feminist Huda Shaarawi refers to the anxiety and shame associated with this trend. She critiques bourgeois men who avoid being seen in public with their unveiled women while shopping ("Mushkilat" 10). In contrast, an advertisement by Sednaoui from 1950 markets a different look for women (fig. 2.17). The ad was placed in the Francophone magazine *La Femme nouvelle*, directed by the renowned feminist Doria Shafik. The ad shows a woman in a swimsuit giving her back to the sea while looking directly at her audience. The advertising reflects the changes in the representation of the Egyptian bourgeoisie, two years before national independence. The model in the image is neither a maternal figure nor a caretaker of the household purchases. The ad projects shopping as a leisure activity: part of a glamorous and individual lifestyle. The model could also be seen as the finalized image stemming from the web of intersectional restations presented in fig 2.16.

Similarly, movies from the early 1950s present the debates and panic over the idea of department stores as feminine spaces. In these representations, the emporium vacillates between being a space of freedom and escape from patriarchy and a space of containment by embourgeoisement. Eventually, the film narratives restore women to their typical national role as caretakers of the household. For instance, *Nashala Hanim* [Lady Pickpocket] (directed by Hassan al-Saifi, 1953) tells the story of a pickpocket and con artist who falls in love with a rich bourgeois Egyptian. The pickpocket finds an ally in the Sednaoui department store delivery person, who helps her transform from a criminal to an attractive bourgeois lady using the store's high fashion. The film portrays Egypt's gendered nationalist project by bringing to the forefront the role of the department store as a custodian of the bourgeois woman and her refined image of elegance and chastity (Bracco 311–12). The department stores stood at the opposite side of another site of obsession of the Egyptian cinema, the cabaret, which came to symbolize corruption and the decadence of the old regime in postindependence cinema (Bracco 316–18).

Purging the National Territory

By the end of the 1950s, department stores in Egypt also became a metonym of a national territory purged from imperial influence, marking a social shift from earlier periods (see chapter 6). For instance, in 1921 when the government called for a boycott of British products, they listed the Cicurel stores as national enterprises (Abd al-Razik 106). The movie *La'bit al-sit* [*The Lady's Puppet*, dir. Wali al-Din Samih, 1946], which partially takes place in a hardware department store, offers a glimpse of the changes that occurred during World War II, before national independence. Once again, the store's map mirrors that of the nation caught in the crossfire among imperial armies. The film focuses on the economic and social crisis facing the *efendiyya*. It centers on a penniless *efendi* Hassan Abu Tabaq, who works in a department store and falls in love with a dancer who abandons him when she becomes a star. The *efendi*'s fate takes a sudden turn when his boss, the Jewish owner of the emporium, decides to escape to South Africa, fearing a German invasion. Following the advice of other Jewish friends, the manager cedes the store's ownership to his honest employee under the sole condition that the latter will transfer some of the store's profits every month, until he pays the full price of the business. This tactic recalls the experience of Galeries Lafayette owner Théophile Bader, who had to find an alternative temporary owner after his escape from Paris. As Hassan ascends the social ladder, he is finally able to be united with his beloved. The movie, produced before Egypt's independence, addresses the economic crisis and the fate of the *efendiyya* facing an economic and a social impasse. He can neither ascend the social ladder nor find the right match. The narrative implicitly hints at the social tension between the disillusioned generation of new *efendiyya*, who lost their prestigious station as government bureaucrats, and the class of entrepreneurs who emerged on the social scene with the development of the commercial sector (see Ryzova). The film does not portray the owner of the store as an outsider or an enemy. He is part of the family who trusts the *effendi* to protect his wealth. As Beinin and Lockman suggest, the later reconfiguration of class divided into ethnic lines eventually led to the subordination of class struggle to the nationalist cause (105; see also Beinin and Lockman). Framed as exogenous enterprises, the sequestration of the stores became part of the semiotics of decolonization. Reclaimed to the national territory, they ushered in symbolically a new postcolonial and socialist era, where they became the stores of the people.

In 1952, most of the stores in Cairo were destroyed by a fire set by anticolonial protesters (Elsheshtawy 8; Reynolds, *City Consumed* 7). However, according to Ronald Cicurel, his father was encouraged by the free officers to rebuild his store, which he did. Although some of the owners held Egyptian citizenship by that time, the stores were cast as foreign colonial businesses. The rising nationalist discourse filtered the class divide into a dialectic of colonizer and colonized, in which the local bourgeoisie increasingly came to be depicted as foreign settlers, while workers were seen as autochthonous Egyptians (Beinin and Lockman 105).

Conclusion

Just as the Chemlas' department store and story began in Egypt with the Suez Canal, it ends with the canal's nationalization and the final departure of many communities from Egypt.[34] In 1957, the Chemla family moved out of Egypt (Shohet, "Communauté Juive d'Egypte après la guerre" 14). Some family members moved across the Mediterranean to France; others went eastward to Israel. After Egyptian independence (1952) and the nationalization of the Suez Canal (1956), all private businesses, including department stores, were nationalized in 1961 (Raafat, "Sednaoui"). Similarly, the Cicurels left in 1957 after acquiring Italian passports. Other networks of department stores, like La Rinascente and L'Innovation, were the source of the family's support and survival (Cicurel 96).

The stores remained sites of ambivalence caught between nation and empire. Despite their nationalization and the ongoing Arab-Israeli conflict, they kept their owners' names. Residents and visitors of downtown Cairo and Alexandria or the various Egyptian provinces still came across the network of department stores named after their owners—Chemla, Ades, Sednaoui, Cicurel, and Benzion. In 1976, Egyptian President Anwar Sadat wrote to Salvator Cicurel, inviting him to return to Egypt and assuring him about his safety. Unfortunately, Salvator had died earlier that year (Cicurel 52–53). In 1987, Ronald Cicurel was the only one from his family to visit Egypt. In 1997, Ronald recounted that he met the director of the Cairo store, who knew his father. The director let him in into his father's office, which had been locked for forty years. Some of his belongings were still there (Cicurel 47). In Israel, the granddaughter of the Chemlas—writer Jacqueline Shohet Kahanoff—continued to advocate for a multicultural Mediterranean lifestyle based on her memories of Egypt and her grandparents' emporium (see chapters 5 and 6).

Figure 3.1. Exterior of Le Bon Marché, catalogue Nouveautés Hiver 1879–1880. *Source*: Ville de Paris, Bibliothèque Forney. Public domain. Used with permission.

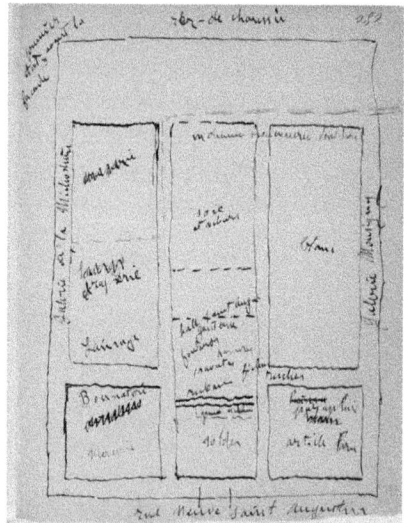

Figure 3.2. Inside map of *Au Bonheur des dames*, by Émile Zola, *Œuvres. Manuscrits et dossiers préparatoires*. *Source*: Bibliothèque Nationale de France. Public domain. Used with permission.

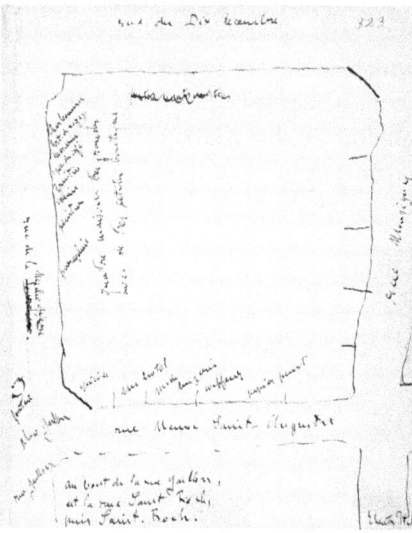

Figure 3.3. Street map for *Au Bonheur des dames*, by Émile Zola, *Œuvres. Manuscrits et dossiers préparatoires*. *Source*: Bibliothèque Nationale de France. Public domain. Used with permission.

Chapter 3

An Empire of Values

The Emporium in Zola's *Au Bonheur des dames*

The Orient at the Heart of Paris

Readers of Émile Zola's *Au Bonheur des dames* (1883) come upon a lavish setting recalling the Orientalist masterpieces of Jean-Auguste-Dominique Ingres and Eugène Delacroix:

> From the middle of Place Gaillon passers-by could catch a glimpse of this oriental hall, composed entirely of carpets and door-curtains.... This sumptuous Pasha's tent was furnished with armchairs and divans made from camel-bags.... Turkey, Arabia, Persia, the Indies were all here. The palaces had been emptied, the mosques and bazaars stripped. Tawny gold was the dominant tone in the worn antique carpets, and their faded tints retained a sombre warmth, the smelting of some extinguished furnace, with the beautiful burnt hue of an old master. Visions of the Orient floated beneath the luxury of this barbarous art, amid the strong odour which the old wools had retained from the land of vermin and sun. (Zola, *The Ladies' Paradise* 87–88)[1]

For all its allusions to painting, Zola's description is neither an account of an artwork nor that of a traveler's experience in the Levant. In the passage, Zola draws a portrait of his fictional department store, Au bonheur des dames, during the Oriental salon, an annual sale event for rugs and Oriental goods, popular among several department stores of the era (see chapter 1). The term *salon*, mainly used to refer to art exhibitions, blurs the distinction between fine art and the sweeping impact of consumerist culture during that era. The emporium brought the distant colonial encounter to the heart of the imperial metropolis. The Oriental salon cast its dominion over the shoppers' senses (sight, smell, touch, hearing). That lavish "Pasha's tent" occupies the Place Gaillon: the center of Haussmann's Paris and an emblematic space of French modernity. Eventually, this new Orientalist department store, a space frequented primarily by women and described as part harem, part bazaar, expands to consume the neighborhood and its traditional way of life.[2] Like the pedestrians and the shoppers, readers encounter a new city map entwined with that of the department store. They confront an ambiguous cartography that distorts and disrupts everyday spatial notions and practices. Significantly, the space that Zola chooses to foreground here is an "Orientalized" one. Strolling through the streets of Paris, Zola's shoppers run into an Oriental oasis at the heart of the French capital, much like the readers, who are taken by surprise in the midst of an unusual text intended to be "a poem of "modern life."[3]

In this chapter, I examine Zola's novel *Au bonheur de dames*. I argue that through the rhetoric of emporialism, mixing imperialist, capitalist and Orientalist imaginaries, Zola transforms the history of the emporium into a Saint-Simonian teleological mythology of empire. In this framework, the novel creates a polarized Manichean world—divided along the lines of East and West, material hedonism and moral restraint, upper and working classes. The narrative resolves these tensions by creating a new hybrid order born through an epic marriage between a spiritual feminine Orient and a technical masculine Occident, a reminder of the French Saint-Simonian Mediterranean project.

A New Commercial and Literary Map

Compared with his other novels of the same series, *Les Rougon-Macquart*, Zola marks in his notes that *Au bonheur des dames* should have an optimistic ending, at least for the protagonists.[4] Yet as the novel reveals, such success comes at a significant price for the community. *Au Bonheur des dames* recounts the social ascension of Denise Baudu, a young provincial worker from Normandy who becomes the mistress of the emporium. The success story follows a Darwinian trajectory crowned and validated by a bourgeois marriage, wealth acquisition, and social prestige. After surviving the ruthless challenges of the modern store, Denise reaches the highest echelons in the enterprise and finally marries the owner, Octave Mouret. Throughout her journey, Denise comes to see the competitive ethos of emporialism as the healthy, unstoppable spirit of the age. She recognizes that the success of modernity is only possible at the expense of the traditional social and urban fabric. She rationalizes the aftermath of emporialism, saying, "every revolution demanded its victims [martyrs]" (375).[5]

Much of Denise's realization materializes before her eyes as the city and its residents fall prey to the modern emporium. In contrast to the fantastic Orientalist image inside the store, near the end of the novel Zola draws another map of Paris: a nightmarish portrait of a city that has become almost unrecognizable. As the voracious, continuously expanding *grand magasin*–bazaar–harem reaches gargantuan proportions, it devours the surrounding traditional businesses and the whole city. To an extent, this spatial predatory trope, in which one urban space consumes another, runs throughout the *Rougon-Macquart* series to mark the tension between past and present (Lumbroso 64). To illustrate this conflict, Zola gives an account of a poster for the fictional Au Bonheur des Dames, emphasizing its antagonistic relation to Paris:

> Then there was a bird's-eye view. . . . Paris stretched out, but a Paris which was dwarfed and eaten by the monster: the houses that surrounding it had the humility of thatched cottages and were scattered beyond it in a dust of blurred chimneys. The monuments seemed to be melting away: two marks on the left-hand side indicated Notre-Dame, there was a circumflex accent on the right for the Invalides, and in the background was the Panthéon lost and shamefaced, no bigger than a pea. The skyline, crumbling into dust, had become nothing but a pathetic frame for the picture . . . as far away as . . . the open country, was now enslaved. (392)[6]

Zola portrays his fictional department store as an out-of-proportion monster that dwarfs the rest of the urban map. His description reiterates the iconography of department stores circulating in the print media of his era. Advertisements frequently amplified the stores' dimension to underscore the emporium's monumental dominance over the cityscape. For instance, a catalogue from Le Bon Marché from 1878 (fig. 3.1) renders the renowned department store in an exaggerated scale in contrast to an out-of-focus background. In the picture, Paris recedes and is almost effaced by a colossal *magasin*. The building with its rectilinear form, surrounded by an orderly line of trees, shows the store as the most modern and organized space in the city. The emporium features as both majestic and ominous: a paradigm of reason and order, overlooking a passive landscape and a muddled expanse of urban sprawl. Through the manipulation of scale between the store and its surroundings, the picture of Le Bon Marché and Zola's fictional poster establish the department store as a central spatial and cultural referent in the city.[7]

Much like the narrator who observes this crumbling cityscape, Zola witnessed the rise and fall of the Second Empire. The growing dominion of the emporium brings to mind Walter Benjamin's description of the Second Empire as a megalomaniac regime. Emporialism in Zola's text embodies this imperial megalomania. Nevertheless, exposing the overreaching power of empire reveals the precarious foundations of imperialism. Zola began writing this novel in 1881, with the aim to document that traumatic history: a time when French national and social maps were in flux both from within and without. Napoleon III's rise to power in 1848 and his subsequent coup d'état were indicative of the destabilizing political power of the voting masses, who had only recently acquired universal suffrage and shifted the balance between the capital and the provinces.[8] The Second Empire ended with the German annexation of Alsace-Lorraine in 1870 after the Battle of Sedan, leading to the chaotic events of the Commune in 1871, when the working class fought over the right to public and social space.[9] Meanwhile, France was also pursuing its colonial project. In that sense, the nation was paradoxically both colonizer and colonized. Inside the metropolis, the Haussmannization of Paris significantly modified the urban map along with the city's social fabric. The nation was disintegrating and expanding simultaneously, just as in Zola's portrait of the department store and the city.

The crumbling urban map in the novel exposes a mind that fails to make sense of the landscape and restore things to order. Derek Gregory dubs this condition "cartographic anxiety": the fear of losing one's social and political agency, which triggers an obsession with the control and reordering of surrounding space as a form of compensation (*Geographical Imaginations* 33). Ann McClintock describes the same phenomenon as the crisis of the imperial man caught between paranoia and megalomania, "suspended between a fantasy of conquest and a dread of engulfment, between rape and emasculation" (*Imperial Leather* 27). As McClintock points out, the colonial map represents a site of failure, where the empire's political and cultural crisis is often displaced onto a symbolically feminized, cannibalistic body: where "the unrepresentable appears on the surfaces of these maps in the form of 'cannibals,' 'savages,' mermaids, and monsters" (*Imperial Leather* 28; "Maidens"). Contrary to this example, Zola's fictional

Orientalized map is not securely located at the remote periphery of the French empire; the harem-like bazaar occupies the center of Haussmann's Paris, which makes its strategic position even more unsettling. Just like the cannibals and savages displayed on the colonial map, the fictional store, depicted as a feminine monster, grows to "devour" the surrounding businesses and neighborhoods. From this perspective, the "body" of Zola's department store, described as a bazaar and a harem—half woman, half machine—marks the failure of the European man to restore national and colonial space to his idealized body politic.

This cartographic anxiety surfaced in various contemporary texts. The notion that the department store was an index for imperial progress and East-West power dynamics also surfaced in other literatures. Albert Robida's humoristic novel *Le Vingtième Siècle* from 1883 gives an opposite account from the other shore of the Mediterranean.[10] He predicts the end of Turkish harems in the twentieth century with the rise of the emporium in Istanbul. New department stores with exaggeratingly Orientalist names like *Le Croissant* [The Crescent] and *Le Sabre Ottoman* [The Ottoman Sabre] popularize shopping and French fashion, which eventually signify the end of women's seclusion (Robida, *Vingtième Siècle* 378). The Ottoman Empire becomes more European under the influence of the emporium. Similarly, in his novel *À Rebours* (1884), naturalist author Joris-Karl Huysmans paints a tableau of modern France using a racialized language of commerce, in which merchants feature as a distinct hostile ethno-class, typically Oriental: "After the aristocracy of birth, it was now the turn of the aristocracy of money; it was the Caliphate of the counting-house [*comptoirs*], the despotism of the Rue de Sentier, the tyranny of commerce with its narrow minded, venal ideas, its ostentatious and rascally instincts" (Huysmans, *Against the Grain* 204).[11] Evoking "the Muslim caliphate" of shop counters, trade counters, and colonial trading posts, [*comptoirs*], and the rue Sentier, near passage du Caire, famous for Jewish merchants, Huysmans cast the French bourgeoisie as outsiders, part of a distinct race, leading to the fall of the nation (see chapter 1). The imaginaries of Zola, Robida, and Huysmans signal the end of a political regime through a triangulated complicity between the body politic, the Orientalized emporium, and the bodies of women or ethnic minorities.

A New Literary Map

Against his landscape of ruins, Zola sets the emporium as an embodiment of a new empire of values on the political and literary fronts. Both the emporium and Zola's novel express a new aesthetic, a reminder of what Marx and Engels once foresaw as the direct correlation between the constant reinvention of capitalism and literature; insofar as modern capital crafts novel cosmopolitan spaces necessary for its circulation, it produces new modes of consumption including new literary and artistic sensibilities (*Communist Manifesto* 64–65; see Introduction). The novel exposes a modern site of capital while crafting a corresponding literary genre that reflects the aesthetics of this new phenomenon. To communicate this message, the passage above treats monuments as "chronotopes" in the Bakhtinian sense, wherein each architectural site serves as a material expression of a specific era and its related aesthetics and context (Bakhtin, *Dialogic Imagination* 257). As a chronotope, the grand emporium contrasts with the surrounding landmarks erected in prior political regimes. The narrator highlights the puny status of three monuments that represent key periods of French history: the Dome des Invalides, a colossal, baroque-style military hospital and the burial place of kings and veterans; the Panthéon, a memorial to great national figures, built in a neoclassical design, where many military heroes, writers, and artists are buried; and the gothic cathedral of Notre Dame. Standing in the middle of ruins, the emporium turns into an antithetical site that challenges traditional sites of power: the Catholic Church and Napoleon's imperial heritage. Zola's description includes the phrases "the skyline crumbling into powder," "lost and shamefaced," "the monuments seemed to be melting away" (392). They reveal a moment of crisis, in which previous sites of memory and power seem to collapse in the face of a growing unstoppable cosmopolitan modernity that elides the distance between empire and colony and brings the Oriental shore of the Mediterranean into the European city.

The text uses the emporium and its surrounding sites as a chronotope to embody the aesthetics of naturalism and earlier literary schools. The author refers to the same public monuments and cityscapes immortalized in the writings of Realists and Romantics: Honoré de Balzac and Victor Hugo. Zola's description of Paris from a bird's-eye view and his depiction of the emporium as a "cathedral of commerce" pay a problematic tribute to Victor Hugo's *Notre Dame de Paris* (1831). Hugo's novel begins also with a bird's-eye panoramic view of Paris from the vantage point of Notre Dame.[12] For him, the cathedral represents the aesthetics of Romanticism, that of the grotesque, with its mélange of gothic and Oriental traits. As Hugo's renowned Romantic map and his cathedral metaphorically "crumble to dust," Zola's naturalist counterpart and his emporium rise to supplant them. The novel also pays a similar problematic tribute to Balzac. Zola explicitly mentions Balzac's *La maison du chat-qui-pelote* (1842) in his preparatory notes as one of the main references on French commercial culture. Balzac's novel depicts a small shop owned by a conservative middle-class family. Augustine, the simple daughter of the boutique owner, falls in love with and marries Théodore, a painter, but eventually loses him to an influential aristocratic woman. Balzac points toward the limitations of the emerging bourgeoisie and their inability to break the tight grasp of the upper classes on art, taste, and manners.

Zola's novel takes the history of this class further by examining the reversal of this situation following the ascension of the bourgeoisie to power and their control over economic and cultural capital. Whereas Balzac's protagonist fails to overcome social barriers, Denise Baudu—the poor niece of a shopkeeper—manages to win Octave Mouret's heart and outmaneuver her upper-class competitor. As modern entrepreneurs and owners of an emporium, Denise and Octave participate in shaping modern France and its urban plan, social structure, and national taste. In another novel, *La Peau de chagrin* (1831), Balzac ties Oriental material culture with bourgeois decadence. The novel narrates the tragic destiny of the protagonist, Raphael de Valentin, a young gambler who comes across a talisman in an antiques store. Covered in Arabic letters, the talisman promises to fulfill his wishes in exchange for a portion of his life. The talisman's power feeds on the protagonist's greed. In this Faustian contract, Valentin's body grows weaker every time his desires are met, eventually leading to his death. In contrast to Balzac's Oriental talisman found in an antiques shop, Zola creates a talismanic shop that grows stronger while fulfilling the desires of an ailing French nation. The Orientalized department store feeds on the greed of the bourgeoisie, foretelling the demise of the French body politic: the old city and eventually the Second Empire.[13] Zola also weaves into his narrative a classical trope of the Orient's invasion, which has frequently surfaced in French literature since its emergence.[14] In so doing, the author frames his literary work as both a continuum and a break from earlier traditions.

A Tableau of Modern France: An Oeuvre of Geography and History

Beyond the literary map, the novel engages in rewriting the history of a nation in crisis when his readers were still grappling with the tragic fate of an ambitious epoch of "progress." Zola's literary project *Les Rougon-Macquart* synchronizes with a parallel academic revision of French history in response to the trauma of defeat and the German annexation of Alsace-Lorraine in 1870. Because of the close linguistic and cultural ties between that region and German culture, France could not claim this territory on the sole basis of a racial or ethnic difference between the Alsatians and the Germans. This dilemma required a new interpretation to the wide linguistic and cultural variations in France without jeopardizing its unity. More so, in the nineteenth-century imperialist purview typically applied to the colonies, the French defeat and territorial loss would classify them as an inferior race to the Germans. In this context, historian Jules Michelet (1798–1874) and geographer Vidal de La Blache (1845–1918) investigated the circumstances that made France and Frenchmen into what they are. Michelet's works, *Introduction à l'histoire universelle* (1831) and *Histoire de la France* (1832–1875), sketch the portrait of France as a transcendent persona surviving the trials of the ages.[15] Michelet relies significantly on visual descriptions and allegories of painting to bring this image to life. As Michèle Hannoosh argues:

> Michelet's pictorial metaphors . . . served a purpose beyond the decorative. . . . Over time, the metaphor of painter and picture became an actual critical practice, as Michelet wrote about works of visual art and made this writing translate the forces and processes of history. . . . In this, he inaugurated a tradition that would be richly renewed well over a century later, as historians and philosophers of history invoked the visual arts to represent historical concepts and notions of history. (*Jules Michelet* 20)

Similarly, Vidal de La Blache reiterated Michelet's gesture of anthropomorphizing France. He incorporated Michelet's pictorial national project into the nascent field of human geography:

> In what sense France is a geographical entity? It seems paradoxical to me even to ask this next question: is France a geographical entity at all? This name, which has taken a concrete shape in our eyes, is embodied in a figure to which maps have accustomed us . . . We gladly incline to consider it as one unit . . . the answer is not as simple as we would at first think. It is not from a geological perspective that France acquires its individuality. Nonetheless, we repeat happily Michelet's statement: "France is a person." (La Blache, *Tableau* 25–26)[16]

In 1903, La Blache published *Tableau de la géographie de la France*, the first volume in a series on the history of France.[17] Since human geography focused on the interaction between individuals and their immediate milieu, La Blache's work shifted the focus from history, with its temporal representation, to space by rendering France into a collection of tableaux, or "landscapes."[18] As Anne Godlewska has demonstrated, the history of mapping and the epistemological approach of studying population through archeological landscapes, monuments and ruins already had roots in the French scientific tradition since Napoleon's mission in Egypt (1798–1801) which produced the profusely detailed encyclopedia *Description de l'Égypte* (Godlewska 129–47). It could also be seen in the writings of geographer Alexander von Humboldt, who was significantly influenced by this imperial magnum opus and whose lectures were translated in French as "Tableaux de la nature" in 1808 (Pratt, *Imperial Eyes* 119–21).[19] In his *Tableau*, La Blache posits that human labor turns a territory into nation, like "a medal coined with the image of a people."[20] La Blache's words imply a reciprocal relation between the individual and their milieu: each influences the other. Under the surface of this nationalist metaphor hides a capitalist logic. Akin to factory workers standing by an imaginary assembly line, the various populations of France participate in producing a transcendent image of their homeland. The French nation crystallizes as a commodity fetish constructed by alienated labor, who, in turn, acquire their unique image as people through this process. As two sides of the coin, the French nation and its people construct what Peter Szendy calls an "iconomic" image: an economically valorized and widely recognized representation. In that sense, national image resembles currency. They are both endowed with "a numismatic" quality. Like capital, this coined image—or "medal"—circulates within national borders and across empires (Szendy 7).

In this new paradigm, La Blache did not discount heredity completely, he subordinated it to culture. This shift created a new perspective of the French nation: one that accommodated the ethnic variations in the French territory but did not undermine Western Europe's racial distinction vis-à-vis the rest of the world.[21] The latter was still necessary to justify French imperialism and colonial expansion.[22] Most important, his work reveals the effect of Saint-Simonian industrial utopianism, wherein the French nation stands for a collective oeuvre, manufactured by the effort of the different provinces. Conceptually, these various geographical tableaux recall the pavilions of the universal exhibition and the corners of the emporium that, in turn, produced a totalized image of the world (Gregory, *Geographical Imaginations* 37–46).

Zola's colossal series *Les Rougon-Macquart* evolves in a similar nationalist and iconographic framework as the works of La Blache and Michelet. Zola wrote *Les Rougon-Maquart* between 1871 and 1893. The series embarks on a study of the people of modern France, who are simultaneously the outcome of their milieu and the eventual alienated producers of a collective transcendent image of their nation. The series comprises twenty novels narrating the society of the Second Empire and the causes of its fall. Following the theories of Hippolyte Taine on social milieux, Zola's series tracks the history of the members of this family and its behavior in different locales (see Savile; Barrows). Just as La Blache analyzes French society by depicting geographic, or spatial, tableaux, Zola depicts iconic sites or spaces of the Second Empire and follows the story of the "evolution" of this family in its relation to them. He dedicates each volume to a specific space: the railways, the mines, the food market, the department store, the stock market, the working-class pub, and the art salon. These sites represent the various milieux that shape and are shaped by the fortunes of the different members of the Rougon-Macquart family. Each landscape stands out as a tableau of human geography produced by the ethos of industrial utopianism. The aggregate sum of these tableaux offers a new founding narrative of national space and its respective collective identity.

Since naturalism prioritized the minute study of social forces and the impact of the milieu on the individual, Zola conducted extensive archival and field research before writing. He observed some of the renowned Parisian stores, such as Le Bon Marché and Les Grands Magasins du Louvre. He interviewed employees and took notes on the merchandise, setting, and working conditions (Zola, *Œuvres. Manuscrits*). Zola even locates his store at the site of an actual *grand magasin* on the rue de la Paix (Marrey 52; Mead, *Charles Garnier's* 44). In his description of the *grands boulevards*, Balzac predicts that in 1860, the heart of Paris would be from rue de la Paix to Place de la Concorde ("Histoire et physiologies" 7). In addition, Octave Mouret evokes the figure of Aristide Boucicaut, the founder of Le Bon Marché. Mouret's friend Baron Hartman is recognizable as an avatar for Baron Haussmann and the Saint-Simonian financiers the Pereire brothers. In this manner, Zola sets his novel against the widely familiar reality and history of the *grand magasin* as it developed in the nation's capital during that era. It is important to note that the novel draws the portrait of the Second Empire using scenes and sights from the Third Republic. The author undertook his fieldwork for *Au Bonheur des dames*, the eleventh volume of the series, more than a decade after the end of the Second Empire. In that sense, this historical work is a multilayered project, which inadvertently overlaps several maps together: those of the Second Empire with those of the Third Republic, all of which came to be amalgamated under the title of la Belle Époque after World War I.

A Saint-Simonian Mediterranean Epic

To relate the phenomenon of the department store during the Second Empire, the text espouses the history of grand magasin with Saint-Simonian Mediterranean utopianism. The narrative plot echoes the writing of Michel Chevalier, the Saint-Simonian counselor to Napoleon III. In a series of writings on the "Système de la Méditerranée" from 1832, Chevalier describes the modern Mediterranean connected via a network of trains and canals:

> The most widespread, monumental and deeply-rooted struggle which has ever made the Earth reverberate with the din of battle is that of the Orient and the Occident. This struggle represents the distinct character of a phase of civilization which has evolved from historical times to the present day. It is the most resounding manifestation of the war that, for six thousand years, has taken place between mind and matter, spirituality and sensuality, a war which we are now bringing to an end.[23]

Chevalier offers a sensational and Manichean worldview in which the interconnected Mediterranean brings about the end of a historical conflict between East and West (29). In his vision, the aesthetics of Delacroix and Ingres converge with the values of capitalism. Painting the portrait of a capitalist world with an Orientalist brush, he depicts the sea basin and its commercial network as a "nuptial bed" uniting a feminine Orient and a masculine Occident ("*Le Globe* 12 février 1832," 116).

Presiding over his emporium, Octave Mouret aspires to cast his commercial dominion over the Saint-Simonian system with its networks of money, people, and trade. Mouret describes himself proudly: "He declared that basically he was more Jewish than all the Jews in the world: he took after his father, a cheery fellow who knew the value of money, whom he resembled in both looks and character; and if he had got his excitable [nervous] imagination from his mother, it was, perhaps, his most obvious asset, for he was aware of the invincible force of his charm in daring everything" (35).[24]

Mouret is not actually Jewish; his words mock French clichés of the era. Zola openly decried French anti-Semitism during the Dreyfus affair (see Zola, *Dreyfus Affair*). In this passage, Mouret adopts a self-perception associated with a nineteenth-century racialized discourse that projects an ambiguously gendered character to Jewish entrepreneurs. Typical of the Saint-Simonian Mediterranean ideal, Mouret embodies a duality of reason and passion that resembles an imagined geography where the sciences of a masculine West meet the sensibility of a feminine East. Mouret's body is also a site of the mythical Saint-Simonian battle between European reason and Eastern sensuality. Having inherited his father's rationality and his mother's "nervous imagination," Mouret's character is a queer mélange, an androgynous one, a woman in a man's body. Mouret is repeatedly given "feminine" characteristics. At a certain moment, the narrator qualifies Mouret as a woman or someone who fully comprehends womanhood: "Il était femme" [He was woman] (Zola, *Au Bonheur des dames*, 137).[25] Mouret can identify with women and understand their thoughts and desires. At his lover's, Henriette's, reception, female guests consider him "one of them" (179). Mouret's character is androgynous: a woman in a man's body, who could translate his vision into an aesthetic tableau. The words "a nervous imagination" attributed to Mouret recall Zola's praise of Delacroix for having an artistic "acute neurosis" [névrose aigüe] (Zola, *Écrits sur l'art* 194). Like Delacroix, who brought the Orientalist gendered fantasy and lush interiors to the French metropole by painting the harems, Mouret's sensual imagination allows him to capture an "irrational, neurotic, and feminine" Orient and reproduce it by means of commodity spectacle (Hannoosh, *Painting*).

Mouret's ultimate goal is to have the city run through the store, making the street, the boulevards, and the *magasin*'s galleries indistinguishable from each other, if not interchangeable (302). He meets with Baron Hartmann (Haussmann's fictional counterpart) to discuss the construction of a new street and the possibility of expanding his department store by taking over the neighboring buildings. Mouret's views bear many resemblances with the actual Baron Haussmann, who was also self-orientalizing figure. As Walter Benjamin indicates, Haussmann nicknamed himself "Pasha Osman ... [the] artist demolitionist" (Benjamin 127). Haussmann's urban plan was another site of battle between the aesthetics of arts and the brutal aggression of capitalism. His framed vistas were designed for the camera and the cannon simultaneously, serving at once as a photographic postcard of the city and a strategic shooting range designed to prevent any possible future riots (Pinon, "Le Project" 74). Department stores were part and parcel of Haussmann's urban plan. As Philip Nord argues:

> The mixture of business and theater concocted by the department store was then a second-hand edition of the genuine article to be found outside on the streets of new Paris. The boulevards of the grand magasin interior were so many extensions of the grands boulevards that stretched from the Madeleine to the Bastille. The department store, the city's new boulevards, the look and structure of Paris nouveau were interlocking phenomena, aspects of a single process. Contemporaries recognized implicitly the interconnectedness of the changes wrought by Haussmannization. Haussmann's Paris, like the department store—the real city like the city in miniature—conjured up images of machines, tentacled creatures, phalansteries, barracks and agglomerations. (133)

Mouret understands the modern Parisian urban plan doubling as a theatrical landscape and a battlefield. The first description of the store in the novel reveals a similar perspective in which the *grand magasin* is perfectly enmeshed into the larger modern urban networks of streets and boulevards. On her way to her uncle's shop, Denise distinguishes the modern store from a significant distance as soon as she reaches Place Gaillon. The text highlights the organization of the department store hinging on the interplay between public and private spaces. Its windows seem to vanish, erasing the borders between the boulevard and the *magasin*. This is a characteristic layout for department stores, of which Michel de Certeau has written: "The department store is inserted into an urban environment . . . with which it is in perfect osmosis. This porousness renders the store infinitely traversable; it is a continuation of the street and one can stroll through it just as one does through sidewalk stalls" (*Practice* 103).[26] In contrast, in chapter 4 the narrator describes Denise's uncle watching the emporium's delivery vehicles on their way toward the grand boulevard. The vehicles deliver merchandise and double as mobile advertisement boards. The emporium's "fleet" invades the neighboring *grand boulevard* and annexes the hub of Parisian public life. This practice reflects the real historical urban context of the time, when Paris attempted to control the torrents of advertisement invading the city. Department stores' owners used their vehicles as moving publicity, impossible to be controlled by the city's regulations (Hahn 144–52). In this sense, department stores owners quickly understood the

Saint-Simonian nature of Haussmann's urban plan, which privileged traffic circulation over that of pedestrians.

Inside the store, Mouret applies the Haussmannian concept of circulation and manipulation of the crowds. He stands on the central staircase, a space that closely recalls the foyer of the opera and the vestibule of the harem, to command the store. From this panoptic vantage point, he studies his clients' behavior and manipulates their circulation (Zola, *Ladies' Paradise* 117; *Au Bonheur des dames* 175). Mouret's organizational strategy follows the quick rhythm of commerce. He constantly anticipates the crowd's practices of space and steps ahead to challenge their sense of orientation. Sometimes he shifts the location of the departments unexpectedly to force them to circulate through the whole store. At other times, he closes an entry door to give an impression of a crowded store and attract curious passers-by (Zola, *Ladies' Paradise* 233–40; *Au Bonheur des dames* 299–306).

The tentacles of Mouret's Saint-Simonian network reach every corner of the Eastern world. Much like the actual department store owners of the epoch, Mouret sends his agents to scour the East to please his French clients (refer to fig. 1.1): "He was ransacking the whole Far East, where travellers were pillaging palaces and temples for him" (408).[27] The language of the text precisely describes Mouret as engaging in an imperialist venture: "Palaces had been emptied, mosques and bazaars plundered" (88).[28] The words *emptied* [*vidé*] and *plundered* [*dévalisé*] emphasize an avid and violent drive for appropriation on the model of the military acquisition of wealth. The words *ransacking* [*remuait*] and *pillaging* [*fouillait*] evoke the operation of an archeological expedition in which the land is dug and destroyed in search of hidden treasures to be displayed and sold to customers.

Emporialism and the Phenomenology of Mass Consumption

Zola's design of the department store and literary imagery are not haphazard. The text's naturalist aesthetics stem from the semiotics of the latest theories in architecture, sociology, and human geography. In a sense, his literary language is an embodiment of its milieu. His language bears the same qualities of his fictional emporium as well as the aesthetics and ideology of emporialism.

To edify his fictional store, Zola sought the advice of architect Frantz Jourdain.[29] In his recommendations, Jourdain stressed the role of "transparency," or the fact that the design of the building should clearly indicate its purported function (Clausen, *Frantz Jourdain* 20–22). Jourdain refers to a dominant architectural aesthetic whose history goes back to architect Jacques François Blondel (1705–1774).³⁰ The best example of this architecture is Victor Baltard's design of Les Halles, made entirely from exposed iron, reflecting its role as a modern marketplace, which Zola portrays later in *Le ventre de Paris* (Mead, *Charles Garnier's* 110–34).³¹ Jourdain translated his own vision into an actual store, that of La Samaritaine in 1905 (Clausen, *Frantz Jourdain* 20–22). Throughout the novel, Zola stresses the elements of transparency in the emporium's design. The department store's aisles and counters mirror the highly organized and controlled Parisian urban plan with its aligned avenues and rectilinear façades. In the author's preparatory notes, Zola includes the blueprint of the store and its location. In the sketches the streets follow a similar pattern and linearity seen in his map for the store's internal layout (figs. 3.2 and 3.3).

The transparency of the emporium is a key element that ties together the interior and exterior of the store. Zola invests further in this aesthetic by weaving in Hippolyte Taine's theories on art. In his lectures at the École des Beaux-Arts, Taine pinpoints the connection between human geography and art. He posits that to understand an artwork, including literature and architecture, one should examine the "essential character" of the milieu in which it was produced, in particular the mindset of the people and their customs (Taine, *Philosophie* 14–15):

> What is a zone, if not a particular temperature, a particular degree of heat and humidity. In one word: a particular set of dominant circumstances, analogous in their type to what we called right now the general mindset [*état d'esprit*] and customs? Just as there exists a physical temperature, whose variations determine the appearance of this or this species of plants, there is a moral temperature whose variations determine the appearance of this or that species of art. Just as we study the physical temperature to understand the appearance of this or that species of plants, on has to study the moral temperature to understand the appearance of a this or that species of art. (9–10)³²

For Taine, the evolution of art is analogous to the evolution of species. By the same token, artists should convey the essential character in their artwork, not by means of pure imitation but by reflecting the milieu in "the interior and exterior logic" of their artwork (Taine, *Philosophie* 29).

Artists and writers should portray "the connections" and relations that tie the various parts of the artwork together to convey an aggregate image of its essential character (Taine, *Philosophie* 28–29).[33] As Christopher Mead argues, Taine foregrounds "empathy" as an expression of transparency. By *empathy*, he means that a building's transparency relies on its way of creating a complex and a multilayered sensorial experience, which emulates the character of the milieu and its inhabitants. One way of achieving this effect is through synesthesia, or producing a complex phenomenological experience that engages many senses simultaneously (Taine, *Philosophie* 41, qtd. in Mead, *Charles Garnier's* 253–59). A good example of empathy in the architecture of the era is Garnier's opera house, finished in 1875, eight years before the publishing of Zola's novel. Garnier collaborated with Jourdain in several projects. For Garnier, the stage was the least important space. The entire monument, with its lighting and grand entrance, was the actual theater made to frame and highlight the everyday life of the bourgeoisie (Mead, *Charles Garnier's* 127).[34] Garnier depicted the opera as an Oriental fantasy and a breathing body that comes to life with "the vapors exhaled from the chests of the spectators, and [the vapors] which escape from the light." As the rays of light fall on the building's golden ornaments, they give the impression of slight vibration. The interplay of air and golden light produces the effect of an "Oriental mirage."[35]

Taine's and Jourdain's aesthetics became the alphabets of the naturalist language that shaped Zola's emporium. For Zola, the emporium is a living being, a species on its own, productive of its milieu, embodying the customs and the mindset of the people. Through transparency and empathy, Zola creates "the interior and exterior logic" of the store. He constructs a psychographic map of the emporium that relies on the analogy between the feminine body and space, between the machine and the body. All of this brings about the various Orientalist imageries of Saint-Simonian mythology. Akin to Garnier's design of the opera, Zola depicts the emporium as a large theatrical space for the bourgeoisie: a space whose features emulate human emotions and sensorial experiences. Inside the store, Zola applies the principles of synesthesia to produce a multisensorial experience, hinging on the interplay of light and the various sensations evoked by Oriental material culture. In chapter 1, Zola describes the emporium in words closely resembling Garnier's description of the opera house, as a human breathing under the light of the gas lamps: "On the other side of the road [The Ladies' Paradise was igniting] the deep rows of gas burners. She [Denise] drew nearer, once more attracted and, as it were, warmed by this source of blazing light.

The machine was still humming, still active, letting off steam in a final roar" (28).³⁶ Later, he re-creates a similar portrait, whereby the internal activity of the store goes in tandem with that of the visitors, who breathe life into the emporium: "It was four o'clock, and the rays of the setting sun were entering obliquely through the wide bays at the front of the shop, lighting up from the side the glazed roofs of the halls; in this fiery brightness, the thick dust, raised from the morning onwards by the trampling of the crowd was floating upwards, like a golden vapour" (264).³⁷

Zola adds a gothic element to the character of the store. He turns the department store into the incarnation of Mouret's dead wife. In the first chapter of the novel, Madame Baudu describes the mysterious death of the owner's wife. The neighborhood residents think that Mouret might have killed her and that her body might be hidden under the store: "There's some of her blood under the foundations of that shop!" (67).³⁸ The emporium is haunted by the spirit of a dead woman, whose body makes the foundation of the edifice while her soul animates it.

The story of the dead wife weaves the store's anthropomorphized image into a larger Orientalist tale, namely, *The Thousand and One Nights*. Zola's text draws on the widely popularized of imaginary of *The Nights* frequently circulated by department stores in their promotional campaigns, at once evoking Oriental despotism and enslavement of women and the fantasy of Eastern commodities, especially rugs (see chapter 1). Much like *The Nights*, "the fairy tale" of the department store centers on a tyrant king. The narrative of both texts is propelled and gains momentum by the death of women. In the *Nights*, Shahryar sentences his first wife to death, marries a new woman every day, then orders his vizier to execute her at dawn (see *Les Mille et une nuits*). Similarly, Mouret is a wealthy widower and an eligible bachelor who refuses to remarry and engages in many romantic affairs. He aspires to cast his seductive web over all women. He builds his commercial empire from his wife's inheritance and develops new strategies to manipulate women's consumerist desires. In the novel, the store is described as a royal court, a harem, a kingdom, and a marketplace. Mouret "reigned over [women] with the brutality of a despot" (427). He ruled Au Bonheur des Dames like an "absolute monarch" with a "council of ministers," overseen by his assistant, Bourdoncle (32).³⁹ In one of the early scenes, the following conversation takes place between him and Bourdoncle: "Mouret became even more expansive, allowing his fundamental brutality to show through his air of sensual adoration [of women]. With a shrug of his shoulders he seemed to declare that he would throw them away like empty sacks on the day when they had finished helping him to make his fortune. Bourdoncle, in his cold way, obstinately repeated: 'They'll have their revenge. There'll be one who'll avenge the others, there's sure to be [*c'est fatal*]'" (33–34).[40] Mouret's commercial odyssey unfolds as a modern Orientalist tale of horror and conquest relying on the extermination and mutilation of women. The vocabulary of commerce stresses Mouret's misogynist character, building his empire at the expense of female shoppers who are like "empty sacks." Like ancient public sites of execution, the store's windows showcase a multitude of headless mannequins, who haunt the streets of modern Paris: "The great velvet coat trimmed with silver fox suggested the curved outline of a headless woman, running through the downpour to some festivity in the mysterious Parisian night" (28).[41]

The emporium, the modern machine, comes to life as more women succumb to Mouret's temptations. Bourdoncle doubles as an "executioner" (the term used for firing underperforming or redundant salesclerks). He is "the man ... whom [Mouret] put in charge of executions" (Zola, *Au Bonheur des dames* 92).[42] As Bethany Hetrick suggests, Bourdoncle's trademark "'passez à la caisse' [go to the till] is itself so sharp and swift that it almost feels like the blade of the guillotine." Bourdoncle has the right to fire, "execute," anyone immediately without giving any reason (Hetrick).

This metaphor hides a deeper Orientalist dimension, as it strikingly reiterates the story of the famous vizier of *The Nights* in charge of the daily execution of the king's wives. Such reference did not go unnoticed for Zola's readers during that time. For example, renowned caricaturist Albert Robida creates a parody of Zola's *Au Bonheur des dames* in one of his works published in *La Caricature* in 1883 ("Au bonheur des dames"). Robida constructs the emporium as a ruthless machine feeding on the bodies of women. The center of the caricature has a phallic-shaped window, aligning the store's image with a heteronormative male gaze that seeks to impose order over an irrational feminized and chaotic space. One of the drawings shows Mouret represented as a king from the Orient while courting Denise. In the cartoon, Bourdoncle, like the famous vizier, stands by the door dressed in Eastern attire, holding a sword.

Bourdoncle prophesies that one day women will seek revenge from Mouret. Soon his words come true, once Denise begins her work at the *grand magasin*. Denise recalls Scheherazade from *The Nights*, who joins Shahryar's harem to avenge the women he killed. Unlike other women, Denise rejects consumerism and resists Mouret's advances, which enables her to rise in the ranks. Significantly, she begins her job at the store during the Oriental sale. On her first day, she literally steps into an overwhelming "décor de harem," which leads her to lose her sense of orientation: "When Denise, who was starting work that very Monday, had crossed the Oriental hall, she had stood still in astonishment, unable to recognize the entrance of the shop, her confusion compounded by the harem scene set up at the door" (Zola, *Ladies Paradise* 88).[43] She checks into the women's dormitory and, by extension, into Mouret's house/harem, since he lives in a connected building. Once admitted into Au Bonheur des dames, she leads a life of seclusion and imprisonment like that of an odalisque, spending her time between the store and the women's dormitory—compared to a harem by the narrator. As she becomes accustomed to the interior of the store and living in confinement, Paris grows distant and foreign: "She was happy in her solitude, in the unsociable [wild] life in which she shut herself away as if in a sanctuary" (133).[44]

At the Heart of the Orient

The synesthetic experience inspired by Taine and Jourdain reaches its epitome during the Oriental salon. In describing this sale event, Zola's language deploys the full rhetoric of emporialism. Obviously, he did not invent the Oriental salon. He based the novel on his observation of similar sales events, which took place in several department stores during that era. Mouret's promotional strategies closely emulate the promotional and setting of the stores during these events. The date of 10 October for his fictive sale takes place the same day as a yearly Oriental salon at Le Bon Marché. The sale at Le Bon Marché included the same goods itemized by Zola, including rugs and *portières* (door-curtains; see refer to fig. 1.11). Mouret, a neurotic investor, converges the romanticized Orientalist visions of materialism with the forces of supply and demand. Akin to Saint-Simonian entrepreneurs, Mouret subjects the sensuality of the Orient to his technical expertise to ensure the maximum circulation of capital, commodities, and people inside the store. He stages the Oriental salon in the "vestibule" (central hall) of the *magasin*. He hangs rugs from the ceiling and decks the corners of the room with door-curtains to give the impression of an Oriental harem or household. Mouret assumes some of the typical Orientalist and colonial roles. On the one hand, he owns and manages a space occupied by a large crowd of women. On the other, acting as an adventurous trader, he bargains for antique rugs in the Levant (Zola, *Ladies Paradise* 87).[45]

Zola applies the principles of synesthesia to create a multisensorial experience that reflects the various sensations triggered by Oriental material culture. Once again, the emporium expresses the Haussmannian duality of artistic landscapes and violent battlefields. The salon inundates all the senses, from the bright color of gold dazzling the eyes, recalling the sunny warm weather of the East and its material riches; to the different tactile aspects of wool, leather, and wood; to the smell of wool. Here, the customer might capture a panoramic view of the entire region via a wide array of Orientalist categories "culture, religion, mind, history, [and] society" (Said, *Orientalism* 239). The following passage describes the clientele's shopping experience while being carefully observed by inspector Jouve, a retired army commander who served in Algeria. The scene reflects the colonial paranoia of luxurious abundance and the fear of loss of control.

> Every time a customer appeared, there was a stir among the page-boys lined up beneath the high porch, dressed in a livery of light green coat and trousers, and yellow and red striped waistcoat. Jouve, the retired captain who worked as a shopwalker, was there too, in frock-coat and white tie, wearing his medal like a sign of respectability and probity, receiving the ladies with an air of solemn politeness, bending over them to point out the various departments. Then they would disappear into the entrance-hall, which had been changed into an Oriental hall.... First of all, the ceiling was covered with carpets from Smyrna, their complicated designs standing out on red backgrounds. Then, on all four sides, were hung door-curtains: door-curtains from Kerman and Syria, striped with green, yellow, and vermillion; door-curtains from Diarkebir, of a commoner type, rough to the touch, like shepherd's cloaks; and still more carpets which could be used as hangings, long carpets from Isphahan, Teheran, and Kermanshah, broader carpets from Schoumaka and Madras, a strange blossoming of peonies and palms, imagination running riot in a dream garden. On the floor there were still more carpets; thick fleeces were strewn there, and in the centre was a carpet from Agra, an extraordinary specimen with a white background and a broad border of soft blue, through which ran purplish embellishments of exquisite design. There were other marvels displayed everywhere, carpets from Mecca with a velvet reflection, prayer rugs from Daghestan with a symbolic pointed design, carpets from Kurdistan covered with flowers in full bloom; finally, in a corner, there was a large pile of cheap rugs, from Geurdis, Kula, and

Kirghehir, priced from fifteen francs upwards. This sumptuous Pasha's tent was furnished with armchairs and divans made from camel-bags, some ornamented with multi-colored lozenges, others with simple [naive] roses. Turkey, Arabia, Persia, the Indies were all here. (87–88)[46]

Zola's style and syntax emulate the sensory overload experience productive of the massive commodity spectacle in the emporium. Readers find themselves confronting an overwhelming text abundant with microscopic sensorial details, which they have to process to construct the larger (macroscopic) image of the salon. In this way, Zola translates the modern practice of urban space into a phenomenological grueling practice of reading. He forces his readers to encounter the unfamiliar and vertiginous world of the Oriental salon, just like modern shoppers who had to adapt their senses to this new hyperstimulating commercial milieu. The emporium and the text retrain the senses by bringing a set of intense novel sensations, often associated with the colonial adventure. The description of the salon is at once highly sensorial and desensitizing, abundant with geographic references and disorienting.

The entire emporium comes to represent the Orient along with its colonial dynamics of policing and control. Mouret's layers of rugs and woolen door-coverings serve as a metonym for the Middle East; they concoct a homogeneous space where borders collapse and any geographic specificity is lost, despite the seeming abundance of details. In the process of listing and naming the country of origin of every rug, like the act of creation in Genesis, the East is called, named, and summoned into existence for the European consumer. With this detailed, encyclopedic indexing, the Orient features as a reified space with "imaginative geographies" and "dramatic boundaries" (Said, *Orientalism* 73). As Edward Said claims: "The Orient [represents a] stage on which the whole East is confined.... The Orient... seems to be, not an unlimited extension beyond the familiar European world, but rather a close field, a theatrical stage affixed to Europe" (63). Every rug recalls a painting and a repertoire of Orientalist themes and characters: the enchanting rose garden, the pilgrimage to Mecca, the mountains, the desert, the different Oriental "types" (Said, *Orientalism* 259), the Arab Bedouin, the shepherd, the Pasha, and the despotic ruler, but also, as the narrator and visitors describe it, the "harem" and old master paintings. The vocabulary dominating the passage, borrowed from Orientalist fiction and travel narratives, highlights the luxurious and dreamy aspect of the place: "the imagination running riot," "garden of dreams," "marvels," "sumptuous tent," "visions of the Orient floated," "luxury."[47] Through Zola's brush, the Oriental salon transports the shoppers and the readers into the French imaginary of *The Nights*, with its fantasies strongly connected to the exuberant details of its material culture, as later portrayed in Orientalist art and literature.

The language brings to the forefront the dream-like aspect of that simulacrum and the sensual pleasure derived from that visual and tactile experience. The salon is at once luxurious, animalistic, and barbaric. It embodies the double aspect of the Orient seen simultaneously as a site of fascination and abjection, or as Zola puts it: "the land of vermin and suns" (88). Just like the disoriented colonial explorer, the store's clients are engulfed in this reconstructed Orient. They literally "disappear" in that fantasy world of the senses. In the midst of the modern city, they find themselves immersed in a polychromatic Orientalist tableau: an enchanting garden, surrounded by flowers in full blossom and thick foliage evoked by the different decorative details and patterns on the carpets of "strange blossoming of peonies," "palms," and [naïve] "simple roses." The author communicates this overwhelming experience that inundates the shoppers' senses with an endless listing of details and a syntactic structure that does not allow the reader any respite. He proceeds through a spectrum of textures, smells, and colors: "velvet," "camel hair," "thick fleece," "coarse wool," "red," "yellow," "vermillion," "purplish," and "tawny gold" supplied with the "velvet reflection."

The rhythm and visions inspired by the salon keep on changing, like pictures from a panorama, another popular invention of Zola's time.[48] As Mouret reconfigures the store's map into that of colonies, he paralyzes his clients' sense of reason, urging them to follow their impulses. The loud voices of the crowd attending the sales event evoke the soundscape of the colonies: the casbah, the *medina*, the bazaar, and the *souk*. Switching from this scenery, Zola reconstructs the biblical narrative of Exodus. He describes the store as a temple for the golden calf, toward which the voice of the crowd rises in worship: "With every step he took the noise increased, becoming the uproar of a nation bowing down to the golden calf" (430).[49] The clients' behavior recalls Taine's depiction of crowds during the revolution: "Besides, passions are exalted by mutual contagion; the crowding, the clamor, the disorder, the wait, and the fasting grow to compose a state of drunkenness from which nothing can come out other than vertigo and fury" (*Les Origines de la France* 158–59).[50] In a later passage, the synesthetic experience reaches its crescendo, when Zola brings the store's landscape and soundscape in unison. He portrays the shopping experience as a Bacchic ritual whose participants have reached a frenzied state and fallen under the spell of their leader: "gold was clinking in the cash-desks; while the customers despoiled and violated, were going away in disarray, their desires satisfied, and with the secret shame of having yielded to temptation in the depths of some sleazy hotel. And it was he who possessed them all like that, who held them at his mercy" (427).[51] The rising clamor of the inebriated, uncontrolled crowd is paired with the metallic ringing of golden coins, as if the crowd's desire were literally and instantly transformed into economic gain. The shoppers' multilayered and complex phenomenological experience is reduced to mere digits in the register. The shoppers are objectified, prostituted, enslaved, and swindled. They leave the store-brothel-temple with mixed feelings of sexual satisfaction and shame.

Typical of emporialism, the salon acquires an illusion of authenticity by virtue of its reference to an Orientalist body of knowledge and a set of fantastic projections that displaces the actual Orient altogether. Emporialism emulates the discursive practices and politics of Orientalism. As Said notes, Orientalism "[puts] into cultural circulation a form of discursive currency by whose presence the Orient henceforth would be spoken for" (*Orientalism* 93). Zola indirectly alludes to the tension between Orientalist art and modern consumerism. A bourgeois customer standing in the Oriental salon exclaims to her friends that the salon resembles the paintings of "Delacroix" (116).[52] Through that naïve comment, Zola ridicules bourgeois taste, which values art according to its ability to replicate prolific material details. In his critique of French art, the author has mocked Orientalist artists, whose works reproduce the aesthetics of commercial utopianism and serve to "decorate the bourgeois salon." This generation of artists, Zola claims, strive to copy Delacroix but lack his talent (Écrits *sur l'art* 194). Unlike their master, they commodify the Orient and produce dull paintings replete with Oriental goods resembling at most a warehouse. Some of the artists that Zola frequently critiques, like Gérome and Édouard Détaille, were often cited in department stores catalogues (Écrits *sur l'art* 185, 340–41).[53] Expressing his contempt to bourgeois taste, Zola writes:

> The truth is that the public is infatuated purely and simply by the artist's games of hide and seek. They recognize very well the buttons on a cardigan, the charms in a chain watch; no detail is lost on them. This is what brings about their admiration ... The crowd feels flattered for their infantile instincts, for their admiration of a surmounted hardship, for their love of insignificant tableaux, well-painted and above all rich in details. They only understand this in art. (Écrits *sur l'art* 384)[54]

130 | Emporialism

The Oriental salon with its prolific details resembles at best the artwork of mediocre painters whose tableaux offer nothing but a commodified experience of the East. The client's comment comes to demystify the theatricality of emporialism, exposing it as a commodity spectacle.

Nevertheless, this commercial version of the Orient anchors itself in the space of the city space and that of the text, taking control simultaneously of both the urban crowd and the readers. The readers by this point are caught in a dizzying space, far away from the transparent, rectilinear façade that connects seamlessly to the Haussmannian geometrical urban plan, seen in Zola's blueprint (fig. 3.3). Mouret constantly changes the setting to hide the legible linearity of the space. While the store arranges objects based on their potential to capture the shopper's attention, it consciously designs the itinerary and the shopping experience of its visitors. Zola's ambiguous layout of the emporium emulates the conflicting architectural aesthetics of the Second Empire, divided between the uniformity of the exterior and the theatricality of the interior. David Van Zanten describes this tension between the sober exterior and the immersive theatrical interior: "it is the nature of this promenade through the consumerist fantasyland that gives us the quality of Second Empire building (*Building Paris* 43). This spatial dichotomy shows best when Madame Marty finds herself trapped in the new setting of the store, inciting her to make more purchases:

> But on the landing of the big, central staircase, [Japan stopped her again.][55] This counter had grown since the day when Mouret had amused himself by setting up in the same place a little auction stall. . . . [H]e was ransacking the whole Far East, where travellers were pillaging palaces and temples for him. And new departments were still being opened: they had tried two new ones in December . . . a book department and a children's toy department, which would certainly grow and sweep away more businesses in the neighbourhood. In four years [Japan] had succeeded in attracting all the artistic clientele of Paris. (418–19)[56]

Mouret redesigns the Oriental map to ensnare the shopper. Madame Marty's experience resembles that of an Orientalist traveler lost in an adventure that promises excitement and riches. She roams the aisles of the store, unable to find an exit from the Oriental maze. Similarly, throughout the novel the scenery shifts from one passage to another, throwing the reader, like the shoppers, into unexpected corners of the world. Both lose their sense of geographical reference, wondering whether it is still the store or the Universal Exhibition, a library, or a toy department. Zola reverses the relationship between subject and object. He places Japan as the subject of the sentence, and Madame Marty as the object: "Japan stopped her again." Not only does Madame Marty lose control over her surrounding space, finding herself in a distant East engulfing her, she also falls under the power of a phantasmatic Orient and its commodities. Madame Marty's experience exposes the paranoia of the imperialist capitalist man, wherein the initial violence of wealth acquisition from the East gives way, back at home, to the commodity fetish, which in its turn takes control of the French consumer.

Mouret manipulates the desires and passions of his public. He renders them mindless and childlike, "orientalizing" them. He turns against Europe the strategies of control intended for the Orient. Exploiting the stereotype of the Jew in the European imaginary, the narrator describes Mouret as a modern Shylock who transforms women's bodies and desires into financial profit. The text draws attention to the connection between the circulation of capital and the circulation of women in the city and the store: "She [the Woman] reigned there [the department store] as an amorous queen whose subjects trade on her, and who pays for every whim with a drop of her own blood. Beneath the very charm of his gallantry, Mouret thus allowed the brutality of a Jew selling woman by the pound: he was building a temple to Woman, making a legion of shop assistants burn incense before her" (77).[57] That passage suggests that the female shopper quickly passes from being the "queen" of the store and a goddess in a temple to being sacrificed at the altar of the temple built for her, for the sake of Mouret's profit. Greeted as a queen by Mouret's "army," she is sold by the pound, and she pays for her desire with her blood. Mouret brings to the forefront the history of European paranoia. The store projects a double form of European anti-Semitism, one from within, the other from without (Anidjar 33). If the store's commodities and setting summon the specter of the Arab-Muslim world, Europe's outside enemy, the image of the powerful Jewish entrepreneur re-creates Europe's internal enemy. In Shakespeare's *The Merchant of Venice*, Shylock loses his wealth, status, and descendants; he roams the city lamenting his loss. Zola offers readers the reverse example. The modern Shylock returns with an army of salesclerks to conquer the nation's capital. He takes revenge on the woman, who now must pay with her flesh. In a sense, inside the store, the European shoppers' status recalls Shylock's fate at the end of the play. They turn into "wandering Jews" who have lost their money, reputation, and future. The crowds are consumed by the salon, engulfed in its elaborate and convoluted setting, just at the readers are engulfed in the elaborate Orientalist maze of Zola's naturalist text. Gradually, Zola pushes the imaginary of the imperial paranoia, inverting the relationship between center and periphery, empire, and colony. The ever-expanding Orientalized store claims control over its economic and cultural capital; it comes to dominate the French nation.

Along with this paradisiacal, decadent space comes the opposite imperialist drive for imposing control and order. Like a two-headed snake, the elements of colonial fantasy and control work in tandem in the text. The Orientalist layout of the department store, including that of the fictional emporium Au Bonheur des dames applies colonial mechanisms of power and control in modern European spaces. Mouret's favorite spot in the store is the central stairs offering a bird's-eye view of the entire place (Zola, *Ladies' Paradise* 117; *Au Bonheur des dames* 175). Standing on the stairs, he occupies the powerful position of the "Orientalist [who] surveys the Orient from above, with the aim of getting hold of the whole sprawling panorama" (Said, *Orientalism* 239). Nothing is more indicative of this than the line of salesclerks dressed in green, yellow, and red, acting like dragomans (Levantine interpreters and guides) waiting in a servile manner to assist the clients in navigating the store.[58]

Commander Jouve, who stands at the door wearing war medals from his battles in Algeria, embodies a long imperialist legacy of control and surveillance and its theatrical display of power. Jouve circulates through the shop, greeting and monitoring employees and customers: "Jouve the shopwalker [inspector] was slowly pacing up and down with his military air, flaunting his medal, watching over those fine, precious goods which were so easy to conceal up a sleeve" (111).[59] Sometimes he wanders quietly, observing customers and eavesdropping on salesclerks; at other times he parades across the store with a militaristic gait, reminding the crowd of his presence, reaffirming the panoptic illusion of constant surveillance. Through his militaristic mien and surveillance strategies, Jouve subjects the store to strict regulatory measures to keep the desiring crowd in check. These images of the ancient commander and war overlap the map of the metropolis with that of the colonies and enforce a parallelism between the imperialist mechanism of control and the chaotic space of the department store.

The arousal of the shoppers' desires announces the simultaneous birth of a mechanism of power reflecting the anxiety produced by an unruly crowd. Indeed, Zola writes at a time when the image of crowds recalls the still-present memory of the Commune of 1871 and the myth of "les femmes pétroleuses" [female arsonists] who supposedly instigated the crowds to set Paris on fire (Gullickson 159–90). In her analysis of iconographic representation of nineteenth-century crowds, Ann McClintock explains: "the crowd became the metonymic symbol of the unemployed and unruly poor; who were associated with criminals and the insane, who were in turn associated with women, particularly prostitutes and alcoholics, who were in turn associated with children; who were associated with 'primitives' and the realm of empire" (*Imperial Leather* 119).

Similarly, as the novel collapses the borders between the Orient and the French metropolis, between the working class and the bourgeoisie, Zola's crowd projects a multitude of images and voices connected with transgression and chaos. One of the recurring incidents in the novel is shoplifting by Madame de Boves, a bourgeois woman whose cryptic behavior is presented through the framework of hysteria and rampant eroticism. She takes pleasure in stealing petty items. She stuffs her red leather bag with stolen merchandise:

> Madame de Boves had been stealing like this for a year. The attacks had been getting worse, increasing until they had become a sensual pleasure necessary to her existence, sweeping away all the reasonings of prudence and giving her enjoyment which was all the more keen because she was risking, under the very eyes of the crowd, her name, her pride and her husband's important position. Now that her husband let her take money from his drawers, she was stealing with her pockets full of money, stealing for stealing's sake as people love for the sake of loving, spurred on by desire, possessed by the neurosis which had been developed within her in the past by her unsatisfied desire for luxury when confronted by the enormous, violent temptation of the big stores. (422)[60]

Zola's depiction of Madame de Boves expresses the masculine anxiety that conflates a gendered imaginary of empire with that of the emporium, wherein the unhindered greed for colonial acquisition is matched with an uninhibited voracity of national material consumption. The masculine-gendered paranoia of losing control over unruly sexualized conquered distant lands parallels a gendered paranoia of modern domestic consumerism, wherein the department store, the unruly bazaar stacked with foreign goods, haunted by the violent traces of the colonial venture, comes to dominate the bourgeois shopper's behavior and reason, especially women (see chapter 1). The imaginary of the rational and timely process of capitalist production centered on the synchronization of world time and division of labor is beset on both ends of the production arc by a feminized unruly body: the distant colonies on the supply side and the consuming bourgeois woman at home on the demand side. In this logic, just as the distant land consumes the bodies and mind of the imperial man, the bourgeois woman avidly devours his material wealth at home. In this passage, "the big stores" emerge as the specter of a hypersexualized colonial Arab man taking possession of European women's bodies. Such imperial paranoia is best summarized by Frantz Fanon's words in the *Wretched of the Earth*: "The look that the native turns on the settler's town is a look of lust, a look of envy; it expresses his dreams of possession—all manner of possession: to sit at the settler's table, to sleep in the settler's bed, with his wife if possible. The colonized man is an envious man. And this the settler knows very well" (39). The Parisian stores feature as a site of a colonial revenge executed over the bodies of European women.

Madame de Boves's shoplifting features as an irrational erotic impulse that does not conform to bourgeois propriety; it is a source of an inexplicable unruly pleasure that is not put into the service of capitalism, patriarchy, or the nation. As a compulsive shoplifter, Madame de Boves transgresses a distinction between social classes that associates morality with the bourgeoisie and criminality with the working classes. Her red leather bag stuffed with her plunders re-creates the image of the unruly womb typically associated with nineteenth-century hysteria. As Zola puts it, she "was risking before the eyes of the crowd her name, her pride, and her husband's important position." At the center of this anxiety is the exposure of the husband's name and title. When Madame de Boves becomes subject to the gaze of the crowd and its judgment, she inadvertently reverses the role between the ruling class and the masses.

Most important, the image of the hysterical and compulsive Madame de Boves brings to the metropolis the masculine cartographic anxiety of the colonial venture, whereby the constant greed of colonial acquisition is paralleled by that of the hysterical, shoplifting, compulsive, middle-class woman within national borders. Zola's novel exposes the paranoid nightmare of imperialism: In his quest to "civilize" the colonies and its populations, the man of empire is conquered by the object of his conquest, devolving into a colonial subject himself. Meanwhile, in her role as a domesticator of the empire, the bourgeois woman devolves into a hysterical, uncontrollable individual, a reminder of the working class and the colonized. The man of empire is engulfed by his colonial space, the woman of empire by colonial objects. They both bring the collapse of order and the failure of their mutual civilizing mission, inside and outside.

From another perspective, the exploitation of female shoppers in the department store, whom Zola depicts as an unruly force, draws attention to the place of desire in the political economy. Gayle Rubin examines the location of women and the function of desire in the patriarchal economic system. She draws on structural anthropology to underscore the unstated economic role of women, not as unpaid housewives and mothers, or even as enslaved women and prostitutes but just as women whose exchange, through matrimony, was the basic form of establishing kinship and political status in early patriarchal societies (Rubin 158). In addressing the question of desire and capital, the novel deploys the Orientalist imagery of the harem portraying women as objects of possession, exchanged as property. In this context, female bodies and desire are strongly suppressed and controlled by the patriarch. Zola's text, however, hints to a parallel violent political economy of gender underlying the French capitalist system. His novel is filled with examples that associate "the exchange of women" with men's political, social, and spatial control. For instance, Mouret and Baron Hartmann, the director of the Crédit Immobilier, are introduced by a common lover, Henriette Desforges: "No doubt he could have seen the financier in his office and discussed at leisure the big deal he wanted to propose to him. But he felt more confident in Henriette's house; he knew how much the possession of a mistress in common brings men together and softens them. For them both to be in her house, amid the beloved perfume of her presence . . . seemed to him a guarantee of success" (71–72).[61] Implicit in the business transaction between Hartmann and Mouret is that common intimate relationship that tied both men to Henriette. Her presence is necessary to facilitate the agreement between the men, who make crucial decisions on their future investment and the planning of modern Paris. In another sense, Henriette's body figures as a double for the two kinds of capital: Haussmann's Paris and the new financial investment in the department store.

The same type of relationship finds its echo in the patriarchal business tradition. Mouret marries his wife and takes over her uncle's boutique. Denise's uncle marries Hauchecorne's daughter, who passes the shop to her husband, who will then offer it to his salesclerk Colomban, along with his daughter. Circulating almost like currency among men, the female body is continuously entwined with that of money and property. In contrast, Rubin sets female desire as the antithesis to the patriarchal tradition of establishing social classes and order, where the exchange of women provides for social and economic bonding between men. In this context, the suppression and control of female desire is necessary to the maintenance of the patriarchy, since female desire could contradict the father's decision to give his daughter to a specific man (Rubin 172–76). Similarly, in the novel, Baudu's daughter, Geneviève, is entangled in this patriarchal network of relations. She is expected to be in love with and dedicated to Colomban while initially her betrothal to him is also a business agreement between the salesclerk and the father. Here the system breaks down in the face of modernity's relentless pursuit of capital. Entranced by one of the salesgirls from Au Bonheur des Dames, Colomban cannot control his impulses even as he knows that he risks his reputation and his future. Like the many shoppers and workers of the emporium, Colomban falls under the seductive spell of the department store. The sickly Geneviève dies out of sorrow for not being able to gain Colomban's love. Her desire fails to engender an economic value within this new patriarchal capitalist system.

The Resolution of the Saint-Simonian Mediterranean Epic

To reach the aspired "happy ending" that Zola intended, the novel resolves its various tensions by adopting the teleology of the Saint-Simonian Mediterranean utopia, purporting to end the eternal battle between East and West. This psychosexual geographic fantasy is enacted inside the department store, whose hallways have metamorphosed clearly into a vision of the East. The vivid language of war frames the day of the Oriental salon as a day of confrontation between the gendered poles of the world: the Orient and the Occident. Here desire aligns with economic profit.

> In the [slowly deserted] departments there only remained a few belated customers.... It was like a battlefield still hot from the massacre of materials.... Liénard was dozing on a sea of materials in which some half-destroyed stacks of cloth were still standing, like ruined houses about to be carried away by an overflown river; further along, ... white ... had snowed all over the ground ... ready-made clothes were heaped up like the greatcoats [*capotes*] of disabled soldiers.... An army of women had undressed there haphazardly in a wave of desire; while downstairs ... the dispatch department, operating at full stretch, was still disgorging parcels with which it was bursting, and these were being carried away by the delivery vans in a final

[jerk] [*branle*] of the overheated machine.... [T]he hall was bare. The whole colossal stock of Paris-Paradise has just been torn to pieces and carried away, as if by a swarm of ravenous locusts. In the midst of this emptiness Hutin and Favier, out of breath from the struggle, were turning the pages of their cashbooks. (116–17)[62]

The erotic Saint-Simonian armageddon is depicted via the semiotics of emporialism: the language of empire, material culture, and desire. The scene sketches a clash between shoppers, employees, and goods. The emporium's Orient is exemplified by "an army" of "undressed" women, whose voracious and highly seductive femininity feeds on the spoils of empire. Zola depicts the aftermath of the oriental salon as a battlefield conquered by an army of female shoppers, who like a "swarm of ravenous locusts" consume the inside of the store. At the end of the Oriental salon, the inside of the store falls into ruins; the employees, like dead and mutilated soldiers, lie in the middle of a void. Fabrics and a "sea of materials" resemble a sea of blood, houses in ruins, barricades, and the greatcoats of soldiers; the hallway is devoured by a swarm of women.[63] The white snow on the battlefield evokes in particular paintings of Napoleon's defeat in Russia's snowy plains in 1812.[64] The text marks the end of the feminine invasion with an imposing act of masculine rationalism and European industrialism, wherein the salesclerks rise from among the spoils of the battle, holding their cashbooks. The scene's imagery operates on various levels simultaneously. The passage is replete with sexual innuendos. The phrases "undressed women," "the service department operating full stretch," "disgorging parcels," "white ... snowed all over the ground," "heaped up ... capotes" (in the nineteenth-century colloquial French, this already meant "condoms"), and the final jerk [*branle*] of the overheated machine" construct a second image of an orgiastic night with hypersexualized army soldiers and women.[65] Read together, both levels of imageries complete the portrait of an imagined Saint-Simonian erotic battle between a masculine Occident and a feminine Orient in which the Mediterranean stands for both a "nuptial bed" and a site of war (Chevalier, "*Le Globe* 5 février 1832" 116 and "*Le Globe* 12 février 1832" 117).

Denise: From Odalisque to Social Utopian

Only one character in the novel is resistant to emporialism. Neither its advanced and innovative techniques nor its sensational aspect excite Denise's imagination or arouse her senses or desire. She lives a life structured around moral propriety. The orphaned Denise stands for an example of a female desire that is not integrated in a European patriarchal political economy. Having lost her father and maintaining a draconian control over her desire, she becomes the only female who is not appropriable. This fact makes her an object of obsession for Mouret, who continuously tries to seduce her. But his calculated strategies fail to ensnare her. Unlike the other female characters in the novel, she is the only one who resists his advances. This resistance is linked to her resistance to consumption, for Mouret's ultimate strategy is to buy her affection by offering her whatever she wants, no matter how much it costs. As Denise becomes an obstacle in the desire-profit machine, she renders capitalism impotent. In the end, Mouret realizes that he must marry Denise to prove his love. In doing so, he helps her ascend the social ladder and become a partner in managing the Saint-Simonian network. Their marriage strangely reverses the patriarchal tradition, since it is she who acquires Mouret and the store.

Mouret and Denise's alliance emulate the Saint-Simonian gendered imaginary. While Mouret is cast as an androgynous man, Denise's femininity is highly ambiguous, much like the image of the Saint-Simonian Orientalized "priestess" or "mother," which the Saint-Simonians hoped to find in Egypt (see chapter 2). She is more of an abstract ideal than a sexual being (Riot-Sarcey 48). In her initial scene, she is described as puny and lacking beauty in contrast to her adolescent, more feminine brother. From the beginning, she is set as a virginal mother figure who takes care of her brothers (50). She is depicted as having a masculine figure, which contrasts with that of her brother's soft feminine features: "He had the beauty of a girl, beauty which he seemed to have stolen from his sister—dazzling skin, curly auburn hair, lips and eyes moist with love. Denise, by his side, in her astonishment, looked even thinner, her mouth too large in her long face, her complexion already sallow beneath her light-coloured head of hair" (6).[66] Throughout the text, Denise is mocked for her unkempt hair and her heavy work boots ("sabots," "galoches"). She is derided by the others as "la mal peignée" [badly combed] and "tête de pioche" [pickaxe-head] (179).[67] While Mouret's androgyny highlights his transgressive character of mastering reason and passion and turning them into tools for making profit, Denise's androgyny stands for another hybrid Saint-Simonian Mediterranean character. She overcomes class barriers and believes in the value of industry and social responsibility.

Denise is part of an emerging group who blurs the distinction between the working class and the bourgeoisie. Her job as a salesgirl provides an opportunity for the worker to master the subtle distinctions that mark the difference between the two classes. Salesgirls at the time constituted a novel group, which shared traits from both the working class and the bourgeoisie. By not fitting completely with either group, salesgirls enjoyed an unusual mobility, which challenged the firmly established marks of distinction. Despite the rules and restrictions imposed on the workers' movements, the shop girls manage to disturb the established social hierarchies. Zola underscores the threat that the salesgirls embody to bourgeois women: "From their daily contact with rich customers, nearly all the salesgirls had acquired airs and graces, and had ended up by forming a vague class between the working and middle classes; and often, beneath their dress sense, beneath the manners and phrases they had learned, there was nothing but a false, superficial education, picked up from reading cheap newspapers, from tirades in the theatre, and from all the latest follies of the Paris streets" (155).[68] The salesgirls pertain to a modern world that challenges the traditional optics of distinction. Having the opportunity to interact with bourgeois clients daily, they manage to transgress class lines and become part of a liminal group that "floats" between classes. They are neither marginalized prostitutes who exist at the fringes of the social order nor domestics who live under the complete control of the bourgeoisie. Inside the carefully designed setting of the store, the new group lives in an ambiguous zone between the public and private. The daily interaction with the bourgeoisie in the store creates an opportunity for performance, where salesgirls in their expensive silk dresses mimic middle-class manners. Zola is clear about the superficiality of this performance, its "falseness" and silliness, derived from the culture of the music hall and the illustrated journal. The salesgirls do not have control over their surrounding space; the displayed merchandise is part of an act. Only Denise, from the provinces, exceeds this performance.

With the popularization of luxury, art, and means of information via newspapers, modern Paris is no longer under the complete control of the bourgeoisie. The streets of the city, like the aisles of the store, present a new phenomenon: a crowd more challenging to read and categorize socially. The tension and power struggle between the working class and the bourgeoisie over the mastery of cultural capital unravels over the course of the novel. In the following passage, Denise is asked to model a coat for a bourgeois woman, Madame Desforges, Mouret's lover. The coat is too large and looks awkward on the slim Denise. As an inexperienced model, she becomes the laughingstock of the store: "And she [Madame Desforges] gave Mouret the mocking look of a Parisian amused by the ridiculous get-up of a girl from the provinces [Denise]. He felt the amorous caress of this glance, the triumph of a woman proud of her beauty and her art. Therefore, in gratitude for being adored . . . he felt obliged to laugh at her in his turn. 'And she should have combed her hair,' he murmured" (114).[69] In the beginning of the novel, Denise lacks the knowledge of upper-class manners. The expensive coat she clumsily models for her client stands for the bourgeois culture that she cannot master. In Pierre Bourdieu's term, the coat symbolizes bourgeois cultural capital and "habitus," which she cannot comfortably appropriate.[70] Her performative attempt at elegance fails miserably, exposing her working-class origins. Mouret's constant obsession with fixing her hair, which he does frequently, underscores his desire to tame her behavior to conform to the norms of the bourgeoisie and erase her connection to her peasant past and her working-class present. Denise at first fails to fit in the normative standards of the bourgeoisie. Coming from a provincial background, she does not know the subtle traits of bourgeois distinction. Her boots, her hair, and her old woolen dress contradict the measures of modern normativity offered in the store, in which the body has to conform to the newly standardized material culture.

Like a colonial subject, Denise undergoes a sort of civilizing mission that seeks to shape her in the image of the bourgeoisie. As a salesgirl, she must wear a black silk dress, a uniform that represents the regulatory measures taken by Mouret's emporium to purge all signs of manual labor, poverty, and the flaws of capitalism. That elegant attire serves to appease the sensibility of middle-class clients, who should find in the department store an uncanny resemblance to their own household. The black silk uniform both accentuates and assuages class tension in the store. For Denise, the silk dress symbolizes an oppressive conformity to bourgeois sensibility. She would rather wear her old woolen dress that betrays her origins than the silk uniform, which anchors her in the bourgeois culture of the department store. The luxurious silk dress represents an illusion of wealth and comfort that hides the exploitation of labor. The salesgirls' condition—dressed in expensive silk but paradoxically at the mercy of Mouret's draconian power—is compared to the life of odalisques who live in abundance in a wealthy harem but cannot control their own lives. Denise is constantly struggling to adjust between her old woolen dress and her new black silk uniform. "Then she noticed that she was dressed in silk; her uniform depressed her, and before unpacking her trunk she had a childish desire to put on her old woolen dress, which had been left on the back of a chair. But when she was once more dressed in her own poor garment she was overcome with emotion, and the sobs which she had been holding back since the morning suddenly burst forth in a flood of bitter tears" (118–19).[71] Denise's new uniform, her old boots, and her woolen dress come to symbolize her double, hybrid life as a suffering working-class woman attempting to master the visible traits of bourgeois "respectability" to appeal to her customers. Her heavy work boots and unruly hair carry the traces of her provincial origins and her working-class present. She brings into the store the memory of manual labor, which the bourgeoisie seeks to forget. The boots are a constant reminder of the relationship between the provinces, the factories of Parisian taste and culture, and the theatrical, "civilized" space of the metropolis. In other words, what hinders Denise's movement is the heavy burden of French social, economic, and political history, which should be kept at the threshold of the department store.

As Denise learns bourgeois etiquette, she fulfills the Saint-Simonian desire of destabilizing the power of the dominant classes by means of adopting a new work ethos. When Mouret falls in love with Denise, Madame Deforges calls her to her luxurious apartment for the fitting of another coat. The bourgeois woman's household, filled as it is with classical Louis XV furniture, stands in stark contrast with the protean Oriental space of the department store. Denise moves from the highly theatrical space in which the distinction between workers and customers is blurred, to an apartment that embodies rigid class traditions. Madame Desforges seeks to humiliate Denise in front of Mouret by stressing the social gap between them. Denise, however, gets her revenge:

> "It's absurd, girl . . . look how tight it is. I look like a wet nurse."
> "Madame is a little plump . . . And unfortunately we can't make madame any slimmer." (318)[72]

This scene mirrors the previous one, when Denise failed to model a coat. This time the narrative reverses the power dynamics between Denise and her bourgeois competitor. Like the earlier coat, the latter one also represents bourgeois cultural capital or habitus. Denise comments that Desforges is too big for the coat, implying that she does not fit her social role anymore. Denise metaphorically dethrones Madame Desforges from her position. She announces her "déclassement," or fall along the social ladder, by reducing her to a "wet nurse." Since the emporium popularized the rules of taste and elegance, it turned fashion into a double-edged sword which can be used against the class that has created it. Denise's experience at the department store helps her defeat Madame Desforges by means of the same rules that the latter enforced earlier in the novel when she mocked Denise's gauche manners.

A Modern Social Order: The Rise of the Saint-Simonian-Fourierist Phalanx

At the end of the novel, Denise successfully emerges from the store's civilizing mission. As a model entrepreneur, the proud product of emporialism, she proves to be the right match for Mouret. Zola returns to the Orientalist motif to suggest a new national and social order. He stages another exhibition, also based on the actual annual sales events of the era, the "white sale." This scene foreshadows Denise's marriage with Mouret. Unlike the previous salon, described as a harem, the white sale is replete with references to matrimony and procreation: "It looked like a great white bed, vast and virginal, awaiting as in legends, for the *white* princess, for she would one day come, all powerful, in her white bridal veil" (398; emphasis added).[73] In today's context, one cannot help but notice the racialized nuances in the title of the sales events, which frame the narrative of progress in the novel, caught between a harem-like Oriental Salon and a "white" sale, awaiting the victorious "white" princess. The two titles allude to the shores of the Mediterranean: divided between Europe and the Middle East. The monochromatic white sale starkly contrasts with the colorful palette of the Oriental salon. References to the Orient are minimized in favor of a fairy-tale setting of marriage. Sexual desire is finally contained, policed, and placed in the service of the nation through bourgeois matrimony. The white sale, then, marks the beginning of a modern phase modeled on the Saint-Simonian ideal. It represents the victory of European reason over an irrational Orient, carefully contained in the larger system. This modern French *Nights* reaches its conclusion when Denise manages to survive in the competitive culture of the store, win Mouret's heart, and become the head salesgirl, "la première" (and later a full partner personally and professionally). Like Scheherazade, who succeeds in controlling the king's wrath, Denise attenuates Mouret's brutal business strategies by modifying the store's policies to improve the life of workers and clients.

Zola's text suggests that this new phase would not have been possible without Denise's moral mission, which sought to improve the industrial machine: "Sometimes, she would become quite excited, imagining a huge, ideal emporium, a phalanstery of trade, in which everyone would have a fair share of the profits according to merit.... Mouret would brighten up when she spoke like this, in spite of his misery. He would accuse her of socialism" (355).[74] As a manager, or *première*, Denise restores balance in the store; she introduces innovative social reforms resembling the principles of the civilizing mission. She hosts concerts, creates a library, and offers classes in English, German, geography, and mathematics to the workers (431). In her analysis of the novel, Anne Friedberg draws attention to the parallelism between "'the horizontal expansion' of the store [and] the 'vertical momentum'" of Denise's career rise in store management (43). The vertical momentum of her ascension symbolizes a moral feminine order, which counterbalances the masculine capitalist "horizontal expansion" of the emporium.[75] In fact, Denise's rise changes the architectural and urban significance of the store altogether. Under the collaborative management of Mouret and Denise, the department store's story becomes an allegory for an alternative national patriarchal model of containment, discipline, and order. Aligning the ideology of empire with that of the emporium, Mouret and Denise establish the modern language of emporialism. They transform the Orientalized store into a miniature imperial utopia. Denise's reform takes on the aspect of an eclectic utopianism, that of an interconnected Saint-Simonian-Fourierist phalanstery, presided over by an entrepreneurial couple. The same eclectic utopian image and ideology was upheld by actual department store owners of the era, such as Le Bon Marché and La Samaritaine (see chapter 1).[76]

Conclusion

In the *Arcades Project*, Benjamin notes that "if we had to define, in a word, the new spirit that was coming to preside over the transformation of Paris, we would have to call it megalomania. The emperor and his prefect aim to make Paris the capital not only of France but of the world" (133).[77] Zola portrays the precarious image of an empire that has suddenly awakened from its megalomaniacal Saint-Simonian imperial dream onto the trauma of German occupation. Zola's emporium mirrors the divided ideologies of the Second Empire. It closely resembles Nouveau Paris, a modern amalgam of old Paris with its boulevards and Haussmann's project concocted of various elements: a city swerving between utopianism and despotism (Schwartz 20; Nord 133). Haussmann's urban plan of Paris, with its oblique angled avenues imposed onto the landscape, aimed to fashion at once the illusion of romantic vistas and the necessary space to coerce rioters into submission.[78] Likewise, Zola's emporium is simultaneously a highly artificial aestheticized space, an oversized monster devouring the city, and a social utopian hybrid: a Saint-Simonian-Fourierist phalanstery that rises to dominate and reorganize the city (see chapter 1).

Although Zola does not speak of the Mediterranean per se, his focus on Oriental trade and material culture reveals the strong impact of Saint-Simon utopianism on Second Empire France. Zola speaks of Suez and Levantinism in his eighteenth volume, *L'Argent* (1891).[79] In Zola's oeuvre, the highly organized commercial and social hub turns into a nightmare exposing the discrepancy between French national culture, informed by Saint-Simonian utopianism, and its actual effect on people's lives. As Palmira Brummett indicates, European narratives about the Mediterranean frequently adopt an itinerary that goes eastward: "the takers of the Grand Oriental tour (always going 'east,' more or less, and returning 'west,' if they can)" (Brummett 10). In contrast to this trajectory, *Au Bonheur des dames* brings the readers back to the French metropolis following the path of a material culture that makes its way from the East to Europe. The novel describes a dialectical process of destruction and creation, where the French notion of industrial capitalism takes shape by incorporating and manipulating the irrational, sensual, and fetishistic forces of a phantasmatic Orient. This battle leads to an unsettling present founded on the violent obliteration of traditions and an anxious, yet hopeful outlook toward an unknown future.

The love story of Denise and Mouret, taking place in the department store between two sales events, "the Oriental salon" (set as a harem) and "the white sale" (the European wedding trousseau), rewrites a progressive history of the modern transformation of a nation reeling between several political, social, and economic regimes of values. The giant harem-bazaar gives birth to a new French society and its leaders. Denise and Mouret, the modern French counterparts of Scheherazade and Shahryar, become the orchestrators of a once envisioned Mediterranean system. Cast as androgynous, both Eastern and Western, they are the site of a struggle between the dissonant and ambivalent elements that were once the foundation of the Saint-Simonian Mediterranean project.

Mouret and Denise are two of the few characters from the entire Rougon-Macquart series who are unaffected by the fall of the Second Empire. Remarkably, this process is not without ambiguity, for Denise's espousal of industrial progress is presented as a submission to "necessity," as making the best of the "inevitable" by infusing it with humanity. The happy ending of the novel, which weaves the fantasy of *The Nights* onto the fairy-tale character of the white sale's commercial illusionism, still conceals a history of violence and calculated manipulations. Zola's Oriental bazaar that takes over the French metropolis may unwittingly raise the question of whether it is actually the Orient that is consuming France or the other way around. The reader is left wondering to what extent this new industrialist social ethos ever truly transforms the fantasy or, worse, the exploitation on which, as the Orientalist theme brings out, its success depends.

Figure 4.1. Magazine cover, *L'Egyptienne*, January 1932. *Source*: Centre d'Etudes Alexandrines. Public domain. Used with permission.

Figure 4.2. Nahdat Misr, *Egypt's Awakening*, Mahmud Mukhtar, *L'Egyptienne*, June 1928. *Source*: Centre d'Etudes Alexandrines. Public domain. Used with permission.

Figure 4.3. A play at a kermess, *L'Egyptienne*, March 1927. *Source*: Centre d'Etudes Alexandrines. Public domain. Used with permission.

Figure 4.4. A play at a kermess, performers in costumes, *L'Egyptienne* March 1927. *Source*: Centre d'Etudes Alexandrines. Public domain. Used with permission.

Figure 4.5. Avril de Sainte Croix pensive at her desk. *Source*: Bibliothèque Nationale de France. Public domain. Used with permission.

Figure 4.6. Juliette Adam pensive at her desk, *L'Egyptienne*, February 1925. *Source*: Women and Memory Forum, Cairo. Public domain. Used with permission.

Figure 4.7. Huda Shaarawi pensive at her desk. *Source*: Women and Memory Forum, Cairo. Public domain. Used with permission.

Figure 4.8. Huda Shaarawi, standing portrait, *L'Egyptienne*, June 1926. *Source*: Bibliothèque Nationale de France. Public domain. Used with permission.

Figure 4.9. Julie Siegfried, standing portrait. *Source*: Bibliothèque Marguerite Durant, Paris. Public domain. Used with permission.

Figure 4.10. Kamala Nehru, *L'Egyptienne*, July 1932. *Source*: Centre d'Etudes Alexandrines. Public domain. Used with permission.

Figure 4.11. Jehan d'Ivray, *L'Egyptienne*, March–April 1928. *Source*: Centre d'Etudes Alexandrines. Public domain. Used with permission.

Figure 4.12. Ehsan al-Koussi, *L'Eyptienne*, May 1929. *Source*: Centre d'Etudes Alexandrines. Public domain. Used with permission.

Figure 4.13. Madame Rouchdi Pacha, *L'Egyptienne*, March 1926. *Source*: Centre d'Etudes Alexandrines. Public domain. Used with permission.

Chapter 4

Modeling Empire

Emporialism and Transnational Feminism

I liked everything about Paris, even the ferocious manners of the rabble. However, despite this fact, I was pained by the outcome of extreme liberty at the beginning of my visit there. I used to think that the young and the old from every class of this nation have a great deal of kindness and good manners... I remember that when I wanted to visit one Parisian *grand magasin* during a sales event, I found a large crowd at the entrance. So, I stood next to the door to give way to others, as it is our custom in the East, thinking that my turn would come when one of the shoppers would return the courtesy to me. Unfortunately, I noticed that no one realized my presence and I found myself pushed violently among these stormy waves of human bodies, tossed by a wave and received by another with punches and stepping on my feet. I almost started to burst in tears. When I found myself before a table surrounded by shoppers... and when I extended my arm gently to reach a piece of fabric that I liked, one of the shoppers snatched it so aggressively from my hands that I almost cried again... In the beginning, I did not like this kind of thing, but I ended up understanding that competition in life is the reason for the progress and success of nations, and that the tolerance and sensitivity of the East is the reason for its decline.[1]

In her memoirs, Egyptian feminist Huda Shaarawi narrates her experiences in French and Egyptian emporia. When she steps into a Parisian department store on a sale day in the summer of 1909, her experience does not differ from that of the many shoppers documented by Émile Zola's novel (chapter 3).² By shopping in the Parisian department store, Shaarawi learns the values imparted by emporialism. Much like Zola's female protagonist Denise Baudu in *Au bonheur des dames*, Shaarawi perceives the intertwined cosmology of empire and emporium. They both witness a moment when the veneer of agora-cosmopolitanism—that is, marketplace civility—in the department store shatters to expose a capitalist Darwinian social model. The store swarms with customers, who conduct their shopping in an aggressive, self-absorbed manner. Shaarawi is shocked by the unexpectedly rude behavior of the Parisian crowd. The store brings to life an unfamiliar facet of French culture that she had not learned from her education or her French acquaintances. The word *rabble* (riʿāʿ الرعاع) to refer to the French crowd is telling of Shaarawi's social status as an elite not accustomed to mixing with the masses. For an aristocratic woman living in a traditional Ottoman-Egyptian house and with limited access to public spaces, shopping in Paris is a Darwinian experience, asserting the survival of the fittest. Faced with this intimidating behavior, Shaarawi flees the *grand magasin* and returns to her hotel, acknowledging her inadequacy to confront the mob.

Like Zola's protagonist Denise, Shaarawi concludes that the store expresses the inescapable spirit of the age. Most important, she deems her experience in the French emporium a valuable lesson on the politics of the empire and the crucial importance of competition. For Zola and Shaarawi, the department store symbolizes progress but strangely evokes the other side of the Mediterranean. And in each case, it is an object of fascination and repulsion: the manifestation of a double-edged modernity with its excesses and promises. Nevertheless, whereas Zola likens the chaotic space of the department store to an Oriental bazaar and a harem, Shaarawi does not recall anything of these places during her shopping trip. For her, the store represents a modern European aggressive ethos, diametrically opposite to the "kind" temperament of the East. Shaarawi's worldview, informed by emporialism, points her toward the importance of resistance as a colonial subject and as a woman to protect one's place in the world. For her, emporialism is an expression of a wider Saint-Simonian taxonomy of relations and a pathway for transnational feminism.

In this chapter, I examine the role of emporialism in the life of Huda Shaarawi. My objective is to show how the emporium served as a space for renegotiating social and political position on the local and international levels. The emporium also mediated the distance between the members of the middle class across empires. The emporium was a cultural referent at the intersection of the individual and the social, the national and the imperial. In this context, emporialism became part of a common mythology and iconography that could be recognized by a global bourgeoisie in the making, including feminists. In examining the relation between Egyptian feminism and emporialism as a multivalent international phenomenon, I hope, as Ellen L. Fleischmann has argued, "not only to 'include' Third World Women but also entirely reconceptualize feminism as a plural(istic) heterogenous set of practices with a long rich history worldwide" (171) (see Paletschek amd Pietrow-Emmler; Amireh and Majaj; McCann and Kim). Straddling the lines between several imperial traditions and political currents, the emporium allowed Shaarawi to rethink and reorder gender, class, and ethnic relations across these domains simultaneously. In so doing, she reconciled a global bourgeois feminist paternalistic ideology with a rising Egyptian nationalist movement—also paternalistic in its outlook.

Much has been written on Shaarawi's life as an Egyptian feminist. Some of these studies reiterate the hierarchical relations between European feminism and other feminist movements. Shaarawi's portrait as a modern Arab Muslim feminist provided a set of familiar iconographic elements that could be quickly deciphered and integrated in national and international feminist narratives. The circulation and production of knowledge around her image as a key figure for Muslim and Arab feminism continues to occupy a significant space in academic circles.[3] The recent interest in her memoirs brings to light the intersectional context of that history that challenges the scope of Eurocentric and imperialist influence of the first and second waves of feminism. Notably, Shaarawi's activism emerged in close contact with (and sometimes in response to) feminist movements originating from the imperial metropolises, Paris and London. Another point of contention, Mohja Kahf suggests, is the selective translation of her memoirs in English under the title *Harem Years* (1987). The translation might have played a role in emphasizing European influence and framing Shaarawi's life in an Orientalist narrative of liberation, which appealed to American and European audiences, especially after the Iranian revolution (Kahf, "Packaging 'Huda'" 140–50). The nationalist framing of her story also undermined the role of other feminist figures during that era. Finally, the recent revisions of Shaarawi's memoirs underscore her class status, which shaped her views and allowed her to occupy a key feminist role and acquire recognition on the national and international stages.

By analyzing the role emporialism in Shaarawi's journey, I aim to situate Shaarawi at the intersection of the formation of global feminism and the global bourgeoisie across empires. Examining Shaarawi's various accounts of the department store offers insight into the elite transnational and interconnected world of the nineteenth century in which Shaarawi's career took flight. Shaarawi hailed from an upper-class background, and precisely for this reason the emporium—in contrast to the factory, the farmland, or the school—served as a primary educational site that mirrored her class and feminist experience, both in Egypt and abroad. Shaarawi began her activism at a key epoch of Egyptian history, from the turn of the century to the end of World War II. This included various moments of upheavals, strikes, economic crisis, and unemployment. The department store, in contrast, captured at once the abstract image of empire and the quotidian experience of women from her social group beyond a national framework.

Most studies of Egyptian history and feminism focus on her early experience in the Alexandrian *grand magasin* Chalon, as an example of a pioneering gesture by a Muslim feminist seeking to assert her presence in public spaces.[4] However, her interaction with the emporium was not limited to the national sphere. She refers to Egyptian and French department stores more than once in her published Arabic memoirs. Her anecdotes about the emporium bring to light several aspects of her personal growth, her worldview informed by the emporium, and her image as a public persona. They reveal her complex life productive of various intermingled political regimes: those of the Ottoman, British, and French empires, plus Egyptian nationalism. For instance, Shaarawi actively used the network of department stores in Egypt and abroad to support the feminist and anticolonial cause. She marketed the products of her vocational school in Istanbul, Washington, and New York. She also sold them at Le Bon Marché in Cairo and Paris (Sharawi Lanfranchi 150).[5] Her anecdotes on the department store shed light on different territories and scales of interaction: the body, household, the nation-state, and the empire. These stories crystallized an important aspect of what she believed to be the role of the modern Egyptian woman during this critical era, one that was crafted after the image of the bourgeoisie.

Life and Career

Shaarawi's memoirs were published posthumously from a manuscript provided by her secretary, Abd al-Hamid Fahmi Mursi. The publication of the Arabic memoirs in 1981 took place during the presidency of Anwar al-Sadat (1970–1981), at the same time as significant modifications in family laws and the reintegration of Egypt in global economy.[6] The work appeared under the title *Mudhakkarat ra'idat al-Mar'a al-Haditha: Huda Shaarawi* [Memoirs of the Pioneer Leader of the Modern Woman: Huda Shaarawi].

The book recounts her personal experience and her political journey. It begins with the first major demonstration against the Egyptian khedive in 1882 and the death of Shaarawi's father two years later. The work includes anecdotes, diary entries, articles from newspapers and magazines, briefings from her political party meetings, and speeches conducted in Egypt and abroad. Shaarawi died before finishing the memoirs (Kahf, "Packaging 'Huda'" 152). Among the many events it documents are her impressions of department stores in Paris and Egypt and her travels and conferences around the world. Although the Arabic memoirs conclude with a random notice of Shaarawi's cousin's wedding, this piece of information signals how the author's life-long activism had come full circle. Shaarawi's engagement with the feminist cause began with her early marriage experience, on which she had no choice. The announcement specifies that Shaarawi's cousin Huriyya Idris chose her future spouse and gave consent for the marriage. The recently published memoirs of Shaarawi's cousin Hawwa' Idris cast light on other aspects of Shaarawi's activism that were not included in the Arabic memoirs and are often overlooked. For instance, Idris narrates the active engagement of the Egyptian Feminist Union (EFU) in the Arab world during the mid-1940s, in Syria, Lebanon, and Mandatory Palestine, under Shaarawi's leadership. This brings to light the multilateral role of the Egyptian feminist movement in the Pan-Arab context and outside the empire/colony binary (Shaarawi, *Mudhakkarat* 53–82).

During Shaarawi's time, Egypt became a semi-independent Ottoman province under British colonial rule with a significant French cultural influence. Cairo and Alexandria were cosmopolitan cities, with a diverse population hailing from the various corners of the Ottoman Empire. This society included migrants from Europe as well as formerly enslaved Africans and Circassians.[7] The Suez Canal was controlled by the British and French empires, and a considerable number of the aristocratic class and the bourgeoisie were fluent in French; they traveled and had connections across the sea. In many cases, men pursued their education in France. Despite being a colony, Egypt was also an empire colonizing the Sudan.[8] By 1923, the Ottoman provinces witnessed the declaration of the Turkish Republic. The nascent Turkish state shed its Ottoman past as the upholder of the Islamic caliphate and pursued unprecedented reforms spearheaded by Kemal Atatürk, distancing itself from its Islamic and Arabic influences.[9]

Huda Shaarawi (1879–1947) belonged to this complex world. She was born into an aristocratic Ottoman Egyptian family. From a young age, she received the typical education for girls in her social stratum. She was tutored in Arabic, Ottoman, Persian, and French. Her father, Omar Pasha

Sultan, was from the landed gentry and participated actively in Egypt's political life and the resistance against British colonization (Shaarawi, *Mudhakkarat* 21). Her activism was initially propelled by her life-changing experience of early marriage to fulfill her mother's wishes of keeping the family wealth under control. Married at the age of thirteen to her forty-year-old cousin, Shaarawi Pasha, she discovered the injustice of traditional customs. At fourteen, she separated from her husband for a period of seven years (1893–1900), during which she cultivated her knowledge of the arts and music, as well as French and Arabic literature. She took her first steps in the public sphere by organizing philanthropic projects. After resuming her marital life, Shaarawi continued her career as a prominent feminist and politician. In 1919, she took to the streets, leading women protesters against British occupation. The 1919 revolution was a turning point in Egyptian history and for Egyptian women. It marked their active participation in the anticolonial struggle and their presence in public space (Shaarawi, *Harem Years* 5–22; Baron, *Egypt as a Woman* 1–12).[10] The events reinforced the entwinement of feminism and nationalism. Afterward, through her writings and association with the leading al-Wafd party, Shaarawi built a strong presence on the political stage. She founded the EFU and was elected vice president of the International Alliance of Women (Badran, *Mudhakkarat* 135). One of the most iconic moments of Shaarawi's life was in 1923, when she led the Egyptian delegation to the first feminist convention in Rome, the only Muslim and Middle Eastern group to join this event. Upon their return, Shaarawi and her protégée, Céza Nabaraoui, took off their face veils and greeted the crowds, projecting what was later crystallized in national memory and reproduced in the media as a new image of the Egyptian woman (Sharawi Lanfranchi 98).

This trans-imperial positioning was key to Shaarawi, since her first steps in activism as a young woman were also born through the navigation of regional and imperial politics. For instance, in his writings, Evelyn Baring, Earl of Cromer, justifies British occupation as a necessary resort to bring Egyptians into modernity. He associates women's seclusion—namely, the harem and the veil—with the deterioration of their influence. He sees this as a major cause of the decline of Eastern societies: "Inasmuch as women, in their capacities as wives and mothers, exercise a great influence over the characters of their husbands and sons, it is obvious that the seclusion of women must produce a deteriorating effect on the male population, in whose interests the custom was originally established, and is still maintained . . . Moslem women in Egypt are secluded, and . . . their influence, partly by reason of their seclusion, is, in all political and administrative matters, generally bad" (Cromer 155–57). He presents the Ottoman tradition of the harem as a cause of Egyptian degeneracy and backwardness. He premises the rise of a modern Egyptian nation on women's mobility as well as their civic and cultural education. In the typical British view of the time, Baring defines a woman's role as that of wife and mother. He depicts Egyptian bourgeois women as cut off from the world: they have no way of arriving at informed views on politics, society, and administration.

The same idea surfaced in the early views of Egyptian feminism. Writers like Qasim Amin, the leading upper-class Egyptian male proponent of women's rights at that time, published a number of controversial Arabic books, including *The Liberation of Women* (1899). Like Baring, the French-educated Amin praises rural women for not covering their faces in public and for their work outside the household, and he calls for a new yet limited role for Egyptian women, especially those of the upper classes. In the same vein as the Earl of Cromer, Amin subsumes the role of women in Egyptian society to that of mothers. He argues for the reform of the traditional Egyptian family and the extension of women's tasks to encompass the actual control over household management and children's education (Shaarawi, *Mudhakkarat* 471).[11] Amin urges bourgeois women to develop the social skills and civic knowledge necessary to serve the modern nation, namely, by raising a strong new generation of men and participating in the political future of the nation.

Even within the confines of her homeland, Shaarawi confronted a set of feminist critiques from bourgeois British, French, and Arabic standpoints. She competed with European women, who were in the process of crafting their own space at the center and the margins of their respective empires. Shaarawi's early activities involved charity work, which was then under the dominion of British middle-class women. As Mary Poovey indicates, the "ideological work of gender" for British women revolved around the domestication of empire by laying claim to a custodian role vis-à-vis the working classes and colonial subjects in the fields of medical care and charity work. Serving the nation through the scripted role of the nurse and the patron of the poor, British women simultaneously upheld the gendered division of spheres and undermined British patriarchy by taking control of the civilizing mission, a social charge previously reserved for men (Poovey 196). Shaarawi opposed the monopoly of charity by British women and founded the first Egyptian charity organization, Mabarrat Mohamed Ali, to wrest this domain from them (Sharawi Lanfranchi 42).

The competition between colonial upper-class women and their British counterparts exposes an intersectional dynamic, constructed along an intricate hierarchy of race and class, wherein feminism strategically relied on taking custody of the subaltern as a way to secure its power against local patriarchy or imperialism. Shaarawi's new social organization transferred this type of control to Egyptian bourgeois women. She founded a workshop, a clinic, a reform house, and a museum for hygiene as a pedagogical site for the poor. In doing so, her project integrated the strategies of biopower, or the management and regulation of marginalized bodies, as a part of the modern nationalist Egyptian "ideological work of gender."[12] This role justified and affirmed the presence of Egyptian bourgeois women in public spaces (Sharawi Lanfranchi 109; Idris 44; Marsot, *Short History* 200).

Shaarawi was not necessarily the first feminist to call for women's rights. During her time, other Egyptian women writers engaged in an active debate on the question of education, women's presence in public spaces, and veiling practices. Nevertheless, her performative gesture crafted her image as a model of the modern Egyptian woman. Contrary to the nationalist purview, before this moment, many women from various social and cultural backgrounds had already stopped using the face veil. As Baron explains:

> When Huda Sha'rawi cast off the veil in 1923, it signaled the end of an era not the beginning of a new one, as the most resistant groups were finally breaking with the habit. Peasants covered their heads but not their faces, for it would have been impossible when working outdoors; urban working women also found the practice impractical; Christian and Jewish women had stopped veiling earlier; and younger Muslims had already begun to reject the tradition.. ... Egyptian women unveiled metaphorically over the course of decades when they put their pens to paper and published their ideas. ("Unveiling" 382–83)

Eventually, Shaarawi became the iconic unveiled face of the Egyptian Arab Muslim woman, an image that conformed to a nationalist middle and upper-class ethos in Egypt and abroad. A significant part of her views was the outcome of prior exchange among many people from diverse backgrounds whose approach to feminism varied greatly. For instance, her social reform program was also inspired by the work of Malak Hifni Nassif, who wrote under the pen name Bahithat al-Badiya [the seeker of the desert] and refused to appear on the public stage (Sharawi Lanfranchi 46–47). In contrast to Shaarawi's activism, Nassif sought to reclaim a space for women by arguing from within Muslim tradition (Ahmed 179–80). Nabawiyya Musa was another prominent and active feminist from Shaarawi's circle. She was born in an Egyptian village and came from a modest background. She accompanied Shaarawi to the 1923 convention in Rome. Musa, the first Egyptian woman to earn a high school diploma, pursued a different path by working as a school director and later school inspector. She called for the education of women and for their participation in the workforce.[13]

Other women from Egypt had already participated in international conferences before Shaarawi did. In 1893, a delegation of Syrian women from Egypt attended the Chicago World's Fair. The group included Esther Azhari Moyal, a Syrian Jewish woman writer. In 1900, Alexandra Avierino, a Syrian Egyptian woman from the Greek Orthodox faith and founder of another early Arabic magazine for women, *Anis al-Jalis*, attended l'Alliance Universelle des femmes pour la Paix at the Universal Exhibition in Paris in 1900 (Baron, *Women's Awakening* 20–21; Badran, *Feminists* 65).[14] Moyal and Avierino established Arabic magazines in Egypt dedicated to women at the end of the nineteenth century. Shaarawi's aristocratic position as a Muslim Ottoman Egyptian elite fulfilled several nationalist expectations that came to be associated with modern Egyptian women. Precisely, Shaarawi was a vocal and influential political figure who used the education, resources, and privileged connections from her class to gain rights for women. Yet the call for gender parity does not automatically imply a universal demand for class or racial equality. These causes might intersect but not necessarily overlap; this was the case with early feminist activism in Egypt as in Europe and the United States. Just like the dominant global wave of bourgeois feminism of her era, Shaarawi's feminist circle abided a patriarchal ideology and assumed a similar paternalistic role toward the working classes and the poor.

Emporialism between Local and International Feminism

From the outset, Shaarawi's feminist experiences involved negotiations with various political and social forces. Her first account of the department store early in her youth is a case in point. In the memoirs, Shaarawi recalls the story of her neighbor and friend, Louisette (the daughter of a high-ranking French officer) who was seduced by a salesclerk and eloped to France. After discovering her fiancé's infidelity, Louisette returned to Egypt but failed to acquire her father's forgiveness. She worked as a governess and died miserably from fever. Shaarawi narrates the story of Louisette and the clerk as an example of the dire consequences that follow the seclusion and overprotection of women (*Mudhakkarat* 89). In her assessment of this moment, Sania Sharawi Lanfranchi situates this early vicarious experience at the emporium as a turning point in her grandmother's personal and political life:

> The death of Louisette ... brought home to [Huda] the fact that her predicament was not entirely due to the oriental environment of Egypt in which she lived. The plight of women, she saw, was the same all over the world. But this meant that it was susceptible to improvement, in Egypt as elsewhere. She began to think, at first inarticulately, in terms of what would later come to be called a feminist approach to women's problems and rights. (26)

Interestingly, Louisette's tragic life strikingly echoes the plots of nineteenth-century romantic or naturalist novels, which circulated widely among the bourgeoisie. Stories around department stores, such as Zola's *Au bonheur des dames*, fed onto the public's moral panic. Arabic, French, and British literature with moral messages on chastity and adherence to patriarchy circulated among the bourgeoisie. Arabic novels of moral corruption—especially of young bourgeois women—went hand in hand with economic destitution and an implied national decline (Johnson 202; Booth, "Between Harem" 343). Shaarawi's anecdote recalls what Marilyn Booth suggests about other Arabic writings of that epoch:

> These "memoirs" recenter the female body ... as they assert both the failure of the harem system for young women from elite families and the lack of a socially and psychologically acceptable alternative. They show the false respectability of a system of enclosure in a feminized space of "protection" and exclusion (in other words, the harem) ... They expose a discourse of privileged social respectability—of honor based on female chastity and obedience, and also (crucially) on economic privilege—by narrating the "futures" of young women of the elite and middle strata as shaped by choice, but only a choice between equally painful alternatives. They displace the blame that was put on young women (and, to a lesser extent, young men) in much rhetoric of the time onto the figure of the father and the space of the paternal home, represented as the harem but only in its negative possibilities. (Booth, "Between Harem" 366)[15]

Narratives revolving around female morality and fear of *déclassement* (losing one's social station) were already taking an important place in the repertoire of bourgeois knowledge. Louisette's story reveals the affinity between historical and literary accounts of the emporium, but also between the point of intersection between upper-class ethos across cultures. The story exposes the widespread masculine anxieties around department stores in France and Egypt as spaces of seduction, moral corruption, and social class transgression (see chapters 1 and 2). Just as the space of the emporium was a widely recognized referent, narratives about the store operated as a transnational cultural vehicle for didactic messages: easy, recognizable, and decipherable.

Louisette's cautionary tale indicates an already ongoing process of exchange leading to the making of a global bourgeoisie, where the emporium and its imaginary had a shared, mutually translatable interpretation. As a bourgeois narrative, Louisette's experience in the emporium unites men, regardless of nationality and religious beliefs, under the banner of patriarchal fear of losing control over women's bodies. It produces a common ground that situates Shaarawi's feminist cause in a framework where European, Ottoman, and Egyptian patriarchal systems overlapped. In addition, her narrative on the department store redeems an Islamic tradition from a European critique that condemned Islam as a despotic faith and a source of backwardness. In so doing, Shaarawi reframes the Egyptian feminist question as a transnational one. She subtracts the question of women's rights in Egypt from an Orientalist narrative, constructed along a fictive historical temporal line dividing a backward East and a progressive West. Instead, akin to the typical circulating moralistic Arabic novel of the era, Shaarawi levels the difference between European and Egyptian bourgeois patriarchies by locating Egypt's feminist question in the popular cause of family reform. This type of positioning reconciles her conservative tradition with feminism by aligning local and international views of gender roles. It also gives the opportunity to engage in a wider debate for social change without offending Egyptian and Islamic customs or being accused of mimicking the colonizer.

Emporialism and the National Political Economy

In 1901, Shaarawi walked into a department store in Alexandria for the first time (Sharawi Lanfranchi 30).[16] Her decision to do so marked another development in her life. Her trip to Alexandria was an escape from her family's pressure to return to her husband. As the patriarch in control of the family's wealth, he refused to provide her with money unless she reconciled with him. Some family members tried to persuade her by claiming that her husband might resort to legal action and limit her freedom and movement by forcing her into what was known as an "obedience house." As Egyptian law dictated, *Bayt al-ṭāʿa* [obedience house] gave the husband the right to limit his wife's mobility by forcing her to abide in a household of his choice (Shaarawi, *Mudhakkarat* 86). Elsewhere in her memoirs, she denounces that law as a form of "blackmail" and coercion which keeps women into a place "more dangerous than prison." Shaarawi adds that the husbands would leave their wives in the direst conditions until they either submitted to their will or negotiated their divorce (*Mudhakkarat* 362). Following these threatening conversations, Shaarawi procured a sum of money from her mother and traveled to Alexandria. She gives an account of her first trip to a department store there:

> In Alexandria in this particular summer, I had the first experience of its kind when I decided to buy things by myself from the *grands magasins* despite Said Agha's objections and my family's aversion to, and surprise at, this step. They talked about it as though I had transgressed the interpretation of Islamic laws (*shariʿa*).... And I was asked to bring along my maidens and Said Agha because it was inappropriate to go alone. I had to drop my wraparound cloak (*izār*) over my face and cover myself so nothing from my hair or my clothes would show. When we stepped inside the store, this unusual sight startled the workers and customers, especially when they saw the eunuch giving them sharp looks as if he was threatening them against looking at us. Then he dashed toward a department manager asking him in one breath: "do you have a place for women?" So, he pointed toward the women's department. They called the female vendors to assist me after they have placed two screens between the others and me.[17]

For Shaarawi, shopping in the department store exceeds the question of occupying a public space. "Buying things for herself," or gaining autonomy in shopping, is a response to a patriarchal claim of control through the regulation of household budget and consumption. The emporium is an anathema, an antithesis to the patriarch's house and the legal machinery that establishes its dominion.

At the beginning of the passage, Shaarawi emphasizes that her shopping trip was "in that particular summer," implying that it was a response to her husband's attempt to limit her mobility. Going into the department store signifies a challenge to the restrictions of women's seclusion and mobility imposed on the upper classes. The visit reconfigures where and how Egyptian women of Shaarawi's pedigree were allowed to be seen. In general, not all presence in public spaces implied an act of transgression. For example, Shaarawi frequently attended events at the opera house with her friends, most likely in a designated loge (Sharawi Lanfranchi 22). The emporium, as a marketplace, allowed for the intermingling of men and women and, above all, people of different classes and backgrounds.

Although this type of urban interaction would be considered a social downgrade for a member of her class, Shaarawi's account of her first visit reveals a schematic shift in the narrative about department stores. In Louisette's story, which she mentions a few pages before recounting her experience in Alexandria, the emporium stands for a fall from grace. In Shaarawi's case, the store features as a valorizing experience necessary for the upper-class women. In both anecdotes, the department store functions as an escape from patriarchal oppression. In Louisette's anecdote, the household guards against the moral temptations of the department store; in the latter, the household is an ominous space, founded on the corruption of a wider legal patriarchal system and its measures of biopower over women's bodies. The emporium in the latter narrative provides a sanctuary, a site of liberation.

To appease her family, Shaarawi had to uphold and exaggerate all signs of her refined status as an Ottoman Egyptian aristocrat. In this key incident, the cinematics and performativity of upper-class distinction encounter the theatricality of the emporium and its setting. Each has its own social regime of values. The economic transaction, supposedly the actual purpose of the visit, recedes in term of importance. The displayed commodities and their price tags are superfluous details. Shaarawi goes to the store chaperoned by maids and the family head eunuch, Said Agha. Said Agha tries to re-create a private space for women inside the store by asking the managers to surround her with screens. His anger and his eagerness to enforce the codes of gender segregation only emphasize the stark difference between the open layout of the modern store and the divided space of the Egypto-Ottoman household. Contrary to his main objective, Said Agha's demands draw more attention to Shaarawi and make her the subject of curiosity of the onlookers. Akin to a comedy skit, Said Agha's actions trigger a series of embarrassing incidents that even put the status of the patriarch into question, when a female vendor dares to ask him about Shaarawi's family's name and origins.

Shaarawi's trip to the department store marks a shift toward a more European political economy. However, as Booth suggests, this social change does not imply that one system was supplanted by another. Rather, it involved a multilayered transformation and various negotiations between the different notions of public and private (Booth, *May Her Likes* xxviii). This is particularly clear in the Arabic memoirs, where the view of Egyptian private space does not match a Eurocentric perspective of the Middle East. For instance, Shaarawi does not use the word *harem*. She mostly talks about the household. In the passage quoted above, Said Agha does not refer to a harem in the European sense of the term, as in, a distinct feminine quarter existing in the household. He asks the store's manager if they had a store/place [*maḥal*] dedicated to women.[18] In Arab and Muslim traditions, the household was neither a feminine nor a fully secluded space, as was imagined by the European mind.[19] As Yaseen Noorani insightfully argues, "The Western idea of the harem is in many ways parallel yet antithetical to the bourgeois ideal of private domesticity. The harem is conceived of as a private space defined by concupiscence rather than love and sentiment; indolence and excess rather than thrift; confinement rather than freedom; and sensual pleasure rather than spiritual fulfillment" (52). The harem was an alter ego of a gendered bourgeois European household based on containment and division of labor. In the European political economy, the household is a space of reproduction of the bourgeois family as a social and economic unit, where each member in the household has a distinct function that corresponds to their role in the public sphere (Noorani 51).[20]

Shaarawi's experience underscores a conceptual and public shift away from the Ottoman gendered spatial configurations. Shopping at the emporium was a public performance that brought the practice of space a step closer to its gendered European counterpart. Shopping in public at the department store projected a defined role for bourgeois women as administrators of the nuclear family's household and budget. A few decades later, in 1921, Shaarawi used the same strategy from the emporium in her struggle against British imperialism. Taking interest in the nation's finances, she participated in a national boycott of foreign businesses to resist occupation (Shaarawi, *Harem Years* 125; Sharawi Lanfranchi 129; M. Russell 89). The boycott mainly targeted British goods and enterprises, not necessarily department stores. Stores like Mawardi or Cicurel were considered national enterprises (Abd al-Razik 106; Reynolds, *City Consumed* 82–98).

The location of the department store visited by Shaarawi bears an importance. Her "public transgression" does not take place in her hometown, Cairo, home to many department stores as well. It unfolds during the summer in Alexandria, a city with a different culture, human geography, and urban plan, where there would be fewer restraints and less social scrutiny of her actions. The employees' surprise and the shopgirl's questions indicate different social codes. In this context, Alexandria functions as a liminal space between the familiar and the foreign, where the negotiation of rules is possible. Whereas the emporium is a counterpoint to the house, the Mediterranean city of Alexandria stands opposite to the traditional position of Cairo.

Shopping at the department store implies a new gendered economic relation closer to the European model that ties women public role to consumerism (Domosh 148). Justifying her decision to her readers, Shaarawi stresses that shopping at the department store saves money. This lesson reframes the role of women in the patriarchal system as main administrators of the household. Her act embodies a capitalist definition of money and value, where consumption is a calculated work. Such a concept contrasts with her earlier references to money, when she gives an account of her paternal grandfather, a wealthy landlord renowned for his kindness and generosity. Shaarawi recalls that merchants and workers would ask her grandfather to pay them their fees more than once. Faking forgetfulness, he repaid them as many times as they asked, ignoring what his assistant already had in the ledgers. The grandfather saw his workers' action as an indirect request for charity and took their game as a cue to help them without offending them. After her grandfather's death, Shaarawi's father, Mohamed Sultan Pacha, could not find the necessary money to secure a piece of land. One day, he met a worker whom his father had helped. Learning the reason for the pacha's worries, he led him to a sealed room in his house. There he brought out a set of earthen jars and poured a large pile of silver coins. He explained to him that this was the grandfather's money, which he kept, and that it was now the time to return it (Shaarawi, *Mudhakkarat* 15–16). The reclaimed treasure was a token of gratitude for the generosity of a man who frequently overpaid him during difficult times without objection.

Despite the fairy-tale character of the story, the narrative reveals a different view of economic relations; wealth, status, and charity run counter to the "rational" and calculated view of European theories of capital applied in the emporium. Whereas British values praise thrift, precision of record-keeping, and hard labor as a predicate to financial prosperity, Shaarawi presents charity as a blessing: both a financial and a spiritual investment, a form of transcendental economic system outside the typical purview of a capitalist transaction. Shaarawi's grandfather's story unfolds in a feudal paradigm of social and economic values, where class and wealth differences constitute a natural order of things. Money saving and landownership did not count as an economic capital to be invested toward the accumulation of wealth. The story of a poor man giving money to a rich landlord contradicts the basic rationale of a capitalist system. From a British or French nineteenth-century purview, this anecdote reinforces the colonial stereotype of the irrational, wasteful, Oriental subject in need of correction. Stepping into the department store, Shaarawi embraces a different paradigm of values. Her narrated experience reorders economic priorities to make thrift a calculated action and a key principle for the modern Egyptian woman to uphold. Wealth is no longer a haphazard blessing. Instead, money acquires a concrete, measurable worth that should be controlled and recorded. In other words, the lesson learned at the emporium aligns the value of money with moral values, where economic capital serves as an index of virtue.

In this new alliance, the bourgeois Egyptian woman and the emporium mutually take possession of a liminal space that was once under the custody of the working classes. Said Agha's argument and his ignorance of the code of a modern European world mark the end of his reign. Shaarawi's anecdote explains the social shift that takes place after the visit, wherein the traditional role of the eunuch as a chaperone loses ground. The position of eunuch sheds light on the hierarchy of sexuality that existed in Egypto-Ottoman culture. Despite his class status, asexual position, and racial origins, the eunuch occupied a liminal gendered and social yet key space in the patriarchal system. Eugénie Le Brun, a French writer who lived in Egypt and a friend of Shaarawi, describes the role of the eunuch in her book *Harems et Musulmanes d'Egypte*: "In many rich Muslim households, one or more eunuchs serve as intermediaries between the harem and everything outside."[21] The eunuch was a marker of boundaries, mediating between the outer world and the private space of the harem. He was also the mediator between the aristocratic woman and her male employees (Le Brun 4). According to Le Brun, one of the eunuch's tasks was to lift female visitors over the threshold, marking the distinction between public and private spheres. The eunuch was responsible for facilitating the transition between the exterior public realm and the interior domestic space (Le Brun 19). As a chaperone, the eunuch represented the patriarch. He signaled the high social status of the patriarch and cast an aura of prestige by highlighting the chastity of the female household members. His physical presence defines the position of the aristocratic woman toward the rest of the society, keeping the unwanted, "the rabble," from both genders at bay.

Acting as a "household manager," Said Agha oversees the household budgets, monitors the children's education, and supervises the servants and enslaved workers. He plays a key domestic role, one that nineteenth-century European society would attribute only to the mother. The eunuch's presence obstructed the shift from a traditional Ottoman lifestyle to a European model, consisting of two distinct but complementary gendered spheres: a public one managed by heteronormative men and a private one controlled by heteronormative women (Domosh 148). This does not signify that mothers did not exercise any control over the household. As Leila Ahmed and Mohja Kahf have convincingly argued, women still had an important role in the family decision making (Ahmed 157; Kahf, "Huda Sha'rawi's 'Mudhakkirati'" 61–65).

The account of the Alexandrian department store exposes how Said Agha, a eunuch and a formerly enslaved Sudanese man, exercises a draconian control over Shaarawi's body and space.[22] Said Agha orders her to cover her entire body, including her eyes. His attempt to re-create the traditional Ottoman gendered configuration of space into the emporium shows his iron grip over the life of the female aristocrat. Not only is Shaarawi's physical space under the control of the household eunuch, her access and status in public space in general is also shaped by him. For instance, it is Said Agha who helps persuade Shaarawi to fulfill her mother's request of marrying at a young age (Powell, *Tell This* 135). Shaarawi's connection to Arabic culture is also monitored by Said Agha, divided between a classical traditional upbringing and a modern one. Whereas Shaarawi is encouraged to read and recite the Quran, she is not allowed to learn proper Arabic grammar as a child. When she asks her tutor to be treated on equal footing with her brother and to be taught grammar, Said Agha confiscates the grammar book and announces to the tutor, "Miss Huda will never be *a lawyer* one day" (Shaarawi, *Mudhakkarat* 43). Although memorizing the Quran projected an image of purity for the female aristocrat, secular Arabic language presented a threat to patriarchy. For Said Agha, no proper lady would have to learn Arabic grammar, since she does not need to participate in the public sphere. He specifically associates grammar with legal representation and by extension the advocation for rights. According to Said Agha's point of view, being a "proper lady" should be a passive role of language acquisition: to converse socially, read, and recite in three languages. Shaarawi's linguistic skills in

Arabic should remain divided between the quotidian use of the Egyptian dialect and the classical Quranic register. The restriction of Arabic grammar imposed by the household eunuch, the keeper of diglossic borders, recreates the material conditions necessary to maintain the current gendered social relations in check and reproduce the notions of feminine virtue and piety, central to patriarchal prestige. By prohibiting Shaarawi from studying Arabic grammar, Said Agha restricts her use of formal Arabic to the reproduction of a patriarchal interpretation of Islamic tradition instead of the active production of legal and religious arguments. In so doing, he reinforces the wider gendered segregation of the public sphere: not only the physical space but also the political and literary, since publishing in formal Arabic was another key site to ask for rights. Said Agha's decisions control and set borders to the various aspects of his ward's life, her body, the spaces she frequented, and even the words she could articulate.

During later shopping trips, Shaarawi eliminates the need for his presence by convincing female members of the family to accompany her, making the emporium part of a collective female experience. Shaarawi's and Said Agha's lives are intricately connected and interdependent. As Eve Troutt Powell suggests, "it is Sai'd Aǧa's body, his skin color, and his harsh and protective stare that mark him the most clearly as belonging to an older tradition of slavery. Huda, too, is part of this... although at this moment it brings her shame" (*Tell This* 136). However, Shaarawi's life trajectory is diametrically opposite to that of Said Agha. The official abolition of slavery Egypt took place in 1877 (Troutt Powell, *Different Shade* 1). During Shaarawi's childhood, the narrative suggests, Said Agha lives in a limbo state between servant and slave. Shaarawi is an aristocratic fair-skinned Circassian woman, whose ancestors were enslaved and became concubines in the Ottoman Empire. She ascends the echelons of public life, gaining more visibility and power. In contrast, Said Agha, an African eunuch, descends the social ladder and later vanishes as a visible marker of bourgeois prestige and power in the public sphere (Troutt Powell, *Tell This* 115–47). Most important, through her memoirs and writings, their lives and images will be permanently entwined. As her life story reflects his own, it documents the intersectional roots of an emerging national bourgeoisie, whose violent gendered, class, and interracial traces cannot be easily erased.

In addition to reconfiguring the role inside the household, Shaarawi's trip to the Alexandrian department store redraws the line dividing the marketplace and the household. In her justification of the shopping adventure, Shaarawi underscores door-to-door saleswomen as a danger to the household. Female peddlers moved from one house to another, selling overpriced items while exposing family secrets to grasp their clients' attention and promote their merchandise. Shaarawi's description of them reverberates with the wider discourses on the same issue at that time. Her critique conforms to that of Egyptian feminist Qasim Amin regarding the relationship between aristocratic women and peddlers and domestic servants, who cross the boundaries between public and private and divulged the secrets of the house. Like currency, rumors, secrets, and stories circulated between the household and the marketplace, implicitly framing and aiding the process of economic exchange. Qasim Amin and Shaarawi seek to debunk the myth of security associated with women's staying at home (Amin, *al-A'mal* 391). According to Shaarawi, ambulant sellers spoil the peace of the patriarchal home. Not only do they dictate bourgeois women's choices, they also exploit their situation for economic advantage. In the context of the peddlers, once again the household features as an unsecure site for women, in contrast to the autonomous space of the emporium dedicated for economic exchange. The ambulant sellers, like parasites, infiltrate the domestic space and threaten the disintegration of the family (Shaarawi, *Mudhakkarat* 61–64). Shaarawi exposes her ambivalent stance toward this group, just as she expresses her admiration of one particular ambulant seller, "al-sit al-zahhara," who visits Shaarawi's household and enthralls her with her stories. Female sellers were part of the middle or working class who competed with the female bourgeois over the control of city space and the household (Troutt Powell, *Tell This* 138; Shaarawi, *Mudhakkarat* 60–61).

Inherent in this idea is the view of the modern household as a sealed space that does not overlap with the marketplace, a distinction the ambulant sellers blur by means of the constant movements between aristocratic households and the market. As Baron points out:

> It had been the habit for women to make purchases at home from dallalas, most often Coptic, Jewish or Armenian women who peddled goods (and news) from house to house. But late nineteenth century, Western-style department stores—also often by non-Muslims—opened in the newer sections of Cairo and Alexandria, presenting competition to the itinerant merchants and bazaar keepers. Carrying imported textiles and ready-made clothes, these stores advertised special services such as private home showings for secluded women. Other women went to the stores to find selections, high quality and reasonable prices. ("Unveiling" 371)

The national discourse on *dallalas* reveals a complex intersectional tension, where the working-class ambulant sellers, from different ethnic and religious minorities, controlled a social and public function typically associated with the new role of middle- and upper-class women as shoppers for the household and the leaders of taste and style. The diverse group of door-to-door women represented a parallel multicultural world: a social network under the dominion of working-class women.[23] As a group, they had their own narratives and collective memory. This cosmopolitanism from below, with its distinct social and spatial practices, competed with its upper-class counterpart. The consolidation of one group relied on the marginalization of the other. By separating the public and the private, Shaarawi takes over one of the advantages monopolized by the ambulant seller: movement between the spheres. It is important to note that Shaarawi does not portray Egyptian society as strictly Arab or Muslim. Her memoirs and her magazine *L'Egyptienne* are replete with references to diverse groups of friends and neighbors of her class. These acquaintances were Muslim, Jewish, and Christian and came from Arab and European backgrounds. Her decision to turn away from ambulant sellers primarily constitutes an adoption of a modern political economy centered on the nuclear bourgeois family. In this new paradigm, the values of the emporium coincide seamlessly with those of empire, the nation-state, and the household. The department store shifts from a site that threatens the patriarch's reputation and financial status to one that might safeguard his honor and privacy, just as eunuchs had done in Ottoman Egypt.

Emporialism and the Saint-Simonian World Order

In 1909, almost a decade after her first visit to the Alexandrian department store, Shaarawi traveled to Paris. There, she narrates her traumatic experience during the sale event, shown in the epigraph. In contrast to the Egyptian context, Shaarawi cannot compete with the Parisian masses over space. Her anecdote marks a further development in her feminist journey. Shaarawi's discourse bears the ideological traces of the French sociological discourse of her day. The French emporium reinforces her worldview: divided into East and West and governed by social Darwinism. Her reference to the "French rabble" recalls Gustave Le Bon's social theories on the irrational chaotic behavior of crowds, although her views differ slightly. For Le Bon, the crowd was feminine, irrational, and impulsive, closer to the

Orientalist cliché of the unruly East.²⁴ In the issue for July 1925, Shaarawi's magazine *L'Égyptienne* printed the following lines by Le Bon on international society: "For want of an accepted code, the international moral conscious never accomplished any progress. It kept that of the rest of the animal kingdom: respecting the strong and devouring the weak.... Concessions do not prevent necessary battles. They make them costlier and harsher."²⁵ Shaarawi's magazine uses Le Bon's quote to justify national independence, suggesting that the acceptance of violence could only be a temporary solution that brings about graver consequences. This idea does not differ greatly from the lesson imparted at the Parisian sales event, after which she realizes that conceding to other shoppers only came at the expense of her own security. As mentioned earlier, Shaarawi chooses this incident at the French emporium as an allegory for broader imperial relations. Just as she recoiled before the aggressive shopper, "docile" nations, despite their rightful demands, make concessions to a strong aggressor. In that respect, in Shaarawi's imaginary, the space of the department store represented both the local and the global. The social dynamics in the emporium are analogous to what plays out on the international stage: the competition among empires and the contention between empires and colonies.

For Shaarawi, then, the emporium expresses a way life that extends beyond the obvious antagonism between the social classes. It reflects a wider political and cultural divide between colonizer and colonized and between a figuratively feminine spiritual East and its counterpart, a masculinist industrialist West. Her perception of the emporium corresponded with the Saint-Simonian preview of the Mediterranean, also divided into feminine East and a masculine West. Her description of the "waves of crowds" that she had to navigate at the store recall the imaginary of the sea. Shaarawi's dyadic gendered view could be partially attributable to a Saint-Simonian ideology prevalent in French feminist circles and among her French friends in Egypt. Some of Shaarawi's acquaintances, such as writer Jehan d'Ivray and the Richards, who took care of her as a child, were Saint-Simonians (Sharawi Lanfranchi 180).²⁶ In addition, many of the French feminists she met in Paris, like Juliette Adam, were influenced by Saint-Simonian utopianism (Moses 162–64). In her speech at the American University in Cairo in 1929, Shaarawi recounts the Saint-Simonian utopian adventure in Egypt in 1833, during their quest to construct the Suez Canal and find a female spiritual leader, an Egyptian woman representing the Orient. She reads a chant by the Saint-Simonians, written on the occasion of their trip to Egypt. She also praises the impact of Saint-Simonianism on women's advancement. In the same speech, she projects Saint-Simonian utopianism onto international relations. She expresses her hope that the League of Nations would eventually fulfill the Saint-Simonian dream of world peace.[27]

Shaarawi uses a similar Saint-Simonian lens to map the Mediterranean. She endows the sea with an allochronic temporality and malleable boundaries. During a boat ride across the sea, Shaarawi stops at various European ports. For her, the Orient reaches as far as Marseille. In Naples and Marseille, she does "not feel being at a distance from the East" (Shaarawi, *Mudhakkarat* 124). In Naples, she recognizes the iconographic codes of European Orientalist imaginary. Seeing ambulant sellers, naked children, beggars, women sitting by their house entrances combing their hair, and clotheslines stretching between homes, she considers Marseille another village in the Orient (124). In contrast, Lyon figures as "a strictly European city, which recalls nothing from the East" (126). For Shaarawi, Lyon, a city of commerce, industry, science, and well-organized stores, exhibits the other dialectal pole of Orientalism (126). For her, as well as for the Saint-Simonians and many nineteenth-century travelers from the Arab world, the frontiers of Europe do not automatically align with the imaginary borders of the West. The West begins with the first signs of industrialization, technological advancement, and modern trade, while the littorals of the European Mediterranean recall the familiar cultural and human geography of the East.

Modeling at the Emporium and Modeling the Nation

For Shaarawi, the emporium represented both a global and a national order. In her second anecdote on Parisian department stores, she narrates her experience watching the salesgirls at the emporium modeling the latest trends for the clientele: "I was surprised when I saw some of the established *grands magasins* employ beautiful and elegant girls to model their clothes. This show was not simply to promote the sales of the merchandise but was a lesson for the buyer who could then recognize the necessary accessories to complete her outfit."[28] Shaarawi's remarks expose the key role she ascribes to public representation and visibility. She admires the pedagogical aspect of modeling, which she considers part of a bigger mission that transcends the promotional strategies of the store. Modeling translates aesthetics and social values into a tangible image that could be further recreated by the shopper. By "educating the shopper" through fashion, the store functions as a disciplinary and educational institution contributing to a civilizing mission encompassing the petite bourgeoisie and the working classes. The history of the actual department stores, however, underscores the class tension between the customers and the employees who modeled the clothes (see chapter 1). In many cases, stepping into a store meant a loss of prestige insofar as many bourgeois women pretended to be shopping for their maids. Interestingly, in *Au bonheur des dames*, Zola's account depicts a similar scene, in which the workers at the department store model clothes for the bourgeois female customers. In the novel, this fashion show is not interpreted by its attendees as an expression of civic education and national unity. Instead, it reveals the fractures in the French nation. In Zola's novel, modeling poses a challenge for French bourgeois women, who perceived it as a foretelling of their social displacement, as the store's employees slowly perfect their emulation of bourgeois taste and manners. They constitute an elusive novel class on their own that challenged established French social structures (see chapter 3).

Whereas the Parisian emporium modeled an idealized bourgeois image for the shoppers to emulate, the city urban plans embodied the nation's history and identity. Walking in post-Haussmann Paris, Shaarawi expresses her fascination with the role of public space in educating and shaping the individual:

> Paris is the wide-open page of French history books. A French citizen would grow up in any environment and would be familiar from an early age with his country's history, before going to school or reading in history books. For this reason, you find the French proud of their glorious history and keen to perpetuate this glory. Not only this but also you could observe the French people circulate by all the historic palaces, the archeological sites and centers of learning, art museums, churches, synagogues which open their doors to the public during vacations.[29]

For Shaarawi, the city and the emporium work in tandem. One tailors the body of the citizen, the other their space and collective memory. Shaarawi sees Paris during the Third Republic as a readable text, an official history book crucial to civic education, a school covering a wide range of topics, including the arts, history, religion, and the sciences. Her reference to young children growing up learning their history from their surrounding spaces and being shaped by that emphasizes the central role she gives to urban planning as an instrument of "biopower" in the Foucauldian sense: that is, as the establishment of national sovereignty through the control of the population via diverse educational and disciplinary institutions (Foucault, *Discipline and Punish* 140). In her description, circulation in the capital constitutes a permanent pedagogical act that translates the cityscape into a progressive national narrative accessible to the city residents and visitors. Visiting the different cultural institutions functions as an autonomous ritual for national integration and a self-motivated learning mission overseen by the citizens themselves. Her description, "الصفحة المنشورة" [wide-open page, meaning also published page of French history] highlights the controlled and censored aspect of that educational mission, whose priority is to ensure the perpetuation of the nation-state. For Shaarawi, then, the emporium mirrors the city in its mission. Both are sites of education. Whereas the urban public space gives shape to the image of the nation, the emporium's project is to model the bodies and demeanor of French citizens. The emporium, like the city, actively participates in creating a collective identity and constructing a nationally identifiable image of the French citizen, women in particular.

Shaarawi's comments on the emporium's models and the city urban plan bring to the forefront a major dilemma in Egyptian political life: the absence of a widely recognized female nationalist figure. In fact, the lack of an Egypto-Ottoman bourgeois role model that fulfilled the expectations of a nationalist patriarchal bourgeois framework was key to the emergence of Shaarawi on the public stage. Growing up, Shaarawi tried to find in her immediate surroundings a national female role model who challenged social restrictions. In her memoirs, she briefly mentions two heroic female figures, both of foreign origins. The first woman is a distant Circassian cousin, a warrior who fought alongside Shaarawi's grandfather during the Crimean War (Shaarawi, *Mudhakkarat* 38). This cousin represents a remote non-Egyptian heritage. In another part of her memoirs, she refers to Jeanne d'Arc after visiting Rouen (139).

Shaarawi's later public act of unveiling could be considered a response to the lack of a nationally recognizable public face of Egyptian women.[30] Like the emporium's employees, Shaarawi modeled that image for the nation and the rest of the world. Her action and demeanor embodied a bourgeois nationalist ideal, meant to be emulated by her compatriots. As mentioned earlier, Shaarawi was not the first woman in Egypt to remove the face veil. However, her image is etched in the collective imaginary as the figure of the progressive Egyptian woman. Shaarawi's image of unveiling at the train station was selectively placed on a pedestal because it represented a Muslim woman from the upper classes, and it symbolized a key political moment after the first feminist international convention. It fulfilled the expectation of a Eurocentric feminist narrative of liberation from a harem. One wonders what her companion Nabawiyya Musa was thinking during that moment. Musa organized the press conference and stood next to Shaarawi. She came from a more modest background and was born in an Egyptian village but had already abandoned the practice of using a face veil since 1908, fifteen years before Shaarawi's unveiling (Musa 78–81). In addition, the decision to unveil was initially instigated by her friend and protégée Céza Nabaraoui, who accompanied her to the convention and edited her magazine *L'Egyptienne*. Shaarawi discussed her decision with her son-in-law (Sharawi Lanfranchi 98). The construction of that image relied on crossing class lines. It is noteworthy that Safiyya Zaghloul, wife of the leader of the Wafd party, Saad Zaghloul, was aboard the same ship as Shaarawi returning from their exile in the Seychelles. Safiyya Zaghloul was popularly known as Umm al-Masriyyin (the mother of Egyptians). Although Saad Zaghloul encouraged his wife to remove her face veil, she kept her traditional dress on the request of the Christian prime minster Wasif Ghali Pasha, who intimated to her that "her husband does not work alone" and that he feared the political repercussions of this act on Saad's reputation (Sharawi Lanfranchi 107). Shaarawi's photos sometimes show her wearing a fashionable European hat. These various representations reveal a moment when early feminists negotiated sartorial codes between European and Egyptian cultures. Some later photos show Shaarawi with neither hair covering nor facial veil (figs. 4.6 and 4.7).[31]

If the moment of public unveiling modeled the modern Egyptian woman to the Egyptian public, Shaarawi's Francophone magazine fashioned the image of the modern Egyptian woman to an international audience. The magazine served as a platform to establish a common iconographic language for a transnational bourgeois feminism. In the first issue, dated January 1925, the editors define their mission: "By founding this magazine in a language that is not ours, but it that is spoken in Egypt as elsewhere by the elite, we have a double purpose: to introduce the foreigner to the Egyptian Woman, like she is nowadays—risking to lift all the mystery and charm that her past reclusion endowed her in the eyes of Westerners, and enlighten the European public on the real political and social situation in Egypt."[32] One of the main reasons the founders chose to establish the magazine in French was as an alternative connection to Europe beyond the grasp of the English occupier. Shaarawi and Nabaraoui chose a permanent magazine cover featuring an Orientalized Egyptian woman from the working class standing coquettishly, dressed in European attire but wrapped in the traditional black fabric (*milaya laf*) (fig. 4.1). The model is slightly Europeanized and modernized. She has a slim figure and wears an elegant necklace. In the background, we find a neo-Moorish doorway, an architecture that is more common in the Maghreb and probably better known among French readers than in Egypt. The magazine cover creates a unique Egyptian cityscape, which projects the colonial imaginary of a traditional Egyptian woman. One of the few pointers that brings the reader back to a modern Egyptian urban space is the magazine headquarters' location, typed in bold font on the cover: Kasr El Nil Street, located in the modern Haussmannized district of Cairo.

In contrast to the fictive Orientalist East-West divide, Shaarawi's strategies demonstrate a deeper understanding of the various imperial powers with which she had to negotiate. The imperial "West" did not constitute a single category in her life, and this fact particularly guided her anticolonial resistance and the magazine's mission. In 1919, in the first revolution against the occupation in which women participated, Shaarawi held picket signs in Arabic and French to communicate her message to the different communities in Egypt and foreign journalists (Shaarawi, *Mudhakkarat* 188). The rivalry between the empires and languages as a platform for communication came out when, during the demonstrations, Shaarawi sent a telegram to Lady Stewart Burnett, the American wife of British Commanding Officer Charles Stuart Burnett. Shaarawi decries the violence committed by British soldiers. Lady Burnett ignored the message and intimated to her friends that she could not make sense of what Shaarawi said (185–87). The officer's wife silenced Shaarawi by depicting her as an inarticulate colonial female subject whose language was devoid of any rationality and meaning. With the channels of communication with the colonizer blocked, French was an alternative strategic language to recruit supporters for the Egyptian cause. Egyptian feminists had already played out the rivalry between French and British feminist circles by hosting French feminists such as Marguerite Clément, who gave talks at Shaarawi's house and at the recently established Fouad University. In addition, the university hired Mademoiselle A. Couvreur to lecture Egyptian women. The lectures offered under the rubric of moral studies included the history of French women across the ages, women's psychology, class relations and behavior in France, and feminism (Couvreur; Pollard 124).[33]

In this context, opening a path for trans-imperial recognition through the French language was a predictable strategy to bypass British control.

The magazine established a transnational feminist network, presenting the efforts of feminists around the world. According to Lanfranchi, the magazine was originally the suggestion of Valentine de Saint Point, the great-grandniece of French poet and political figure Lamartine. Saint Point hosted a literary salon. She was a rebellious, eccentric character: a writer, a dancer, and a model. She was a friend of Alexandrian Italian poet Marinetti and enthusiastically supported the futurist movement. Shaarawi gave the editorship to Nabaraoui while Saint Point established her own magazine, *Le Phénix* (Sharawi Lanfranchi 127). *L'Egyptienne* remained a site of transnational and cross-Mediterranean feminist collaboration for fifteen years, showcasing the writing and work of many key French feminist activists, such as Juliette Adam, Maria Vérone (president of the French League for Women's Rights), and Avril de Saint Croix, who presided over the National Council for French Women after Marguerite Durand. Through their participation in *L'Egyptienne*, the writers denounced the British occupation and supported the boycott of British commodities. At the same time, Shaarawi and others assumed an imperialist stance by claiming Egyptian custodian role over Sudan (Baron, *Egypt as a Woman* 73–74, 170–74). The magazine denounced the British annexation of Sudan (Sharawi Lanfranchi 129).

Between the Emporium and the International Stage

Shaarawi's modeling of Egyptian women on the national and international stages did not constitute a mere act of copying European women. Her feminist principle and activism reflect a mutual understanding among international women of the same class. On 30 July 1914, during a visit to Paris, Shaarawi attended a feminist meeting bringing together Julie Siegfried, Avril de Saint Croix, Marguerite Clément, and Louli (Louise) Sanua, the daughter of Egyptian playwright Ya'qub Sanu' (Shaarawi, *Mudhakkarat* 137; Sanua 150). In the bibliographical notes for Sanua's memoirs, Yvonne Ducaris claims that Shaarawi came to the meeting fully veiled and accompanied by a eunuch. She attended alone and unveiled thereafter. If that were really the case, this experience then resembles closely Shaarawi's trip the Alexandrian department store (Ducaris 150). This feminist movement already shared many common ideological grounds with Shaarawi's circles. Most of them aligned their cause with the nation-state. They distanced themselves from socialism and were influenced by Saint-Simonian feminism (Shaarawi, *Mudhakkarat* 137–38; Sanua 85). Three decades earlier, French feminist circles were divided along social questions. By the end of the Second Empire, after the violent events of the Commune in 1871, French feminists split into two irreconcilable factions along issues of class and suffrage. Liberal writers and feminists like Léon Richer and Marie Deraismes allied mostly with the nascent Third Republic and became the dominant voices of feminism until World War II. Republican bourgeois feminists adopted a vision influenced by Saint-Simonian utopian ideology advocating a paternalist stance. They prioritized the maternal role of women in shaping future citizens. Other contending French feminists with a socialist purview, such as Hubertine Auclert, called for suffrage and spoke at the worker's congress (Moses 223). In some cases, the predominantly French bourgeois feminist circles would censor more radical feminist figures like Auclert on questions of voting and economic justice (Moses 214–21).

Richer was one of the major vocal advocates for women's rights in France. His views were strongly affected by French social utopianism. His work drew on Fourier's *Theories of the Four Movements*. Richer and Fourier correlated the liberation and education of women to the advancement of the nation. In *La femme libre*, written after the fall of the Second Empire in 1870, Richer considers the position of French woman as an index to national progress: "It is now time to think that France will not rise up from the profound low state into which it was precipitated and kept by a sequence of painful events unless a better advised and educated woman takes on her share in the common task."[34] He subsumes feminism under the national cause and calls for the education of women, since they were the mothers of future citizens. His publications (especially after 1870) mainly addressed the French middle classes. In contrast to Fourier, who dismissed gender differences and highlighted the expression of desire as a key aspect to an equal society, Richer's notion more closely resembles the Saint-Simonian perspective. He believed in a hierarchal and designated role of women in the society (Moses 133–34, 147, 201).

Shaarawi's bourgeois and multicultural (notably Francophone) background fit easily in the conservative mainstream French feminist movement. For example, the writings of Qasim Amin, who studied in France, reveal the influence of this version of French feminism. Amin's words recall those of Richer in *La femme libre* (1877) [*The Free Woman*] (Moses 199). In his own book *The Liberation of Women* (1899), Amin places the feminist cause at the center of national responsibility. Tracing a direct relationship between women's status and national progress, he claims that "evidence of history confirms and demonstrates that the status of women was inseparably tied to the status of a nation. When the status of the nation is low, reflecting an uncivilized condition for that nation, the status of women was also low" (*The Liberation* 6). Shaarawi's worldview overlapped with that of French bourgeois feminists. The shared beliefs among members of the same social class made this international collaboration possible. For instance, the Franco-Egyptian Louli Sanua established a pioneering professional business school for young women in Paris in 1917 (Milhaud 53–59).[35] The school prepared students for a career in department stores. Sanua assumed a paternalist role toward her students. She actively contacted department stores to persuade them to hire her graduates (Sanua 85; Chessel 283–84). In 1924 and 1925, Sanua traveled to Egypt, Syria, Palestine, Sweden, Norway, and the United States, where she inspected schools (Milhaud 93). In Cairo, she visited Shaarawi's salon and the schools for girls. There, she shared her experience in women's education (Sanua 33; Milhaud 42, 93; "La Mission de Mlle Sanua," 3–4). Perhaps it was Sanua's connections in the *grands magasins* that helped Shaarawi market her atelier's wares in French emporia.

Moreover, transnational feminist ties were guided by a scripted bourgeois protocol of mutual public recognition. For instance, French feminist journal *La Fronde*, founded by Marguerite Durand, pays tribute to various delegates of the International Conference for Women's Suffrage in Paris in 1926 by mentioning their names and their contributions to conference and the feminist cause. The journal praises Shaarawi various times for her generosity as a host and for her activism.[36] In another issue, Durand thanks Shaarawi for her support of a common cause vital to feminist groups in France and in Egypt: the closure of brothels (Durand, "Salut des femmes" 1). Despite their marginality, sex workers were among the most important individuals competing with bourgeois women over public space, since in Egypt and Europe, nineteenth-century public spaces were associated with promiscuity and sexual transgression. Controlling the mobilities of sex workers went hand in hand with bourgeois women's access to civic rights and imperial and national prestige, insofar as the visibility of the bourgeois body relied on the erasure of the sex worker. Abolitionism established a common platform of solidarity and recognition between feminists in Egypt, France, and England (Kozma, *Global Women* 135–55). It aligned the views of Egyptian feminism with its European bourgeois counterpart, while rallying the international public against the British colonizer for legalizing prostitution (Shaarawi, *Mudhakkarat* 305). Abolitionism was a site of collaborative, comparative, and competitive inter-imperial triangular site of morality that operated on the imperial, national, and local levels. Abolitionism pitted one

178 | Emporialism

empire against the other and the colonies against the empire. On the other hand, it pitted the brothel against the bourgeois household in the imperial metropolises and the colonies. Abolitionism was a site of transnational mutual recognition and colonial resistance. In the Egyptian contex, it presented a strong argument against the corruption of mixed courts system, which placed foreign residents under the protection of their respective empires and enabled them to evade Egyptian law (Badran, *Feminists* 192–206).

Like the emporium's civic mission, the act of mutual recognition encompassed a performative task of public self-styling or modeling, which established a common iconography for a transnational bourgeois feminism. *L'Egyptienne* issues are replete with articles, profiles, and photos of women from Egypt and abroad whose portraits starkly contrast with the unchanging illustration on the cover. The magazine deployed what Booth calls the "the rhetoric of exemplarity": a genre of "feminist hagiography" characteristic of early Egyptian feminist biographical writings (Booth, *May Her Likes* 50, 90; Badran, *Feminists* 65).[37] *L'Egyptienne* constituted a transnational "secular" hagiographic and iconographic feminist project where the semiotics of feminism intersects with the semiotics of bourgeois status. The magazine participated in sketching the distinctive traits of feminists around the world as public figures using the decipherable signs of bourgeois propriety and intellectual engagement. An example of this genre are the photos of Avril de Saint Croix (president of the National Council for French Women from 1922 to 1933), Juliette Adam, and Huda Shaarawi at their desks (figs. 4.5–4.7). As published portraits framed in a domestic setting, they occupy a hybrid space between the public and the private, the masculine and the feminine. The portraits sometimes include symbolic objects, such as desks, armchairs, books, or notebooks, that suggest that the subject of the portrait is reclaiming a space typically associated with men. For instance, *L'Egyptienne* portrays Shaarawi in her house standing next to an armchair (fig. 4.8). This pose shares many resemblances with that of Julie Siegfried, president of the National Council for French Women from 1913 to 1922 (fig. 4.9). A typical variation of this photo would have the head of the family sitting in the chair while his partner stands next him, or the opposite. However, in this case the patriarchal chair is empty. The caption details Shaarawi's life achievement: "The great feminist personalities of Egypt ... the founder of that active magazine and president of the Egyptian Feminist Union. She is loved by thousands of foreigners as well as the Egyptian people who consider her an incarnation of patriotism and a heroine of liberty." Another photo of Adam portrays her standing. The caption introduces her as a French patriot, a "spiritual mother to Kemal Atatürk" and an ally to the Egyptian nation.[38] Other portraits present Indian activist Kamala Nehru, the wife of the first prime minister of India, Jawaharlal Nehru (fig. 4.10); Margery Corbett Ashby, the president for the International Women Suffrage Alliance from 1923 to 1946 (*L'Egyptienne*, July 1926); Jehan d'Ivray, the French Saint-Simonian feminist writer who lived in Egypt (fig. 4.11); Ehsan al-Koussi, the assistant director of Sania school and the descendant of Sheikh Ali al-Leissi and Sheikh al-Koussi (fig. 4.12); and Eugénie Le Brun, also known as Madame Rouchdi Pasha and Niyya Salima, who wrote several novels to critique the Egyptian marital and divorce laws (fig. 4.13). The list of figures is extensive and includes Swiss explorer and writer Isabelle Eberdhardt, who converted to Islam and settled in Algeria (*L'Egyptienne*, October 1925); Turkish feminist and writer Halidé Edib (*L'Egyptienne*, December 1926); Francophone novelist Nelly Zananiry (*L'Egyptienne*, February 1927); Egyptian musician Sophie Abdel Messih (*L'Egyptienne*, March 1927); Pantip Tevakul, delegate of Siam to the League of Nations (*L'Egyptienne*, February 1930); Lotfia al-Nadi, the first Egyptian and Arab pilot (*L'Egyptienne*, May 1932); and the first Indian judge, D. H. Khin (*L'Egyptienne*, November 1948).

Despite this mutual understanding, the cause of Egyptian feminists sometimes diverged from that of their French counterparts. During a later stay in France, at the cusp of World War I, Shaarawi asked her feminist French friends if they would oppose the war. Her friends replied that they would stand next to their men (Shaarawi, *Mudhakkarat* 140). Shaarawi expresses her disappointment in French feminists who in times of crisis simply decide to assume a secondary scripted gender role instead of voicing their opinions against the war. Nonetheless, Shaarawi's feminism was not that distant from the viewpoint of her French partners who aligned their movement with the cause of the Third Republic. In principle, Shaarawi also subsumed her activism to Egyptian nationalism. The alliance with the nationalist cause earned both groups popularity and prestige in their respective nations (Moses 218–23). Yet both were unable to secure the right to vote until after World War II: French women in 1945, Egyptian women in 1951 (Rochefort 85–86).[39] The writings of Shaarawi's cousin Ḥawaa' Idris reveal the postcolonial fate of the Egyptian feminist movement. President Gamal Abdel Nasser attempted to restrain the role of the EFU by changing its name to Huda Shaarawi's Association in 1966 (Elsadda, "Hawwa' Idris" 20; Idris 50–91). This symbolic act exposes the end results of aligning feminism with a paternalist national cause. It also sheds light on the subsequent growing tensions between feminism and nationalism after independence.

Amid the effort to model a national image, the magazine revealed an already existing pluralistic and multicultural portrait of Egypt: one that could have served as an alternative model of feminism and national identity. In 1927, the newspaper reported on a kermess fundraising party organized by the EFU founded by Shaarawi. During the event, different Cairene women dressed up as female historical characters to enact a set of eclectic tableaux of Egypt. The show, written by Francophone poet Nelly Zananiry, modeled Egyptian identity through sartorial and spatial design. The kermess gave a glimpse into how the members of Shaarawi's class interpreted their place in the nation's past and present.

The tableaux offered a panorama of pharaonic, Hellenic, Mamluk, and Ottoman periods. The participants included Mademoiselle Solé (a Syrian Egyptian perhaps related to writer Robert Solé), Mademoiselle Jabès (a Francophone Jewish Egyptian, probably a relative of writer Edmond Jabès), Nelly Zananiry, Mlle. Schmeill, Mlle. Generopoulo, Mlle. Habachi, and Madame Eid. The group represents diverse backgrounds—Jewish, Syrian, Germanic, and Greek, among others. The women played various female characters from Egyptian history, such as Cleopatra, Hatshepsut, Teti Sheri, and Shajarat al-dor, or sometimes allegorical figures, such as the Bride of the Nile, Turkish dancers, and the modern Egyptian woman (figs. 4.3 and 4.4). Although the event aimed to provide entertainment for Egyptian elites, the ceremony revealed the dilemma of a society grappling with the definition of modern Egyptian nationalism. In one of the symbolic moments, Zananiry reenacted Mahmud Mukhtar's highly publicized unfinished statue, *Le réveil de l'Egypte*. She stood before a "mute" sphinx and asked about "the future of the Egyptian woman" (Nabaraoui, "Une kermesse" 50).

In "Acting Out Orientalism," Emily Apter analyzes how French celebrities at the turn of the century mobilized Orientalist stereotypes to subvert heteronormative gender roles by staging ambiguously masculinized female Oriental characters (such as Cleopatra or Semiramis). According to Apter, this theatrical Orientalist "camouflage" crafted a clandestine space on stage to question normative gender roles. In many cases, the excessive Orientalist performance served as a code to communicate same-sex desire. By reenacting widely circulated Orientalist clichés of strong women, Apter adds, "the subject poses as an object to become a subject" on its own terms. In contrast to the French context, the Egyptian sketch offered a more nuanced negotiation of gender and national identity.[40] In this moment of auto-Orientalization and the adaptation of an Orientalist fantasy, framed as a series of tableaux from Egyptian history, the participants inadvertently presented the possible tools for its deconstruction. Dressing up as strong female characters with ambiguous sexuality, they called into question heteronormative gender roles (figs. 4.3 and 4.4). In their embodiment of different women from Egypt throughout the ages, the participants established an alternative pluralistic vision of Egyptian nationalism that allowed cultural, ethnic, and religious difference by reclaiming the country's complex Mediterranean history. The show included Muslim, Jewish, Christian, Lebanese, Syrian, Greek, German, Ashkenazi, and Sephardic women from Egypt who reenacted diverse Egyptian historical figures and also belonged to different cultures and histories. As Carmen Gitre has argued, the theatrical space and performance underscore the various social and political currents, contradictions, and dilemmas, underscoring the Egyptian national identity in the making. Indeed, the performers represent the plurality of cultures that composed Egyptian society, which gradually disappeared as a middle-class nationalist narrative, centered on the perception of the *efendiyya* class, became more dominant (Gitre 10). Posing as distant women from Egyptian history, the participants playfully and unwittingly raised many questions against the imperial and colonial notions of feminism and national identity.

A year later, Mukhtar's nationalist representation of Egyptian women, with similar iconographic elements, emerged in public space. In 1928, the Egyptian government celebrated the inauguration of Mahmoud Mukhtar's Statue "Egypt's Awakening" or "Nahdat Misr" (fig. 4.2). The statue featured an Egyptian peasant holding a sphinx with one hand and lifting the veil with the other. Mukhtar sketched his design in 1918 while still in Paris and received a prize for his work at the Grand Palais in 1920 (Colla 227–33). Mukhtar's design was widely advertised years before its inauguration. Most likely Nelly Zananiry, the author of the play at the Kermess, was aware of the design, hence the resemblance between her final tableau and the statue.[41] Mukhtar's statue strongly recalls the creations of his mentor, Jules Coutan, who designed the statue "France Bearing the Torch of Civilization" for the universal exhibition of 1889 (Gershoni and Jankowski 35). It also evokes the Saint-Simonian Mediterranean imaginary of Egypt of Bartholdi's statue "Egypt Carrying Light to Asia" (refer to fig. 2.2). Thematically, the statues symbolize the renaissance of the Egyptian nation. Mukhtar's statue presents Egypt as a native peasant, in the process of unveiling. The choice of location for the statue strikingly echoes the Saint-Simonian worldview: it was originally placed by the gates of Cairo's central train station to be the first image to receive visitors and travelers (Baron, *Egypt as a Woman* 1).

In placing the focus on rural Egypt, Mukhtar's design reiterates a wider national classist discourse. Notably, by putting rural Egyptian women on a pedestal as an image of the nation, the statue does not address the question of social justice. It erases the peasant's material presence in favor of the Orientalist stereotype of the unchanging and permanent Egyptian *fellah*, who remains the same across the ages despite the different regimes that rule the country. This particular image of the *fellah* became fodder for Egyptian and Western social economic and political studies, justifying the subjection of *fellah* to the national elites' civilizing mission (Mitchell, *Rule of Experts* 132). Egyptian literature, as in Muhammad Hussayn Haykal's *Zaynab* (1913), considered the first Egyptian novel, also reiterates a similar rhetoric of nationalism to critique the Ottoman Egyptian elites (see Allen).

In *Egypt as a Woman*, Beth Baron revisits the unveiling of Mahmoud Mukhtar's statue "Nahdat Misr." Baron underscores the irony of this situation, in which Egypt is depicted as a woman, while women were not present at the ceremony, affirming "the inverse relationship between the prominence of female figures in the allegorization of the nation and the degree of access granted women to the political apparatus of the state" (*Egypt as a Woman* 2).[42] Lisa Pollard highlights the cross-gendered iconographic quality of this representation by calling it "a man realm in feminine garb" (87). The statue, however, reveals more than the absence of women; it marks several intersectional tensions and ellipses at once. The statue eclipses the contemporary groups and cultures that do not necessarily associate with either rural or ancient Egyptian heritages: Levantines, Maghrebis, Italians, Greeks, Armenians, Turks, and Circassians, among many others. In other words, its erases the majority of women and faces who constituted Shaarawi's world and played a part in the tableaux at the kermess organized by *L'Egyptienne*. The modern image of the Egyptian woman remained divided between a pastoral ideal of nationalism centering on the female peasant and an emerging feminist movement spearheaded by a diverse multicultural group of upper-class women.

Emporialism and the Bourgeois Household: Modeling the House of the Egyptian Woman

In addition to modeling the public image of Egyptian women, Shaarawi's mission took a parallel spatial design. In Egypt as in France, eclecticism became a design of choice that brought to life the optics of empire and emporialism. The aesthetics of eclecticism showcased the status of the bourgeoisie. In both countries, Orientalism played a key role. The European bourgeois woman re-created a utopian image of empire in her salon, one that glossed over colonial and social tensions. To do so, she favored a design that blended Eastern and Western material culture. Following the model of department stores and design manuals, bourgeois women created a continuum between France's historical periods on the one hand, and between the metropolis and the colonies on the other hand. Similarly, Shaarawi's House of the Egyptian Woman painted a utopian portrait of the Egyptian nation that sought to bridge its internal tensions, connecting past dynasties to the present. Just like in France, collections established a continuum between past and present. Reconnecting with the past involved a reconstruction of an Orientalist image of the Orient, close to that of the emporium.[43]

Just as Shaarawi saw Paris as an expression of French history, she decided to redecorate her house to reflect the new Egyptian woman. She hired Italian architect Antonio Lasciac to take charge of the design. The new house was to be called *Bayt al-Maṣriyya* [the Household of the Egyptian Woman]. According to Sania Sharawi Lanfranchi, the new setting was inspired by her visit to entrepreneur and Arabist Charles Crane's house in the United States. Crane decorated his home with Eastern artifacts collected during his travels (Sharawi Lanfranchi 135). Lasciac was asked to create a reception area with interconnected "French" and "Oriental" salons. Describing the new house, Sharawi Lanfranchi writes:

> [Syrian painted] carved wood was chosen for the ceiling, doors and shutters . . . doors inset with ivory, as well as huge brass chandeliers, marble columns, marble floors and fountains, and Turkish ceramics. . . . This famous Oriental Salon, as it came to be known, [communicated with another salon] in the purest Western style with sofas and gilded armchairs of the Louis XV period, [and] a beautiful piano. The connecting hallway was also decorated in Oriental style with boxed-in painted planks for the ceiling, endless carpets and huge brass chests, with sofas nonchalantly covered with tapestries and cushions that smacked of the *Thousand and One Nights*. (Sharawi Lanfranchi 165–67)

In fact, Shaarawi's Oriental design expressed a wider Arab revival movement in Egypt (Volait, *Fous du Caire* 208). This decorative trend represented a neo-Orientalist revival for conserving Egyptian Arab and Islamic urban heritage, which was propelled further by the aggressive Haussmannization of Cairo. *L'Egyptienne* published several articles on this topic (see Nabaraoui, "La grande pitié"; Marques, "L'Égypte Musulmane). The destruction and sometimes remodeling of old buildings initiated a collection craze among European visitors and residents and the Egyptian bourgeoisie. The movement was spearheaded by French architects and diplomats, Orientalists, and Egyptian elites, such as Ahmad Zaki, prime minister Nubar Pasha, and Ya'qub Artin.[44] Among the many contributors who might have influenced this wave was Gustave Le Bon, who visited Egypt in 1882 and wrote a book discussing art, wherein he photographed Egyptian artifacts as artwork on display (Volait, *Fous du Caire* 218). In addition to Shaarawi's house, Lasciac participated in designing villa Zughayb next door, and the house of Shaarawi's brother Umar Sultan Pacha, who was an avid collector of Arab artifacts. All these households included a Western and an Eastern salon. This trend signaled a key distinction between nineteenth-century homes and their modern counterparts (Hamamsy 173; Volait and Ribelles 38–51; Volait, *Fous du Caire* 181–226).

Many members of the Egyptian bourgeoisie began collecting and displaying Arab antiques and artifacts in the 1920s. The Oriental decor in Shaarawi's house, as well as in the houses of her bourgeois acquaintances, represented an eclectic style that blended diverse Arab motifs and aesthetics. Egypt's bourgeois reconstruction of its Arab past was not distant from Lanfranchi's fantastical reference to *The Nights*. This new neo-Orientalist eclectic design was mediated by various artists and architects whose trajectory crisscrossed the Mediterranean, and whose attempts of reconstruction was based as much on the Universal Exhibition as on Egyptian heritage. House designs varied between the neo-Moorish and the neo-Mamluk, or neo-Byzantine (Volait, *Fous du Caire* 202). The construction of the Heliopolis quarter by the Belgian company of Baron Empain in 1905 takes neo-Orientalism to another scale. In addition to adopting neo-Byzantine and neo-Moorish designs, Baron Empain added a palace in a Hindu style for himself (Ilbert, *Héliopolis* 164; Raymond 321–33; see also Van Loo and Bruwier). Shaarawi's house decor, like the Parisian decor on the other side of the sea, brought in one space many Easts and Wests: not just that of France and Egypt.[45] Through this neo-Orientalist self-styling, the houses of Egyptian elites edged closer to the imaginary eclectic Orient constructed by the emporium and the Universal Exhibition (see chapter 1).

Conclusion

For Shaarawi, emporialism constructed a divided cosmos between East and West, a perspective that informed her assessment of the larger Mediterranean. Her visit at the emporium confirmed a dominant ideology of empire, hinging on social Darwinism. Seeing the world through the emporium and its rhetoric of emporialism, she understood the necessity of competing over public and space. Similarly, her feminism developed with an interconnected world. It was developed mutually with a liberal bourgeois feminism that dominated European circles. Just as she navigated the boundaries between empires and nations, between the household and the city space, she encountered these various maps reflected inside the emporium. Her attempt to model the modern Egyptian woman revealed a richer context and a complex intersectional dynamic that conflicted with the tunnel vision of imperialism and its commercial alter ego, emporialism. In reconstructing the public and private spheres, she competed, contested, and collaborated with subjects from different empires: French and British feminists, eunuchs safeguarding the honor of the patriarch, women peddlers, and sex workers, all of whom would have told different stories of Egypt and the Mediterranean.

Emporialism reveals how Shaarawi's development as a feminist and her views from the outset were the amalgam of transnational and intersectional relations that exceeded the Egyptian and Muslim contexts. In some cases, creating a public image for Egyptian women and constructing bourgeois national space revealed a complex process, including the back-and-forth circulation of Orientalist representations and material culture, across the Mediterranean, between Egypt and Europe. Revisiting Shaarawi's experience at the emporium reveals that feminism in the Middle East and elsewhere, like the history of the bourgeoisie and the middle classes, did not emerge "sui generis" in the sealed borders of the nation-state and then shined outward, to borrow Simon Gunn's words (70). Shaarawi's feminism was not an insular nationalist perspective that later earned the stamp of approval from European international circles.

Shaarawi's class-based movement did not constitute a unique Egyptian phenomenon; rather, it reflected global feminist dynamics, strongly tied to the formation of the global middle and middle-upper classes. It was not a passive colonial imitation either. In many cases, Shaarawi's anticolonial activism was a point of contention between her group and French, British, or American feminists (Badran, *Feminists* 108–9). It was a process of an interdependent construction, beyond the binaries of national/foreign, internal/external, or empire/colony (Gunn 66). Her views and actions developed through the mutual exchange with a wider international circles of liberal bourgeois feminists who dominated European and American spheres of influence and who came to establish their ideals along national, racial, and class lines. In Egypt, as in elsewhere, the formation of gender, race, and class relations relied on the intermixing of local, regional, and imperial forces.

Chapter 5

Jacqueline Kahanoff's *Jacob's Ladder*

Between Emporialism and Levantinism

In my youth, I considered it natural that the residents of Cairo understood each other, although they spoke different languages and used different appellations: Muslim, Arab, Christian, Jewish, Syrian, Greek, Armenian, Italian. The names of cities like Baghdad, Tunis, Aleppo, Beirut, Damascus, Istanbul, Thessaloniki, Casablanca, and Jerusalem, were all too familiar because people, especially relatives, would enjoy the company of each other as if they were roaming around through the rooms of one big house. Only "Paris" was different—a distant name shining in gilded letters on the labels in Nono and Uncle David's department store [Kol-Bo].[1]

In her memoirs of cosmopolitan Cairo, Jacqueline Shohet Kahanoff reconstructs her city of birth through the lens of emporialism. Writing from Beersheba, the Israeli Egyptian writer was the granddaughter of the founders of the Chemla department store in Egypt (refer to fig. 6.1). Using her grandparents' department store as a point of reference, she lists the national and religious epithets constituting the diverse populations of the eastern Mediterranean. In her portrait, the cosmography of the emporium overlaps with the city's human and cultural geography. Like the aisles and walkways of the *grand magasin* Chemla, the streets of Cairo brought together a diverse world (see chapter 2). Despite their differences, people understood tacitly that they were the members of one family, strolling in the different rooms of one big house. In her description, Kahanoff, like Émile Zola in *Au Bonheur des dames*, conflates the image of the street, the store, and the house. Her account does not aim to analyze an imperial modernity informed by Orientalist aesthetics and the paranoia of conquest; rather, it seeks to highlight the dynamics of Francophone and Levantine cultures in Egypt. Yet in an unexpected turn, Kahanoff detaches her images from the politics of European cosmopolitanism. After giving an account of the city's human geography, she pauses at the French labels in her grandparents' department store. By contrasting the store's French labels and life in the street, she adeptly marks the gap between the reductive representation of a culture and its practice: between a French homogenizing system of value, especially its optics of cosmopolitanism, and the Egyptian practice of multiculturalism. Kahanoff exposes how the standardized price labels cannot encompass the plethora of epithets and identities that make up the eastern Mediterranean. Beyond the promising name of "Paris," inscribed on the price tags and the typical scope of emporialism, she perceives a different lifestyle taking shape through the daily interaction among Cairene residents over the store's counters, and likewise in the streets of Cairo, where French was the social language of a diverse elite. As a Cairene woman, Kahanoff reads her city's social map in a manner that challenges the clichéd European perspective of diversity centered on the optics of visibility. For instance, she recognizes the various cultural, regional, and religious affiliations of Cairene residents. She does not conflate Arabness with Muslim faith, and even under the rubric of Arab culture, she acknowledges many groups that escape the European eye. Years later, Kahanoff named this unique culture—irreducible to the word *Paris*—Levantinism, which for her constitutes the seeds of a new Eastern Mediterranean lifestyle that she documents in her writings. She later introduced this concept to Israel in 1954 after settling in Beersheba (Starr and Somekh xvi).

In this chapter, I explore Jacqueline Shohet Kahanoff's concept of Levantinism, expressed in her English novel *Jacob's Ladder* (1951) and her other writings, developed in accordance with her childhood experience in Cairo where she takes her grandfather's department store as a model for that lifestyle. She began writing her novel in the United States and finished it during a brief stay in England in 1951, three years after the declaration of the state of Israel and a year before Egyptian independence (Starr and Somekh xvi). In that sense, the novel was caught in a liminal space between imperialism and nationalism, between the fall of the Ottoman Empire and the failure of Francophone culture, between the dusk of British imperialism and the rise of American hegemony. After Egyptian independence in 1952 and the Suez Canal crisis of 1956, the novel gained another meaning, as it records the history of Jews from Egypt, the dispersion of the Egyptian cosmopolitan Levantine society, and the dismissal of Levantine culture in Israel at the height of Zionism and Nasserist pan-Arabism.

In my analysis of emporialism in Kahanoff's novel, I aim to examine the distinctive aspects of Levantine culture and its aesthetics produced and showcased by the emporium. I seek to excavate the underpinning intersectional layers of the romanticized portrait of Francophone Levantinism that came to be associated with the Egyptian department store. In contrast to the various romanticized narratives on Levantinism, Kahanoff's depiction of Levantine spaces of cultural production, including the department store, adeptly reveals a double image of Levantinism divided along class lines and often reduced to the cosmopolitan middle-class image. The text addresses the frequently overlooked role of the labor force in shaping the image of the cosmopolitan elites. The novel narrates the often marginalized role of working-class Levantines in the elites' acquisition of cultural capital and consolidation of status in an intercolonial and interimperial context. It reveals how the frequently invoked memory of Levantinism carries the colonial traces of racialization of labor, or what I dub "ethno-classism," a process that foregrounds a Europeanized cosmopolitan portrait of Levantine elites by means of a representational slippage, which simultaneously Orientalizes European and Middle Eastern members of the working class and draws the image of the bourgeoisie closer to its white European counterpart.[2]

Emporialism and the Dynamics of Ethno-Classism

Addressing the institutional and social bias in the representation of Levantine and Mizrahi cultural production, Ammiel Alcalay has critiqued the paucity of circulated literary and academic texts attending to the contributions of Mizrahi Jews to Arab and Israeli cultures, which complicate the standard tropes and binaries in political and cultural representations of the Middle East (*Keys* v–vi). Many works, especially memoirs, in Arabic, Hebrew, English, and French have been published to document and in some cases come to terms with the cosmopolitan life and Levantine culture of colonial Egypt and other parts of the Middle East. These texts cover the experiences of a wide range of communities, including the expatriation of Arab Jews from various Arab countries and their migration to different regions of the world, including Israel.[3] Most of the widely known representations of Levantine culture, however, come from Francophone middle-class or elite authors such as Kahanoff who possess the agency to document their experiences. As a result, these representations have perpetuated the common association of Levantinism with the image of a rootless Francophile socialite (Durrell; Cialente, *The Levantines*). A number of recent academic works have analyzed such literary texts to explore Levantinisim as an active space of cultural production and cultural memory that challenges reductive notions of Jewish and Arab identity in Zionist and Arab nationalist discourse.[4] In prioritizing this perspective, however, they overlook the actual material history to an extent, including social and colonial dynamics, that led to its construction. Much remains to be said about the origins of Levantinism, the agents who participated in its production, and the politics of memory that contributes to its current framing.[5] Recent scholarship in history, literature, and cultural studies shed more light on these works by drawing attention to the class relations implicit in some of these memoirs. They question the historical accuracy of this romanticized Francophile Egyptian cosmopolitan experience (Fahmy "The Essence," pt. 1 65–72; Halim 8; Mabro 251, Starr, *Remembering*; Miccoli, 54). This scholarship shows that, contrary to this representation, the Levantine community, including Egyptian Jews, was divided by culture, social class, and geographic origins (Krämer 8–67; Mabro 238). Most of the widely known representations of Levantine culture come from Francophone middle-class or elite authors (such as Kahanoff) who have the agency to document their experiences. Consequently, these representations have perpetuated the common association of Levantinism with the image of a rootless polyglot cosmopolitan figure. In many of these narratives the image of the domestic servant surfaces as an alter ego to the Levantine middle-class characters and as the faithful guardians of Levantine memory.[6] Examining the portrait and memory of Levantinism requires paying special attention to the intersectional relations that produced it in order to highlight the implicit racial and class tensions that underlie the romanticized memory of a Francophone bourgeois Levantine past that became dominant in post-1960s memoirs and novels.

Though often unnoticed, the literary texts in question contain a recurring motif of domestic workers and other working-class laborers from different ethnic communities—Greeks, Italians, Syrians, Lebanese, Sudanese, Egyptians, and others. It is often through domestics and workers that the protagonists of these works define their ties to their immediate surroundings. Domestic workers also play the role of parental figures, informal teachers of Arabic, Orientalized representatives of local culture, and even keepers of memory for the Levantine employer who departed, voluntarily or involuntarily, as part of the broader dislocation of many ethnic communities in the late 1950s.⁷ Despite their diverse cultural backgrounds and important roles, servants appear in these texts only as a ghostly presence or fleeting reference. Rather than being an important part of the bygone, bourgeois, or middle-class cosmopolitan life described by the narrator, they serve as the backdrop of that image.

In *Outline of a Theory of Practice* and *Distinction*, Pierre Bourdieu explores the class tension implicit in the construction of an idealized portrait of the bourgeoisie. He traces the intricate relationship between cultural production and class formation. To distinguish between the consolidated image of a group and the actual history of its construction, Bourdieu defines the *habitus* as "the subjective but not individual system of internalized structures, schemes of perception, conception, and action common to all members of the same group or class and constituting the precondition for all objectification and apperception" (*Outline* 86). Habitus constitutes the standards, ethos, expertise, and material culture that shape a group and inform its views and representation. It is constructed and enforced by means of control and exchange of "economic" and "cultural" capital and creates the markers of distinction characteristic of each social group. Whereas economic capital refers to financial resources and assets, cultural capital stands for the overall knowledge, manners, and taste (education, aesthetics, fashion, music, art) that a group adopts or internalizes for self-representation and social interaction. Bourdieu warns against treating the histories of culture and social class separately, since the image of a class rests on the culture it produces and performs to maintain its dominance. He draws our attention to "genesis amnesia," a common process in the representation of class where the focus is directed toward the finalized picture created by different social groups, in contrast to the "modus operandi," which charts the process and the artifice underlying the formation of this image and its corresponding habitus (*Outline* 78–79). For instance, what we recognize as bourgeois culture depends primarily on a successfully erased history of material acquisition, education, and interclass relations. How could we consider bourgeois culture without the army of workers that participated in producing it: the governess, the domestic help, or the private tutor? How could we give an account of the unrecorded hours spent during childhood to learn table manners, practice a musical instrument, attend a painting workshop, or study a foreign language? These seemingly marginal elements, often expunged from the final portrait of a bourgeois family, are central to the affirmation of its social and economic status. Similarly, could we think of Levantinism as part of a cultural capital that contributed to the construction of social classes in Egypt and vice versa? If I may rephrase

Simone de Beauvoir's famous sentence, "One is not born *Levantine*, but rather becomes one," precisely through a long process of learning and intersectional social interactions.

What stands out in *Jacob's Ladder* is the fact that the author does not present the cosmopolitan background of the young protagonist, Rachel, as a seamless natural condition. She considers it the complex outcome of a long struggle and continuous work to consolidate the family's social status via economic and cultural capital by navigating a complex colonial system produced by the overlapping French, the British, and the Ottoman empires. In that sense, the family's situation evokes the mimetic gesture of the department store where the French façade hides the invisible or undocumented effort involved in putting that image together. In my reading, I explore the department store and the household in *Jacob's Ladder* as complementary sites for the production and performance of Levantine culture. In so doing, I seek to reinscribe an erased history related to the process, agents, and spaces of the construction of that culture. Among those agents are servants, nannies, salesclerks, and other colonial subjects, whose faces are later blurred while painting the portrait of an elite Levantine society.

In its depiction of Levantinism, *Jacob's Ladder* aptly records the mechanization of emporialism, which subjects the residents of the empire (colonials and middle-class Europeans) to an intertwined discourse of ethnic and class purity that seeks to cast the members of the colonial middle class into its white European corresponding image by adopting European material culture or a consumption pattern valorized by European standards. The novel reflects a complex process of alienation, corresponding to Deborah Starr's and Sasson Somekh's description of Kahanoff as never being "at home" in Hebrew, Arabic, French, or English. Kahanoff spoke French at home and in school in Egypt. She mastered English by communicating with her British governess. She studied elementary Arabic when she lived in France. She was not fluent in Hebrew either, since she did not foresee her later immigration to Israel. To publish in Israel, her writings were translated from the English to Hebrew ("Editor's Introduction" xiv–xv). Not being at home in language or nation-states makes most of her writing revolve around the image of the household, with the desire to anchor it in the history and geography of the surrounding milieu. In her novel, the department store overlaps with the map of the household, creating an unsettling image that reveals the fragility of both spaces. It is precisely this narrative strategy that shifts the lens between the household and the department store that enables Kahanoff to capture the implicit and unrecorded tensions in a complex Levantine colonial culture, forced to fit into the Procrustean bed of European cosmopolitanism, even though it operates in a complex interimperial, colonial, and regional Mediterranean framework that challenges the paradigmatic limits of Eurocentrism.

Reconstructing Kahanoff's Levantinisms

Before analyzing the image of the department store in Kahanoff's work as a model for Levantinism, I give a brief survey of her concept. In assessing Levantine culture, I argue that it is not a single category but a multiplicity of perspectives and experiences enmeshed in a social, political, and economic system subject to different variables, such as class, gender, ethnicity, and colonial relations. Likewise, tracing the history of Kahanoff's concept of Levantinism through her writings, starting with *Jacob's Ladder*, shows the progress of this idea largely informed by the author's experiences. Just as there are many Levantine communities, there also exist many phases of Kahanoff's Levantinisms, mostly connected to her memories of Egypt and her goal of anchoring this lifestyle in the Mediterranean.

The epithet Israeli Egyptian I used above cannot summarize Jacqueline Shohet Kahanoff's complex and rich experience. She was born in Cairo in 1917 to a Jewish Iraqi father and a Jewish Tunisian mother. Her family's life depended on extraterritorial dynamics born from the unique interlacing of Ottoman, British, and French empires in Egypt. Her Tunisian family, who held French passports, moved to Egypt to be part of a growing urban economy. Her maternal grandfather began as a street vendor in Tunisia and moved to Cairo, where in 1907 he established the famous department store Chemla Brothers, which constitutes the inspiration for Smadja Brothers in her novel (Reynolds, *Commodity Communities* 129). As French subjects, they benefited from various legal privileges and protections granted to foreigners, including the mixed court system established by the Ottomans and kept by the British. Kahanoff attended a French *lycée* founded by l'Alliance Israelite Universelle (Kahanoff, "A Culture Stillborn" 123). In 1937, she attended a French law school to prepare for a career in the mixed courts, a legal system abolished by 1949.[8] In 1940, Kahanoff moved to San Francisco and then studied journalism at Columbia University in New York City between 1942 and 1945 (Starr and Somekh, "Editor's Introduction" xi–vii). There, she published several short stories in English. The Chemla department store, which inspired her novel, was sold to an investor in 1946.

Kahanoff's story "Such Is Rachel," the kernel of *Jacob's Ladder*, received a prize from the *Atlantic Monthly* in 1947 (Starr and Somekh, "Editor's Introduction" xix). Although she grew up familiar with British culture, her writing bears the influence of American culture, which had a different sociopolitical context and a distinct notion of race and class (Starr and Somekh, "Editor's Introduction" xvi). Views toward class relations, work ethics, and social integration differed from those of the Sephardi and Mizrahi Egyptian elites living in colonial Egypt, whose population reflected the human geography of the Ottoman Empire. Among the many differences at that time would be the question of segregation and the filtering of Jewish identity through European—especially Eastern European—history, including the traumatic impact of World War II, which does not fit into the writer's background or experience. In 1951, she moved to Paris to join her younger sister and eventually came to reside in Israel in 1954. Her parents remained in Cairo until 1957, when they too settled in Israel (Starr and Somekh, "Editor's Introduction" xi–vii; Shohet, "Communauté Juive," 14 Dec 1964). After Egyptian independence in 1952, the Chemla store was nationalized, but it operates under the same name to the present day.

In Israel, Kahanoff encountered new political and social dynamics between the Mizrahi and Ashkenazi communities. However, her writing remained strongly connected to Egypt and its Levantine culture. At the height of Zionism, Levantinism, seen strictly from a Eurocentric view, posed a social and political threat, a sign of regression that did not match a Zionist utopian vision of a homogeneous modern state modeled after Europe. As Gil Hochberg pinpoints, after the influx of Moroccan Jewish immigrants to Israel, Israeli newspaper *Ha'aretz* quotes a French diplomat warning the new state that "the immigration of certain human material is liable to bring the Jewish nation down and make it into a Levantine nightmare" ("Permanent Immigration" 219). In another incident, British newspaper *Manchester Guardian* claims that David Ben-Gurion, the Israeli prime minister, is "plunging the new nation into Levantinism." Ben-Gurion once vowed that he would "prevent Levantinism from creeping into [Israel's] national life" (219).

In this very politically charged climate, where Mizrahi culture was disparaged and repressed, Kahanoff once again turns to her childhood memories in Egypt to reclaim Levantinism as a critical term to question the Eurocentric vision of the Levant and the social and political relations between Ashkenazi and Mizrahi communities in Israel. Her memories of the cultural and urban geography of Cairo and Alexandria, as well as her early struggles to define her national and cultural belonging in Egypt, serve as a useful experience for questioning citizenship in Israel. In Egypt, Kahanoff witnessed the coexistence of many groups from various Middle Eastern and European cultures. In contrast to the dominant aversion to Levantinism, she suggests it as a solution for the impasse of Zionism anxiously seeking to distance Israel from its milieu by creating a double standard in the treatment of European and Middle Eastern immigrants. In her essay "From East the Sun," Kahanoff claims that Israel's "best chance for peace and survival may be to transform the Zionist revolution into a Levantine one" ("Afterword" 251). This idea, however, precedes her immigration to Israel, where she encounters the sharp schism between Mizrahi and Ashkenazi societies. In *Jacob's Ladder*, Kahanoff already experiments with this idea while rethinking the position of Jews in modern Egypt and Palestine. In the novel, set before the establishment of the Israeli state, Rachel, the protagonist, receives four dolls as a gift from her uncle, who just has returned from Palestine:

> Uncle Moses came to see her, and brought her little dolls from Palestine, two Jewish *Kibboutzniks*, a man and a woman, with little Russian blouses embroidered at the collar, and two Arab ones. Rachel played with them, while the family chatted. She married the Arab man, thinking perhaps of her beggar, to the Jewish woman, and the Jewish man to the Arab woman. Uncle Moses noticed her game, and said, half-laughing, half-cross, that she was an incorrigible dreamer like her father. (*Jacob's Ladder* 349; emphasis in original)

The image of Uncle Moses returning to Cairo cannot help but strike a comic chord by recalling the biblical story of Exodus in which the prophet leads the Hebrews out of Egypt. In this case, modern Moses makes his way back from Palestine with a set of dolls of Ashkenazi Jews and "Arabs," reflecting—and questioning—the situation in the 1950s. Rachel's game provides insight into Kahanoff's early perception of Levantine culture in the Middle East, right after the founding of the Israeli state. Kahanoff wrote these lines from the United States, before Egyptian independence, still not having planned her migration to Israel. This complex and ambiguous scene, then, is an early attempt to present her cosmopolitan experience in Egypt, without necessarily anticipating the later development of the Israeli-Arab crisis, or the tension between Mizrahi and Ashkenazi communities in Israel. In addition, reading this child play with the specter of World War II eugenics in the background renders the scene even more thorny to navigate, given the many entangled civic and interracial experiences of that time.

Looking at the Arab dolls, Rachel recalls a young Egyptian beggar, whom she has seen in the streets of Cairo while walking with her Irish governess. She immediately identifies with the homeless child and realizes that she is "brown," in contrast to the governess. The identification with the beggar becomes the first moment of recognition of a divide in Egyptian colonial culture, between Rachel's European education and her Middle Eastern heritage. In that context, she sees the image of the Arab dolls from Palestine and the Egyptian beggar as interchangeable. Her words reveal an intersectional slippage and an act of erasure, where the figure of Arabness is reified into a specific image of class, namely, that of the poor. Rachel conflates Arabness with the Orientalist and classist image of the beggar, a process that I call ethno-classism. This struggle continues throughout the novel until in another incident Rachel shouts, "Egypt for Egyptians" in support of a public demonstration (364). This identification shows ambivalence toward Middle Eastern and Egyptian heritage, or an inability to perceive Egyptian and Arabic cultures other than antithetical to their European counterpart and diametrically opposite to the image and culture capital of the middle class. Despite Rachel's Orientalist association of "Arabs" with beggars, she perceives a society where both Arabs and Europeans, vaguely defined, create "a hybrid" culture. Her likening of the Arab doll to a native Egyptian "beggar"—whom she considers a reflection of herself—suggests an even broader outlook, in which she imagines a utopian space that overcomes race and class differences. The uncle's comments reveal the author's consciousness of the daring aspect of this ideal. Rachel's actions elicit an ambivalent reaction from her uncle, who is at once amused and annoyed. He calls his niece an "incorrigible dreamer," suggesting that her imagined society is merely utopian (349). This sentence leads the contemporary reader to wonder whether Kahanoff, who had not yet settled in Israel, is subtly contemplating the possible connection between Palestinians and Israelis in the 1950s.

Jacob's Ladder

Jacob's Ladder is a semi-autobiographical novel that narrates the coming of age of Rachel Gaon, a young Jewish girl "from Egypt," the granddaughter of two merchant families, the Gaons and the Smadjas. Rachel's Jewish Iraqi paternal grandfather, Jacob Gaon, features as both a business patriarch and a prophetic figure akin to the biblical Jacob. Rachel's Jewish maternal grandfather, Nathan Smadja, migrates to Cairo from Tunisia to establish a chain of department stores, Smadja Brothers. Growing up in colonial Cairo, Rachel struggles to reconcile her Middle Eastern Jewish heritages and her multicultural European education. In her eyes, both European and Arab cultures in Egypt break down into many subcategories: French, English, Italian, Greek, Muslim, Arab, Jewish, Christian.[9] Rachel questions her national belonging to Egypt and her cultural affiliation with France and Britain; she identifies neither as Egyptian nor as European, since she does not speak Arabic fluently, and her grandparents come from a traditional Iraqi and poor Francophone Tunisian background, respectively. On the other hand, she attempts to understand the place of her Jewish Tunisian and Iraqi families in modern Egypt and the meaning of celebrating Passover in Cairo, a situation she deems paradoxical to the biblical narrative of Exodus. Rachel's family strives to ascend the social ladder by emulating a European lifestyle. To do so, the family depends primarily on the working class. They hire Egyptian servants who worked in British households and English nannies who give Rachel and her brother access to parts of the city limited to British citizens. They also fashion their new European image by dressing from the atelier of the grandfather's store, which employs Syrian, Greek, and Italian seamstresses, who constitute the workforce of the Levantine community.

In her attempt to rewrite her experience through the story of Rachel, Kahanoff uses the department store as a key space to document the history of Levantine Egypt. Via a technique of doubling, the reader can discern various foil characters as the many sides of the protagonist.[10] The same pattern applies to the central spaces in the novel. For instance, Kahanoff plays on the multiple meanings of "The House of Gaons" and "the House of Smadja," as the department store, the household and the family lineage. She invents a protagonist whose paternal and maternal grandparents are each building a chain of stores. This allows her to write a multilayered history of Jews in Egypt where each house presents a different perspective: mythological on the one hand and materialist on the other. Whereas the House of Gaon stands for a mythological space that creates a continuum between biblical history and the situation of modern Jews in Egypt, the House of Smadja, based on the Chemla store, refers to an actual urban site through which she traces the daily life of cosmopolitan Cairo. Central to Levantine culture is the tension productive of a Eurocentric perspective, in which Levantinism represents a threatening backward lifestyle. Its mixture of European and Middle Eastern traits gives no clear indication of national or cultural belonging to either Europe or a cliché Orient. This makes Levantine culture a site of division between an idealized modern European image and a marginalized Middle Eastern double. Writing in 1946, Albert Hourani sheds light on this divide existing in the perception of Levantine culture: "To be a Levantine [is] to live in two or more worlds at once without belonging to either, to go through the external forms ... of a certain national identity, religion or culture, without actually possessing it. Not to be able to create, but only to imitate; and so not even to imitate correctly, since that also necessitates originality. It reveals itself in lostness, pretentiousness, cynicism and despair" (Hourani 70–71). For Hourani, Levantine culture symbolizes "the crisis" of Arab society, a form of alienation brought about by the political and social changes in the Eastern Mediterranean during the nineteenth century (Hourani 71). He associates Levantine life with commercial culture developed from the trade networks connecting Eastern Mediterranean ports with Europe. The Levantine way of life constitutes an impasse, a desperate gesture of mimicry seeking to reconcile old Arab and modern European customs but producing sterile clichés. Hourani's definition, however, presupposes the presence of an authentic Arab and European identity—each belonging to a different temporality, which Levantine culture fails to capture—and only manages to create what Bruno Latour might call a "hybrid monster," an ambiguous representation that does not conform to a strict form of modernity that seeks to sever all connections with the past (Latour 12-13). In other words, one can either be a traditional atemporal nondescript Arab or a modern European.

Reading Kahanoff in 2004, Hochberg reviews Hourani's words in light of the contemporary situation in Israel in which Levantinism has been thought of as a means to reintegrate Mizrahi culture in Israeli society and reclaim a marginalized Arab heritage ("Permanent Immigration"), as suggested by the writings of Ammiel Alcalay, Ronit Matalon, and Nessim Rejouan.[11] Hochberg's reading is part of a body of literature that sheds light on the dynamics of Levantinism as a cultural notion that challenges the reductive aspects of national, religious, and social affiliations. She contends that Levantinism is not a geographical concept but a complex "performance of culture" ("Permanent Immigration" 220). She shifts the focus onto Levantinism as a cultural category. Yet this lens overlooks that what is now dubbed Levantinism is not a homogeneous category; it expresses a wide range of cultural and economic exchanges between various social and ethnic groups in different social, historical, and political contexts. Nevertheless, most of its representation comes from middle and upper social strata who have the agency to document their experience and whose image, including that of the Francophone "rootless Levantine," has come to be associated with Levantinism in general. Although Levantinism offers a sense of mobility by means of allegiance to many groups at once, it is itself contingent on a set of colonial, legal, and economic circumstances particular to the social classes that contributed to its emergence and historization. For this reason, the department store, with its manicured organization, class relations, and promise of social mobility, emerges as a key site to analyze Levantinism and Levantine society.

Return to the *Grand Magasin*: In Search of Lost Time, but Which One?

In terms of themes, language, structure, and the history of its reception, *Jacob's Ladder* documents many losses at once. As a literary work, it embodies Levantine aesthetics with many of its complexities. Kahanoff writes in British English in the United States but emulates Marcel Proust's *À la recherche du temps perdu* (1913–1927), where a nostalgic narrator reconstructs the French past by entwining personal and social history. Kahanoff titles her chapters: "The World of Rachel Gaon," "The Stranger," "The Invader," and "a World Regained," recalling the final volume of Proust's *Recherche, Le temps retrouvé*. She frequently refers to Proust in the novel and compares Rachel's experience in Alexandria to Marcel's summer at Balbec.[12] Just as Rachel sits on the ruins of an old city giving way to the modern Levantine one, Marcel, Proust's narrator, acts as witness and historian of a romanticized bygone Belle Époque (1871–1914). He decides to impersonate the famous French memoirist Duc de Saint-Simon (1608–1693),[13] and Scheherazade, to write the story of a nation that has turned Levantine (Proust, *Recherche* 2398). Proust evokes the urban changes after World War I by describing the image of the crescent dominating the Parisian sky as he imagines the Seine becoming the Bosporus (Proust, *Recherche* 2218).[14] In contrast, Rachel documents her family's Arab heritage before it is swept away by Levantinism by weaving together oral stories transmitted from one generation to another, as well as Egyptian colonial and social history. Like Proust before her, Kahanoff highlights the effect of material culture in the life of their respective societies and on class and national representation.

Jacob's Ladder re-creates the modern history of the Chemla family in Egypt while giving insight into the process of creation of their unique cosmopolitan lifestyle that mixes Eastern and Western traditions. Near the end of the novel, Kahanoff resorts to the technique described above to paint the Smadja department store in a new light, signaling as such Rachel's coming of age. Like Zola, Kahanoff uses the purview of emporialism to express the passage of time by collapsing the distance between the department store and the bazaar (see chapter 3). In the following passage, the narrator casts an Orientalist light onto the cosmopolitan department store, transforming it into its dreaded Other, the bazaar: "Back in Cairo, if ever she went to Smadja Brothers, a run-down store with the air of a bazaar, she wondered how, in the old days, marching down the creaking aisles with her grandfather, she had believed this was the grandest place on earth. Well she thought disdainfully, she had grown up now, and lost all her silly illusions" (*Jacob's Ladder* 394). At first glance, the description of the European department store condemned to deteriorate to the status of a bazaar could be interpreted as a lament for a bygone Levantine culture. But this Orientalized framing of the store serves another purpose. The customary nostalgic trope for Levantinism associated with the novel is more likely to be a product of the recent reading of *Jacob's Ladder* seen retrospectively through the lens of contemporary Egyptian and Israeli cultures, in which Egyptian intellectuals mourn the disappearance of cosmopolitanism, while Israeli intellectuals critique the marginal position of Mizrahi culture in Israel.[15] In fact, in contrast to this idea, the novel primarily laments the birth of a modern Levantine culture at the expense of a lost Arab Jewish heritage. In a later passage Rachel sits on the stairs of her Iraqi grandparents' house, located in a traditional Egyptian neighborhood, and ruminates on the past: "She sat down on the crumbling steps and closed her eyes to savour and remember its silence, so that it should not be engulfed in the clamour of the Levantine city . . . All this was gone, but perhaps, she told herself passionately nothing, no one, could ever wholly die as long as the living remembered, and she must keep alive in her heart's memory all that had been of this world, lest it perish through her neglect" (407). Following a long tradition of French writers, such as Victor Hugo and Émile Zola, Kahanoff uses a spatial metaphor: the image of a building in ruins devoured by the modern cityscape. Zola's *Au bonheur des dames* depicts an outgrowing bazaar dominating the Parisian landscape (see chapter 3). In contrast, in Kahanoff's text the utopian Levantine *grand magasin* metamorphoses into an Oriental space to register the end of an era. The passage aligns with the common European depiction of the

Mediterranean city as a decaying archeological site to be reconstructed by the European writer or painter. In this novel, the modern Levantine city takes over what the narrator dubs old Cairo with its rich multicultural lifestyle. Kahanoff's account of Levantinism is imbued with nostalgia for a way of life the protagonist could never recover, due to—as she explains in the text—a colonial system that taught her to internalize an Orientalist reductive view of Middle Eastern culture. In this ambivalent context, Rachel accepts Levantine culture as an expression of her time while acknowledging loss of and rupture from her grandparents' Arab heritage. Perceiving the bazaar at the heart of the department store stands for understanding the double aspect of Levantinism as both European and Oriental. Ironically, Kahanoff's description unwittingly exposes the actual origins of the department store initially designed after Oriental bazaars, which kept haunting the French urban imaginary (see chapters 1 and 2).

In addition to the disconnection from a Middle Eastern heritage, the novel documents several ruptures and losses, such as the writer's disappointment in Francophone culture or, more accurately, the recognition of its failure to create a coherent Egyptian urban class, much like Huda Shaarawi, who realized the limitation of French culture in ensuring a universal transnational feminist solidarity (see chapter 4). Kahanoff wrote first in French in Francophone newspapers in Egypt. After a few attempts, she found it futile to write in French, since her Levantine audience was made up of many cultures. In her essay "A Culture Stillborn," Kahanoff claims: "Many people in this milieu were well-read in all three languages. Italian, English and French. This complexity gave this minority a subtlety, diversity, and refinement rarely matched elsewhere, but no ethnic element or language was actually strong enough to weld these disparate groups into some kind of unity" (114–15). For Kahanoff, Egyptian Francophone culture breaks down into many subcategories and represents many communities with more diverse and complex backgrounds that transcend the limits of the French language. Questioning the effectiveness of French in uniting these communities, a situation that led her to write in English, she says: "The Jews were so intoxicated by French culture that they did not pay attention to the advice of the Alliance for the Jews to learn the language of the land in which they lived. In the eyes of the middle-class Egyptian Jews of my generation, speaking Arabic was considered outdated and old-fashioned. Only the lower classes, that is to say Jews from the ghetto, spoke Arabic" (123–24).

The Original Portrait of *Grand Magasin* Chemla: A Mimesis of French Culture

Most of Kahanoff's examples of Levantinism revolve around the construction and reconstruction of maps and urban spaces, through which she introduces her concept and subtly negotiates questions of national, social, and cultural belonging. This pattern appears in *Jacob's Ladder*, where the department store and its double, the household, are two sites for analyzing Levantine society. Like many Cairene *grands magasins*, Chemla Brothers stressed its French aspect. An advertisement for the store, published in Shaarawi's Francophone magazine *L'Egyptienne* (refer to fig. 6.1), borrows its design and iconography from Parisian posters, which manipulate the picture's scale by foregrounding the department store and dwarfing the surrounding urban monuments to give the impression of a colossal building dominating the horizon. The picture evokes Zola's description of an ad campaign for his fictional department store (refer to fig. 3.1), Au Bonheur des dames: "Then came a bird's-eye view of the buildings themselves, of an exaggerated immensity... Beyond, stretched forth Paris, but Paris diminished, eaten by the monster... The horizon crumbled into powder" (Zola, *Ladies' Paradise* 383).[16] This advertising technique elides the specificity of the urban map and its human geography, where the store comes to displace the entire city. The hyphenated words "Paris-Cairo," positioned at top center, and the script affirming the regular connection with Paris, emphasizes the store's role as mediator of French culture in Egypt, almost reducing its commercial activities to a bilateral exchange between the nations.

The store positions itself as a metonymy for France in Egypt, an idea also expressed through its merchandise, architectural design, and setting. This is how Kahanoff's mother, Yvonne Shohet, remembers her father's store, Chemla Frères, the first department store built in 1907 on Boulac Street (later known Avenue Fouad), in a French fin-de-siècle style:

> All the tiles in marble, the columns in style Louis XVI with acanthus leaves, for that period it was an incomparable luxury, the display windows... The store was constructed with our own [design] plans. It means that the ground and first floors were spacious... There were three floors above.... Very beautiful large apartments. On the ground floor there was... first [the department for] notions... very well-stocked, fabrics, on the right and the left there was the department for knitwear and hosiery for men and women. A little farther then there

were special articles for men, and more toward the inside lingerie. The back of the store was occupied by furniture on the left and shoes department on the right. And all that with the counters in polished mahogany, and with ravishing display cases. . . . There were very large ateliers for the haute couture. We also had two department managers from Paris. We also had a very good milliner from Paris, and a corset maker from Paris.[17]

The interview, conducted in 1964 in Israel, documents the history of the *grand magasin* Chemla tailored after a Parisian space (Shohet, "Communauté Juive," November 1964, 1–90). As Nancy Reynolds indicates, like many of its competitors located on the same street, the store's design and layout was part of the mimetic gesture to emphasize its connection to France (*City Consumed* 77). The language of the interview, French, is central to the re-creation of the store's image. The store was a French space memorialized in the language of the culture it represented. In the same way, the department store's activities and commercial culture sought to reconcile a modern European tradition with a local one. Reynolds explains: "multilingualism and ethnic intermixing dominated the store floors and the store shelves of much urban commerce" (*City Consumed* 224). In other words, neither the products sold nor the employees or clientele were exclusively Francophone, despite the emphasis on the French aspect of the store. The everyday reality in the store was different from the romanticized French image. Many of the employees spoke several languages, including Arabic, and used them according to specific contexts, such as the cultural background of their clients or their colleagues (Reynolds, *City Consumed* 65–69).

The *Grand Magasin* as a Mirror to Levantinism

The motif of the department store as a reflection of Egyptian society already existed in the Egyptian cultural repertoire. In using the department store to mirror Egyptian cosmopolitanism, Kahanoff draws from the popular Kish-Kish Bey plays starring the famous actor Najib al-Rihani and directed by Togo Mizrahi, which she describes in other writings:

In Cairo, Kish-Kish Bey's popular theater provided the one setting where people of various backgrounds met and laughed together and at themselves and one another. These unpretentious, lively, funny, partly improvised playlets were produced by a young Jew called Mizrahi. Vivid recognizable types were portrayed on the stage: the Greek grocer, with his funny lisp in Arabic, having a passionate argument with his customers, the Jew from harat-al-yahud [the Jewish quarter], with a rose or twig of jasmine behind his ear, which he passed under his nose whenever he felt embarrassed or told a fib; and the middle-aged, veiled Moslem lady, venturing into a department store, entranced by Western goods, asking the cheeky little Italian salesgirls whether one puts a girdle over or under a petticoat, and at what moment one puts on or takes off a bed jacket in bed. Kish-Kish Bey reflected our simple origins, stripped of pretense. ("Culture Stillborn" 116)

Najib al-Rihani was an Egyptian Francophone actor with an Iraqi father and Egyptian mother. He adapted many plays from French and starred in many theatrical works and movies representing the Egyptian Levantine community, such as "Hassan, Morcos, and Cohen" and "Kish-Kish Bey in Paris." The playlets center on the naïve but cunning Kish-Kish Bey, a provincial landowner who travels to Cairo to squander his profits from the cotton harvest.[18] Ironically, the Renaissance theater where Rihani performed his early vaudeville plays was later replaced by the *grand magasin* Chemla owned by Kahanoff's grandparents (al-Rihani 68). Togo Mizrahi's and al-Rihani's portrayal of the department stores on the theater stage showcased the different Levantine "types" who made up modern Egyptian cosmopolitan society to critique the cultural transformation of this community, which had suddenly prospered in the early twentieth century and found itself before an unprecedented economic and cultural capital due to the commercial activity revived by the Suez Canal and the cotton trade boom. In the scene described above, the play ridicules not only the Muslim woman unable to understand the purpose of a girdle but a modern Egyptian society trying to force itself into a new form. Kahanoff's description of the woman as Muslim reflects an ethno-class slippage whereby an Egyptian woman from the petty bourgeoisie dressed in a traditional ottoman attire is automatically associated with her faith rather than her class.[19]

Building on the above repertoire, Kahanoff presents a similar idea from the perspective of a Jewish woman from Egypt and the daughter of the owners of a department store. Just as Najib al-Rihani mocks the unfamiliarity of the Muslim client with a girdle, Kahanoff narrates a Jewish middle-class family's comic struggle to master European material culture imported and marketed by their own department stores and necessary for acquiring social status in a colonial context. In the novel, Rachel describes the ways the Smadjas try to understand and adopt French and later English cultural capital. In one of the passages, Nathan Smadja asks: "What's that Proust, Alice, benti [my daughter]? I don't remember eating it" (*Jacob's Ladder* 211). By weaving her family history as owners of *grands magasins*, and that of Egyptian Jews, Kahanoff expands al-Rihani's narrative to shed light on another side of the prism that makes the Levantine community.

Mapping Levantinism through the Department Store: A Biblical Teleology

While narrating the social ascension of the Gaons and the Smadjas in Egypt, *Jacob's Ladder* switches between three sites of Levantine culture: the house, the department store, and the city at large. For Kahanoff, both the domestic and public spaces record the tensions between the sought-after European lifestyle and the actual culture created during that process of mimicry. The novel does not begin in the department store. Instead, it offers a detailed description of the House of Gaon, located in the Abbasieh [Abbasiyya] quarter, a "traditional" neighborhood. With a cinematic scene, the narrator introduces the Gaons and their patriarch, the traditional man from Iraq:

> Horses' hooves clattered through the silence of the narrow lanes, and Jacob Gaon made ready to receive his sons. He pictured them in their European suits, coming from their modern homes to the timelessness of this lane, with its houses withdrawn behind high walls, flowering with Jasmin [sic] and Honeysuckle, its echoes of grave voices exchanging the Arab greeting: "Peace be upon you"; in it no woman walked unless she were draped in habbara.[20] The old man heard the carriage pull to a stop, heard steps on the path, and the hushed whispers of his sons while they waited for the servant to answer their knock. He detected the urgent note in their tone.... But Jacob soon drove worry from his fine old face, and composed it into lines of majestic serenity. Whatever his doubts, his sons must always see him stern and detached, the Patriarch. (3)

Jacob Gaon resides in a reclusive, idyllic traditional house that exists in harmony with its geographical and cultural location. The house blends perfectly with the surroundings. The neighborhood dwellers speak Arabic; men and women live according to age-old religious customs. The clattering of the horses' hooves announces the advent of guests who are, in this case, Jacob's sons. The sons here are both insiders and outsiders. Their European attire and their homes in the English-style suburb Garden City mark another spatial and temporal rupture created by a European lifestyle. The image of the sons carries an ambiguous connotation of continuity and rupture; while it suggests the projection of Jacob's family line into the future and their success in developing the father's enterprise, it also bears a nostalgic tone that laments the separation from an earlier state of things, or a "fall" into a European way of life that distances the sons from this old, serene, paradisiacal quarter. The House of Gaon suffers from a divide between two generations and traditions.

The spatial description and the linguistic register bring out another aspect of the patriarch's image. Jacob sits in a room where the texts of the Ten Commandments and the Balfour Declaration hang on the wall.[21] The documents anchor the family in a specific sociopolitical context, by bringing to the forefront the British imperial presence, the recent memory of world wars and the emergence of the newly founded Israeli nation.

When his sons ask him for advice, Jacob replies in a cryptic language, using biblical metaphors: "We must think of lean years, and prepare for them in the prosperous one" (6). The allusion to the biblical story of Jacob's ladder aligned with the British promise to create a modern nation for Israel entwines modern and biblical history.[22] The reference to the story of Jacob creates an imaginary continuum between the ancient House of Israel (Jacob) and the modern House of Jacob Gaon in Egypt. However, the text also predicts a forthcoming historical caesura in Arab-Jewish (Mizrahi) experience. By highlighting the Balfour Declaration on the wall, the text underscores the dissonance between the politics of that document and the patriarch's lifestyle and heritage. This symbolic setting raises the question whether the traditional Arab Iraqi-Egyptian patriarch fits in the ideological imaginary projected by the Balfour Declaration, which would come to consider Jewish faith and Arab culture mutually exclusive (see chapter 6). This dilemma later took center stage in Kahanoff's writing.

Soon enough the readers realize that despite the religious tone recalling the biblical East, the conversation between the modern Jacob and his sons revolves around their commercial enterprise, more specifically around the operation of their new stores. In contrast to the biblical Jacob, the modern Jacob is a merchant and should be the future owner of a chain of stores.

"The House of Gaon" evokes both a household and a shop.[23] The depiction of the Gaons as merchants in modern Egypt, which simultaneously refers to scriptures, reconstructs the family's profession as a divine predestination. Jacob's sons attempt to anchor themselves in Egypt by building many houses, or stores. The debate between father and sons regarding their dream of commercial expansion re-creates an overall map of Egypt outlined by the sons' future project of building a store in every town. This plan triggers Jacob's refusal because it does not conform to traditional commercial conventions. The father, who knows every town and hamlet and speaks various Egyptian dialects, operates in tandem with local merchants (11). The sons' commercial aspirations, however, consist of acquiring a large market share by disrupting this custom and building their own retail centers, placing competition before social collaboration.

The scene follows Zola's pattern in staging the department store as a rupture in the social fabric of the community. The text emphasizes this fact by shifting the focus from Jacob to his servant: "Ahmed the servant, a tall and severe man, came in with Turkish coffee. He had been with Jacob since the day of his arrival in Egypt, and had come to look like him, except that he was younger, and wore finer galabiehs" (14). Standing silently in the shadow of Jacob Gaon, the Muslim servant appears to be Jacob's alter ego, a reminder of Jacob's humble beginnings. Both share an Arab background but are separated by social class and religion. Ahmed more closely resembles Jacob than his sons do.

Despite Ahmed's position as a servant, he has a central role that even Jacob could not perform: "In this part of Cairo, where Moslem and Jew sent servants bearing gifts to his neighbor on religious holidays, where everyone lived by the peace handed down to him by his forbears, obeyed an ancient order and accepted the fortunes and the misfortunes of life as the will of God, women still lived in the seclusion of their own quarter" (4). The text suggests that the serenity of the neighborhood rests on another world, on the presence of domestic help who act as a liaison between Muslim and Jewish neighbors. As Stoler points out, "servants policed the borders of the private, mediated between the 'street' and the home, and occupied the inner recesses of bourgeois life; they were, in short, the subaltern gatekeepers of gender, class and racial distinctions that by their very presence they transgressed" (133). The servants' mobility contrasts with the age-old quarter's stability. In contrast to their patrons, servants can cross social, spatial, and cultural boundaries and bridge the distances between the separate groups. Servants move among houses but also in the gender-segregated quarters of the household. Unlike the department store's recorded economic transactions, the circulation of gifts between neighbors represents an unregistered economic exchange beyond the goods sold in the marketplace.[24] The stability of the Gaons depends on these invisible connections maintained and established by the servants who represent, or replace, their masters in these moments. By introducing the servants, the sentence inverts the capitalist economic paradigm, where now the Gaon's wealth and prosperity appear to be a surplus value to this unrecorded economic transaction. Via this game of doubling and the creation of foil characters, Kahanoff initiates a central theme that runs throughout the text to highlight the tension between the visible and invisible, between what is officially acknowledged and recorded and what is only implicitly understood and erased from memory.

As the conversation between father and sons progresses on the possible location of the future stores, the passage switches from evoking an overall map of the country to that of Cairo divided between modern and traditional neighborhoods:

> Couldn't we go half-way to meet him by starting one new branch . . . perhaps at the intersection of Sharia Boulac and Sharia Emad el-Din, the heart of new Cairo?[25] . . .
>
> "Our business is in old Cairo," David said, "but people are moving to the modern part of town, and it's precisely because a new city is growing that you brought us here. Our new branch would be to the parent house what the child is to the father." (9, 11)

In her focus on the divide between the two sides of the city, Kahanoff creates her novel over a stereotypically colonial map that structures the city into two sites antagonistic to each other: a modern European side and an antiquated Oriental one. The Abbassieh [Abbasiyya] quarter, which Kahanoff describes as traditional, was built in 1848–1852, during the Khedive Abbas's life, and its plan does not necessarily conform to an old, antiquated Cairene quarter.[26] In the context of Kahanoff's novel, the intergenerational argument between Jacob and his sons is reflected in the cityscape as an urban schism where Cairo is divided between a new culture taking shape and a traditional one that functions according to different rules. The location of the future store stands for the sons' desire to prosper and acquire social status by being part of modern Cairo. Yet the son's choice to "meet half-way" and locate the store where both cities intersect suggests that the department store would be a blend of both lifestyles, projecting as such the traits of a Levantine culture situated at the intersection of old and new, "Oriental" and European.

Levantinism between Empires and Emporium

In chapter 2 of *Jacob's Ladder*, the text takes the readers to Smadja Brothers, the store owned by Rachel's maternal grandparents. As mentioned earlier, this is based on the writer's memory of Chemla Frères, which was located on the same street mentioned by the Gaons as the midpoint between the two sides of Cairo. The narrator describes the department store as a place of openness and calm, in contrast to the bustle and din of the street.

> Nathan Smadja stood at the entrance of his store, smiling at the life of the sunny street flowing by him, "A bargain, a good bargain, my lady!" the pedlars [sic] cried, and the fat, handsome women shouted back, "Go on, away with you, you rascals! Thieves!" His thick thumb crooked over the gold chain of his watch taut across his big paunch, he smiled guilelessly at all the people who came in, as if to tell them "Don't worry, we have everything you need, and at a good price too," and people smiled back at him. (22)

In contrast to the sacred halo surrounding Jacob Gaon, Nathan Smadja is described in comic, banal terms. He neither sits on a throne-like chair in a reclusive paradisiacal house nor speaks in a refined cryptic language with biblical metaphors. The readers encounter Nathan for the first time as he stands at the doorway of the store. He is dwarfed by the large entrance and embodies a very stereotypical racialized Mizrahi look: a large paunch, a gold watch, and a crooked thumb, talking to customers, and in other passages shouting at peddlers (25). Unlike Jacob, he does not have servants to open the big gates of his secluded, sheltered house to lead the guests to his room. Nathan's speech is a mix of languages: French, Arabic, and perhaps some Italian (while talking to Mrs. Biagiotti), to communicate with clients and peddlers. His linguistic register is that of the everyday, a colloquial idiom delivered in a theatrical manner marked by short sentences and interjections, a reminder of the *souk*, the traditional marketplace, or of advertisements: "Don't worry, we have everything you need, and at a good price too.... Come I'll show you the new lace we're unpacking—a dream! Extraordinary! The finest! Just arrived from France for your trousseau!" (22).

The Smadja Brothers store does not resemble a modern business enterprise with a clearly marked hierarchy between employees. Instead, it is a family-oriented venture, mixing traditional and modern management. Nathan occupies an awkward position between a manager of a "Parisian" department store and a peddler promoting his merchandise on the street, serving as doorman, vendor, and store manager. He even feels more comfortable in the streets, shouting and competing with street vendors than enacting the role of a typical department store manager:

> Nathan forgot his troubles as soon as he was in the streets. He shouted at the small beggars, glued to the display windows by their running [sic] noses and sticky fingers, "What! Soiling our windows! Let me catch you at it again, and I'll beat you to death!" They laughed, because he was good-natured, but ran out of his reach... A young pedlar came up boldly, the basket strapped around his neck full of threads, needles, elastics, buttons.
> "For your daughters, sir?" He asked impudently.
> Nathan laughed. "You can try to undersell me, you rogue, but don't expect me to undersell myself. Off with you!" Then he called, "You there, with the balloons! That's something I don't sell. Give me a red one for my grandchild." (25)

As foil characters, the young street peddlers reflect Nathan's childhood. In fact, the narrator stresses that the Smadja brothers themselves had earlier been "two small, ragged pedlars in the streets of Tunis" (23). The finger marks made by the beggars on Nathan's modern vitrine evoke the traces of his past as a young street vendor, his beginnings, and the history of his family's social ascension. The scene reveals the fragile class distinction that separates him from the young street vendors surrounding his store, especially since he does not act in an aloof manner, as expected from a member of the upper class. The finger marks soiling the windows destroy the illusion of the seemingly invisible glass pane, which connects the store to streets. The fingermarks remind the readers of the class divide that separates the two sides of the windowpane. Metaphorically, the fingerprints construct an unpronounced implicit stop sign understood by the passersby for whom the transparent window materializes as a solid barrier that keeps the unwanted outside.

Leaving the description of the store's semi-closed barriers, which separates the city and the store, the narrator swiftly moves inside the store:

> The pair [Rachel and her grandfather, Nathan Smadja] marched down the central aisle of the store in stately procession, and the employees dropped the merchandise they were showing to customers, crossed their hands on their hearts and exclaimed, "Isn't she a darling!" Even the customers participated in the ritual as Nathan, his face beaming, picked on an enormously fat Moslem woman, knowing their love for children and the generosity of their praise ... The woman laughed, her face half visible under the veil, and said ... "May Allah protect her from the Evil Eye!" ... "You can have ten per cent off that handbag you're buying! We just received this lot from Paris, first quality, my lady, the latest fashion, the finest in Cairo." (56)

Nathan uses traditional ways to market his store, hinging on developing personal connections with the clientele, greeting them, and exchanging news. Whereas French department stores built their image by stressing fixed prices and eliminating bargaining, Nathan promotes his French merchandise by offering an instant discount to the customers he likes. French department stores appealed to families by creating play spaces for children, selling toys, and giving away balloons and trinkets. Nathan's strategy is reminiscent of such an idea. However, he translates this mechanism into the local context. Talking about Rachel in the department store and exchanging compliments with the shoppers is a marketing technique that revolves around the theme of family and children, which appeals to a middle-class clientele.

For Rachel, the department store represents a private kingdom where she receives exceptional attention from both customers and employees. Unlike the clearly marked spaces in the city divided by class, ethnicity, and citizenship, between old and new, here she can wander with few restrictions. "Rachel was free to dash through the aisles on a scooter, to touch everything" in that miniature world that mimicked the larger social and economic structure of the nation, and the larger empire: "lead soldiers ... bright firemen ... trumpets ... tea sets ... [a] train winding its way through green board pastures" (57).[27] In contrast to this childish utopia in the eyes of Rachel, the narrator reveals another dimension of the store that reflects a more realistic image of Egyptian society, when Nathan takes his granddaughter to the workshop, or atelier:

> He marched her off to the workroom, where new pleasures awaited Rachel, as her grandfather entrusted her to the care of young seamstresses. The big sunny room exploded with laughter, the gay whirr

and purr of the sewing machines, of scissors crissing through bright wools, velvets, laces, and silks, the quick movements of pulling threaded needles, of feet busy on the treadle machines. That the girls were pale, smelling of sweat, cheap perfume and bad breath, was something Rachel did not notice when Nathan opened the door and a great shout greeted her . . . "Here's Mascotte, to bring us luck!"

The girls cleared a space on the long table, and hoisted up the child, to sit enthroned among the fabrics, the ribbons, the flowers, the cushions bristling with pins and needles, and the light spools of thread. Even Madame Marthe, the stern première, who had been with the Smadjas since Tunis days, relented in her discipline, and let the girls drape Rachel in rolls of fabric, which trailed regally behind her as she paraded up and down the table, stumbling over obstacles, dragging her doll after her. They laughed and clapped their hands, exclaiming, "Will we be bridesmaids at your wedding, Mascotte?" (57)

Just as the real store serves a cosmopolitan Levantine crowd, the atelier depends on a large group of Levantine employees who are the workforce that re-creates Parisian fashion for their clientele. For Rachel, the atelier appears as a fairytale space, full of laughter and conviviality. The House of Smadja materializes as both a department store and a household where the employees are part of one family. Despite its happy tone, the scene retains the grim traces of manual labor and class distinction: "the pale" workers, the "stern" look of Madame Marthe, "the smell of sweat," the "cheap perfume," and the busy feet on the treadle. The image of the atelier workers contrasts with the playful aspect of the scene and most important with that of the socialite Levantines.

Objects and Subjects of Display

The description of young Rachel draped in fabric and pretending to be a bride foreshadows another moment in the novel, in which the family celebrates the wedding of Rachel's aunt. The workers of the atelier are in charge of making the family's outfits for this significant social event. The narrator gives the following critique of the elite Levantine society attending the wedding:

> Something had happened in this society, which made money the yardstick of all values. This was a liberated society, acquisitive, competitive,

but also fluid, and doubtful of itself. Old values were breaking down, and there was a lack of new ones to fill the empty space. Money was there, as a common language between the once segregated communities, money was the symbol of power, esteem, love given and received, money was the measure of things. Yet people who made such remarks felt a vague shame in doing so, while longing to feel again what they had felt in the synagogue. (135)

In this description, the narrator stresses the transformation of an ambitious and self-doubting class that needs the affirmation of material wealth to consolidate their newly found status. In this highly fragmented elite Levantine world that has lost contact with its respective roots, money becomes a common denominator that replaces cultural capital. Unlike the traditional household of Jacob Gaon that seems anchored in space, fixed and unchanging, the new Levantine community is as dynamic and fluid as the image of money it represents. Whereas the crowded atelier smells of sweat, bad breath, and cheap perfume, a space crammed with fabrics and sewing machines, the elegant wedding represents the final visible product put together in the store's atelier, whose workers do not attend the ceremony.

Rachel's family members, however, are neither working class nor established colonial elites. Midway on the social ladder, they must work hard to secure their social status in the emerging cosmopolitan community. The Gaons and the Smadjas find themselves in a paradoxical position, both constricting and strategic, in relation to the society of which they wish to be a part. Being constantly under public scrutiny as promoters of the latest trends and fashion, their command of European material culture is crucial to their social appearance and their financial progress. Because of their dependence on commerce, they are forced, in a sense, to model European material culture for others and spearhead the social and cultural transformation of the city regardless of its impact on their lives. The narrator emphasizes the role of the store in transforming Egyptian society, through their imports: "Smadja Brothers were the first in Cairo to import American sheer silk stockings, lastex [sic] girdles, polo shirts, plastic cigarette cases" (402).

The family members are themselves objects of display both inside and outside the department store. By taking on that role, they also invent themselves as colonial elites. For instance, Rachel's position as the daughter of department store owners and merchants prescribes her social and gender image. As a member of the Smadja and Gaon families, Rachel embodies this double position that shapes her social representation but also her situation as a woman. For instance, she obtains permission to wear lipstick because of "the part [that] the sales of lipstick had played in promoting the Gaons' prosperity" (421). Being the daughter of department store owners marks her social and gender representation. This middle position of women, as producers and consumers of material culture, reflects the Kahanoff's family's real experience tethered to the politics of empire. At first, they model French material culture. Later they contribute to the popularization of American fashion with the ascendance of the United States as a major power.

The situation narrated in the novel closely resembles what the author's family experienced while establishing their elite social position. Kahanoff's mother, Yvonne Shohet (née Chemla), describes the connection between the Chemla households and the House of the Chemla Brothers (the department store):

> Our parents insisted that my female cousins and I were dressed very elegantly. First, because it was an advertisement for them. People asked: "Where does this dress come from? Ah, naturally, it's evident. She is a Chemla daughter; it's a sure thing that she has pretty dresses with the couture atelier that they have!" Also, mother and my aunt, then later, my aunt Pia, my uncle's Clément's wife, when he got married, dressed from the store. (Yvonne Shohet "Communauté Juive," 20 November 1964, Tape 1 17)[28]

Following the tradition of family-owned shops, women from the Chemla family married the head salesclerks to keep the business in the household (Reynolds, *Commodity Communities* 268). Dressing from the atelier promoted the store's merchandise and highlighted the family status. By wearing the stores' merchandise, the public would also know that the wearer is a "Chemla daughter." In this case, family lineage and social position become entwined with the store's employees and the image of merchandise. Rachel's situation does not differ from the previous description. She is the product of the store and the household. She represents a unique embodiment of cultural and economic capital: an intersection between the two faces of "the House of Smadja," the household and the marketplace. As a child, she is a marketing device that allows the grandfather to chat and bond with his clients and sell merchandise. In addition, she reveals herself as an example of a new elite Levantine class, who is actually another "product" of the atelier. As the seamstresses describe her, Rachel is truly a "mascotte" [mascot] of the Levantine community in the double sense that as a bourgeois Levantine she is being transformed into the visible and marketable emblem of Levantinism.

Beyond the Vitrine: Mastering European Material Culture

Despite the strategic social position of the narrator's family, Kahanoff reveals the artificiality and fragility of their new social image, which is a product of a continuous conscious effort and separation from their heritage. In her description of Hattouna, her Iraqi grandmother, Rachel stresses the grandmother's belonging to a distant "dead" "world" that had its proper customs, manners, and aesthetics, but lost their significance in this new society:

> He [Rachel's father] bowed before the aged woman, who sat in the attitude of a Persian miniature, her back upright, never leaning against the cushions of the low divan, her legs folded beneath her with dainty slippers peeping out from the sides of her dove-grey silk habbara.... Tiny violet flowers trimmed the mauve kerchief Hattouna wore over the wig of an orthodox Jewish matron, and her graceful, stylized movements set them dancing on her forehead ... Smaller silk rugs of delicate shades hung on the walls, and ebony tables inlaid with ivory and mother-of-pearl were strewn among the divans. Near the latticed window, precocious apricot blossoms shot out from an enameled Persian vase ... She returned carrying a brocade of pale almond green and white gold wrapped in russet silk.
>
> "How beautiful! But really, you shouldn't do this! It'll look handsome draped over my piano!" Alice exclaimed enthusiastically.
>
> Hattouna's fingertips caressed the sumptuous material. "In Baghdad, it would have made a bride's dress." (20)

Dressed in a traditional Iraqi Jewish manner, Hattouna sits in a secluded quarter, which resembles an Oriental tableau that highlights a luxurious but different materiality. The delicate lady, who moves gracefully in that familiar elegant place, belongs to another social space that has a different relation to material culture. Hattouna offers a sumptuous piece of fabric to Alice, Rachel's mother. Whereas the grandmother sees the fabric as the material for a luxurious "bride's dress," Alice, the Francophone Tunisian daughter-in-law, assigns a different use value that reflects the family's wealth. For her, the brocade will make an elegant cover for the piano. In Hattouna's description, her own "world is dead" not just because it belongs to a remote life in Baghdad but also because it has lost its cultural and economic value in this new society. Outside her house, despite her elite status, Hattouna seems out of place. During her own daughter's wedding, she is treated condescendingly by the Levantine Jewish community. Her upper-class culture capital has become obsolete. Sitting in her quarter, a harem-like space, Hattouna appears to be "a Persian miniature," an object in a museum.

Whereas the Gaons' life belongs to a distant, extinct, and comfortable world, Smadjas' house represents comic and gauche attempts to adopt a French lifestyle. The narrator describes Nathans "Grand Salon":

> [Nathan] looked with pleasure at his table, opened at full length to seat nearly twenty people, adorned with the best tablecloth with two big soup tureens ... overflowing with couscous ... He walked around the table, and bumped into a sculptured bronze corner of the sideboard, but its style, which Nathan proudly though inexactly called "Louis XV" was worth all the bruises it inflicted on the family ... Sandra, a chubby girl of twelve, with blue eyes and black hair ... saw him throw the stone into one of the Chinese vases on the sideboard. Everything went into those vases except flowers, she thought. When she married and had her own house, she would not allow people to do such things, nor to yell from one room to another. Throwing herself on her bed, she began to read a French novel, longing for the elegant world it described. (28–30)

The paragraph highlights the often undocumented efforts and pains involved in becoming bourgeois. Just as the family members use their own bodies as living advertisements and wear Chemla's merchandise, the narrator describes the same corporeality in relation to other European objects. The bruises made by the new furniture on the Smadjas' bodies mark an invisible struggle and a muted pain as they force themselves into this new lifestyle. The mistakenly identified "Louis XV" sideboard and the Chinese vase that has been assigned different functions from its original purpose (in contrast to Hattouna's Persian vase) reveal the gap between the family's social aspirations and their actual failure to master cultural capital. In her rejection of her family's old habits and gauche manners,

Sandra, Rachel's aunt, escapes her immediate surroundings to sink into a French novel; she creates a distant imaginary European world based on fictional literature, hoping that one day her future family will have more French manners. The shiny golden furniture, the large table laden with couscous, the misused Chinese vase, and the entire Smadja family are as close to French culture as the shiny golden word *Paris* featured on the department store façade.

The Gaons and the Smadjas, despite their ambitious aspirations, only manage to live in a culture that is neither European nor Middle Eastern. As Homi Bhabha indicates, the civilizing mission always functions with a deferral, an engrained failure that prevents it from reaching its claimed goal, justifying as such the continuous presence of the colonizer. It turns the colonized subject into a "subject of difference that is almost the same but not quite" (Bhabha, *Location* 122). Finding themselves midway on the social ladder, the Gaons attempt to overcome the disparity of the civilizing mission and guarantee their transformation to colonial elite by seeking the expertise of domestic help. During her trip to London, Alice, Rachel's mother, decides to hire a nanny. The following debate takes place between Rachel's parents:

> "I'll need someone then to help me with Rachel."
>
> "But why not an Italian nursemaid?" David suggested. "It's an English woman, criticizing, looking down on us, drawing the child away. I don't care for . . . " he said lamely, and appealed to Moses, who shook his head.
>
> Alice argued heatedly. "The children who have English nurses won't play with those who don't, and the English nurses won't even talk to Italian nursemaids. They aren't admitted to the same playgrounds either. It just isn't fair to the child. We must think of her future and give her the best advantages . . . "
>
> "Rather." Moses stopped his brother's protest. "Our Children must become European, civilized. It's their only way to defend themselves in the modern world. Look at Samuel's daughter. She is marrying into one of the best families in Cairo . . . Dinah has manners and that makes the difference." (116)[29]

By bringing to light Alice's words, the novel offers insight into the fine lines of the colonial legal system hinging on the control of minorities shaped by emporialism. On first glance, in contrast to the "natives," the protégés of the

British Empire seem to enjoy a distinct social and legal status in Egypt. Yet these minorities are also subject to a minute hierarchy and classification, which regulates their privileges, including their spatial and social movement. Kahanoff's text records a colonial dynamics and pressure of intersectional slippage and erasure, which relies not solely on consumerism but also on the racialization of labor relations, especially that of domestic servants. The intersectional slippage carries out a process of ethno-classism, a situation where ethnicity comes to embody class, in contrast to a situation where ethnicity and class would be perceived as two distinct and independent social relations.

Typically, ethno-classism constructs an imagined universal hierarchy of race and class, with European bourgeoisie, whiteness, and cosmopolitanism at the high end of the social and ethnic ladder and working-class colonial subjects at the bottom.[30] In the novel, Alice refers to Ḥārat el-Yahūd, the Jewish quarter, as a dreaded Oriental space, whose residents mark the fate of Gaon were they not to acquire European cultural capital through colonial education: "Did we give our girls a good schooling for them to live like Hara Jews?" (211). The memory of the Jewish quarter is brought forth as a typical Orientalist landscape: "Alice shuddered recalling those who have come to be interviewed, gaunt, haggard women, their eyes blurred by ophthalmia" (78). Jews from the Hara mark a regression on the colonial social ladder, a situation that is closer to the faceless "natives." Unlike the British-style neighborhood of Garden City, where Alice resides, or even the traditional affluent Arab Abbasiyya quarter where Jacob lives, Jews from *al-Hara*, transliterated in Arabic in the text, embodies the phantasmatic threat of becoming Arabized (Abu-Lughod 142). To return to Harat al-Yahud is a reminder of Nathan Smadja's beginning as a poor peddler: a native, an Oriental expunged from the colonial social map, if not from history itself. The contrast between the two positions is startling, between the imaginary confines of Harat al-Yahud rendered monolithic and monolingual through its Arabic transliteration, and the rich cosmopolitan suburb of Garden City. In reality, unlike the image suggested by the novel, Harat al-Yahud harbored a diverse poor cosmopolitan community with different social, cultural, and religious backgrounds, including Egyptian Muslims and Mizrahi and Ashkenazi Jews.[31]

Notably, the ethno-class hierarchy of empire comprises several minute classifications for Europeans and other colonial subjects. In the Gaons' cosmopolitan context, the Mediterranean Greek and Italian nursemaids from Orientalized parts of Europe—in contrast to English ones—cannot guarantee the family's social ascension and prestige in a British colonial context. This passage exposes another ethno-classist ghostly phenomenon, "Aleksandrism," underscoring the glamorous image of cosmopolitan Levantinism. Most likely, by "Italian nursemaid," Alice means a Slovenian woman from Trieste or its rural surroundings, who were frequently hired by affluent families in Egypt. As Biancani points out, Slovenian domestics migrating to Egypt (called in Slovenian *Aleksandrinke*) played a role in crystallizing the image of the bourgeois cosmopolitanism in Egypt, a phenomenon that came to be known in Slovenian cultural memory as Aleksandrism. The representation of these Slovenian governesses veered between Orientalism and Europeanness (Biancani, "Gender" 713).[32] Most likely, for this reason, Rachel's mother insists on hiring an English governess who could project a European image devoid of any Orientalist traces.

Rachel's mother's words reflect the changing optics of visibility in the Cairene cityscape, marking a parallel shift in codes of status along racial and gender lines. In the actual historical context of the city, among upper-class Muslim families, eunuchs ceded their role to old maids, who were then supplanted by European governesses (Hamamsy 142; Pollard 44). The European governess served as a shared visible capital that taped together the fragmented image of a diverse elite who embraced the worldview of British imperialism. In her account of interwar Egypt, Chafika Hamamsy suggests that this new social code relied on symbiotic intersectional exchange: governesses gained status by carefully selecting highly ranked families who, in their turn, consolidated their prestige by hiring them (146). As Rachel's mother indicates, the mere presence of an English nursemaid has the potential of transforming her daughter's status, since she would give her access to certain public places designated for English citizens. Like the *grand magasin* whose glass barriers keep the "unwanted" native beggars and peddlers away, the city space is also subject to a more intricate colonial system dividing the elite Levantine community into even smaller subgroups and controlling their mobility according to ethnicity and economic status. The Azbakiyya garden, where Rachel and her brother go to play, turns into a colonial grid divided along lines of race and ethnicity. The segregated children's playground becomes a microcosm, or an incubator, in which the colonizer shapes the habitus of the different minorities and consolidates them into distinct groups and races. The *grand magasin*, despite its restrictions, forges a relatively fluid culture different from that of the colonizer's, since its main criterion of discrimination is wealth.[33]

The Gaons' conversation reveals the key role that domestic help plays in the civilizing mission. Governesses embody the colonizer in the intimate space of the household. David's protests expose the colonial aspect of hiring an English nanny and its direct influence in instituting the rigid dichotomy between colonizer and colonized, Western and "Oriental." Positioned inside the house, the governess becomes the colonial agent that places the colonized Orientals under her constant gaze and marks their "need" for "corrective study by the West," creating the traumatic "inferiority complex" or splitting of consciousness (Said, *Orientalism* 41; Fanon, *Black Skin* 7–8).

From a sociological perspective, the governess assists the schooling system and the household in creating the distinct reified image of the bourgeoisie. Pierre Bourdieu posits that "the ideology of natural taste contrasts . . . two modes of acquisition of culture": one that is produced at an early stage of life and accompanied by a schooling system and a "belated" one that communicates the knowledge of manner and taste but does not allow its complete internalization by the subject. The former "confers the self-certainty which accompanies the certainty of possessing legitimacy, and the ease of which is the touchstone of excellence; it produces the paradoxical relationship to culture made up of self-confidence amid (relative) ignorance and of casualness amid familiarity, which bourgeois families hand down to their offspring as if it were an heirloom" (Bourdieu, *Distinction* 66). Being a part of an ascending social class, Alice and David do not have a strong enough knowledge of British culture to be able to transfer it comfortably to their daughter. The nursemaid then would substitute for the parent and transmit a ghostly, English bourgeois "heirloom" that could distinguish Rachel from the rest of her original society. By hiring a British nursemaid, Alice Gaon takes control of her children's education to ensure that the colonial civilizing mission reaches its presumed goal of transforming her children into Europeans.

Rachel's mother crosses class boundaries and turns colonialism against itself. Alice consciously chooses a British nanny as her substitute. By incorporating a British woman in the household, she takes control of the imperial optics of visibility relying on the minute classification of race, class, and gender, wherein the British nanny is showcased or window displayed as part of the bourgeois family cultural capital. Alice occupies a double position: one of ultimate powerlessness, since she decides to give her agency as a mother to the nursemaid, but also a position of control vis-à-vis the colonial civilizing mission as the employer of her colonizer. Growing up with the nursemaid corresponds to Ann McClintock's claim:

> In a very real sense, these children grew up with two (or more) mothers, whom they learned to distinguish by learning the social scripts of class difference, the meaning of uniforms, curtseys and bows, the rituals of recognition and deference that separated the two most powerful figures in the child's life. The contradictions were sharp ... On the one hand, the Nanny's power was absolute. On the other hand, she could be rebuked, demeaned or dismissed at a word from the mistress. (*Imperial Leather* 86)

As Rachel internalizes colonial values and language through the help of her nursemaid, she can stand out as the modern European civilized subject amid the "natives" and the rest of the Levantine community. However, for Rachel, the governess's presence reveals a more complex connotation than the simple blurring of lines between authenticity and mimicry across race and class. Moses, Rachel's uncle, affirms that having a nanny is a significant investment, since it can help Rachel marry into the "best families." The nanny plays an essential role in instituting and internalizing colonial and gender performance, a combination that can turn Rachel into a profitable piece of economic capital for the family and hence be of a great advantage to consolidate the family's social and financial situation in Egypt.

A rich colonial subject, Rachel's mother uses the resources available to turn the colonial model upside down and fulfill her social ambitions. The paradoxical effort to hire an English nanny to reach the aspired objective of the civilizing mission recalls Stoler and Cooper's analysis of the tension between discipline and desire in colonial relations: "The ambiguous lines that divided engagement from appropriation, deflection from denial, and desire from discipline not only confounded the colonial encounter, it [*sic*] positioned the contestation over the very categories of ruler and ruled at the heart of colonial politics" (Stoler and Cooper, "Between" 6). The nanny serves as a self-imposed, financially rewarded, panoptic eye that operates by "distributing individuals, fixing them in space, classifying them ... training their bodies, coding their behavior [and] maintaining them in perfect visibility" (Foucault, *Discipline and Punish* 231). She embodies the quintessential Foucauldian nightmare of biopolitics.

The story takes an ironic turn when Rachel's parents realize that Miss O'Brien, the nanny they hired, is actually Irish, and that her connection to English culture is thus colonial: the presence of a governess does not suffice to acquire British cultural capital. Ireland had fought a tumultuous war of independence ending in 1921, a period that overlaps with the historical time frame of Kahanoff's novel between the great wars. Miss O'Brien does not have perfect command or knowledge of aristocratic English cultural capital, nor its subculture of colonial etiquette sought by the Gaons. This incident reveals the family's weak grasp on Cairene cultural capital. In the actual historical context of colonial Egypt, most aristocratic families had already devised an intricate system of interviews to hire a governess (Hamamsy 146). Alice's ambition for social ascension pushes her to seek the help of a Sudanese servant who worked previously in British houses:

> Hassan, now secure in his position, introduced into this most un-English household all he had previously learned, with an enthusiasm, which might have been his way of catching up with years of restraint. He washed fruit in permanganate-tinted water, and had Anna sew squares of fine net, trimmed with green wooden beads, to cover the children's food and drink. They were copies of those bought by British officers at the supply centers in their camps and came to replace Miss O'Brien's more casual cheese-cloth.
> "He's far more meticulous than nanny," Alice remarked. (209)

Hassan, who occupies an inferior position on the colonial ladder, has the expertise that can perfect the colonial simulacrum. The family's contact with English society remains limited to social events, a situation that hinders the complete internalization of English etiquette. The presence of Hassan is crucial to the construction of the fantasy of the European bourgeoisie and its racial and class hierarchies. The Sudanese servant appears to be more English than the English; he executes English manners to the minutest details far better than the Irish nanny. Ironically, the fantasized English etiquette becomes a puzzle whose parts are pieced together by the various colonial subjects of the novel: Egyptians, Sudanese, and Irish. It is through the contribution of a Sudanese man and an Irish woman that the Gaons can move up the social ladder and, by extension, modify their image from faceless Orientals to bourgeois Europeans. Ironically, in their effort to create themselves as model colonial subjects, the Gaons also define and reaffirm what it is to be British middle class by following Hassan's exaggerated practice of English etiquette.

The Other Levantines

The presence of the "British" nanny heralds the end of Rachel's Levantine multicultural world. If the space of the *Hara* in the novel is constructed as a fictive monolithic poor Arab culture, the British nanny's upbringing leads to another restricted monolingual culture.

> She didn't go to see Nonino and the girls in his store, or to uncle Joseph's house on Saturday afternoons, or eat things good enough to give her indigestion. She didn't speak Arabic, Italian, or even French anymore, but only English, even with Papa and Mamma. She never did things that made her feel happy, only sometimes on Nanny's Day off, when she was left with her mother, she became again Caline, who spoke French. The other days were sad and ugly, like the old sewing basket in Nonina's house. (161)

Rachel's world is reduced to becoming a copy of the British middle class as she gains access to more places in colonial Cairo designated for British citizens. Walking in colonial Cairo with her nanny, wearing a white panama hat and a blue muslin veil, Rachel internalizes the British colonial consciousness, which constructs her as inferior and different. She suddenly identifies with a beggar:

> She caught sight of a band of beggars hardly older than herself, their bodies showing through torn rags, besieging passers-by, fighting among themselves in their hunt for cigarette butts, scattering quickly when a Shawish [police officer] descended upon them with a stick ... except for one who never ran away ... he stopped to see her go by, and smiled at her just as she smiled at him, a little bit only, from the corner of the eye. But now, with the blue veil, she could not even do that ... the little beggar was more handsome than her cousins Henry and Claud, with his flashing white teeth and black eyes, and far braver ... She loved him even more than Mamma, and she thought he loved her too ... She didn't want him to be locked up, because he was brown, as she was, and they were together against *shawishes* and pink people who spoke English ... Nonino and Aunt Rene's skins were fairer than Nanny's, but it wasn't the same thing, they must be brown inside, and she loved brown people, not the pink and pale ones. (167)

Strolling the streets of Cairo, Rachel begins to see the city and herself through a blue veil, which stands for the blue eyes of the colonizer, and adopts colonial binaries and hierarchies. Her realization recalls Frantz Fanon's *Black Skin, White Masks*, in which he describes the psychological divide in the colonized subject who perceives herself through the European

Other (9–11). The passage most likely alludes to W. E. B. Du Bois's renowned description of "double consciousness," or the alienation experienced by an individual of color who internalizes the dominant racist view of herself and begins to watch the world from the perspective of the marginalized, as if through "a vast veil" (38).[34] When Rachel, donning an English lens, recognizes herself in the image of a poor "brown" beggar, she also adopts an ethno-classist perspective that equates bourgeois with European and white, and native and local with other races and poverty. Following this logic, Egyptian identity becomes incongruous with material wealth, European education, and multiculturalism, since from a Eurocentric perspective to be an "authentic" native is tantamount to being poor and Oriental.

What remains untold in the story is that Rachel's alienation was not particular to the Jewish community or foreign residents. Rather, it was a question of class: precisely, a new bourgeoisie in the making, constituted of entrepreneurs, landlords, and former Ottoman elites.[35] In fact, what Rachel describes was a common situation for many Egyptian elites, regardless of their faith or cultural background. Chafika Hamamsy provides prolific details on the experience of her family members and her acquaintances growing up with foreign governesses. She calls this Egyptian generation "Europeans with Egyptians passports (141). In a sense, Rachel is caught in the same liminal position of many Egyptian children of that interwar generation who grew up after the fall of the Ottoman Empire. They witnessed a long-established Ottoman Egyptian tradition giving way to a Mediterranean/Levantine Egyptian context divided between nationalism and colonialism.[36]

At this point of the story, Rachel does not yet recognize the significance of her nanny being Irish. The nanny's origins add another layer of complexity, since Miss O'Brien is another subject of the British colonial mission: a subject whose representation in nineteenth-century British culture was constructed to resemble that of Africans from the colonies. The Irish were subjected to colonial mechanisms of control (McClintock, *Imperial Leather* 52). Rachel, however, perceives being British as a single category: that is, being white and Anglophone. This is another moment where Kahanoff subtly highlights the difference between the visible and invisible, between the performance—or the labeling—of a culture and the hidden distinctions that exist in the group embodying that culture.

Although Rachel internalizes British colonial racial categories, her previous experiences allow her to see a third perspective, invisible for the Eurocentric colonial Orientalizing lens that divides the population into natives and Europeans. She could clearly read the fine distinctions that make the social web of Levantine colonial culture. One of the most interesting moments of this passage is Rachel's realization that the Levant falls outside of the typical binary racial classifications. Instead, she identifies as "brown." Kahanoff's text was published in 1951, when that particular racial identification had not yet gained political and social traction. On their way back home from the British section in the park, Miss O'Brien is startled by Rachel's ability to read the Cairene cityscape distinctively: "'How do you know he's Syrian [a shopkeeper],' Miss O'Brien asked puzzled. Except for the lower-class Arabs, she could not tell people apart, and it had intrigued her not only that Rachel knew these things, but that there were so many shades of familiarity, respect, condescension, in her manner of saluting people in the street; more than once, when in her own unavoidable dealings with natives, servants and such, Rachel had acted as interpreter, she had instinctively modelled her conduct upon the child's" (168). Rachel gives Miss O'Brien a lesson in human geography as she introduces Egypt's Levantine commercial class: the Syrian, Greek, and Armenian shopkeepers whom Miss O'Brien could not differentiate. Miss O'Brien's consciousness thus awakens to discern the complex culture of Egypt beyond the distinctions of native/European and rich/poor, as she becomes the pupil and Rachel the teacher. Rachel's self-recognition as "brown" precedes a sequence of events that exposes the racial and class anxiety of a Levantine culture that has adopted the European bourgeoisie as its model. When Miss O'Brien comes to understand the makeup of Egyptian society, she helps Rachel reconnect with the multicultural domestic helpers who make up the other Levantine world found in the Gaon household, despite the disapproval of Rachel's mother:

> "Where's Rachel?" "I sent her to the kitchen on an errand, Mrs. Gaon." Alice frowned. "You could ring for Mahmoud to come." "I know, but she so enjoys looking about in the kitchen. And it would be a pity if she forgot Arabic and Italian, it's so lovely that she can speak them! Those are the people she's always known and will always live with, and I think she misses them." Alice's frown deepened, and she sounded displeased. "I want Rachel to speak English without a trace of an Egyptian accent, without Arabic words creeping in." (170)

Seeing Rachel's attachment to her Levantine world, Miss O'Brien starts to appreciate the value of that cosmopolitan milieu. She allows her more freedom in speaking other languages and communicating with the domestics.

In her attempt to restrict Rachel's milieu, Alice Gaon tries to create a rigid spatial control of the household, between the servants' Levantine kitchen and the masters' quarters. Alice seeks to sever the connection between her emerging bourgeois family and the working class, that other Levantine life that exists in the household and reflects a threat to the family's social ascension since it is contaminated by Arabic culture.

By using a bell to communicate with her servants, Alice silences Levantine polyglossia and reduces it to the monotone sound of the bell. This cold metallic sound connecting the kitchen and the salon alerts the reader to the fact that Levantine culture, unlike its elitist reputation, actually exists in many contexts not necessarily related to the upper classes. The workers hidden in the kitchen, Maria and Donia the Italian and Lebanese maids, and Hassan the Sudanese servant also construct another version of Levantine culture beyond the grasp of their employers.

The novel stresses the competition between these Levantine, socially divided, worlds. Rachel's family decides to hire a poor Syrian wet nurse for her newborn brother: "she is a Syrian Christian, a pearl of a woman, clean, strong, healthy, honest. Her milk is good ... it would revive a corpse!" (180). Rachel is fascinated by this new mother, who stands in contrast to the British governess, and she grows attached to her:

> Amina ... reminded her of the pictures of the Madonna ... it was while the baby greedily clung to Amina's big breast that arrangements were made.
>
> "What will you do with your own child?" Alice nervously asked her.
>
> "I'll leave him with my cousin. We gave birth at the same time," she spoke quietly, "But could I go home once a week to see my husband and my son?" (181)

Amina, who dedicates herself to feeding Rachel's brother, loses her own child to malnutrition. The text suggests that the interdependence of both Levantine worlds is almost parasitic, where the elite Levantine class feeds on its working-class other. At the same time, that working-class Levantine Other is caught between intimacy and Otherness. Rachel and her brother, as upper-middle-class colonial cosmopolitan children from Egypt, have several competing mothers: the Francophone Tunisian Egyptian mother, the British nanny, and the Syrian wet nurse, from which, to borrow McClintock's words, "they learned to distinguish ... the social scripts of class difference" (*Imperial Leather* 86). Each mother has her own geographic, linguistic, class, ethnic, and religious affiliations that mediate between the children and their surroundings.[37]

The racial and class anxiety reaches its height when Alice discovers that Donia, the Lebanese Christian maid, is in love with Hassan, the Muslim, "black Sudanese servant" (383). Hassan and Donia elope and take Donia's daughter, Angèle, with them. Rachel's family experiences a great shock:

> Donia and Hassan said they were leaving and getting married, and that she had become Muslim. The little girl [Angèle] cried, and her mother slapped her face ... Hassan tried to console the child, and promised she would still go to [her French] school and be a Frankish lady. Then Donia was angry and said, "No, she won't go back to school. If I'm good enough to live with a Sudanese, so is Angèle" .... Mother [Alice] cried, "if only I had listened when you said that I was all Angèle had in the world! None of this would have happened." (399)

The passage cleverly exposes the convoluted and intertwined roots of emporialism and Levantinism. Donia's Francophone daughter, Angèle, "who was practically brought up" with Rachel, serves as another cultural double for the protagonist. For Alice, Hassan's and Donia's marriage embodies many taboos at once; it is a relationship that transgresses the colonial hierarchy of religion and culture. Angèle follows the opposite trajectory of Rachel's. While Angèle begins her life as a Levantine Francophone girl, she descends the social ladder as her mother marries a Sudanese Muslim. From a Eurocentric perspective, Levantinism stands for a temporary stage in the dynamics of emporialism and its civilizing mission: a transitional phase in which the modern colonial subject gradually sheds a Middle Eastern heritage toward adopting an idealized, homogeneous European lifestyle. Angèle, on the other hand, represents the dreaded outcome of Levantinism. While Angèle moves closer to a dismissed African, Arab, and Muslim culture, Rachel follows the British colonial trajectory, which seeks to conform to a British middle-class ethos. If, according to the famous anecdote of Khedive Ismail, the construction of the Suez Canal distanced Egypt from Africa and made it part of Europe, Donia and Angèle, who quits her French school, stand for the reversal of the French Mediterranean project:

a dreaded outcome in which Egypt has turned its back to the Mediterranean shore to anchor itself in African soil.[38] Donia embraces a cultural and racial "hybridity" that rejects European values and adopts a cultural form that cannot be considered cosmopolitan, since it detaches itself from the Eurocentric paradigm.

Recording the Lost Time: Another Scheherazade, Another Saint-Simon

In the third part of the book, titled "The Invader," Rachel's mother hires an "authentic" English governess. In her attempt to perfect her children's British education and purge it of Arabic traces, Alice hires another nanny after the departure of Miss O'Brien. This time, Alice ensures that the new hire, Miss Nutting, is English. Miss Nutting's draconian measures and racist views sharpen Rachel's double consciousness and ambivalence toward her heritage and colonialism: "Bound together by the violent emotions they had awakened in each other, Miss Nutting and Rachel became the protagonists of a relentless, underhand struggle, where each symbolized to the other evil herself, which must be uprooted and destroyed" (324). As her resentment escalates, Rachel falls ill and for the first time, her father, sitting by her bed, narrates her grandfather Jacob Gaon's journey through the desert in a caravan from Baghdad to Cairo. On the same occasion, she reads her great-grandmother's letters from Tunisia, written in a hybrid of French and Arabic transliterated in the French alphabet. The letters could only be deciphered when read aloud. Both narratives—the letters of Mama Zeiza, the crude Arab Jewish woman from al-Hara,[39] and the story of Jacob Gaon—exist in the margins of history and can only be transmitted as part of oral tradition, a lost heritage, threatened by the French and British colonial project:

> In the evenings, the story cycle continued, with David telling his daughter stories about the Gaons and Baghdad. He passed abruptly from those about the family to those of the great days of Baghdad Jewry under the rule of the Great Caliphs.... Her father's learning, Rachel discovered, was not the kind she could acquire at the *Lycée Français,* for the little she knew of Eastern history had come to her in a back-handed way, only in so far as it concerned the Crusades.

> Through all her father narrated, an oral tradition was handed down to Rachel, as of old. . . . She knew the name "Gaon" was handed down from those who had founded in Baghdad the university to which Jews from all over the Diaspora came to receive instruction. . . . At school, she had been taught to say, "*Nos ancêtres les Gaulois*," and had had doubts about her ancestors because they were not Gauls. Now she knew she would rather be a Gaon than a Gaul. (348–49)

This passage recalls Proust's conclusion of his novel *In Search of Lost Time*, when the narrator compares Paris, full of "Levantines" and Africans during World War I, to Baghdad of the same epoch from the *Thousand and One Nights*. He decides to embody a Levantine hybrid French Arab persona, that of Scheherazade and French historian Saint-Simon, to write the history of his epoch.[40] Shifting between history and myth, between poetry and storytelling, Scheherazade-like, Rachel's father creates a semi-fantastic narrative of origin by retelling the memoirs of his father and ancestors. This alternative imaginary allows her to anchor herself in an anticolonial history in which she could perceive herself as Jewish and Middle Eastern. After she recovers from her illness, Rachel decides to force Miss Nutting to leave.

During one of her confrontations with Miss Nutting, Rachel sees some "street rioters" and joins them in chanting "Egypt for the Egyptians" (364). She finally slaps the nanny on her face and forces her to quit (366). By using the word *invader* to refer to the arrival of the new nanny, and by synchronizing Rachel's confrontation with her with a public condemnation of the British occupation, the text clearly parallels her action with the Egyptian nationalist project. On the surface, the scene reads as a rebellious gesture made by a colonial subject seeking to reclaim a national identity. But by identifying momentarily as Egyptian, Rachel actually seeks to resolve a colonial dilemma—the mutual exclusivity of European modernity and national belonging to Egypt. In addition, she tries to come to terms with the "effendification" of Egyptian culture, described by Miccoli as "the social and historical process leading to the creation of a new national middle class, whose identity was rooted in the figure of the Egyptian peasants, 'repositories of eternal truths'" (Miccoli 70). This ethno-classist representation divides the population into Europeans and Levantine subjects on one hand, and Orientalized natives on the other hand: A binary that casts Egyptians who possess European education as outsiders.

The Department Store as a Mirror to the Self

In this context, expelling the British nanny expresses the awakening of a colonial subject who seeks to reclaim her history and space. It is only at that moment that Rachel views her grandparents' "French" department store as a bazaar: "Back in Cairo, if ever she went to Smadja Brothers, a run-down store with the air of a bazaar, she wondered how, in the old days, marching down the creaking aisles with her grandfather, she had believed this was the grandest place on earth. Well, she thought disdainfully, she had grown up now, and lost all her silly illusions" (394). Rachel finally manages to resist her British nanny's orders and prejudices against Middle Eastern culture. As she learns to differentiate between the Gaons and the Gauls, she begins to see Smadja Brothers differently. The utopian store changes its appearance before her eyes and becomes an Oriental space onto which she projects her new self-perception (394).[41] She also accepts that as a subject of the colonial "civilizing mission," she remains "Oriental," despite her European cosmopolitan education. Unlike the cosmopolitan department store, the bazaar is endowed with a geographical and cultural origin and connects to a local imaginary and history. Most important, seeing the bazaar beneath the department store's façade highlights her recognition of the double nature of the Levantine world combining East and West. This realization is not without ambivalence, since Rachel's account of "the run-down bazaar" is rather pejorative and marks her disillusionment with her recent self-discovery.

Next Year Not in Jerusalem

The hidden nature of the department store comes with more disillusionment than just disappointment in the European colonial promise. Synchronizing with the new realization, the novel also presents an ambivalent stand toward Zionism. The work begins with the framing of the biblical and the British imperial commitment to the founding of a Jewish state in Palestine, by depicting Jacob Gaon, the patriarch, sitting in front of the Ten Commandments and the Balfour Declaration. Throughout the story, Rachel and her brother save money for the future nation. As Jacob grows old, he decides to move to Jerusalem to die and be buried in the Holy Land:

David [Jacob's son] too had reasons for gloom. He had returned from Jerusalem appalled by the squalor of the Jewish quarter in the old city... He [Jacob] wrote asking me to bring him back to Cairo, but of course, these people [Jacob's relatives in Jerusalem] did not send the letter... what will and courage he has! He clung to life, so that his death would not be sullied by such indignities. And those people dare call themselves religious, because they live in Jerusalem... How shameful! How revolting!... Your grandfather, old as Methuselah, dashing off to die in Jerusalem... I [Alice] was sure no good could come out of it. (417)

Jerusalem comes to represent another nightmare for the family. Unlike cosmopolitan Cairo and Alexandria, the city turns out to be a stereotypical Oriental town rather than a utopia. After traveling to Jerusalem, Jacob feels betrayed by his religious relatives and decides to return to Egypt. His life takes a comic and anti-Zionist turn: contradictory to the biblical Exodus, modern Jacob rejects Palestine and goes back to Cairo! Just as the Hebrews, wandering in the desert, regretted leaving Egypt and aspired to return to the comfort of their old life, Jacob actually turns back and settles in Egypt.

Rearranging the World Order

Kahanoff concludes her novel in Rachel's house with the Gaons and the Smadjas celebrating Passover. Alice, struggles to set the table the proper way for that big event. Only Ahmed, Jacob's servant, knows the fine details of this ceremony. Rachel rebukes him for not cooperating with her mother and showing her the proper way to set the table. Ahmed finally agrees to help: "Rachel assisted Ahmed in preparing all the things necessary for the prayer and setting them as they should be. Thus, she learned from the old Moslem all that she as a Jewish woman needed to know" (424).

The Hebrew word *le-seder* (לסדר), which shares etymological roots with the Hebrew words for order, arrangement, regulation, annals, and history, gives insight into the broader meaning of that scene. Setting the table for the Seder stands for putting things in order (Klein 435–36). By concluding with a ceremony that unites the Gaons, the Smadjas, and the domestics, Kahanoff rewrites the history of Egyptian Jews in Egypt according to her own perspective and narrative temporal sequence. In the scene, everything returns to a new order. The family is united. Rachel reconnects with her Jewish heritage, and the Moslem servant, who teaches her the rites of her religion, vows to obey her and send his sons to serve in her house. If symbolically the Gaons stand for a mythical history of Rachel's family and the Smadjas for quotidian history, the table, which reunites the families, resolves the tension between the biblical narrative of Exodus and the quotidian situation of modern Jews in Egypt. Rachel's family reconnects with their Jewish heritage while still being cosmopolitan. They accept their life as Jews living in Egypt after Exodus. In other words, they now live under a Levantine order of things. They mirror the social structure in the grandparents' emporium: precisely a situation where all cultures are mixed. Rachel's English education was transmitted by an Irish nanny, and the table for the Seder is set by a Moslem servant.

Similarly, Jacob Gaon, who returned from Palestine to live in Egypt, is not out of place. The empty seat left as a part of the ritual, symbolizing the wait for the unannounced visitor, Elijah the Prophet, reconstructs the family as both guests and hosts, in the double Derridean sense of hospitality (Derrida and Dufourmantelle 17–28). Hosting a guest stands for a performative act that claims one's ownership of a house. Ahmed says to Rachel: "When you marry . . . I shall send you for servant a son of our house" (424). It might not have been unusual that servants have their own children and relatives hired by the same employers. However, this thorny class- and race-loaded statement brings to the forefront the staunch legacy of an imperial culture, from which Levantinism seeks to detach itself.

Conclusion

In its attempt to narrate her childhood experience, Kahanoff's novel deconstructs the rhetoric of emporialism and its complex ethno-classist promise of social ascension. Her narrative travels between two symbolic spaces making up the Levantine habitus: the household and the department store. She creates a house of mirrors, in which each character finds foils in a series of competing and complementing Others. As they follow the colonial promise of social ascension and financial progress, Jacob, Alice, Nathan, and Rachel catch their own reflections in many parts of the city and in the image of workers, servants, nannies, and beggars. Each character—Ahmed, Miss O'Brien, Angèle—represents an erased history, a future aspiration, or a feared outcome. Using the department store/house as a model, the novel manages to register the hidden processes through which colonial culture is created and negotiated. In turn, the novel reveals the colonial mechanisms that seek to consolidate different minorities into distinct races: Arab and Jew, bourgeois and working class, European, cosmopolitan, and Levantine. For Kahanoff, Smadja Brothers represents the intersection of many histories and cultures—a Levantine world that exceeds a Eurocentric cosmopolitanism. But even Levantinism, that East-West amalgam, features as a game of doubles divided between the bourgeoisie and the working class. The atelier's workers and the domestic servants often relegated to the background have constructed their own Levantine life that does not necessarily conform to a bourgeois paradigm. The clear contribution of servants and governesses in reshaping the culture of the Egyptian middle class demonstrates the fragility of the aforementioned categories, since the same markers of distinction adopted by the Levantine colonial bourgeoisie depend on the presence of servants who share their knowledge and navigate the spaces that their masters could not reach.

Kahanoff reclaims Levantinism as a way to distinguish and separate an Egyptian urban lifestyle from a strictly Eurocentric vision of cosmopolitanism. The novel brings out the distinction between the shining cosmopolitan lure of emporialism, akin to the golden letters displayed on the emporium's labels, and the actual life of the community that has adapted this notion creatively to suit their own circumstances. A life that is distinct from their past but also different from a romanticized European utopian image. From an imperialist perspective, Levantinism is a transitional stage, a failure of the civilizing mission, born under the auspices of emporialism and its convoluted hierarchy of class, race, ethnicity, faith, and gender. Levantinism bears the traces of a Eurocentric colonial system of race and class, frequently amplified and exploited by emporialism. In contrast, for Kahanoff, Levantinism as culture is an end in itself: a lifestyle that intentionally keeps its Eastern Mediterranean and Middle Eastern roots. Kahanoff's novel, however, reveals that Levantinism comes at the expense of alienation and a traumatic disconnection from one's origins and culture. Despite its classist and colonial influences that still exclude some groups, this Levantinism points toward a different social order outside the path traced by the colonizer: a lifestyle that could only be perpetuated by the crisscrossing of religions, classes, and cultures and the acknowledgment of the parallel and interconnected histories of the many groups that make up the Levantine world. Through this Levantine interdependence, the various coexisting groups could survive and reconnect with part of their lost heritage and history and redraw the contours of post–World War II Egyptian nationalism.

Five years after the publication of her novel, Kahanoff had to confront once more the question of national belonging and integration, this time as a Mizrahi woman in Israel under the pressure of Zionism. There she retells the story of Levantinism in Egypt. Once more, emporialism acquires a new meaning in a different context, as the next chapter shows.

Figure 6.1. Advertisement, Chemla Frères, *L'Egyptienne*, February 1927. *Source*: Centre d'Etudes Alexandrines. Public domain. Used with permission.

Figure 6.2. Façade Bazar Hotel de Ville Paris, 2022. *Source*: Photo by author.

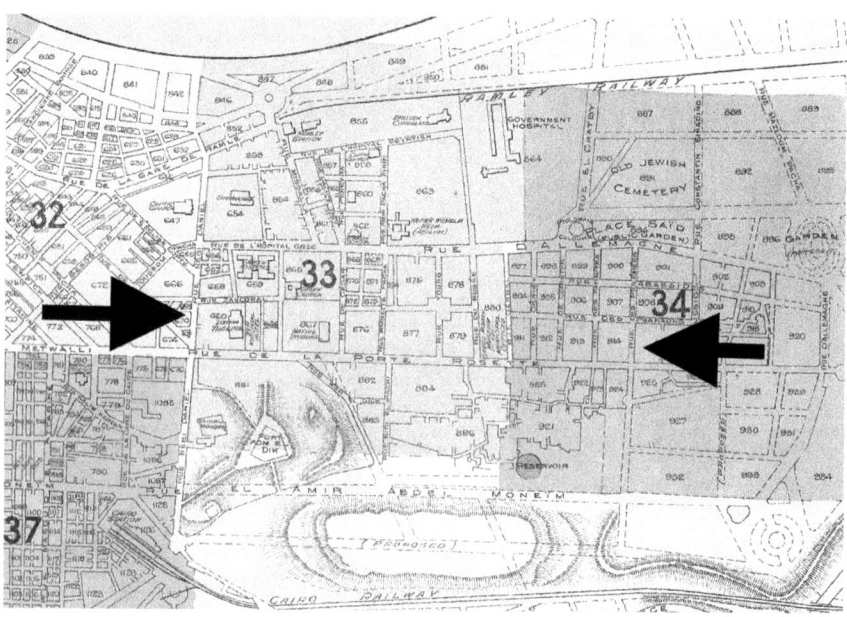

Figure 6.3. Map of Alexandria, 1905. Left arrow: Nebi Daniel Street; right arrow: Ptolemies Street. *Source*: Harvard University. Public domain.

Chapter 6

Neo-Emporialism and the Politics of Memory

In 2011, the Egyptian government began the renovation of Sednaoui al-Khazindar department store. Often depicted as Egypt's Galeries Lafayette, Sednaoui acquired a nostalgic aura, referring to an unrecoverable history and geography: a colonial past, a time when Cairo's cityscape overlapped with that of Paris (refer to figs 2.3 and 2.4) (see Elkadi and Kerdany; Moustapha; Myntti; Raafat, *Cairo* and *Maadi*; Rafik; Volait, "Reclaiming" and *Le Caire-Alexandrie*). Similarly, in 2020, the French government finished a ten-year restoration project of La Samaritaine (see Dicharry). Both restorations were part of "heritage (re)making," a return to a *belle époque*—a bygone golden era—colonial Cairo and Paris of the Second Empire–Third Republic, respectively. The stores were not meant to be transformed into museums. They resumed their function as marketplaces, adding nostalgia as another exchange value to the displayed merchandise.

What makes the emporium a global site of nostalgia after the end of empire? In this chapter, I focus on emporialism and nostalgia as a narrative framework for collective memory across political regimes. Through a survey of writings spanning from post–World War II to present day, I hope to illuminate how nostalgia for the emporium, under the banner of the return to a golden age or the *belle époque*, serves as a platform for re-evaluating history and social belonging. In the following context, longing for a past era and its regime of values is expressed through the nostalgia for the emporium, whose phantasmatic map converges many spaces and histories. In their reconstruction of the emporium, these authors re-create home and homeland, while inevitably summoning the ghost of empire. In the Egyptian and French contexts, what came to be called the *belle époque* marked a time fraught with struggles and tensions, defeat, and occupation, leading one to question, as Vanessa Schwartz insightfully does, whether it was indeed a "belle," or a "beleaguered," epoch to which the writers seek to return (7).[1] One might ask even whose *belle époque* to begin with, or according to which bourgeoisie: the one that lived through that era, or another that emerged after its fall? To whom does this memory belong, and whose interests does it serve in later periods?

Emporial nostalgia has persistently occupied a unique position in cultural memory. Television shows spun around (or at least referencing) department stores are still produced globally. Christmas window displays in department stores, such as Macy's, Harrods, Galeries Lafayette, and El Corte Inglés or the perennially popular Macy's Thanksgiving Day parade are still popular attractions.[2] These rituals make the emporium, and by extension emporialism, a part of an invented tradition, always in the making. In contemporary literary and visual narratives, the reconstruction of a collective experience through department stores does not entail a detailed account of these spaces. Sometimes the name of a store as a reference stands out as a loaded signifier from which the reader can unpack its multilayered history. As Michel de Certeau puts it: "to walk is to lack a site. It is the indeterminate process of being both absent and in search of the proper, of one's own" (*Practice* 139). Similarly, to utter a name is to pronounce a lack. To write about a missing space implies an act of reappropriation. To be nostalgic—to express one's lack of home—is a manifold performative act. Paradoxically, by claiming the absence of home, one retrospectively creates and establishes a point of origin. Nostalgia, or homesickness, is a double enunciation that enables the individual to reconfigure and repossess the past and the present simultaneously.

In the texts I explore here, emporia appear as a fleeting reference, sometimes by name only. However, the act of naming summons the entangled history of emporialism from collective memory. Andreea Deciu Ritivoi suggests that nostalgia functions as a "type of autobiographical memory," a coping mechanism that distances the present in favor of a romanticized past (30). Similarly, the texts I examine are structured around an imaginary temporal caesura. They attempt to recuperate or reflect on a "lost" time, structured around a postcolonial or postmodern moment. They depict the emporium as the surviving ruins of fallen empires, even though most of these spaces are still operating. In this context, the lens of nostalgia overlaps with the vantage points of "postcolonialism" and "postmodernism," which, as fictive markers of time, indicate a symbolic crossing from one ideology to another, a change in the regimes of values, presaging the redefinition of collective identity and memory.

A closer inspection reveals that all the above terms—nostalgia, post-colonialism, and postmodernism—are sites of ambivalence. They denote at once a rupture and a strong fixation with a prior condition. Nostalgia, post-colonialism, and postmodernism have become the key words of a paradigm shift. They refer to an imaginary threshold that promises a separation from an earlier period haunting the psyches of the survivors. Conversely, they project a Janus-faced subjective position of someone "in between," straddling the line of before and after, and have come to look at a nebulous future through the lens of the past (Bhabha, *Location* 1–2). The three terms bear the burden of an epistemological crisis and an obsession with memory or, as Pierre Nora puts it, a "historiographical anxiety" produced by the heightened tension between the homogenizing hand of history and the multifaceted disruptive memories it seeks to control (10). For Nora, memory "remains in permanent evolution, open to the dialectic of remembering and forgetting of its successive deformations, vulnerable to manipulation and appropriation, susceptible to being long dormant and periodically revived" (8). Memory, as Nora suggests, is a vivid polymorphous category that changes continuously over time to serve different purposes and groups, whereas history is an impersonal narrative that tries to destroy it (9). This condition calls for the need for *lieux de mémoire*, or "material" sites that, because of their multifunctionality, could conserve the traces of the past while escaping the scrutiny of history. These sites, existing at the crucible between memory and history, provide a *mise en abyme* that allows for the reconstruction of collective memory and identity in a new sociocultural context (19–20).

For Nora, history is arguably an impersonal category against which he erects various romanticized sites of memory. As François Hartog suggests, Nora's *lieux de mémoire* function in a binary paradigm divided between past and present. There is "no question of a progressive time" (103). Yet history is a dynamic narrative: always evolving, producing new accounts, sometimes competing, or colluding with sites of memory. This historical narrative is informed by changing paradigms and regimes of values: political, academic, and social. The tension between the various paradigms shapes our perception of the past. In that context, I would like to draw attention to Thomas Dodman's phrase "historicity of nostalgia" (Dodman 10, 14; Hartog xv–xvii).[3] In so doing, I seek to highlight the underpinning regimes of values or the ideological and epistemological aspect of a constructed nostalgic narrative in circulation. National history is a good example of a discursive reordering of time that conforms to the edicts of a political power and the frontiers of a territory. By the same token, sites of memory and regimes of histories are "invented traditions," to borrow Eric Hobsbawm's words. "They are set of practices ... which imply continuity with ... a suitable historic past" (Hobsbawm and Ranger 1). If one aspect of a nationalist history, like that of the archive, gives the false impression of moving forward toward an "open future," concepts like "national heritage sites" or *lieux de mémoire* could serve as sites of contention and erasure of memory in that regime of historicity, with the potential of turning the gaze to a different present that does not fit the dominant narrative (Crownshaw 215–22; Hartog 115). Likewise, one can see the historicity of nostalgia at work in emporial nostalgia. Emporial nostalgia is a variegated discourse that operates on several scales, mirroring the history of empire but also reflecting and navigating various regimes of historicity made of temporal cesurae, moments of crises, momenta of nationalism, or hopes of diasporic returns. In the same way, the following texts designate the emporium as a site of nostalgia—a *lieu de mémoire*—to revisit, comply with, or contend with a regime of historicity (Hartog 120–43). Emporialism, in this case, serves as a rhetoric of *translatio imperii*, marking a regime change, or the supplantation of one empire by another (Hartog 13; 164).

Emporial Nostalgia or Translatio Imperii: Remembering a Mediterranean Belle Époque

Using emporialism as a guiding lens, Ilios Yannakakis gives an account of the cosmopolitan Mediterranean past of his city of birth:

> Mohammed Ali Square lights up other avenues in my memory. I remember the department stores over towards Saint Catherine's Square: Hannaux, Chalon, Sednaoui. The salesgirls were Jewish, Italian, Armenian, Greek, Maltese; some consigned to spinsterhood by meager dowries, others young and hopeful of the promised but ever postponed marriage. They all spoke French, the foundation of their polyglot world. They were the very image of their juniors, those pupils of the Christian schools whose studies scarcely reached the level of *certificat d'études*. They were part of Alexandria's European proletariat of diverse ethnic and religious backgrounds, who could take credit for having perpetuated the lingua franca—French—over generations. ("Farewell" 110)

In his portrait, the department store offers a microcosm of the city's human and cultural geography, all cemented together by Francophone culture. Yannakakis's descriptions bring to mind the old connection between the emporium and the theater. As the avenue lights up, the store transforms into a stage, a consumer utopia, not far from its Saint-Simonian antecedent, or the *tableau vivant* of the Universal Exhibition (see chapter 1). Once we tear through this nostalgic image, the French utopian veneer gives way to a much richer lifestyle that does not fit the imperial European purview of cosmopolitanism (see chapter 2; Delanty; Brown and Held). At the same time, this portrait of the emporium gives way to another set of possible underlying tensions. Yannakakis brings to the forefront the various middle agents, or intermediaries, whose lives relied on being caught in the machinery and dynamics of emporialism and who forged an unexpected social network born from the specific political circumstances in Egypt located at the interplay of three empires. The author mentions the diverse origins and cultures of the salesgirls: Greek, Italian, Maltese, and other residents who communicate via French, a foreign language that relates neither to their national backgrounds, nor to their English colonizer, nor to the Arab locale where they live. French education and the emporium were two of the few available channels to fulfill a dream of social mobility for the Alexandrian petty bourgeoisie, especially women. The text suggests that the now-romanticized bourgeois Francophone Alexandrian culture depended paradoxically on the aspirations and gendered labor of the marginal and the underprivileged: the members of the Alexandrian working class and lower middle class, many of whom migrated from poor cities around the Mediterranean. They forged their connection to French culture neither in their European countries of origin nor in France. For most of them, the access to Francophonie could have been only possible across the Mediterranean. Their view of France was primarily mediated and shaped by an Egyptian imaginary.

Framed as it is, as a reconstruction of time past, Yannakakis's narrative of the emporium foretells its conclusion. The readers understand that once the lights of the stores go out, the story will end. The faces of those who made Alexandrian cosmopolitanism possible will swiftly vanish, after being caught in between two political regimes. Arguably, as the emporium falls in the dark, so do the days of empire, which ushers into the postcolonial moment. The author's cosmography of Alexandrian department stores reflects that nationalist political shift. In his description, the writer mobilizes a selective map of Alexandria. He calls the square by an older name,

"Square Mohammed Ali," referring to the Albanian Ottoman founder of the last Egypto-Ottoman dynasty (1805–1953) and considered by many the patriarch and founder of modern Egypt. Throughout the years, the same square was given many names, such as "la Place des Consuls," and Manshiyya Square after independence. The site witnessed the Egyptian president Gamal Abdel Nasser's famous postindependence speech announcing the nationalization of the Suez Canal in 1956. This emblematic moment and its site mark the end of French and British control over the canal, inaugurated in 1869, and the departure of the author's own Greek Alexandrian community, as well as many other groups mentioned in the passage above. The space, with its multiple names, bears the colonial and postcolonial histories of Egypt and its Mediterranean connections. The author's depiction of the stores re-creates the history of Alexandria and the larger national territory. By returning to the department stores as a site of memory, Yannakakis's text draws a parallel between the end of emporialism and decolonization. The nationalization (sequestration) of department stores signals the decline of a cosmopolitan Franco-Mediterranean society, giving way to a nationalist Arab culture.

One can understand the significance of the utopian image shaped by emporialism for Yannakakis when, in a later essay in the same book, he describes his life after his migration to Czechoslovakia:

> In 1952, the ideological conference of the communist party of Czechoslovakia... announced a war without quarter against "cosmopolitanism" and "cosmopolitans." Fear grew and gripped all those who did not feel themselves to be "ethnically pure and culturally pure." Arrest followed arrest at a frantic pace. Kangaroo courts condemned dozens of "cosmopolitans" to death, "traitors" to their homeland, which was thus no longer theirs.... The "new order" orchestrated its auto da fé to the applause of the "new man."... In the middle of this torment, I went to earth. I changed my CV. I erased my "cosmopolitan" origins, my multiculturalism.... I "nationalised," "aryanised," "proletarianized" myself. There I was, metamorphosed into an "authentic" Greek, born by accident in Egypt to poverty-stricken parents. ("Death" 190)

Yannakakis's works are caught between various regimes of power and regimes of historicities, between the memory of Egyptian cosmopolitanism, Francophone culture on one side, and communism and national independence on the other. His emporial nostalgia lies at the crossroads of all these paradigms and experiences. For Yannakakis, the Eastern bloc features as a dystopian space, the opposite image of an Alexandrian cultural life mirrored by the emporium. In Czechoslovakia, he actively purges any traces of cosmopolitanism from his life. His new condition parallels that of the many middle agents and intermediaries he mentions in the earlier passage—the salesclerks and salesgirls whose lives gave emporialism its social and cultural materiality. He finds himself caught in the middle of contending ideologies that erase his former memories and experiences. The same cultural capital that once secured his status and in which he took pride becomes a source of disenfranchisement.

On the other side of the Mediterranean, almost a century earlier, French writer Émile Zola paints a similar portrait, as a part of a large-scale geohistorical memory project. In Zola's text, the stores represent a microcosm of the various members of French urban society during the Second Empire. In his cosmography of the Parisian department store, he portrays the *grand magasin* as an invasive, constantly expanding, "Oriental" space, akin to bazaars and harems: a site of excessive greed and decadence, at the heart of the French metropolis, foretelling the French defeat by the Prussians in 1870 and the annexation of Alsace-Lorraine (see chapter 3).

Each author re-creates the emporium to document the rise and fall of empire, along with its related values, and in both texts, emporialism represents a critical experience that redefines social and political relations. Whereas Zola reassesses the trauma of German occupation, Yannakakis retraces the end of British control (1882–1952) and the fall of the Egypto-Ottoman monarchy (1922–1953). In Czechoslovakia, Yannakakis's cosmopolitan Alexandrian background undergoes a symbolic "aryanization" in the name of ethnic and cultural purity. This term brings the specter of another regime: the Nazi invasion of Europe and its racial project during World War II. Conversely, it also underscores Alexandrian cosmopolitanism as diametrically opposite from European purity. Yannakakis's and Zola's accounts offer insight into the history of their respective nations, specifically of two eras that remarkably came to be dubbed by French and Egyptian bourgeoisie the Belle Époque. The authors remember their nation's history through the lens of emporialism. Seen separately, Zola's and Yannakakis's texts could be considered accounts and critiques of France's and Egypt's histories. Read together, these works give insight into the cultural memory of the larger Mediterranean. The authors' portraits of the emporium rely on the association of their respective stores with the opposite shore of the Mediterranean. Whereas Yannakakis's Alexandrian department stores mirror an exogenous French culture, Zola's Parisian counterpart evoke an exotic Orient. Such trends are still operative in the contemporary culture of emporia.

In 2022, Parisian department store Bazar de l'Hotel de Ville set up its seasonal promotional campaign revolving around Indonesian culture (fig. 6.2). Akin to the pavilions of the Universal Exhibition or Zola's Oriental salon, the display windows showcased a set of Indonesian artifacts. Whereas the store's main door was adorned with a caricatural image of an Indonesian dancer, the main promotional poster showed a blonde European woman dressed in a beach dress made from a sarong fabric, holding an Asian mask. The poster reiterates the temporal fantasy of the masquerade, hinging on the bygone dreams of empire, of becoming and acquiring the Other (see chapter 1).

By reconstructing these allotopic Mediterranean geographies, that is, the Mediterranean of the other shore, Yannakakis and Zola use the emporium as a space that is other, or a "heterotopia," to borrow Michel Foucault's term. For Foucault, heterotopias are "counter-sites" whose significance is based on their juxtaposition with the surroundings. While utopias are non-sites, heterotopias provide a "mixed" experience between the imaginary and the real (Foucault and Miskowiec 24). Heterotopias are "capable of juxtaposing in a single real place, several sites that are in themselves incompatible" (25). As differential spaces, they function as rich sites of memory, open for a multiplicity of interpretations. Nora points out that the rich significance of a *lieu de mémoire* stems from its ambiguity as "a site of excess" that doggedly refuses to vanish, enabling different communities to mobilize the different meanings and histories related to these sites (24). Reflecting and refracting a variegated image of empire, the nation, the city, the household, and even the body, emporialism turns the department store into a *lieu de mémoire*, a multivalent "enunciatory" site that opens up possibilities for other "times of cultural meaning . . . and other narrative spaces" (Bhabha, *Location* 255).

Heterotopias are strategic spaces that mold the social experience. They function through a mechanism of inclusion and exclusion (Foucault and Miskowiec 26). To inhabit a heterotopia is to be part of a collective that understands how to decipher its history and practice of space. In his study of collective memory, James Wertsch argues that "remembering is a form of mediated action, which entails the involvement of active agents and cultural tools" (13). This becomes possible, as Maurice Halbwachs suggests, when individuals act and respond to the sociocultural and political "framework" of their social milieu (Halbwachs 51). He adds, "a recollection is the richer when it reappears at the junction of a greater number of these frameworks, which in effect intersect each other and overlap in part" (172). Such a quality enables those who are reconstructing their memories to use heterotopia as a juncture between competing social frameworks and a point of departure for developing a "dialogical" narrative that engages and critiques other narratives (Wertsch 58). From the kaleidoscopic heterotopia of the emporium, then, springs a proliferation of collective narratives that share the experience of inhabiting or interacting with the site, but each account responds to a different sociocultural and political framework and recalls a different ideology. The practice of space, that is, heterotopic space, strategically consolidates memory into a "usable past" that can help root the collective to their current social milieu (Wertsch 31).

Above all, the re-creation of heterotopias in literature and visual culture charts new paths for remembering and dismembering the past, opening up to different possibilities of belonging. As Michael Rothberg posits, the varied media representations of sites of memory develop into a "rhizomatic" multidirectional memory formation, leading to unexpected alliances and connections. Memory of the emporium-heterotopia, then, develops more like a *"noeud de mémoire*, that is a 'knot' or a 'node of memory,' shaped and reshaped by a web of 'rhizomatic' connections extended amid diverse elements." In that sense, memory of the emporium "emerges from unexpected, multidirectional encounters—encounters between diverse pasts and a conflictual present ... between different agents or catalysts of memory" (Rothberg 9).

Such memory, however, is from the onset multilayered and multiple, relying on the imaginary of other stories and sites, as the previous chapters have shown. Astrid Erll argues that the representation of an earlier event provides a narrative structure, namely, "schemata," for subsequent experiences and their representations. In its visual or literary afterlives, the memory of the emporium refers "not so much to what one might cautiously call the 'actual event' but instead to a canon of existent medial constructions, to the narratives, images and myths circulating in a memory culture" (Erll 110–11; see Rigney). As a site of memory, the emporium is "remediated" or re-created across time to serve as an underpinning narrative structure for other memories. In this context, emporialism functions as a memory schema enabling the construction of further narratives and mythologies around the emporium, as the following examples will show.

Emporialism: An Embattled National Territory

As an iconographic and narrative schema, the French emporium is haunted by the prior imaginary of emporialism swerving between the megalomania of empire and the delusion of its collapse. The emporium mirrored the precarity of the national territory. In 1929, synchronizing with the Great Depression, Julien Duvivier adapted Zola's novel for the cinema.[4] The movie, screened in July 1930, was filmed against the modern Parisian cityscape (Niogret 78). The events took place at Galeries Lafayette, but Duvivier added some shots of the exterior of the Samaritaine. The film was one of the last silent movies produced (McGrath 656–57). In this sense, the film itself resembled the old businesses in Zola's novel, which faced extinction (Flinn 64; Walter 127, 135). In the film, Duvivier offers the spectator sweeping panoramic shots showing the store as an interconnected and highly industrialized machine. This rendition of Zola's novel captures the sharp difference between a world on the edge of economic stagnation and the endless motions within the store and the city (McGrath 251–52). Unlike other countries, France's economy was more robust and did not sense the effect of the market crash immediately (S. Reynolds 111; see Rothermund). Nevertheless, the story of the social ascension of Denise, who moved from the province to the city, contrasted with the experience of many women who were pressured to quit their jobs during that era (S. Reynolds 109–18). In fact, Duvivier's adaptation, as Peter Klaus Walter suggests, prioritizes the role of women in the modern economy by highlighting Denise and her moral role in introducing social reforms to the workplace (133–37).

Beyond this context, the actual emporium and its further representations in cinema continued to be the chessboard for rival empires. In 1943, André Cayatte directed another film based on Zola's novel. Cayatte's Janus-faced film documents the fall of the Second Empire while contemplating the surrounding ruins of the Third Republic, when Paris yielded to another German occupation. On the one hand, the movie's focus on the illusionism of the commodity spectacle offered the viewers a momentary escape from the dire conditions of their existence. Nevertheless, the movie marks the emporium as a site of imperial battle (Wolter 141). Shot during the German occupation of Paris by a German-directed company, the context of the movie production and the narrative lend themselves to be deciphered as a subtle resistance to occupation (Wolter 140–41). The triumph of the protagonist in the "commerce war" and their survival amid the ruins of old Paris offered an example of resilience in the face of death and destruction (Wolter 142–44). As Jennifer Wolter argues, throughout the film, French spectators could find glimpses of their daily struggle during occupied France, including the lack of resources, power outage, fear of surveillance and betrayal by friends and colleagues, and the need challenge injustices and authority (Wolter 145–48).

The battle over the department store took place on the cinema screen and inside the emporium. The historical narrative of Galeries Lafayette became a symbolic territory of imperial wars. The published history of the stores stresses the origins of its owner, Théophile Bader, a Jewish man from Alsace who, after the German annexation of Alsace-Lorraine, proudly chose to keep his French citizenship and moved to the French part of Lorraine (Gaston-Breton 14). The insistence on the French identity of the owner replicates a larger national discourse after the Franco-Prussian war, which rejected the German claim over the areas and emphasized that the residents of Alsace-Lorraine were French. To a certain extent, Lafayette's historical narrative suggests that Bader's decision represents a symbolic return of the lost province to French territory.

A few decades later, during the German occupation of France in World War II, the German authorities took control of Galeries Lafayette as part of a process of "Aryanization." This was an anti-Semitic project to purge the French economy of any Jewish influence. Like Yannakakis's account of communism, Nazi ideology and policy is expressed as a process of Aryanization of the emporium. In this process of expunging Europe of any signs of the Orient, the Parisian store was decorated with oversized columns and other iconographic elements, emphasizing Nazi aesthetics. Through a subtle accord with the French banks, the owners of Lafayette transferred their ownership temporarily to the banks to protect it from German control. The owners reclaimed their stores after the French liberation, having participated actively in the resistance. After liberation, in 1950 singer Edith Piaf stood before the gates of Galeries Lafayette to sing the national anthem, once more reaffirming the entwined imaginary of the emporium, women's bodies, and that of the nation-state (Gaston-Breton 63, 68–84). For Yannakakis, the Alexandrian emporia were sites that resisted the claims of ethnic and cultural purity. The historical narrative of Lafayette reiterates a similar stance. Piaf's gesture marked the end of a tragic period in European history and the German occupation of Paris. One can see the distinctive iconographic element of emporialism in this event. Typically, emporialism overlaps the body of women, with the maps of the city, the nation, and the store. Piaf's body and voice as a symbol of France converged with the image of the department store and that of the nation-state. Her act symbolically reclaimed the nation's territory and purged the invader from France and its mirror map, the emporium.

248 | Emporialism

From Emporialism to Neo-Emporialism: Neo-Emporial Others

In contemporary media, emporialism embodies a multilateral discourse that overlaps the maps of contemporary France, neo-imperialism, and consumerism. Bertrand Bonello's French film *Nocturama* (2016), shot in La Samaritaine, re-creates a postmodern image of Zola's emporium, protesting the simulacra of modern-day capitalism. The film revolves around a group of young Parisians from different racial origins who break into a department store during the night to execute a terrorist plan to bomb the city. Once again, the store overlaps with the map of the city and of the nation facing the threat of annihilation. André, one of the attackers, announces the main premise of the plot: "The twentieth century is the proof that democracy makes its own enemy, and, above all, democracy cannot and need not to be judged by its results rather by its adversaries.... Civilization is the sufficient condition of the end of the civilization."[5] Just like Zola's narrative, the film intentionally critiques the megalomania of emporialism and destroys its illusion of commercial utopianism. The young Parisians wander into the emporium, turning the marketplace into part household part playground. They momentarily reactivate the phantasmagoria of consumerism prior to their incumbent death at the hands of the police. The police finally reclaim the emporium-city-nation by purging the consumer utopia of its usurpers. At the end, the film brings back the specter of the Orient to the heart of the store and the metropolis. The final scene concludes with the camera focusing on the remaining survivor, a young man of Maghrebi origins crying desperately for help. In so doing, the movie questions the future of France and its complex relation with migration, which have deep-seated roots in its imperialist past.

In the contemporary context, nineteenth-century emporialism has come to represent the French imperial past prior to the staggering effect of globalization. In some cases, emporialism plays a concrete role beyond the limit of a fictional narrative or the cinema screen. The restoration of La Samaritaine in 2020 is good example of a rhetoric of neo-emporialism that seeks to appropriate, if not completely rewrite, the past. The photos of the inauguration portray French President Emmanuel Macron surrounded by hundreds of employees standing on the central stairs. Such a theatrical posture frames the project as a return to the social utopianism of the Second Empire, exemplified in the visions of La Samaritaine's founders Ernest Cognacq and Louise Jay, and that of its architect, Frantz

Jourdain. In its attempt to turn back the clock, the store rehired some of its past employees, aiming to create 3,000 jobs in total (Dicharry). The nostalgia for empire synchronizes with France's decline as a global power. The project takes place at a troubled moment, fraught with class tension and demonstrations, when the French government is actively and quickly distancing itself from its socialist past.[6] With the purported revival, the store shifts its mission by specializing in luxury brands and catering to the upper classes and tourists. Indeed, the twenty-first century, as Thomas Piketty suggests, marks a return to the gilded age of the Belle Époque, specifically the widening wealth gap between a global capitalist class and the rest of the population. Although the restoration project has been celebrated as a revival of the Belle Époque, it has reclaimed that past while underhandedly erasing its connection to working-class history, precisely to social equality. One wonders whether the nostalgic utopian photo of the newly restored *grand magasin* brings to life France's golden past or its deep-buried class tensions. In this context, the emporium's image does not veer away from Zola's description of the emporium as an emblem of a destructive yet inevitable march of progress: an ambivalent image wavering between commercial utopianism and social Darwinism. In other words, President Macron's photo at the Samaritaine raises the question of whether it was meant to celebrate a return to the glorified past of emporialism or a symbolic dance over the rubble of a vanishing socialist legacy dismantled in the name of progress.

In its construction of allotopic geographies, the rhetoric of emporialism produces its European Other inside and outside the emporium. Emporialism partly produces its map of empire and hierarchy of race through the fetishization and racialization of other commercial spaces. Whereas in the past the distant Oriental bazaar served as foil to the emporium, currently, the nearby corner store plays that role. France's omnipresent yet invisible *arabe du coin*, or corner stores mostly managed by North African immigrants and immortalized by their racialized moniker, carry out an intersectional slippage, a process of ethno-classism, where the gendered image of the North African man is reified into class. To be North African is to be, by extension, Arab and working class. The Arab on the corner—referring simultaneously to the owner of the store and to the store itself—reactivates the paranoiac image of a Muslim invasion. The store/Arab symbolizes "*homo islamicus*," whose character evoked a series of work ethos, maps, and temporalities excluded from the valorized chronology and geography of capitalist modernity (Rodinson 60).

The French movie *Monsieur Ibrahim et les fleurs du Coran* (2002), based on the novel of the same name by Éric-Emmanuel Schmitt (2001), addresses this particular image of the convenience store in the French imaginary. The book and the movie narrate the coming of age of Moise (Momo), who realizes his situation as a poor Jewish young man in 1960s France. Momo befriends Monsieur Ibrahim, an *arabe du coin*, the owner of a convenience store. Monsieur Ibrahim addresses Moise as "Momo," a typical nickname for Mohamed. The movie highlights the interchangeable racialized and class structured imaginary of Muslims and Jews central to the construction of European modernity.

As the story progresses, Momo becomes aware of the intertwinement between the fate and the image of the Jew and the Arab in the European imaginary of race. In the movie, the Turkish owner of the convenience store, Monsieur Ibrahim, brings this racialized imaginary to the forefront. He explains to his young Jewish protégé Momo: "Je ne suis pas Arabe Momo.... Un Arabe ça veut dire horaire de huit heures du matin jusqu'à minuit et même le dimanche dans l'épicerie" ["I am not an Arab Momo.... Being an Arab means working hours from 8 a.m. until midnight, even Sunday, at the convenience store" (*Monsieur Ibrahim* 17:30–17:47). Monsieur Ibrahim's words expose the subtle Eurocentric distinctions underlying emporialism. On one hand, Muslims and Jews are cast as Orientals and Semites as Edward Said might suggest (Said, *Orientalism* 102). On the other hand, they are located in an intricate grid of racial and class hierarchies among different minorities: the Arab, the Turk, and the Jew. The image of the network of corner stores strung across Parisian streets, evoked by this mundane expression, packs many tensions at once. The store inhabited by the lurking Arab subtly occupies the contemporary metropolis. To an extent, this racialized contemporary discourse on the Arab corner store recalls Joris Karl Huysmans's xenophobic panic that marks the decadence of his era with the social ascension of small Jewish shopkeepers from Rue Sentier (see chapter 3). In this context, the sight of monsieur Ibrahim and his Jewish protégé Momo standing at the entrance of the corner store overlaps past and present xenophobia. On the one hand, it highlights the ambiguous and clichéd position of Arab immigrants conveniently present yet kept at a distance. On the other hand, it brings to the mind the anti-Semitic history of Europe. The corner store, the modern emporial other, omnipresent across the French cityscape, brings back the anxieties of imperialism and its fear of engulfment. But even the imaginary of the other space constructs its own hierarchies of race, class, and gender. Momo's coming of age experience begins with his first sexual experience with a sex worker. In that respect, the representation of both geographies of emporialism (that of the emporium and its Other) still relies on the metonymic association between the body of women and that of the city. Ironically, the character of Monsieur Ibrahim is played by Omar Sharif, a Francophone Egyptian American actor of Lebanese origins, who grew up in the multicultural context of Levantine colonial Egypt. Sharif is one of the emblematic figures of that eastern Mediterranean culture that was often exoticized, Orientalized, or deemed inferior.[7] He also represents the same era the various authors and filmmakers mentioned in this chapter attempt to document by taking the department store as a symbolic key space for this epoch.

The Gendered Bodies of Neo-Emporialism

In the imaginary emporialism, the bodies of women are caught at the crossfire between empires. A case in point, mentioned earlier, is Edith Piaf singing the national anthem in front of the department store. Her body and voice recuperate both the emporium and Paris to the national territory from the German invader. Piaf's body melds the emporium, the maps of the city, the nation, and the empire. The historical affinity between the department store, the city, and the body of women remains another active iconographic element in postmodern French culture. One of the most widespread advertisements is by renowned photographer Jean-Paul Goude for the Galeries Lafayette campaign (2001–2015). The campaign features model Laetitia Casta. In the image, Casta is pictured in profile, her hair tied in a bun. On top of her head stands a giant Eiffel tower. A red, white, and blue ribbon, representing the French flag, ties the Eiffel tower to her head, chin, and hair. Her head is slightly tilted downward as if to balance the weight of the metal structure on top of her hair. The poster cleverly and uncannily captures the history of urban and commercial representation of emporialism, in which a woman's body is conflated with that of the emporium, the city, nation, and empire. Casta wears a shiny black dress, a reminder of the black silk uniform typically worn by nineteenth-century salesclerks to appease a middle-class sense of propriety and taste.[8] Serving as a metonym for the department store and the French territory, the model's head is tethered to that of the nation and the department store. Like the early catalogue covers featuring giant women from Printemps and Sednaoui (refer to figs 1.2 and 2.14), Casta resembles a mythical hybrid creature, between women and nature: a human unicorn, a half-human, half-fantastic-animal. She reflects the volatile nature of the consumer and nationalist utopia of emporialism which, as a woman, she is expected to embody.

The tripartite alliance between woman, nation-state, and the emporium is not a unique image particular to France. It is part of an imaginary that transcends national borders and political regimes. One can see similar images operating along the two sides of the Mediterranean. In 1954, two years after Egyptian national independence, the representation of the department store in Egyptian cinema marks a significant gendered shift. Various European film productions and television series set in department stores portray the emporium as a brutal space controlled by a man. Eventually a woman manages to win that man's heart and introduces a more humane order to the workspace. Egyptian comic movie *Banat Hawwa* [Daughters of Eve] is one of the rare works that goes against this typical narrative grain. The movie is shot in the Chemla department store. In contrast to other stories, the movie presents the modern emporium as a bastion of feminism rather than exploitation: a utopian space fully managed by women and forbidden to men. In the movie, the male protagonist tries to seduce the store manager, a leader of a radical feminist group. He finally succeeds in conquering her heart by conquering the emporium: that is, by securing a job there despite being a man. The film ends with the typical bourgeois marriage of the manager and the employee, who restores the feminist woman to a traditional patriarchal order. The film takes place at a critical political moment—two years after independence, during an active feminist movement led by Doria Shafik, who stormed parliament in 1951 demanding the right to vote. In 1954, the same year as the movie's release, Shafik undertook a hunger strike to force Mohamed Naguib, the first Egyptian president, to include women's rights and equal status in the new constitution (C. Nelson 167–208).

The intricate connection between women's bodies, the nation, and the store is frequently reflected in Egyptian postcolonial literature. The novel *Ramza* by Out-el-Kouloub (1958) reiterates a triangulated connection sometimes between the department store, the city, and women's bodies and in other times between the department store, the body of women, and the nation. Out-el-Kouloub was an aristocratic Egyptian Francophone woman who published her books in France. The novel begins in the late nineteenth century, around 1877, the date of the Ottoman abolition of slavery, and takes the reader through several decades. The eponymous protagonist tells her story to a female writer belonging to a new generation of Muslim women, who reap the fruit of the previous generation's struggle against oppression:

> It was the time when the department stores had just begun to open in Cairo, and I still remember my happiness when I received a red silk dress from chez Pascal, a sport jacket from Dé Rouge, and a parasol... from Omar Effendi. I only knew these department stores from having passed in front of them on those rare occasions when I was driven by car around the districts of Muski, al-Azbakiyya, or Wagh al-Birka. I had never been inside, nor had any woman or young girl of status. The salesgirls used to come to the house. As a special favor, against custom, my father consulted me on these purchases. Oh! It was never in a direct manner! It was by some sort of coincidence that I would find some catalogues, and I would mark with a pencil what I liked.[9]

Ramza specifically associates her freedom with her ability to control her purchases and her mobility in the city. In the passage, the department stores figure as forbidden and desired spaces, which she only knows through the products that her father buys. Her father displays his generosity by indirectly giving his daughter a choice in selecting the items he buys for her. The mutual understanding between them and the silence surrounding Ramza's perusal of the catalogues cast her act as a transgression of the patriarch's honor. In contrast to the European context, going to the department store was a role scripted for men, who shopped on behalf of the whole family. Like Egyptian feminist Huda Shaarawi, Ramza only sets foot in the *grand magasin* when she travels to Alexandria. Before eloping with her lover, an army officer, Ramza purchases a white dress on her own, after leaving behind the large trousseau her father selected for her (174).

The novel sets the department store as a space of feminist agency and patriarchal transgression. Even so, published six years after the Egyptian independence movement led by the Free Officers, the text reinscribes the department store in a new framework that acknowledges the postcolonial moment and the change of regimes of values. Emporialism marks the newfound alliance between a rising postcolonial class and a feudal aristocratic colonial one through intermarriage. In this broader context, the emporium serves a site that bridges the time before and after empire. In the novel, the body of the bourgeois woman emerges as another parallel site that links the colonial and the postcolonial worlds. The same body records a lateral social and economic transaction between patriarchies, between a rising power and an eclipsed one.

All Memories Lead to Cicurel

The iconographic complicity between the emporium and women's bodies remains at work in Egyptian narrative schemata of the department store. In the memory of the Egyptian emporium, the Cicurel stores became a narrative schema, a knot of collective memory at the crossroads of Egypt, France, and Israel. One of the most telling texts that announces the postcolonial moment and the key shift in the perception of the department stores features in Latifa al-Zayyat's *Al-Bab al-Maftuh* [The Open Door] (1956). The novel reactivates the discursive praxes of emporialism that overlap the city, the nation, and women's bodies. The novel, set between 1946 and 1956, narrates the memory of Egyptian independence, including that of the Cairo fire of 1952, which targeted "foreign" business enterprises and resulted in the ruin of most department stores located in Cairo's city center. *Al-Bab al-Maftuh* is often hailed as a piece of remarkable feminist literature that captured the spirit of the postcolonial moment. Al-Zayyat was an active participant in the anticolonial struggle and was arrested in 1949 and again in 1981, while opposing the context of the Egyptian-Israeli peace agreement. Her novel aligns the feminist cause with the wider nationalist one, wherein both nation and women strive for independence. In this context, the aspired social and gender equality would be the outcome of the anticolonial movement (Nasser 55; Elsadda, *Gender* 97).

In al-Zayyat's novel, as in Shaarawi's memoirs and Zola's *Au bonheur des dames*, emporialism comes to express a symbolic battle among empires fought around the emporium and women's bodies (103). In the novel, Layla helps her cousin Gamila prepare for her wedding. Gamila represents an ideal young woman who complies with expected gender roles as a middle-class Egyptian woman. Gamila's mother buys her daughter's dresses and trousseau from Cicurel stores to fashion her into a beautiful bride that could please her future husband. Preparing for the wedding, Layla watches her cousin trying on her wedding dress, made of fabric from Cicurel.[10] In a typical Zolaesque and a Shaarawi moment, the novel depicts the Cicurel store during a sales event as a battlefield on which crowds of women meet (see chapters 3 and 4). Layla's friend jokingly compares the sale event to the colonial resistance in Suez. Cicurel stands in opposition to the Suez Canal zone, a site of colonial resistance from which women are excluded.

During Gamila's wedding party, Gamila and Layla learn about the Cairo fire. Layla watches the fire consuming the department store from her building rooftop (148). Layla goes away, leaving Gamila standing in her wedding dress, framed by the thick smoke. Layla decides then to join the anticolonial struggle in Suez. There she watches the destruction of the statue of Ferdinand de Lesseps by the resistance, marking the end of a colonial story that began with the Saint-Simonian project of Suez (349). In the text, the destruction symbolically creates a historical line for emporialism beginning from the Saint-Simonian dream of Suez up to the burning of the department stores. In this context, the Cicurel building and Gamila's body wearing the wedding dress, like Ramza's body as well, are two parallel sites of resistance, announcing the end of a political and patriarchal regime and the rise of another.

The novel complicates the notion of social belonging, which the Cairo fire sought to reduce into colonizer and colonized. The following dialogue takes place: "The people are burning the city." Layla asks: "Why are we burning our city?" (145). As Nancy Reynolds suggests, the Cairo fire was meant to reconfigure collective and national memory by marking the stores as imperial spaces to be purged from the Egyptian national narrative and the urban map. In this situation, the Jewish community and the stores are suddenly proclaimed as intruders. "The sense of loss and self-destruction wrought by the fire is magnified by the passage's dialogue, which Layla shifts rapidly from the general political level of the [colonial] struggle, expressed in the neutral third person, to an immediate, emotional, and possessive first-person" (N. Reynolds, *City Consumed* 196). Reynolds adds that moving from the third-person "the city" to the collective "our" reframes the stores and colonial Cairo as a national common heritage rather than a foreign site built by foreign intruders as the fire meant to highlight. Layla's words restore the various families who built the Egyptian stores into a collective nationalist narrative.

The alliance between body, nation, and emporium resurfaces in the work of French Egyptian writer Paula Jacques. Writing from Paris, Jacques, a contemporary novelist and radio presenter, documents the history of departure of the Jewish Egyptian community. In her first novel *Lumière de l'oeil*, Jacques narrates the story of the Castros, a middle-class Jewish family in the final years before they migrate to France, between 1952 and 1957. The family's language and customs are a mélange of Franco-Arab-Jewish

Egyptian culture. The novel begins with the family dressed in their most elegant clothes on their way to a photographer's studio for a family portrait. For this portrait, the mother has bought an expensive dress from Cicurel. As the family passes by Suleiman Pacha Square, the father looks at the Pacha's statue in the center. He remembers that Suleiman Pacha was a French soldier in Napoleon's army before he settled in Egypt and became the chief organizer of Mehmet Ali's army. Jacques mobilizes the history of Franco-Egyptian exchanges and collaboration that started during the nineteenth century (12). Later, Becky Castro shows off her dress, also from Cicurel, to an acquaintance: "The Bey's wife asked me where I bought my dress. At Cicurel, my dear, but the price is piping hot like a burning coal!"[11] The dress from Cicurel represents the habit (the clothes) and the habitus of the Jewish family constructed out of its imaginary connection to the Jewish Egyptian bourgeoisie (the Cicurels, the Chemlas, etc.) and Egyptian cosmopolitan culture. Listening to her mother, Mona Castro fantasizes about burning her dresses (18). The description of the cost of the dress as piping hot like a "burning coal" and Mona's idea of her mother's wardrobe being set on fire foreshadows a passage on the Cairo fire, which the family watches from their roof of their house a few days later. Interestingly, the scenes set on the rooftop during the Cairo fire, from both Jacques and al-Zayyat, re-create the same political turning point from the perspective of the postcolonial middle class and that of the Jewish Egyptian community. Just like Gamila's wedding dress from Cicurel engulfed in smoke, Mrs. Castro's dress, from the same store, is hypothetically set on fire. Both dresses serve as a site of memory for the store, the city, and its multicultural past.

For the Castros, this significant event marks the beginning of the end as they prepare to leave Egypt. The novel concludes with the departure of the family, while Om Sayyeda, the housekeeper, guards their photo album (274). The image of domestic servants is tightly connected to the memory of Egypt's Mediterranean middle-class past. Paradoxically, the servant—the excluded Other from the story of emporialism—becomes the guardian of memory.

In another novel by Jacques, *Gilda Stambouli souffre et se plaint*, [Gilda Stambouli Suffers and Complains], Jacques begins with a reference to Cicurel. Gilda, a middle-class Jewish Egyptian widow, leaves Egypt in 1956 and settles in France in 1957. In between, she moves to Israel to live in a kibbutz. Disappointed with her situation, Gilda decides to migrate to France, leaving her young daughter behind. A bureaucrat from the Jewish agency for Israel in Jerusalem tries to dissuade her: "You will see, in fifty years this country will be a paradise." Gilda sarcastically answers: "in this case, I will come back in fifty years."[12] Gilda spends her time in Paris trying to bring back her daughter, who finally dies in the kibbutz. The novel marks the protagonist alienated position from the Egyptian nationalist project and Zionism.

In her attempt to find a job, Gilda applies to an atelier that had hired a previous owner of Cicurel as a seamstress. She exclaims: "Cicurel in Cairo was a replica of Galeries Lafayette. Do you see how fate is!"[13] The brief reference to the "lady" from Cicurel, now hired as a seamstress, becomes a symbolic reference for Jewish Egyptians as a collective. By evoking the comparison between Galeries Lafayette and Cicurel, Jacques reactivates the particular rhetoric of emporialism in Egypt to overlap the French and Egyptian maps. In doing so, the author highlights the displacement of Egyptian Jews and the stark contrast between their central position in Egypt and their marginal situation in Paris. Gilda, like the "lady" from Cicurel, embodies a postcolonial condition in which French language and culture lose their crucial role as a means of integration. Instead, Gilda finds herself on the margins of three nations and a memory of an unrecoverable past.

The pattern of documenting a community's legacy by referencing the emporium continues in other Francophone Egyptian literary works. In his novel *Le Tarbouche*, Robert Solé uses the imaginary of emporialism to reconstruct Egypt's colonial past. Solé is a Francophone Egyptian of Syrian Christian origin. He moved from Cairo to France at the age of eighteen. *Le Tarbouche* documents the role of the Syrian community in modern Egypt. Writing from France, Solé presents another competing perspective for the official national narrative. The Egyptian imaginary of emporialism tightly connected to Francophone culture serves to question his belonging to France and the emerging Egyptian nation. Whereas previously mentioned writers take the wedding dress and the emporium as a symbolic representation of a changing political and a patriarchal regime, Solé takes the fez, an obsolete dress item for men, and the department stores as a reference to the memory of empire. To mark this displacement, the writer selects an Arabic name for the French novel. The fez is an iconic item unique to a bygone colonial Egypto-Ottoman era. The novel title is at once polyglossic and heteroglossic. In addition to the French language, it exploits different registers of Arabic cultures and dialects. In Egyptian colloquial speech, the word *tarbouche* contains a sexual innuendo, implying the glans penis. This double entendre casts a different light onto the narrative, as it mocks the construction of nationalism altogether.

In the novel, set in colonial Egypt, the Batrakani family struggles to navigate the different currents between an emerging Egyptian nationalism, British imperialism, Francophone culture, and their Syrian heritage. Although they had settled in Egypt three generations earlier, the Batrakanis are considered neither locals nor foreigners. In the novel, consumer culture becomes the key element around which they weave their national belonging to Egypt through the promotion of a new brand of fez (*tarbouche*) to the Egyptian public as authentic Egyptian attire. After the fall of the Ottoman Empire, the fez became a multivalent sign of modernity: imposed in the 1820s as the symbol of a modern Ottoman citizen, it was later banned by Kemal Atatürk as part of an outmoded past. Solé chooses an image fraught with ambiguity and irony. In the beginning of the narrative, Solé illustrates the competitive colonial relationship between Syrians and Egyptian Jews through a list of rival department stores. He parodies this situation in the following lines: "What do they want these accursed Jews? They own all the department stores in Egypt. Cicurel is theirs, Chemla is theirs. Gattegno is theirs. And Orosdi-Back, don't they own that too by any chance? Lucky we've still got Sednaoui."[14]

In this satirical passage, Georges Batrakani, the family patriarch, expresses his frustration at the control of commerce by Jews in Egypt. The listing of the cosmopolitan stores comes in contrast with the family's comic attempt to promote the traditional Turkish headdress as a symbol of Egyptian nationalism. This incident recalls the actual history of the Omar Effendi department store, which promoted the sale of the fez to distance itself from its European past and establish itself an Egyptian business (see chapter 2). More important, by melding the image of the emporium and that of the fez, Solé connects the history of his community to the rise of the first modern urban generation of Egyptian men, the *efendiyya*, whose experience became part and parcel of the nationalist narrative.[15] By evoking (albeit comically) the past commercial rivalry between Sednaoui and Cicurel, the text succinctly restores to the national memory the history of Syrian Egyptians. Solé's distinction brings attention to the broader colonial and postcolonial contexts of Egyptian Jews and Syrians in Egypt. In the eyes of the British occupier, both groups—who shared French as a lingua franca—brought about the imperial rivalry between England and France. In *Modern Egypt*, the Earl of Cromer comments: "Amongst the obstacles which have stood in the way of the British reformer in Egypt, none is more noteworthy than that both Europeanized Egyptians and Levantines are impregnated with French rather than English habits of thought" (236). On the other hand, Sednaoui in contemporary Egyptian culture is often mistakenly associated with the history of Egyptian Jews. This comic moment in the novel, then, points out the lapses and elision in the contemporary Egyptian popular memory of both communities.

The Aftermath of Emporialism

The Egyptian emporium also operated as a structuring narrative and iconographic schema grounded in the ethnic and classist inclusion/exclusion of Muslims, Arabs, and Jews from a European discourse on modernity. This is precisely the tension that triggered Jacqueline Kahanoff's formulation of the concept of Levantinism based on the memory of her grandparents' department store in Egypt. Kahanoff saw the store as a site of an alternative non-Eurocentric civic relation that distances itself from the colonial intertwinement of race and class. *Jacob's Ladder* sheds light on the different individuals that Yannakakis depicts in his account of Alexandria. For Kahanoff, the Levantine department store produces its own version of cosmopolitanism shaped by the various communities and intermediaries caught in the machinery of empires and emporialism. Most of the store's employees and clients exist and negotiate between the different forces and regimes at play. Their lives are irreducible to the gilded French labels affixed to the products sold at the store. They embody an eastern Mediterranean regime of values that does not define itself according to a European paradigm of modernity and cosmopolitanism (see chapter 5). Kahanoff takes this memory from Egypt to Israel to critique a Eurocentric national culture that marginalizes Mizrahi history. In a later work from 1968 (published in 1976), fourteen years after her migration to Israel, Kahanoff revisits her vision of the Levant that she began in *Jacob's Ladder*. She stresses the obsolescence of nationalism in comparison to the multilayered nature of Levantine eastern Mediterranean culture:

> [While] the Levant cannot be sharply differentiated from the Mediterranean world, it is not synonymous [with it]. The Levant has a character and a history of its own. It is called "Near" or "Middle" East in relationship to Europe, not to itself. Seen from Asia, it could just as well be called the "Middle West." Here, indeed, Europe and Asia have encroached on one another, giving rise to world civilizations, fracturing into stubborn local subcultures and multi-layered identities . . .

> [The Levant] is not exclusively eastern or western, Christian, Jewish, or Moslem.... Because of its diversity, the Levant has been compared to a mosaic—bits of stones of different colors assembled into a flat picture. To me it is more like a prism whose various facets are joined by a sharp edge of differences, but each of which according to its position in a time-space continuum, reflects or refracts light... and perhaps the time has come for the Levant to reevaluate itself according to its own light, rather than see itself through Europe's sights, as something quaintly exotic, tired, sick, and almost lifeless. ("Afterword" 247)

In this passage, Kahanoff critiques the European construction of the "Near East" as a reductive geographic label for a rich and complex culture. She locates the Levant culturally at the intersection of Europe and Asia. By defining Levantinism as part of Mediterranean cultural geography, she reinscribes the modern history of Sephardic and Mizrahi communities into that of the Mediterranean. For Kahanoff, the Mediterranean represents a space of movement and exchange, where the Levant stands as a culture "on its own," one that does not belong to a single empire or people and can be claimed by many. The metaphor of the prism evokes Lawrence Durrell's description of Alexandria in *Justine* (1957), published six years after *Jacob's Ladder* but 19 years before the text above. In that respect, the text above marks an evolution of her view on Levantine culture, bearing the marks of Durrell's Alexandria. Durrell's text describes the city as neither "Greek, Syrian, or Egyptian, but a hybrid, a joint" (26). Like the city, Alexandria's Levantine residents negotiate their diverse social space by selectively projecting one side of their persona. Their "multidimensional" character takes on the quality of a prism, reflecting a variegated image that changes according to the perceiver's angle of vision. In the narrator's words, "to everyone we turn a different face of the prism" (26, 119). In contrast to Durrell's description, Kahanoff's metaphor of the Levant as a prism "whose various facets are joined by a sharp edge of differences" suggests a social contract that takes account of differences rather than erasing them.

To illustrate her concept, Kahanoff refers to the urban map of Egypt and Alexandria. A later short story, "To Remember Alexandria" (1976), set between 1967 and 1973, depicts a romantic encounter in Tel Aviv between Antonia Ferrar and Josh. Antonia is a middle-aged Jewish Italian woman from Egypt who has settled in Rome and is struggling with cancer. Josh is a young Israeli pilot, a "healthy, cocky... never doubting" Sabra (220). The depiction of Josh matches the stereotypical nationalist description of the modern Israeli, or Sabra. In Zionist discourse, a Sabra is depicted as "young and robust, daring and resourceful, down to earth, honest and loyal, ideologically committed and ready to defend his people to the bitter end" (Zerubavel 116). Correspondingly, Antonia's physical representation conforms to a stereotypical nationalist description of the sickly, frail wandering Jew. In contrast to Josh's seemingly solid world rooted in the new culture of his nation-state, Antonia, an interpreter for international organizations, lives in a bygone ghostly Mediterranean world, between nations and languages, between her memories of Alexandria, her new life in Italy, and her trip to Tel Aviv (218). Josh invites her to visit Jerusalem, the inland city, as a way of forgetting the Mediterranean. The text aligns nationalism with the act of turning away from the sea toward the sealed culture of the inlands. Trapped in her memories, Antonia foresees Tel Aviv as the continuum of where she came from: "To remember. For we were all here before. Here and in Egypt. And so I wished, crazily wished to plant a seed of Alexandria in the soil of Israel, for Alexandria was once almost a Jewish city as much as it was Greek. Where else in the world does the street of the Ptolemies bisect Nebi Daniel Street in the heart of the city? Probably their names have been erased. Those streets are probably called Liberation Street and Arab Brotherhood Street" (224). Kahanoff chooses a fatalist conclusion to the story, in which both characters remain victims of their separate worlds and fulfill their stereotypical destinies. Antonia dies in exile from cancer. Josh, the modern nationalist, dies during the Yom Kippur War, leaving behind a wife and a daughter who feel at home in Tel Aviv. In contrast to *Jacob's Ladder*, where Kahanoff announces the birth of modern Levantine culture at the expense of a Middle Eastern heritage, here she mourns the end of Levantine culture ruined by nationalism. Whereas *Jacob's Ladder* was written as an attempt to situate herself in a national Egyptian culture, "To Remember Alexandria" rewrites her experience in Israel. The decision to kill off both characters, the frail Levantine and the resilient Sabra, points toward the condemnation of a Eurocentric Zionist purview of national identity, which distances itself from the Levantine past. Josh's daughter, who feels "at home" in Tel Aviv, is part of a new generation who has neither memories of nor a personal connection to that cosmopolitan past. Her belonging to the land comes at the price of a symbolic amnesia and the erasure of history. The only traces of that bygone culture that might unsettle her illusion of stability are Antonia's letters from Italy, locked in Josh's desk.

In an unfinished novel, *Tamra*, depicting another impossible love story, this time between a Muslim young man and a Jewish young woman, Kahanoff draws the same map as above:

> Cairo is an Arab city, Alexandria in many ways Greek, a Mediterranean one. *Where else in the world would the street of the Ptolemies intersect with Nebi Daniel, the Prophet Daniel?* And there stands the great synagogue. From the center of town, all along the Corniche, a string of Greek casinos and cafés. . . . Alexandria is the most European of Egypt's cities, but a Europe that was always part of the Mediterranean world. It has its Greeks living here since antiquity, its Italian colony and its Italian Jewish community. It is really a city of the Levant. . . . In high society, Greek men are supposed to have Jewish mistresses, and Jewish men have Greek mistresses. It is whispered that the mothers themselves do not always know who fathered what child. They are almost a race apart, Greco-Jewish. We are so ignorant of the past, but Alexandria is so much older than the Arab Moslem conquest. It is still a Greco-Jewish city. ("Alexandria" 79; emphasis added)

Kahanoff turns to the Egyptian map as an artifact, or an archeological site, to highlight her paradigm of Levantinism structured on Greco-Jewish culture. Taking a Braudelian stance, she distinguishes between the shores of the Mediterranean and the inlands by polarizing the differences between Cairo and Alexandria. Likewise, Kahanoff claims "that the great historical lesson of the Levant [is that] . . . each entity has had to renounce part of its claim to an all-embracing universality" ("Afterword" 250). Although Kahanoff is a native of Cairo and Levantinism existed where she lived, she later reconfigures Egyptian cultural geography to stress Alexandria's character as a Mediterranean port facing the sea and looking toward Europe, detached from the Egyptian territory and beyond the claims of nationalism and Nasserist pan-Arabism.

After this process of rezoning, the narrator grounds her idea by marking the hub of Jewish and Greek culture on the map of Alexandria. But a quick consultation of the actual map of the city reveals that the two main roads, "Nebi Daniel and Ptolemies," do not intersect as Kahanoff claims in the various texts that she drafts later in her life (fig. 6.2). They are two distant parallel roads. Although the streets rightfully highlight Alexandria's Greco-Jewish heritage, this example shows how Kahanoff's selective memory reconstructs an imaginary urban plan for Alexandria, one she places in the service of her vision of Levantinism. In fact, the road that actually intersects with Ptolemies Street is called Abbasid Street—a street that refers to the same epoch that Kahanoff exalted in *Jacob's Ladder* as the golden epoch of Iraqi Jews, and as part of her family Arab heritage. In so doing, Kahanoff forces Arab culture into the background,[16] making it an outsider colonial power, and emphasizes a Greco-Jewish cultural *métissage*. Levantinism lies at the crossroads of two central streams that make the fabric of a European modernity specific to the Mediterranean: Greek and Jewish. Both survive resiliently and assimilate to the main culture regardless of the ruling powers, transforming it from within. The text is not clear about whether she suggests that a mélange of Mizrahi and Ashkenazi culture in Israel should be the substructure for Levantinism, equivalent of the Greco-Jewish intersection.

Kahanoff proceeds to reconfigure Alexandria's human geography in correspondence with her imaginary map. In the guise of Mediterranean tableaux of classical civilizations, she connects the contemporary Greek and Italian residents to the Hellenic and Roman empires: "Alexandria is the most European of Egypt's cities, but a Europe that was always part of the Mediterranean world. It has its Greeks living here since antiquity, its Italian colony and its Italian Jewish community" ("Alexandria" 79). In this key sentence, Kahanoff establishes a historical and geographical continuum between Egypt and the imaginary historical timeline of European civilization. She depicts the Mediterranean city as a fallen cradle of European and Mediterranean civilization and projects onto Cairo an Arabic/Muslim identity. Recalling Durrell's Quartet, Kahanoff brings forth another ethnographic tableau of interracial lovers: "In high society, Greek men are supposed to have Jewish mistresses, and Jewish men have Greek mistresses" ("Alexandria" 79).[17] Just like Kahanoff's early example of the intermarrying Arab and Ashkenazi dolls, the romantic metaphor of Greek and Jewish lovers transforms Egyptian Levantinism into what Mary Louise Pratt calls a "transracial love story" in which "the love relationships unfold in some marginal or privileged space where relations of labor and property are suspended" (see chapter 5) (*Imperial Eyes* 100). The display of Levantinism, as an Alexandrian summer "fling," a fleeting love affair between Greeks and Jews, where cultural and social lines are transgressed secretly and delightfully but still kept intact on the surface, overshadows the economic and colonial networks underpinning Levantinism.

Not only does Kahanoff reinscribe Alexandria in the Mediterranean, she subtly reverses the relationship between land and sea. In her later writings, the Mediterranean returns to center stage, whereby the sea ceases to be the southern water frontier of Europe, separating it from the third world. In this reversal, the European continent, like Alexandria, becomes annexed to the sea. This is a reminder of Fernand Braudel's historical project which, as Palmira Brummet posits, subordinates European history to that of the sea (37). Situating Alexandria in a Braudelian paradigm allows a simultaneous implicit reconfiguration of the Israeli cultural map. By stressing the differences between Cairo and Alexandria, she suggests a parallel division between Jerusalem and the Mediterranean city of Tel Aviv. Just as Alexandria should turn toward the Mediterranean, so should Tel Aviv, wherein both cities belong to a heterotopic cultural space distinct from their homogenizing national narrative.[18]

In the article where Kahanoff attempts to redefine the ties between Israel and the surrounding Arab nations, she proposes Levantinism as a framework for equality and an alternative to imperialism and neocolonialism. Nevertheless, she reproduces the discourse of the colonial civilizing mission, giving Israel a role previously reserved for imperial powers. In describing the role of Israel in promoting Levantinism, she says, "The Six-Day War has catapulted Israel as a force in the Levant; whatever arrangements are finally made about our as yet unrecognized borders, the imbalance between our different societies remains, leaving us little choice except to modernize the Levant while remaining respectful of its diversity" ("Afterword" 254). Kahanoff's English writings on Egyptian Levantinism pave the way for reclaiming Arab Mizrahi culture as a valuable component of a non-Eurocentric cosmopolitanism. Yet it seems with the pressures of the Arab-Israeli conflict and Zionism, her Levantine project gradually evolves away from its early inception in Egypt. On one hand she places more emphasis on Greco-Jewish connections. On the other hand, in her definition of a new Israeli role in the Middle East, Kahanoff constructs a hierarchical relation of power between Arab Mizrahi culture and the rest of the Arab world.

Counteremporialism: The Skeletons in the Levantine Closet

The traces of the Levantine past, with its colonial anxieties in the Israeli context, resurfaces in the works of Ronit Matalon and Orly Castel-Bloom.[19] Both are Israeli writers born to Egyptian parents. In her Hebrew novel *The One Facing Us*, Matalon narrates the fate of Levantinism after the departure of the Jewish community from Egypt.[20] The story centers on the Sicourelles, a Francophone Jewish family who left Egypt in the 1950s. Esther tries to piece together her family history, transmitted to her mainly by oral narratives and photographs. The novel pays tribute to Kahanoff by forging a link between her and the fictional Sicourelle family. As Hochberg convincingly argues, Kahanoff's "presence in the novel is elevated to the status of myth. She takes the places of the 'spokeswoman of Levantinism,' which as such can never be fully captured but rather forever remains a missing photo" (*In Spite* 54). In addition to referring to Kahanoff as a brand name of Levantinism, Matalon uses the name Sicourelle (an alternative spelling to Cicurel), recalling the prestigious Jewish Egyptian family and their department store. Cicurel/Sikourel is another competitive emblematic site of bourgeois Levantine culture in Egypt, which frequently surfaces in the memory of that era. In that sense, the imaginary of emporialism and its connection to Levantine culture and empire finds its way in Matalon's novel.

Beginning with this reference, which evokes the memory of one emporium against another, and by extension pits one site of Levantinism against another, the novel sets the stage to offer an alternative narrative for Kahanoff's Levantinism. *Jacob's Ladder* ends with a scene of the Seder dinner in the family's Cairene household. Rachel takes charge of setting the table by giving orders to the household staff. The Sudanese servant happily promises Rachel that one day his own children will serve in her house when she grows up. In contrast, *The One Facing Us* begins with a reversal of this racialized confusing moment that concludes Kahanoff's novel. In Matalon's novel, the Sicourelles leave Egypt and finally settle in Cameroon. By planting this symbolic name of Egyptian Levantinism in Cameroon, the narrative underscores a pivotal constitutive moment, when Levantinism separates from the African continent and directs itself toward Europe. Whereas Levantinism defines itself via its connection to the shores of the Mediterranean Sea, the Sicourelle family turns away from the Mediterranean to settle in sub-Saharan Africa, exposing one of Levantinism's original colonial fears.

Furthermore, the structure of the narrative emulates the nature of Levantinism, which itself is concocted from disparate elements. Levantinism establishes its elitist status by referring to a phantasmatic connection to a French culture that does not reflect that of France and does not come with a "French citizenship" (80). The Sicourelles guard the memory of the Levantine past and their lives in Egypt by an equally phantasmatic relation with a collection of disparate unreliable photos that tell a partial story, leaving the rest to the imagination of the spectator. In describing the photographs, Esther says: "The photograph resonated with me: after all, the blurring of figures and landscape, of general and specific, is exactly what typified our Levantine experience.... Questions—What is our language? Our nationality? Our place?—rise from the painfully beautiful haze of these photograph" (126). Shimrit Peled argues, "the bringing together of the pictures and their interpretation and the various family stories that accompany them ... make up a novel that creates a new nonterritorial alternative to 'home' within a postcolonial reality" (344). Matalon's photographs astutely sum up the complex history of Levantinism, caught as it is between the imaginaries of the Mediterranean Sea and the African territory, a memory that swerves between an aestheticized Francophile elitist image and an unresolved colonial past. Matalon's text creates an alternative territory that brings together the photos with their missing captions. The novel doubles as a space of encounter where the celebrated Francophile bourgeois image of Levantinism is complemented by its frequently erased colonial subtext. Hochberg suggests that Matalon's text is "a reminder of a lost historical opportunity through which the present victory of Zionist nationalism reemerges in the ghostly form of failed Levantinism" (*In Spite* 57). Esther's encounter with the photograph compels her to compare the marketable image of Levantinism and its reality. In her effort to piece together the family history, she simultaneously questions the Levantine past, its potential future, and its limits in a context marked with the tensions among Ashkenazim, Mizrahim, and Palestinians. The novel highlights this tension through the story of Uncle Edouard, who tries to find a space in the new ethno-class structure of Israeli society, where his Francophone and Arab backgrounds become obsolete forms of cultural capital (Matalon, *One Facing* 127–38). Edouard ends up working in the secret service extracting information from Palestinians. In this brutal and liminal position of power he comes to be nicknamed "king of Gaza" (Hochberg, *In Spite* 57; Matalon, *One Facing* 137).

In her short story "Ummi fi Shughl," Castel-Bloom also summons the ghost of another cliché featured in *Jacob's Ladder*. Castel-Bloom opts for an Arabic title, which she transliterates into Hebrew letters as "ummy fi shughl" [My mother is at work]. In the story, the narrator, a paranoiac woman, sits on a bench while waiting for the bus. The narrator is bitten by a sixty-year-old Arab widow, dressed in mourning clothes, hiding under the bench. The Arab woman claims to be the narrator's mother, which the narrator denies. The woman asks where she is from; the protagonist answers that her parents are from Cairo and that she is not a Shoah survivor but lately she has been dreaming of that. The rest of the conversation takes place in Arabic, transcribed in the text in the Hebrew alphabet: "Who are you" "I am your mother." "No, my mother is at work" [ummy fi shughl]. "I am your sister." "No my sister is at work" [ukhty fi shughl]" (10). In her analysis of the passage, Hochberg points out that the transliteration of Arabic into Hebrew returns to the repressed memory of affinity, between Jews and Arabs, especially in the collective memory of the Mizrahi community (*In Spite* 1–4). A similar incident takes place in Matalon's novel. Like Castel-Bloom's ghostly Arab woman, Esther's uncle interpellates his niece in Arabic, bringing the specter of a Levantine past which she did not live. Describing that incident, Esther says: "He speaks in Arabic, forcing on me an intimacy with a world that has never been mine" (Matalon, *One Facing* 16).[21] In both incidents, language, as Hochberg suggests, serves as a site to revive the modern history of Mizrahi Levantine culture and its roots in Arabic culture: "Castel-Bloom's absurd representation . . . unleashes this repressed memory (which could be called the repressed memory of the Semite) by introducing it as an unexpected threat: a fleeting memory that might flash up at any given moment and 'bite.' It is a memory that emerges from underneath momentarily, only to be immediately pushed back under the bench, sealed in the dark abyss of national amnesia" (*In Spite* 2).

Matalon's and Castel-Bloom's narratives perform an exercise of interpellation that requires the listener to answer to, or define, their subjective position.[22] In Matalon's novel, Esther mentions that Uncle Sicourelle addresses her in Arabic, compelling her to recognize (and by extension be part) of a forgotten Arab/Levantine past unknown to her. In Castel-Bloom's story, the Arab woman calls on the Mizrahi narrator about twenty times in Arabic, forcing the protagonist to speak in the language of her parents, which quickly reveals her struggle to situate herself in her parent's Egyptian past and in the Israeli national narrative. The protagonist's immediate response "I am not a Sho'ah survivor . . . My parents are from Cairo," marks the pressure exercised by a Zionist nationalist narrative calling for the Mizrahi community's disavowal of their Arab origins and an assimilation by integrating the traumatic European history of the Shoah, as part of personal and collective memory (10). As Ella Shohat argues, in the national and cultural paradigms of Israeli and Arab nationalism, the identification "Arab Jew" became "an oxymoronic entity" ("Dislocated Identities" 78). Cast as outsiders amid the currents of pan-Arabism, Arab nationalism, and Zionism, Arab Jews experienced simultaneous geographical and cultural "dislocation" and "displacement" (Shohat, "Rupture and Return," 49–52).[23] After facing social and political pressure to leave their countries of origin, those who settled in Israel were forced to suppress their memories of the Arab world when these memories contradicted the foundational Ashkenazi Zionist narrative of exile and return, depicted in Zionist discourse as a journey from "diaspora to redemption" (Shohat, "Rupture and Return" 49 and "Dislocated Identities" 77–79). Shohat points out that in its approach to Arab Jews, Zionism adapted a colonial perspective of race and class to produce what she describes as "Zionist Orientalism" (*Israeli Cinema* 106–7). The depiction of Arab Jews in reductive Orientalist terms and the constant association of them with manual labor regardless of background forecloses the possibility of recognizing Arab Jewish heritage, including Levantine culture, in any positive way (*Israeli Cinema* 9).[24]

The encounter between the paranoiac narrator and the lurking Arab woman recalls the ethno-classist ghostly image from Kahanoff's *Jacob's Ladder* and *Monsieur Ibrahim et les fleurs du Coran*, wherein being from the working class comes to be associated in particular with the image of a faceless "Oriental" (see chapter 5). In his study of class structure and labor relations in Israel, Shlomo Swirski draws attention to similar social dynamics that reproduce a chain of hierarchical classification encompassing Ashkenazim (Jews of European origins), Mizrahim (Jews of Arabic backgrounds), and Palestinians. In this taxonomy of race and class, the image of the bourgeoisie is associated with Ashkenazim, while that of the proletariat is tightly connected to the Mizrahi population. This class divide is further reproduced and safeguarded by an "class-ethnic division of labour," which frames Ashkenazim as the custodians of a neo-colonial civilizing mission where they "transmit the protestant ethic . . . to Orientals" (44–45). Swirski explains: "In Israel, the Jewish labourer is Oriental despite the fact that he was born to parents who in all likelihood were not employed as labourers . . . He is Oriental because . . . [he] is representative of his 'race'—the ethnic group as a whole" (Swirski 45; Alcalay, *After Jews* 26). The Arabic exchange in Castel-Bloom's story brings this anxiety to the forefront. In the dialogue, the Arab woman refers to a different family member every time. One time she claims to be the protagonist's mother, another time her sister. Nevertheless, each time the narrator answers her, only the word *shughl* [work] remains unchanged. The repeated Arabic word for work reverberates in the text as if it were the echo of a stubborn inner voice, which the protagonist struggles to suppress in her attempt to liberate herself from this racialized image. The dialogue points out to the reification of the imaginary of labor as Arab. To be Arab is to be a worker and to do Arab work, or in Hebrew *Avoda Aravit*, to recall the Israeli sitcom of the same title, a satirical program that discussed the image of Palestinians in Israeli culture.[25] In *Jacob's Ladder*, Kahanoff also summons the specter of the Arab working woman in contrast to the emporium's owners' image. Rachel's family decides to hire a poor Syrian wet nurse for her newborn brother: Rachel is fascinated by this alternative maternal figure, who stands in contrast to the British governess. Amina loses her own child due to malnutrition (*Jacob's Ladder* 181). The text suggests the interdependence of a Levantine world divided along ethnic and class lines, where the glamorous elite Levantine class feeds on its working-class other.

Amina in *Jacob's Ladder*, Castel-Bloom's Arab woman reeking of sweat and hiding under a bench, and Matalon's unreliable photos of the Sicourelles all point toward the suppressed image of a working-class Arab/Levantine Other: A figure caught between intimacy and Otherness, an "intimate outsider," to use Mary Roberts's term (11) (see Roberts 1–16). Yet Castel-Bloom's story turns Levantine history upside down. The Arab woman asks the protagonist to take her home with her. In this case, Jews and Arabs exchange roles. In contrast to the Levantine past, the Jewish protagonist is expected to host the Arab woman. The protagonist refuses to do so. The story ends with an impasse, a symbolic dislocation and displacement of the characters. The Arab woman returns under the bench while the protagonist remains seated at the bus stop, fearing to be bitten again but refusing to go home.

Emporialism Mending the Present

Just as in any site of memory, emporialism has many lives and keeps producing further meanings and connections transmitting the memory of the past from one group to another, from one bourgeoisie to the subsequent one. Writing in English, Egyptian journalist Samir Raafat revisits colonial sites in Egypt and documents their stories on his website and in his book *Cairo, the Glory Years*. Raafat's nostalgic work filters many of the social and historical tensions expressed by the previous authors. He laments the passing of the Belle Époque and criticizes the indifference of young generations toward their national urban heritage (*Cairo* 9). Raafat re-creates the map of cosmopolitan Cairo through the history of Egyptian emporia and their founding families:

> In 1910, Moreno Cicurel opened Au Petit Bazar in Cairo's European Ismailia district at No. 3 Avenue Boulac (later Avenue Fouad) next to

> Chemla Frères (No. 11) one of Cairo's oldest department stores.... At Cicurel everything could be bought and the range was endless, from lavish glass, crockery, fabrics, cosmetics to the latest Parisian fashions. Many a high society lady's trousseau was prepared entirely at Cicurel. But before all this came to be, Moreno Cicurel launched several other ventures including Au Rêve des Dames, a haberdashery and ladies wear at No.19 Kasr al-Nil Street. As his business expanded and as the Cicurels, père & fils, bought off and merged with, smaller competitors, Cicurel became Egypt's leading department store with branches in several towns and cities. ("The House of Cicurel")

Through the nostalgic lens of emporialism, the text establishes the position of the current postcolonial bourgeoisie as heir and protector of that past. On his website and in his book, Raafat delves into the history of Cairo, revealing the stories and mysteries encrypted on the walls of the houses and monuments that once belonged to the colonial bourgeoisie, including the proprietors of Egypt's emporia. Some of his articles adopt mysterious titles, such as "Murder at Villa Cicurel," recalling the genres of detective and romance novels. Among the many stories he brings to life is that of the murder of the family's patriarch by his chauffeur: "Not since the May 1921 Alexandria trial of murderesses Raya and Sakina had Egyptian society been so gruesomely entertained. And now it was the brutal Hollywood-type murder of Solomon Cicurel that would absorb the nation's attention for the next few months" ("Murder"). Raafat retells the murder incident and contacts the grandson of the alleged murderer to update the story. In this context, the reconstruction of the narrative creates an imaginary continuum that bypasses the postcolonial rupture.

On the other hand, emporialism as *lieux de mémoire* has mobilized and brought several communities into contact with each other. Emporial nostalgia became a site of contention, and connection, with the past. Websites like the Historical Society of Jews from Egypt (www.hsje.org) give an account of Egyptian department stores to reclaim the history of Egyptian Jews before Egyptian independence. Similarly, Raafat's website led many members of the Jewish Egyptian diaspora to correspond with the writer and post their updated news. The site mediates a complex history of unresolved political tensions. It was only the beginning of a other social media outlets and literary and media productions, which connected Egyptian Jews around the world but also with Egypt. They share memories of their childhood and those of their parents in Egypt and afterward. They upload official documents, photos, and ads of that history. They document a charged history filled with pain and nostalgia: that of Egyptian Jews and of many communities who lived in Egypt before1956 or the nationalization of the Suez Canal.[26]

Since 2019, the internal spaces of the Sednaoui and Chemla department stores have been divided into small spaces and rented as boutiques catering to the masses. They become Mall Sednaoui and Mall Chemla (Hamdi and Gamal; Hifzi; Moustapha; Saleh). The façade of the stores and their founders' names remain intact, but the site the of emporia remains in flux, taking other narratives and experiences of the city.

Conclusion

In *Geographical Imaginations*, Derek Gregory posits:

> The task of a critical human geography—of a geographical imagination—is ... to unfold that utopian gesture and replace it with another: one that recognizes *the corporeality of vision* and reaches out, *from one body to another*, not in a mood of arrogance, aggression, and conquest but in a spirit of humility, understanding, and care. This is not an individualism; neither is it a corporatism. If it dispenses with the privileges traditionally accorded to "History," it nonetheless requires a scrupulous attention to the junctures and fissures between many different histories: a multileveled dialogue between past and present conducted as a history (or an historical geography) of the present. (416)

Inherent in this argument is what Gregory calls "the decorporealization" of space, which obscures the materiality of the body and its central role as both subject and object of space. He suggests that this tension calls for the need to relocate the human body at the center of these narratives to reinscribe in these various maps the complexity of human experience.

In my introduction, I called for a multiscalar and a multiplanar reading of literature. The planes I have retraced in these chapters include a close reading of emporialism inscribed in the space of the department store as a heterotopia, the history of French-Egyptian cultural and urban exchange, and the various representations of the stores in literature and visual media, including fragmented references to these spaces, which in their turn operate as sites of memory. In so doing I ask a set of questions. Department stores are primarily spaces for producing and consuming cosmopolitan and arguably colonial "cultural capital." What happens when the memory of consumption functions as a cultural product making its way back into the political economy as a fetishized good, to be consumed by readers? Can memory of consumption serve as a superstructure to reorder social relations of production through the theme of a nostalgic return to a bygone past embodied in the memory of material culture, rather than the actual material culture?

My project began with the final chapter, with the narrative fragments on department stores found in contemporary literature. Throughout the book, I hoped to undo the "utopian gesture" implicit in these narratives. Revisiting emporialism means revisiting the spaces of its production and reactivating several material and symbolic regimes of values, on the economic, political, social, and aesthetic fronts. That encounter has allowed various authors to write and contest history, negotiate between past and present, history and memory, between a space that was conceived as an embodiment of a modern urban and national culture and the individuals who shaped, have been shaped by, or subverted the function and symbolic significance of these spaces. Each investigation traces a different map, shaped by intersecting regimes of value, which offer insight into the multidirectional and intersectional process of memory that informs our understanding of the Mediterranean and of contemporary culture and political economy.

Finally, one of my objectives has been to examine not only the circulation of goods and people in the Mediterranean, that is, the trade network, but also the "iconomic" quality of the Mediterranean. That is, the Mediterranean in circulation, as myth and imaginary used by various people to forge in their turn their own economic, social, and political relations. In all these situations, the space of the department store, and consequently that of the Mediterranean, is not considered an object of a lost past or an excavated fossil. Thinking of emporialism as a part of a modern spatial schema/heterotopia and as a narrative and iconographic schema brings to light another area where the circulation of capital collides with that of literature and memory. In each new location, the emporium is enmeshed in a new regime of values, which casts a different light on the space, exceeding the rhetoric and praxes of emporialism. The various narratives spun around it produce various, sometimes competing meanings, each with its own recalibration of race, class, and gender relations. The emporium is part of a multidirectional and intersectional narrative.

Emporialism attests to the enmeshment of maps and histories. In emulating the Saint-Simonian world order of interconnected networks of transport, trade, and people, emporialism projects Saint-Simon's phantasmatic gendered Mediterranean dream of uniting the Orient and Occident. Spanning a sea divided among empires, emporia—and the narratives about them—become the sites of many contested ideologies and spatial practices. Emporialism reveals a complex interconnected history bridging industrial capitalism to global culture through its large-scale institutionalization of commercial heterotopias that create a shopping experience centered around the colonial experience and the optics of industrialism. Yet Mediterranean culture surpasses Saint-Simon's Orientalist binary. For many writers, emporialism serves as a broken mirror, reflecting the failure of imperialism and its ambition of acquisition and professed civilizing mission. This crisscrossing of maps and histories has allowed the various peoples of Egypt and France, navigating between the ebb and flow of nation-states and empires, to reinvent their national identity and interrogate and imagine new forms of modernity, citizenship, cosmopolitanism, and social equality. Most of the widely known representations of emporialism and the Mediterranean come from members of middle-class or elite authors who have the agency to document their experiences. In prioritizing this perspective, they overlook to an extent the actual material history, including social and colonial dynamics, that led to its construction. Much remains to be said about the origins of emporialism, the Mediterranean, Levantinism, the agents who participated in their production, and the "politics of memory" that continue to contribute to their current framing.

Notes

Introduction

1. "Il y a dans un grand magasin [de joujoux] une extraordinaire gaité qui le rend préférable à un bel appartement bourgeois. Toute la vie en miniature ne s'y trouve-t-elle pas, et beaucoup plus colorée, nettoyée et luisante que la vie réelle? On y voit des jardins, des théâtres, de belles toilettes, des yeux comme le diamant, des joues allumés par le fard, des dentelles charmantes, des voitures, des écuries, des étables, des ivrognes, des charlatans, des banquiers, des comédiens, des polichinelles... des cuisines et des armées entières bien disciplinées avec de la cavalerie et de l'artillerie" ("Morale du joujou," 1: 582, in *Oeuvres complètes*)

2. "Toute la vie en miniature ne s'y trouve-t-elle pas, et beaucoup *plus colorée, nettoyée et luisante que la vie elle-même*?" (("Morale du joujou," 1: 582, in *Oeuvres complètes*, emphasis added).

3. "C'est un moi insatiable du non-moi, qui, à chaque instant, le rend et l'exprime *en images plus vivantes que la vie elle-même*" ("Le peintre de la vie moderne," 2: 692, emphasis added).

4. Makdisi examines the history of romanticism as a genre, which developed in tandem with modern imperialism and industrial capitalism.

5. See N. Smith, "Homeless/Global," and *Uneven Development* 131–54;

6. On the transnational history of the middle class, see Lopez and Weinstein.

7. On the distinction between goods and commodities in material culture, see Myers, "Introduction," in *Empire of Things*.

8. See "History of Amazon: From Garage Startup to the Largest E-Commerce Marketplace," https://www.capitalism.com/history-of-amazon/.

9. By "allochronic" I refer to Fabian; Herzfeld, "Practical Mediterraneanism."

10. Beck distinguishes between "cosmopolitanization" and cosmopolitanism. The former is a passive form of cosmopolitanism, a product of globalization, whereas the latter is an active intellectual and political engagement (1–14).

11. The performance was scheduled to run from 2 September 2022 to February 2023. Because of popular demand, it was kept on for two more months, until 23 April 2023. See https://www.lebonmarche.com/fr/lbm_gazette-interview-bonheur-des-dames.html.

12. For more on urban schemata of modernity, see Kamal, "Reflections." For analysis of space, iconography, and connection to both the local and the global, see Amin and Thrift; Bachelard; Bennett; de Certeau 1, 2; Cosgrove, *Geography* and *Social Formation*; Cosgrove and Daniels; Lefebvre; Gregory, *Explorations* and *Geographical Imagination*; Jameson, *Postmodernism* and *Archaeologies*.

13. On the relation between hosts and guests, migrants and citizens, see Derrida and Dufourmantelle.

14. I am referring here to Dipesh Chakrabarty's critique of Eurocentrism in *Provincializing Europe*.

15. On this issue, see Eldem, "Plurality."

16. These complex connections have been at the center of recent studies on Egypt's colonial history. See Jacob; Z. Fahmy, *Ordinary Egyptians*; see also Watenpaugh.

17. Kamal, "Ghostly Labor" 26; By *extraterritoriality*, I refer to the work of Sarah Abrevaya Stein, Ziad Fahmy, and Will Hanley. Stein defines extraterritoriality as both a legal situation and a phenomenon where Ottoman subjects became protégés of French and British empires. Following the capitulation agreement, Ottoman subjects would hold a European passport from one empire while residing in another. See Stein 2–3; Z. Fahmy, "Jurisdictional Borderlands"; Hanley. For the notion of imperial formation, see also Stoler, McGranaham, and Perdue.

18. See also Werner and Zimmermann.

19. For histories and debates about Mediterranean studies, I relied on Braudel, *The Mediterranean and the Mediterranean World* and *La Méditerranée I, II, III*; Abulafia; Balfour; Dakhlia; Danforth; Herzfeld, "Practical Mediterraneanism," "Honour and Shame," and "Horns"; Horden and Purcell; Trevor-Roper; Dobie; Shepard, *French Mediterraneans*; Elhariri and Tamalet, *Critically Mediterranean*; Isabella and Zanou; Tucker, *Making*; Derrida.

20. Spivak refers to Heidegger's notion of "worlding" in "The Origins of the Work of Art" (*Basic Writings* 170). See also Heidegger, "The Age of the World Picture," in *The Question* 115–54; "The World as an Exhibition" in Mitchell, *Colonising Egypt* 10–12.

Chapter 1

1. Zaki occupied various positions in his life, including translator, interpreter, instructor, and secretary for the Egyptian Cabinet. For more information on Zaki's life, see Volait, "Ahmad Zaki."

2. To refer to department stores, Zaki used the word *al-Makhāzin al-kobra*, which is the literal translation of "grands magasins." The word *makhzan* (plural *makhāzin*)

comes from Arabic meaning warehouse. See "Magasin" in *Larousse Dictionnaire étymologique*; see also "Magasin" in *Le Robert: Dictionnaire culturel en langue française*.

3. By *Rūmīs*, Zaki means the members of Greek communities living in the Ottoman Empire.

4. For a translation of this experience, see Zaki et al.

5. On the department store, Baudelaire writes: Toute la vie en miniature ne s'y trouve-t-elle pas, et beaucoup *plus colorée, nettoyée et luisante que la vie elle-même?"* (1:582, emphasis added). Describing modern urban life, Baudelaire says: "C'est un moi insatiable du non-moi, qui, à chaque instant, le rend et l'exprime *en images plus vivantes que la vie elle-même*" (2:692, emphasis added) [He (the modern *flâneur*) is an 'I' with an in insatiable appetite for the 'non-I', at every instant rendering and explaining it [modern crowd] in pictures more living than life itself (Baudelaire, *The Painter* 9).

6. On biopolitics and biopower, see Foucault, *Discipline and Punish* and *History of Sexuality*; Agamben.

7. Mercedes Volait describes Zaki as a man of letters well versed in Orientalism and Occidentalism ("Ahmad Zaki" 21). See also Smail Salhi. For Zaki's worldview through his writings, see Zaki, *Qamus al-Joghraphia*.

8. For Zaki's relation to German culture, see Mangold-Will.

9. For more information on France from 1848 to 1914, see Agulhon, *The French Republic* and *The Republican Experiment*; Clark; Harvey, *Paris*; Fureix and Jarrige; Heath; Mayeur and Reberioux; Rabinow; Shaya; Siegfried; Todd; Woolf.

10. Here I allude to Eugene Weber's book *Peasants into Frenchmen*.

11. Photo of old Paris at the 1900 universal exhibition are available in Martel.

12. In *The Arcades Project*, Benjamin gives a portrait of the tensions in the utopian purview of Saint-Simonian industrialism crafted in the universal exhibitions and the emporium during the Second Empire: "The Saint-Simonians, who envision the industrialization of the earth, take up the idea of world exhibitions. Chevalier, the first authority in the new field, is a student of Enfantin and editor of the Saint-Simonian newspaper The Saint-Simonians anticipated the development of the global economy, but not the class struggle. Next to their active participation in industrial and commercial enterprises around the middle of the century stands their helplessness on all questions concerning the proletariat. World exhibitions glorify the exchange value of the commodity. They create a framework in which its use value recedes into the background. They open a phantasmagoria which a person enters in order to be distracted. The entertainment industry makes this easier by elevating the person to the level of the commodity" (7).

13. For the history of Saint-Simonianism, see Abi-Mershed; Charlety; Chevalier, "*Le Globe*, 31 Janvier 1832," "*Le Globe*, 5 février 1832," and "*Le Globe*, 12 février 1832"; Coilly and Régnier; Musso *Crititique des réseaux* and *Saint Simon*; Pilbeam; Picon, *Les Saint-Simoniens* and "L'utopie spectacle"; Ribeill.

14. Earlier versions of this poster were printed in 1891, and then reprinted in 1897, 1898. For the French translation, see Zaki et al. 157–62. This poster is also available on p. 158 of the French translation.

15. See also Lockman 74–78.

16. In Ovidian myth, Pygmalion was a sculptor who sought to create his dream woman. The narrative represents a masculinist quest for the construction of the perfect woman. The story of Pygmalion was later adapted by George Bernard Shaw into a modern play by the same name in 1913, and into a Broadway play (1954) and a movie *My Fair Lady* (1956). For more on the contemporary impact of this ideal, see Hallstead. For the various adaptations of Shaw's *Pygmalion*, see Ray.

17. For the role of the European bourgeois woman in domesticating empire, see B. Smith; Poovey.

18. Kamal, "Ghostly Labor." My notion of ethno-classism, especially the connection to the civilizing mission and the ambiguous representation of labor in metropole and colonial subjects, draws and elaborates on McClintock's concept of "commodity racism" and Mona Domosh's idea of "flexible racism." For the latter, see Domosh 181–94. Domosh explores the connection between nineteenth- and early twentieth-century racial representation in American society and consumerism, as evidenced in the commercial advertising created for international markets, which promoted the idea that the use of American products embodies the promise of becoming "white through consumption" (189). For the colonial example of ethno-classism, see chapters 2 and 5.

19. "Ajoutez-y des blanchisseuses, des mendiantes, des femmes sans souliers, des poissardes racolées depuis plusieurs jours à prix d'argent.—Tel est le premier noyau, et il va grossissant ; car, de force ou de gré, la troupe s'incorpore les femmes qu'elle rencontre, portières, couturières, femmes de ménage et même des bourgeoises" (*Les Origines* 154).

20. For an example of the department store's use of ethnological exhibit in its promotional campaigns, see Mathur 27–42.

21. My summary of the various traits of department stores around the world relies on Andia; Aunay; Auslander; Berlanstein; Barthes, *Language* and *Fashion System*; Batignani; Caracalla; Clausen, "Department Stores," *Frantz Jourdain*, and "The Department Store"; Crossick and Jaumain; "Hommage à Monsier Boucicaut"; De Grazia; Gaston-Breton; Giffard; Hendrickson; Jarry; Kupferschmidt, *European Department Stores* and "Who Needed?"; MacPherson; Papadia; Pasdermadjian; Rachline; Rappaport; Remus; Reynolds, *City Consumed* and "Entangled Communities"; Siegfried; Tiersten, *Marianne in the Market*; Weiss-Sussex and Zitzlsperger; Weitz; Whitaker; Zola, *Œuvres*.

22. On Les Halles, see Mead, *Making Modern Paris* 193–226, particularly 222–26 for the affinity between the architecture of churches and markets.

23. On the porosity of imperial and colonial territories, see Stoler and Cooper, "Between Metropole"; see also Stoler, McGranaham, and Perdue, *Imperial Formation*.

24. See also "emporium," in the *Oxford Dictionary of English Etymology*; I owe this idea to Samuel Weber, who drew my attention to the etymology of the word.

25. Coffee was available in a limited form before its introduction to the court. Some coffee places already existed in Marseille and Paris. See the following note.

26. For the history of coffee shops in Paris since 1673 and their locations, see Fosca; LeTailleur; Langle. See also Pao.

27. See also Cohen; St-Fulchrand.

28. Al-Musawi describes the European obsession with *The Nights* as "nightism" (19). For more on the history of the *Nights* and its imaginary, see *Les Mille et une nuits*; Chaulet-Achour; Sermain.

29. See B. Anderson. For the role of advertising in shaping the imaginary of consumption, see Hahn.

30. The passage du Caire was photographed by Eugène Atget in 1911 (Benjamin 42). Benjamin notes that the covered arcades were an inspiration from Napoleon's expedition in Italy (102). See also Moncan, *Passages en Europe*; Canac.

31. Benjamin mentions that the printing press took over the arcade and its vicinity in the late eighteenth century (46). For a history of the design of the Universal Exhibition and Napoleon's mission to Egypt, including the introduction of the printing press, see Mitchell, *Colonising Egypt*. He does not mention that the passage du Caire was the first passage in Paris, but he notices that it adjoined the "cour des miracles" (42).

32. For British and French writers' use of the motif of disillusionment and Orientalist narrative structures to frame their visit to Egypt, see Said, *Orientalism* 166–97.

33. This is the original French description by Kermel: "Non, non, m'écrai-je en mettant le pied sur la première d'entrée, il n'y a là ni reflets, ni souvenirs, ni les témoignages de ce que pouvait la main de celui qui immortalisa le nom du Caire. Je ne vois là ni les richesses de l'Égypte, ni ses parfums, ni ses enfants, ni le grandiose des monuments, ni les profondeurs de ses pensées; ce n'est point qui peut poétiser le berceau des sciences et des arts. Profanation des mots!" (68). See also Moncan, *Passages couverts* 260–61.

34. In her lectures for Egyptian women at Cairo University in 1910, Mademoiselle Couvreur, from Lycée Racine in Paris, highlighted the history of the Egyptian shawl in French fashion and Empress Josephine's distinctive flair with this trend. Just as in the case of rugs, this exemplifies how Orientalist material culture would trickle back to its milieu of origins, as a valuable commodity based on the appreciation of the European consumer. See Couvreur esp. fasicule 4; On the various lectures offered to students in that era, including the women's section, see *Annuaire*.

35. Boucicaut became a partner in 1852, at the beginning of the Second Empire. Finally, the store was expanded into a *grand magasin* in 1869.

36. Department stores around the world were sites of transnational exchange, mediating the local and the global. Some stores might have copied the strategies and design of Le Bon Marché, but they were also the products of their own milieux and modernization processes. Likewise, Le Bon Marché emulated its competitors. For instance, the store borrowed the idea of the buffet from the United States (Giffard 25).

37. Many stores used the words *magasin* and *maison* interchangeably. Le Bon Marché stressed its image as a bourgeois household in advertisements (Tiersten, "Marianne in the Department Store" 121).

38. See, Le Bon Marché, Souvenir of the Bon Marché.

39. As Benjamin suggests: "The arcades, which originally were designed to serve commercial ends, become dwelling places in Fourier" (17). See also Fourier, "The Phalanstery," "An Architectural Innovation," and *Théorie de quatre mouvements*; Beecher.

40. For the Saint-Simonian and Fourierist impact on the Parisian urban map, see Papayanis 169–200.

41. On paternalism in Le Bon Marché, see also Miller 75–90; Giffard 225–30; Badel, "Employers' Organisations"; Chessel.

42. For the history of guilds and *campagnonnage* in France, see Sewell. For the image of the couple in French social utopianism, see Moses 90–91; Moses and Rabine 20–21.

43. Giffard gives a detailed account of all the programs Boucicaut set up for his employees. He also mentions that l'Association d'économie sociale visited Le Bon Marché in 1882. The association praised Boucicaut in a newspaper article and mentioned the strong influence of Frédéric le Play on his views (225).

44. For similar Orientalist campaigns in other stores, see Galeries Lafayette, "Galeries Lafayette Tapis," circa 1910; La Samaritaine, "Jouets, étrennes, 1914"; Printemps, "Au Printemps, tapis & ameublements," 1913.

45. "La tyrannie des objets est plus grande que nous ne l'imaginons sur nos habitudes, sur l'ordre et le cours de nos pensées intimes."

46. "Il s'établit entre les hommes et les objets qui les entourent . . . certains rapports harmonieux qui donnent aux habitations un caractère, comme une âme" (Viollet-le-Duc, *Dictionnaire* 400, qtd. in Havard 2). See chapter 3 in this book, where Zola translates this aesthetic into a literary aesthetic.

47. In the Mediterranean system, Michel Chevalier claims: "The most widespread, monumental and deeply-rooted struggle which has ever made the Earth reverberate with the din of battle is that of the Orient and the Occident. This struggle represents the distinct character of a phase of civilization which has evolved from historical times to the present day. It is the most resounding manifestation of the war that, for six thousand years, has taken place between mind and matter, spirituality and sensuality, a war which we are now bringing to an end" ("*Le Globe* 5 février 1832," 114). For the French text, see note 159. For Chevalier's writings on the Mediterranean system, see Musso, *Le Saint-Simonisme L'Europe*.

48. Haussmann's contemporary, architect Viollet-le-Duc, lamented how the Haussmannian building erased every sense of individuality and homeliness: "La personalité de l'individu s'efface et où il n'est guère possible d'admettre l'amour du foyer" (Viollet-le-Duc, *Entretiens* 304, qtd. in Eleb 294). On the tension in the Haussmannian urban plan between outside and inside, see Van Zanten, *Building Paris* 7–45. On eclecticism and the contrast between the bourgeois interior and Haussmann's Paris, see Van Zanten, *Building Paris* 38–43 and *Designing Paris*. See also Hoganson 13–55: Hoganson explores the role of Orientalist material culture and eclecticism in the American household during the nineteenth century. For the French context, see Tiersten, *Marianne in the Market* 155–84; Lasc.

49. The actual lines from the memoirs read: "J'ai encore un autre motif de placer l'obélisque au centre, c'est qu'il ne rappelle aucun événement politique et qu'il est sûr d'y rester, tandis que vous pourriez y voir quelque jour un monument expiatoire ou une statue de liberté" (Rambuteau 388–89). See also Schneider 2:234, n62.

50. See Le Bon Marché, "Arménienne."

51. On the depiction of "demoiselles," see Giffard 89–107.

52. See also Spiekermann. On suffrage in Britain and consumer culture, see Gurney 104–6.

53. McBride covers the social and economic working conditions of female salesclerks in department stores from 1870 to 1920. As she argues, despite the cliché, the social mobility of female clerks was rare, and the hours were not relatively better than that of domestic servants. On history of labor, see also Berlanstein; Redclift and Sinclair.

54. For examples of the panoramic genre, see Benjamin 6–7; Cohen. See also Hahn 20–21. On "Panoramania," see Schwartz 157–76.

55. As Giedion pinpoints, Haussmann's critics, like Adolph Tiers, perceived his city from the purview of the pedestrian. They could not grasp that Haussmann's urban project was geared more for the circulation of vehicles than for residents. See also Ferry 104–6. In 1868, two years before the end of the Second Empire, Ferry's critiques of Haussmann's project confirm the same viewpoint.

56. Under the section "les flâneurs," Giffard gives a detailed account of various types of *flâneurs*, men and women (108–18); Giffard interviews a salesgirl who describes to him the various types of clients she encounters every day, their nationalities, shopping habits, and behavior, from flirting to the way they talk to the employees (189–204). On women as *flâneurs*, or *flâneuses*, see D'Souza and McDonough. For a profile of Parisian urban experience by nineteenth-century writers, see Parmentier.

57. See Rappaport 178–214; Krakauer 291–304.

58. See also Avenel.

Chapter 2

1. For the Saint-Simonian contribution in Egypt and in its subsequent impact on the French empire, see Levallois and Régnier. For the contribution of Saint-Simonians to Egypt's urban and national project, see Volait, *Architectes et architectures* 52–62; Alleaume. For the Saint-Simonian activities in Algeria, after Egypt, see Abi-Mershed.

2. Referring to the digging of the canal (*percement*), Barrault said: "Suez est notre centre de vie et travail. Là nous ferons l'acte que le monde attend pour confesser que nous sommes mâles" [Suez is the center of our life and work. There, we will accomplish the act which the world awaits to attest that we are males] (qtd. in Musso, *Saint-Simon* 115).

3. This idea, I argue, surfaces in Émile Zola's novel *Au Bonheur des dames*, in which the Orientalist *grand magasin* expands to devour the metropolis (see chapter 3).

4. On the Statue of Liberty, see Silverman.

5. "La fellah[a] [sic], c'est la femme du peuple par excellence; elle tient au sol par toutes ses fibres; ses enfants sont les plus vivaces; ils résistent mieux à la misère, au manque d'hygiène, à toutes les causes délétères qui attaquent et font disparaître l'enfant de l'étranger, même celui du riche Turc" (Voilquin 289).

6. For colonial and Ottoman Egypt see Daly; K. Fahmy, *All the Pasha's Men*; El Shakry; Marsot, *Egypt in the Reign of Muhammad Ali*; Tignor, *Modernization*.

7. Gregory refers to Mary Louise Pratt's reading of the colonial discourse of travel writing; see Pratt, "Scratches on the Face."

8. Ismail was a friend of Haussmann. Having met in Paris, the *khedive* hosted the baron in his Istanbul residence after Haussmann left his position in the French government (Des Cars 295, 323).

9. For a detailed mapping of the commercial geography of the area and the locations of the department stores, see Moustapha 125–48.

10. By *extraterritoriality*, I refer to Sarah Abrevaya Stein's definition of the term in *Extraterritorial Dreams*. For the description of the capitulation system and extraterritoriality, see note 20 in the introduction.

11. For instance, the Cairene opera house combined architectural elements from both Opera Garnier and La Scala in Milan (Raymond 312). The Italian urban and cultural influence was ubiquitous in the different aspects of the Egyptian modernity. Mehmet Ali's educational missions started with an academic collaboration with Italy rather than France (Alleaume 120–30). This experience is still marginalized in Egyptian historiography in favor of a Francophile imaginary, which associates the beginning of modern Egyptian history with the French-Egyptian encounter during Napoleon's 1798 expedition. For a detailed account of the diverse and multilayered urban development in modern Egypt since the time of Mehmet Ali, see Abu-Lughod (110–15); Alleaume; Mitchell, *Colonising Egypt*. See also Giacomelli and Godoli; Petricioli; Raymond; Volait, *Architectes et architectures* 81–155 and *Le Caire-Alexandrie*.

12. "L'Égypte, vois-tu, c'est tout simplement une terre africaine, turque de nom, anglaise de droit; on y trouve des Égyptiens qui parlent l'arabe, des hôtels où des cuisiniers allemands vous fabriquent des mets français, servis par des garçons suisses, des tziganes napolitains qui jouent des airs russes, des femmes valaques qui se font passer pour des Parisiennes, et des juifs espagnols qui se disent Anglais. Seuls, les Anglais de toutes marques sont bon teint et le prouvent par la façon dont ils mènent les gens et les choses. Eux seuls, sont rois, parce que, seuls, ils savent être pratiques" (Ivray, *Les Porteuses* 72).

13. Although in the typical history of the Egyptian belle époque, this multicultural aspect is associated with the Suez Canal project, this culture was already in the making before then (see chapter 6). When Maxime Du Camp traveled to Egypt in 1849, he met officers from Napoleon Bonaparte's army: actors and translators who communicated in a multitude of languages and did not fit a typical French national image. He found in

Egypt an Orient full of comic European characters drifting aimlessly and whose fortune ranged from living in unparalleled luxury to extreme misery (Du Camp 118–40).

14. See also Eldem, "Les Ottomans." On the shift in the transformation of the cosmopolitan structure at the end of the Ottoman Empire and the polarization of the Kemalist bourgeoisie, see Göçek 134–41.

15. For a detailed history of the *efendiyya* class, see Ryzova. See also Jacob.

16. The plays of Ya'qub Sanu', written during the second half of the nineteenth century, critiqued the adoption of European fashions and etiquette for men and woman. For an example of these plays, see Sanu', *Al-Amira al-iskandaraniyya* and *Abu ridah wa ka'b al-Khayr*, *Anisa 'ala-l-Moda* [A Fashionable Woman], *Ghandur Masr* [Cairo's Dandy]. See Gendzier; Milhaud 48–49; see also M. Russell 41.

17. See also an advertisement from Le Bon Marché in *L'Egyptienne* (January 1932).

18. For the equivalent French image, see figures 1.3 and 1.4.

19. See *Anis al-Jalis*, vol. 19, 31 October 1907.

20. For the Chemla advertisement, see *al-Lata'if al-Musawwara*, 5 April 1915.

21. See Baron, *Egypt as a Woman*, esp. chap. 1.

22. See *al-Lata'if al-Musawwara*, 14 August 1916; 24 March 1919, 6; 31 March 1919, 5; 28 March 1921, 2; 17 October 1927, 11.

23. The same image is also available in M. Russell 40.

24. "The New Woman," *al-Kashkul al-Musawwar*, 21 November 1921.

25. *Rose al-Yusef*, 13 January 1927, 11.

26. See the 1910 Mitsukoshi advertisement "'Oriental Beauty' Presenting Mitsukoshi Department Store to the World," in Moeran 173. The ad features a woman in kimono looking at the viewer and holding a small model of the department store in her hands. In 1912, Galeries Lafayette published an ad of a woman carrying a small model of the department store. The woman represents the city of Paris, with the motto of the city placed by her feet (Tiersten, *Marianne in the Market* 222). In 1909, Selfridges published a similar advertisement of a woman representing the city of London, carrying a miniature model of the store, to announce the opening of the store. By her feet the caption reads: "London receiving her newest installation" (Wild 2).

27. A *taqtūqa* is a nineteenth-century "light" genre of song that hinges on describing the everyday. A part of Egyptian urban culture, it generally expresses either comic or tragic themes, addressing many social issues at the center of attention of the Egyptian urban community, such as marriage, polygamy, divorce, and the "reconstitution of the family around the nuclear model" (Lagrange, "Women" 229).

28. In French in the original.

29. Abdel Hay, qtd. in Lagrange, *Musiciens* 732. Quotes added for emphasis.

لسه طالعة من البيضة
لسه طالعة من البيضة وعاملة العشرة وذمتها / حقول إيه ياختي أريضة [قريضة] والله بانت لبتها /ع البهلي ماشية من غير بيشة تتغمزلي شمال ويمين / تقولش على راسها ريشة والا ماشية على عجين / تتدلع . . . تتشخلع و لسه طالعة من البيضة / الكاب محزق على جسمها و الشعر مقصوص"ألا جرسون"/ البدع دا من طبعها واللي عشقها صبح مجنون/ تتدلع . . . / من الصبح بدري على شملا و بعدها ع "البون

"مارشيه" / دي تعمل لك كل عامله خلتني يا ناس برّيه/تتدلع . . . / الدانس دا حتما ليلاتي ترقص لي تانجو و شارلستون / مهما أقول وألا أهاتي. دا الرقص من ضمن الفنون/ تتدلع . . .

30. Foreign brothel owners benefited from the capitulation system, which protected them from prosecution (Hammad and Biancani 251). Although the nationalist discourse on prostitution during the late nineteenth and early twentieth centuries constantly claimed that sex work was an imperial influence, centuries before British colonialism sex workers paid taxes, revealing that they were implicitly recognized (Hammad and Biancani 237.). The majority of sex workers were Egyptian women. Police records and reports from World War I mention that "at least 2.300 native plus 800 European women registered as prostitutes" (Biancani, *"Let Down"* 83).

31. The magazine does not state the sources, but the first caricature on the left row was published in *al-Fukaha* magazine, on 10 August 1927. The other cartoons could be also from the same source.

32. For similar processes involving the reconstruction of ethnic representation and nationalism in Iran, see Ebrahim.

33. On enslaved women in domestic spaces, see Tucker 165–72.

34. On the final departure of various communities from Egypt, see Beinin, *Dispersion*; Dalachanis; Ilbert, Yannakakis, and Hassoun; Krämer; Petricioli; Starr, *Remembering*. For narratives, see Aciman; Lagnado, *Arrogant Years* and *Man in the White*; see final note in chapter 6.

Chapter 3

1. "Du milieu de la place Gaillon on apercevait ce salon oriental, fait uniquement de tapis et de portières. . . . Cette tente de pacha somptueux était meublée de fauteuils et de divans, faits avec des sacs de chameau. . . . La Turquie, l'Arabie, la Perse, les Indes étaient là. On avait vidé les palais, dévalisé les mosquées et les bazars. L'or fauve dominait, dans l'effacement des tapis-anciens, dont les teintes fanées gardaient une chaleur sombre, un fondu de fournaise éteinte d'une belle couleur cuite de vieux maître. Et des visions d'Orient flottaient sous le luxe de cet art barbare, au milieu de l'odeur forte que les vieilles laines avaient gardée du pays de la vermine et du soleil" (141). The English translations of Zola in this chapter are from *The Ladies' Paradise*, translated by Brian Nelson. The French version of Zola's novel I cite is the 1998 Librairie Générale Française edition.

2. Notably, Zola exaggerates the conflict between the department store and its surrounding traditional boutiques. The connection between the *grand magasin* and the department store was more complex and multilayered than this. By the end of the century, the city recognized the value of small shops (Badel 300). In some cases, the small stores benefited from the presence of the *grand magasin* in their vicinity, since it brought more clients to the area (Nord 83, 91).

3. "Je veux dans *Au Bonheur des dames* faire le poème de l'activité moderne. Donc, changement complet de la philosophie: Plus de pessimisme, ne pas conclure à

la bêtise et à la mélancolie de la vie, conclure au contraire à son continuel labeur, à la puissance et à la gaité de son enfantement" (Zola, *Au Bonheur des dames* dossiers préparatoires 2). [I want in *Au Bonheur des dames* to write/compose the poem of modern life. Thus, a complete change of philosophy, no more pessimism, not to conclude with human stupidity and life's melancholy, quite the opposite, on life's continuous labor, on the power, and joy of its birth.]

4. Zola, *Au Bonheur des dames* dossiers préparatoires 2.

5. "Martyrs" in the French original: "Toute revolution voulait des martyrs" (451).

6. "Vu à vol d'oiseau. . . . Paris s'étendait, mais un Paris rapetissé, mangé par le monstre: les maisons d'une humilité de chaumières dans le voisinage s'éparpillaient ensuite en une poussière de cheminées indistinctes; les monuments semblaient fondre, à gauche deux traits pour Notre-Dame, à droite un accent circonflexe pour les Invalides, au fond le Panthéon, honteux et perdu, moins gros qu'une lentille. L'horizon tombait en poudre n'était plus qu'un cadre dédaigné . . . jusqu'à la vaste campagne, dont les lointains noyés indiquaient l'esclavage" (468).

7. Zola's description of the feminized gigantic emporium bears a striking resemblance to advertisements portraying a giant woman looking over and almost crushing the cityscape (see chapters 1 and 2).

8. See Agulhon, *Republican Experiment*; E. Weber.

9. See Plessis; K. Ross, *Emergence* and *Communal Luxury*; da Costa Meyer; Harvey, *Paris*.

10. Robida had probably read Zola's novel by that time, when it was published in serial form. As I mention later, Robida sketched a cartoon in 1883 to parody *Au bonheur des dames* (Robida, "Au bonheur des dames").

11. *Comptoirs* could also mean "shop counter" in French. "Après l'aristocratie de la naissance, c'était maintenant l'aristocratie de l'argent; c'était le califat des comptoirs, le despotisme de la rue du Sentier, la tyrannie du commerce aux idées vénales et étroites, aux instincts vaniteux et fourbes" (Huysmans, *À Rebours* 346).

12. On the tension between Hugo's romantic rendition of Notre Dame's architecture and Zola's naturalist depiction of the central markets, see Mead, *Making Modern Paris* 193–226. For more on Zola's writing see Bloom; B. Nelson.

13. See Balzac, *La Peau de chagrin*, in *Oeuvres complètes*. For an analysis of the store in Balzac's novel, see S. Weber esp. chap. 6. For Weber, the store represents the antithesis of the casino.

14. See Said, *Orientalism* 51–110. For examples of the imaginary of psychosexual paranoia of invasion in contemporary French political discourse of immigration, see Lockman 66–99; Shepard, *Sex, France*; Mack; Scott; Kamal, "'A Living Tableau.'" This paranoia is still present in contemporary French literature. See Houellebecq's novel *La Soumission*.

15. "La France a un centre; une identité depuis plusieurs siècles. Elle doit être considérée comme une personne qui vit et se meut" (Michelet, *Introduction* 49) [France has a center, an identity for many centuries. She should be considered like a person who lives and moves]. In the preface to *Histoire de la France* from 1869, Michelet reiterates the

same idea: "Le premier je la vis [France] comme une âme et une personne" (2) [I was the first to see her as a soul and a person].

16. "En quel sens la France est un être géographique? Il me semble presque paradoxal de poser même la question suivante: la France est-elle un être géographique? Ce nom a pris à nos yeux une forme concrète; il s'incarne dans une figure à laquelle les cartes nous ont tellement habitué... Volontiers nous serions portés à la considérer comme une unité... La réponse n'est pas aussi simple qu'on le croirait tout d'abord. Ce n'est pas au point de vue géologique que la France possède ce qu'on peut appeler une individualité... Cependant nous répétons volontiers ce mot de Michelet: 'la France est une personne'" (La Blache, *Tableau* 25–26).

17. Most of the French nationalist discourse and goals featured in Michelet's and La Blache's works resurface implicitly in the framework and methodology of Fernand Braudel's canonical work on the Mediterranean.

18. In this section, I rely on Derek Gregory's analysis of the national projects produced by La Blache and Michelet during the emergence of human geography. Gregory compares Michelet's and La Blache's historical and geographical projects of France after the fall of the Second Empire and considers the role of human geography (*Geographical Imaginations* 37–46).

19. For more on the history of French geographical tradition, Humboldt's work, and their relation to the Egyptian expedition, see Godlewska 149–90. For more on the relationship between the pictorial tradition in geography and imperialism, see Godlewska and Smith. See also Humboldt.

20. "Une individualité géographique ne résulte pas de simples considérations de géologie et de climat. Ce n'est pas une chose donnée d'avance par la nature. Il faut partir de cette idée qu'une contrée est un réservoir où dorment des énergies dont la nature a posé le germe, mais dont l'emploi dépend de l'homme. C'est lui qui, en la pliant à son usage, met en lumière son individualité. Il établit une connexion entre des traits épars; aux effets incohérents de circonstances locales, il substitue un concours systématique de forces. C'est alors qu'une contrée se précise et se différencie, et qu'elle devient à la longue comme une médaille frappée à l'effigie d'un peuple. Ce mot de personnalité appartient au domaine et au vocabulaire de la géographie humaine. Il correspond à un degré de développement déjà avancé de rapports généraux. Ce degré a été atteint de bonne heure par la France" (*Tableau* 26).

21. In *Principes de géographie humaine* (1922), La Blache clearly marks the distinction between both terms: "On peut dès à présent considérer comme acquise, contrairement aux habitudes du langage courant qui les confond sans cesse, la distinction fondamentale du peuplement et de la race. Sous les conformités de langue, de religion et de nationalité, persistent et ne laissent pas de travailler les différences spécifiques implantées en nous par un long atavisme. Cependant ces groupes hétérogènes se combinent dans une organisation sociale qui fait de la population d'une contrée, envisagée dans son ensemble, un corps" (11) [In spite of current usage, which confuses the terms *people* and *race*, the fundamental distinction between them can henceforth be considered

established. Beneath similarities of language, religion and nationality, the specific differences implanted in us by an ancient descent never cease to be operative. Nevertheless, all such heterogeneous groups blend in a social organization, which makes of the population of a country a unit [a body] when looked at its entirety (La Blache, *Principles* 17)].

22. On the French dilemma with the definition of race after the German occupation, see Priest.

23. "La lutte la plus colossale, la plus générale et la plus enracinée, qui ait fait jamais retentir la terre du fracas des batailles, est celle de l'Orient et de l'Occident. Cette lutte est le caractère distinctif de la phase de la civilisation qui s'est écoulée depuis les temps historiques jusqu'à nous. C'est la manifestation la plus éclatante de la guerre que se font depuis six mille ans l'esprit et la matière, le spiritualisme et le sensualisme; guerre à laquelle nous venons à mettre fin" (Chevalier, "*Le Globe* 5 février 1832" 114).

24. "Il déclara qu'il était au fond plus juif que tous les juifs du monde: il tenait de son père, auquel il ressemblait physiquement et moralement, un gaillard qui connaissait le prix des sous; et, s'il avait de sa mère ce brin de fantaisie nerveuse, c'était là peut-être le plus clair de sa chance, car il sentait la force invincible de sa grâce à tout oser" (81).

25. My translation. I rely on the French version of the text. Nelson's translation reads: "He seemed a woman himself" (83).

26. "Les grand magasins sont insérés dans un environnement urbain ... avec lequel [ils] sont en parfaite osmose ... Cette porosité les rend indéfiniment traversables; [ils] sont une continuité de la rue, on s'y promène comme au milieu des étals des trottoirs" (*L'invention* 147). Compare the department store with its successor, the shopping mall. Whereas the department store is enmeshed in the fabric of the modern city, the suburban mall recoils away from the cityscape.

27. "Chaque année, il remuait tout l'Extrême-Orient, où des voyageurs fouillaient pour lui les palais et les temples" (497).

28. "On avait vidé les palais, dévalisé les mosques et les bazars" (*Au Bonheur des dames* 141–42).

29. Initially, Zola pinpointed to Jourdain that the architect's avant-garde views would be anachronistic to his project: "Your superb dream of a grand, modern bazaar does not quite fit my department store." "My scene takes place before 1870, and I cannot create such an anachronism without inviting criticism. Ah! Such beautiful décor I could create with your store were I not bound by my scruples as a historian" (qtd. in Clausen, *Frantz Jourdain* 21). See also Zola, *Correspondance* 303, 376.

30. For a brief account of this history, see Mead, *Charles Garnier's* 253–59.

31. As Mead suggests elsewhere, this industrial element was also integrated in the Cathedral Saint-Eustache opposite the food market. In this sense, Zola's cathedral of commerce expresses the affinity and competition between the church and the market as bourgeois public spaces during the Second Empire (*Making Modern Paris* 223–26).

32. "Or qu'est-ce qu'une zone, sinon une certaine température, un certain dégrée de la chaleur et de l'humidité, en un mot un certain nombre de circonstances régnantes, analogues dans leur genre à ce que nous appelions tout à l'heure l'état général de l'esprit

et des mœurs? De même qu'il y une température physique qui, par ses variations détermine l'apparition de telle ou telle espèce de plantes; de même il y a une température morale qui par ses variations détermine l'apparition de telle ou telle espèce d'art. Et, de même qu'on étudie la température physique pour comprendre l'apparition de telle ou telle espèce de plantes . . . il faut étudier la température morale pour comprendre l'apparition de telle espèce d'art" (Taine, *Philosophie* 9).

33. "Le rapport et les dépendances mutuelles des parties" (*Philosophie* 27). "Dans l'œuvre littéraire comme dans l'œuvre pittoresque, il s'agit de transcrire non le dehors sensible des êtres et des évènements, mais l'ensemble de leurs rapports et de leurs dépendances, c'est à dire leur logique. Ainsi en règle générale, ce qui nous intéresse dans un être réel, et ce que nous prions l'artiste d'extraire et de rendre, c'est la logique intérieure ou extérieure, en d'autres termes, sa structure, sa composition et son agencement" (*Philosophie* 28–29).

34. For the theatrical setting of the opera, see Mead, *Charles Garnier's* 110–34.

35. The entire quotation is as follows: "Lorsque les vapeurs qui s'exhalent des poitrines des spectateurs, et celles qui s'échappent des appareils d'éclairage, viennent à tamiser un peu les rayons qui les pénètrent et s'agitent insensiblement avec les courants qui les transportent, il y a dans cette espèce de vibration de l'air, faisant vibrer à son tour les taches d'or places sur les saillies des ornements, comme un effet de mirage oriental" (Garnier 1:139 qtd. in Mead, *Charles Garnier's* 257). See also Clausen, *Frantz Jourdain* xviii.

36. In the original text, Zola anthropomorphizes the store: "Le Bonheur des Dames allumait les files profondes de ses becs de gaz. Et elle se rapprocha, attirée de nouveau et comme réchauffée à ce foyer d'ardente lumière. La machine ronflait toujours, encore en activité, lâchant sa vapeur dans un dernier grondement" (73).

37. "Il était quatre heures, les rayons du soleil à son coucher entraient obliquement par les larges baies de la façade, éclairaient de biais les vitrages des halls; et, dans cette clarté d'un rouge d'incendie, montaient, pareilles à une vapeur d'or, les poussières épaissies, soulevées depuis le matin par le piétinement de la foule" (335).

38. "Il y a de son sang sous les pierres de la maison" (67).

39. "Il régnait sur toutes avec la brutalité d'un despote" (507). "Gouverner le Bonheur des Dames [était] quelque chose comme un conseil de ministres sou un roi absolu" (79). In another moment the narrator describes Mouret as "Trônant brutalement audessus d'elles, comme le roi despotique de chiffons" (137); "He . . . appeared like some despotic king of fashion" (84).

40. My addition in brackets matches the original French. "Alors, il s'égaya davantage, il laissa percer le fond de sa brutalité, sous son air d'adoration sensuelle. D'un haussement d'épaules, il parut déclarer qu'il les jetterait toutes par terre, comme des sacs vides, le jour où elles l'auraient aidé à bâtir sa fortune. Bourdoncle, entêté, répétait de son air froid: Elles se vengeront . . . Il y en aura une qui vengera les autres, c'est fatal" (80).

41. "Le grand manteau de velours, garni de renard argenté, mettait le profil d'une femme sans tête, qui courait par l'averse à quelque fête, dans l'inconnu des ténèbres de Paris" (73–74).

42. My translation. "l'homme... qu'il chargeait d'ordinaire des exécutions" (92). Nelson's translation is "Bourdoncle... whom he actually charged with the task of reprimanding negligent staff" (43).

43. "Denise, qui allait justement débuter ce lundi-là, avait traversé le salon Oriental, elle était restée saisie, ne reconnaissant plus l'entrée du magasin, achevant de se troubler dans ce décor de harem, planté à la porte" (142).

44. "Elle était heureuse de sa solitude, de cette sauvagerie où elle vivait enfermée, comme au fond d'un refuge" (191).

45. Zola, *Au Bonheur des dames* 141. See the catalogue of Le Bon Marché from 1878, in the previous chapter. The catalogue cover features the inside of a harem with women standing on upper-level balconies looking into a foyer. Just like the catalogue, Zola's clients stand on the upper floors and stairs to enjoy the panoptic pleasure of watching other people navigating the Oriental salon.

46. "Chaque fois qu'une cliente se présentait, il y avait un mouvement parmi les garçons de magasin, rangés sous la haute porte, habillés d'une livrée, l'habit et le pantalon vert clair, le gilet rayé jaune et rouge. Et l'inspecteur Jouve, l'ancien capitaine retraité, était là, en redingote et en cravate blanche, avec sa décoration, comme une enseigne de vieille probité, accueillant les dames d'un air gravement poli, se penchant vers elles pour leur indiquer les rayons. Puis, elles disparaissaient dans le vestibule, changé en un salon oriental sous ses ordres.... D'abord, au plafond, étaient tendus des tapis de Smyrne, dont les dessins compliqués se détachaient sur des fonds rouges. Puis, des quatre côtés, pendaient des portières: les portières de Karamanie et de Syrie, zébrées de vert, de jaune et de vermillon; les portières de Diarbékir, plus communes, rudes à la main, comme des sayons de berger; et encore des tapis pouvant servir de tentures, les longs tapis d'Isphahan, de Téhéran et de Kermancha, les tapis plus larges de Schoumaka et de Madras, floraison étrange de pivoines et de palmes, fantaisie lâchée dans le jardin du rêve. À terre, les tapis recommençaient, une jonchée de toisons grasses: il y avait, au centre, un tapis d'Agra, une pièce extraordinaire à fond blanc et à large bordure bleu tendre, où couraient des ornements violâtres, d'une imagination exquise; partout, ensuite, s'étalaient des merveilles, les tapis de la Mecque aux reflets de velours, les tapis de prière du Daghestan à la pointe symbolique, les tapis du Kurdistan, semés de fleurs épanouies; enfin, dans un coin, un écroulement à bon marché, des tapis de Gheurdès, de Coula et de Kircheer, en tas, depuis quinze francs. Cette tente de pacha somptueux était meublée de fauteuils et de divans, faits avec des sacs de chameau, les uns coupés de losanges bariolés, les autres plantés de roses naïves. La Turquie, l'Arabie, la Perse, les Indes étaient là" (140–41).

47. For example, see Moussa.

48. On panoramas, see Schwartz 149–76.

49. "De proche en proche, le brouhaha s'élevait, devenait une clameur de peuple saluant le veau d'or" (510).

50. "D'ailleurs, les passions s'exaltent par leur contagion mutuelle, et l'attroupement, les clameurs, le désordre, l'attente, le jeûne, finissent par composer une ivresse de

laquelle rien ne peut sortir que le vertige et la fureur" (*Les Origines de la France* 158–59). Taine was one of Zola's favorite historians. See also Barrows 77.

51. "[L]'or sonnait dans les caisses; tandis que la clientèle, dépouillée, violée, s'en allait à moitié défaite, avec la volupté assouvie et la sourde honte d'un désir contenté au fond d'un hôtel louche. C'était lui qui les possédait de la sorte, qui les tenait à sa merci" (507).

52. "Un Delacroix!" (173).

53. For examples of department stores' catalogues associated with these artists, see chapter 1.

54. "La vérité, c'est que le public s'entiche purement et simplement des tours de passe-passe de l'artiste. Il distingue les boutons sur un gilet, les breloques sur une chaîne de montre tant et si bien qu'aucun détail ne s'y perd ; voilà ce qui suscite cette admiration inouïe... La foule est flattée dans ses instincts les plus enfantins, dans son admiration de la difficulté vaincue, dans son amour des tableautins bien dessinés et surtout bien détaillés. Elle ne comprend que cela en art" (384).

55. My translation in brackets. In the original text, Zola uses the active voice.

56. "Mais, sur le palier du grand escalier central, *le Japon l'arrêta encore*. Ce comptoir avait grandi, depuis le jour où Mouret s'était amusé à risquer, au même endroit, une petite table de proposition.... [C]haque année, il remuait tout l'Extrême-Orient, où des voyageurs fouillaient pour lui les palais et les temples. D'ailleurs, les rayons poussaient toujours, on en avait essayé deux nouveaux en décembre... un rayon de livres et un rayon de jouets d'enfants, qui devaient certainement grandir aussi et balayer encore des commerces voisins. Quatre ans venaient de suffire au Japon pour attirer toute la clientèle artistique de Paris" (497; emphasis added).

57. "Elle [la femme] y régnait en reine amoureuse, dont les sujets trafiquent, et qui paye d'une goutte de son sang chacun de ses caprices. Sous la grâce même de sa galanterie, Mouret laissait ainsi passer la brutalité d'un juif vendant de la femme à la livre : il lui élevait un temple, la faisait encenser par une légion de commis" (129). Advertisements of department stores represented their customers as the queens of the department store. Refer to figure 1.2.

58. Providing assistants and interpreters was part of the culture of the department store. In 1878, Printemps hired out its employees as interpreters for the visitors of the Exposition Universelle, an innovation for which it received two silver medals (Caracalla 40).

59. "[L]'inspecteur Jouve se promenait de son allure militaire, étalant sa décoration, gardant ces marchandises précieuses et fines, si faciles à cacher au fond d'une manche" (167).

60. "Depuis un an, Madame de Boves volait ainsi, ravagée d'un besoin furieux, irrésistible. Les crises empiraient, grandissaient, jusqu'à être une volupté nécessaire à son existence, emportant tous les raisonnements de prudence, se satisfaisant avec une jouissance d'autant plus âpre, qu'elle risquait, sous les yeux d'une foule, son nom, son orgueil, la haute situation de son mari. Maintenant que ce dernier lui laissait vider ses tiroirs, elle volait avec de l'argent plein sa poche, elle volait pour voler, comme on aime

pour aimer, sous le coup de fouet du désir, dans le détraquement de la névrose que ses appétits de luxe inassouvis avaient développée en elle, autrefois, à travers l'énorme et brutale tentation des grands magasins" (502).

61. "Sans doute il aurait pu voir le financier dans son cabinet, pour causer à l'aise de la grosse affaire qu'il voulait lui proposer. Mais il se sentait plus fort chez Henriette. Il savait combien la possession commune d'une maîtresse rapproche et attendrit. Être tous les deux chez elle, dans son parfum aimé . . . lui semblait une certitude de succès" (123).

62. My addition in brackets to match the French text. "Dans les rayons, peu à peu déserts, il ne restait que des clientes attardées. . . . C'était comme un champ de bataille du massacre des tissus. . . . Liénard sommeillait au-dessus d'une mer de pièces, où des piles restées debout, à moitié détruites, semblaient des maisons dont un fleuve débordé charrie les ruines; et, plus loin, le blanc avait neigé à terre. . . . [L]es confections s'amoncelaient comme des capotes de soldats mis hors de combat . . . Un peuple de femmes . . . se seraient déshabillé là, dans le désordre d'un coup de désir ; tandis que . . . le service du départ, en pleine activité, dégorgeait toujours les paquets dont il éclatait . . . dernier branle de la machine surchauffée. [L]e hall restait nu, tout le colossal approvisionnement du Paris-Bonheur venait d'être déchiqueté, balayé, comme sous un vol de sauterelles dévorantes. Et, au milieu de ce vide, Hutin et Favier feuilletaient leurs cahiers de débits" (173–74).

63. For more on the language of war in *Au bonheur des dames*, see Ramazani.

64. See for instance Swebach; Charlet; Marbach; Foord.

65. "Capote" in Delveau 87; *branler* in colloquial French refers to masturbation (Delveau 77–78).

66. "Il avait la beauté d'une fille, une beauté qu'il semblait avoir volée à sa sœur, la peau éclatante, les cheveux roux et frisés, les lèvres et les yeux mouillés de tendresse. Près de lui, dans son étonnement, Denise paraissait plus mince encore, avec son visage long à bouche trop grande, son teint fatigué déjà, sa chevelure pâle" (48).

67. "Words like 'clogs' and 'gollywogs' circulated" (122).

68. "Presque toutes les vendeuses, dans leur frottement quotidien avec la clientèle riche, prenaient des grâces, finissaient par être d'une classe vague, flottant entre l'ouvrière et la bourgeoise; et, sous leur art de s'habiller, sous les manières et les phrases apprises, il n'y avait souvent qu'une instruction fausse, la lecture des petits journaux, des tirades de drame, toutes les sottises courantes du pavé de Paris" (215–16).

69. "Et elle [Madame Desforges] jetait à Mouret le regard moqueur d'une Parisienne, que l'attifement ridicule d'une provinciale [Denise] égayait. Celui-ci sentit la caresse amoureuse de ce coup d'œil, le triomphe de la femme heureuse de sa beauté et de son art. Aussi, par gratitude d'homme adoré, crut-il devoir railler à son tour . . . Puis, il faudrait être peignée, murmura-t-il" (171).

70. Habitus constitutes the standards, ethos, expertise, and material culture that shape a group and inform its views and representation (Bourdieu, *Outline* 86). The word *habit*, in French meaning clothing, shares the same etymology as *habitus*. On the coded social language of fashion see also Barthes, *Fashion System* and *Language*.

71. "Puis, elle s'aperçut qu'elle était vêtue de soie; cet uniforme l'accablait, elle eut l'enfantillage, pour défaire sa malle, de vouloir remettre sa vieille robe de laine, restée au dossier d'une chaise. Mais quand elle fut rentrée dans ce pauvre vêtement à elle, une émotion l'étrangla, les sanglots qu'elle contenait depuis le matin crevèrent brusquement en un flot de larmes chaudes" (176).

72. "C'est une plaisanterie, mademoiselle.... Regardez comme il me bride la poitrine. J'ai l'air d'une nourrice."

"Madame est un peu forte... Nous ne pouvons pourtant pas faire que madame soit moins forte" (393).

73. "On aurait dit un grand lit blanc, dont l'énormité virginale attendait, comme dans les légendes, la princesse *blanche*, celle qui devait devenir un jour, toute-puissante, avec le voile blanc des épousées" (475; emphasis added).

74. "Parfois, elle s'animait, elle voyait l'immense bazar idéal, le phalanstère du négoce ... où chacun aurait sa part exacte des bénéfices, selon ses mérites.... Mouret alors s'égayait malgré sa fièvre. Il l'accusait de socialisme" (430).

75. Friedberg here quotes Ross, "Introduction" xiii.

76. See Miller on Le Bon Marché; Caracalla on Printemps; Jarry on La Samaritaine.

77. Benjamin quotes Dubech and d'Espezel (404) in describing the modern condition of the city.

78. For the history of the creation of Nouveau Paris and the design challenges that it represented, such as the limitations imposed by the topography of Paris and the creation of fake vistas, see Van Zanten, *Building Paris* 6–45. See also Garnier's opera placement and design in Mead, *Charles Garnier's* 106–10.

79. In *L'Argent*, Zola presents the character of Georges Hamelin, who is engaged in the Suez Canal project and adopts a Saint-Simonian worldview and mission toward the East. He also presents the enigmatic Levantine character Sabatini, who trades in the French stock market.

Chapter 4

1.

قد أعجبنى فى باريس كل شىء حتى شراسة أخلاق الرعاع فيها . . . و مع ذلك فقد تألمت من نتائج التطرف فى تلك الحرية فى بدء عهدى بزيارتها، إذ كنت أظن أن الصغير و الكبير من كل طبقة فى تلك الأمة على جانب عظيم من الرقة و حسن المعاملة . . و أذكر بهذه المناسبة أننى عندما أردت لأول مرة زيارة أحد حوانيت باريس الكبرى فى يوم حدد لتخفيض أثمان البضائع، وجدت على أبواب الحانوت زحاماً شديداً، فوقفت عند الباب لأمكن بعض الداخلين من المرور مجاملة كما هى عادتنا فى بلاد الشرق، ظانة أنه سياتى دورى و أجد من بين الداخلين من يرد لى تلك المجاملة، و لكنى لاحظت للأسف أنه لم يشعر بوجودى أحد، و رأيتنى مدفوعة بشدة بين تلك الأمواج المتلاطمة من الأجسام البشرية، تتقذفنى موجة و تتلاقفنى أخرى باللكم والسير على قدمى فكادت تنهمر دموعى [. . .] لما وجدت نفسى أمام منضدة محاطة بالمتفرجين[. . .] وقد مددت يدى بلطف إلى قطعة من القماش أعجبتنى، و لكن سرعان ما اختطفتها من يدى احدى المتفرجات بغلظة حتى كادت الدموع تفر من عينى مرة أخرى [. . .]. مثل هذه الأشياء لم

ترقني أول الأمر و لكنني أنتهيت منها إلى أن أفهم أن التزاحم فى الحياة هو سبب نهضة تلك الأمم و تفوقها، و ان تسامح الشرق و رقة شعوره هما سبب تأخره وأضمحلاله . . .

(Shaarawi, *Mudhakkarat* 129; my translation).

2. Shaarawi's Arabic memoirs mention that her first trip to Europe was in 1909 (124); Margot Badran's chronology in the English version, *Harem Years*, places her first trip in 1914 ("Introduction" 5).

3. On the academic framing of Shaarawi's feminist experience, see Kahf, "Packaging 'Huda.'"

4. See M. Russell; Shaarawi, *Harem Years*. The English memoirs mention the trip to the Alexandrian store and refer briefly to Shaarawi's visit to the Parisian *grand magasin*, but the text does not contain her reflections over this experience.

5. See an advertisement for Le Bon Marché in Cairo and another for her vocational school's ceramic wares at Le Bon Marché in Paris, in *L'Egyptienne*, no. 49, May 1929.

6. On the Sadat era, see Tignor 274–81.

7. The Circassians, or the Adyghes, were people from the northwestern Caucasus forced into mass migration by tsarist Russia during the Caucasus Wars (1817–1864). In 2011, the Georgian parliament recognized the persecution of the Circassians and the destruction of their homeland in 1864 as the "Circassian genocide" (Richmond 1). See also Hille and Gendron.

8. See Trout Powell, *Different Shades*; Baron, *Egypt as a Woman* 73–74.

9. For the history of modern Turkey, see Turnaoğlu.

10. This information can be found in detail in the memoirs; also see Badran, "Introduction."

11. See Q. Amin, *al-A'mal*; see also Pollard 152–65; M. Russell 100–125.

12. On biopolitics and biopower, see Foucault, *Discipline and Punish* and *History of Sexuality*.

13. See the memoirs of Nabawiyya Musa; Badran also gives an account of Musa's life (*Feminists* 58).

14. See Avierino for details of the summit. For details on the various debates and writing by women during the turn of the century, see Baron, *Women's Awakening* 13–35.

15. For examples of this narrative genre, see Booth, "Between Harem"; see also Johnson 170–203. Another example of an adapted text that contributed to a transnational bourgeois imaginary of girls' modern edification is Fénelon, *Traité de l'éducation des filles*. As Booth indicates, Rifa'a al-Tahtawi's adaptation of Fénelon's work into Arabic was a prominent text in the debates over girls' education in colonial Egypt. *L'éducation* was also a popular text in France for girls' education until 1870: namely, during the rise of the Third Republic (Booth, "Girlhood Translated?"); see also Mikhail; al-Jumayyil.

16. Sania Sharawi Lanfranchi, Huda Shaarawi's granddaughter, situates this event in 1901. The Arabic and English memoirs do not give the year. They only specify that it was in the summer. Only the English translation of the memoirs refers to the name of the store: Chalon.

17.

و فى الأسكندرية و فى هذا الصيف بالذات . . . كانت لى أول تجربة من نوعها . . . فقد قررت أن أشترى لوازمى بنفسى من المحلات الكبيرة. بالرغم من تذمر «سعيد أغا» رغم امتعاض أهل المنزل من هذه الخطوة ودهشتهم من هذه الخطوة و تحدثهم عنها و كأننى قد خالفت قوانين الشريعة.وكان على أن أصحب وصيفاتى و سعيد أغا لأنه لا يليق التوجه بمفردي. و كان على أن أسدل أزارى على حاجبي و أن ألتف بحيث لا يظهر من شعرى و ملابسي أي شيء.. و عندما دخلنا المحل، دهش الموظفون والمشترون كأنما الغير مألوفة، و بخاصة عندما رأوا الأغا يحملق بنظراته الحادة في وجوه الناس وكأنه يحذرهم من النظر الينا. ثم اندفع نحو أحدى مديري الأقسام يسأله في لهفة واحدة : ألا يوجد عندكم محل للحريم؟ فأشار له إلى قسم السيدات. ونادوا على الفتيات البائعات ليتولين خدمتي بعد أن وضعن حاجزين يحول بيني و بين الموجودين.

(Shaarawi, *Mudhakkarat* 88; my translation)

18. The word *maḥal* in Egyptian Arabic could mean a shop, a location.

19. For example, the Mamluk Ottoman household served as a public and a private space. See M. Russell 4.

20. As Noorani suggests, the traditional Arab domestic sphere "does not determine an ideal of femininity in the manner of the bourgeois notion of the private sphere. It does not set up a specific lifestyle, role, attributes, and purpose as essential to successful womanhood" (65).

21. "Chez un nombre de riche musulmans, un ou plusieurs eunuques servent d'intermédiaire entre le harem et tout ce qui vient dehors" (4).

22. See "Huda and Halida and the Slaves at Bedtimes," in Trout Powell, *Tell This* 115–47; For examples of the status of eunuchs in the Ottoman Empire, see Hathaway.

23. On *dallalas*, see Tucker, *Women* 81–82.

24. See Le Bon. As an avid reader, Shaarawi, who was fluent in French and grew up among many French residents in Egypt, should have been familiar with Le Bon's work. Le Bon visited Egypt in 1882 and published *The Civilization of the Arab* in 1884, which circulated in Egyptian circles for its praise of Arab artistic heritage (Volait, *Fous du Caire* 218). Madame de Couvreur, who lectured women at Cairo University, ordered Le Bon's book for the library. Shaarawi attended some of Couvreur's lectures (Pollard 124).

25. "Faute d'un code accepté, la morale internationale n'a réalisé aucun progrès. Elle est restée celle de tout le règne animal : respecter les forts, dévorer les faibles. . . . Les concessions n'empêchent pas les batailles nécessaires. Elles les rendent plus couteuses et plus dures" (*L'Égyptienne*, 1 July 1925).

26. Ivray wrote a book on Saint-Simonianism and women: *L'aventure Saint-Simonienne et les femmes*.

27. See Shaarawi's speech at Ewart Hall at the American University in Cairo, "Conférence prononcée par Mme Houda Charaoui au 'Mémorial Ewart Hall' de L'université américaine, le 12 Novembre 1929," *L'Egyptienne*, November 1929, 2–18, esp. 5–6 and 12.

28. و كم عجبت عندما رأيت محلات الأزياء الكبرى تعرض الملابس على فتيات جميلات أنيقات و لم يكن هذا العرض لمجرد الترغيب فى شراء الملابس، بل فيه دروس للمشترية تمكنها من تمييز ما يلائم هذه الملابس من باقى اللوازم التى تحتاجها لتكملة أناقة الملبس

(Shaarawi, *Mudhakkarat* 127, my translation)

29. باريس هي الصفحة المنشورة من سجل تاريخ الفرنسيين، حيث يشب الفرنسي في أية بيئة ملماً منذ نعومة أظافره بتاريخ بلاده، قبل أن يدخل المدارس ويتعلم هذا التاريخ في الكتب. ولذلك تراه فخوراً بتاريخها المجيد، حريصاً على خلود هذا المجد وليس هذا فحسب، بل ترى الشعب الفرنسي يطوف بكل القصور التاريخيّة ودور الآثار والعلم والمتاحف الفنيّة والكنائس والمعابد التي تفتح له أبواها في أيام العطلات.

(Shaarawi, *Mudhakkarat* 129, my translation.).

30. Musa still covered her hair. Shaarawi was photographed both with and without head covers. These covers varied; they included traditional styled head covers and European hats. These variations shed light on the different sartorial negotiations undertaken by Egyptian women during that era. I use the words *facial veil* to make it easier for English readers to follow the argument. However, at the turn of the century, various words were used to refer to the facial veil; each had a different social connotation. For instance, Qasim Amin uses the words *burquʻ* and *niqāb* in *The Liberation of Woman*. The former referred to the small facial veil used by the middle class, the latter to the translucent white facial veil used by the upper classes, also known as *yashmak*. Both terms should not be confused with the contemporary English notion of *burka* or the *niqāb* used by women in contemporary Egypt. The Arabic term *burquʻ* encompasses any form of facial covering regardless of class-related dress code. This includes the *yashmak* as well as the *bisha* used by the working class. For examples of usage of these terms, see Amin *al-Aʻmal* 356–57; Shaarawi, *Muthakkarat* 95; Badran, *Feminists* 22–23; Baron, "Unveiling" 370–71.

31. See also a photo of Shaarawi in Idris 229.

32. "En fondant cette revue dans une langue qui n'est pas la nôtre, mais qui est en Égypte comme ailleurs parlée par toute l'Élite, notre but est double: faire connaître à l'étranger la Femme Égyptienne, telle qu'elle est de nos jours—quitte à lui enlever tout le mystère et le charme que sa réclusion passée lui prêtait aux yeux des occidentaux—et éclairer l'opinion publique européenne sur le véritable état politique et social de l'Égypte" (2; my translation). For a detailed profile of the magazine, see Fenoglio Abd El Al.

33. On the selection of Couvreur and other instructors for the women's section, see Badran, *Feminists* 54.

34. "Il est temps d'y songer la France ne se relèvera de l'abaissement profond dans lequel l'ont précipitée et maintenue une triste succession d'évènements douloureuses, que si la femme mieux dirigée, plus instruite, prend sa part de la tâche commune" (Richer 10).

35. *Haut Enseignement Commercial pour les Jeunes Filles* (Milhaud 53–59). Sanua mentions Shaarawi in an entry of her memoirs from 18 April 1942 (Sanua 33).

36. In *La Fronde*, see Brémontier; see also Durand, "Salut des femmes" and "Autour du congrès"; for other public recognition of Shaarawi see "La Mission de Mlle Sanua"; Chandet, "Chronique étrangère" and "L'émancipation."

37. See also Booth, "Biography" and *Writing*.

38. See Adam, "La grande amie."

39. See also P. Smith 104–62.

40. Apter refers to Craig Owens's words. See also Butler on performance of gender.

41. See Mukhtar, "Nahdat Masr" the cover of *al-Kashkul*, 28 November 1924, and the cover of *al-Mussawar*, 6 February 1925.

42. Baron quotes Pierson 44.

43. On the conservation of Arab heritage in Egypt and the collection and re-creation of Orientalist decor, see Volait, *Fous du Caire* and Émile Prisse; Oulebsir and Volait; Giese, Volait, and Braga; Crosnier Leconte and Volait, *Maisons de France* and *L'Égypte*.

44. The Committee for the Conservation of Arab Artistic Monuments was established on 18 December 1881 (Volait, *Fous du Caire* 74–75). See also Volait, *Antique Dealing*.

45. As Volait indicates, Shaarawi's house was in the neo-Mamluk style, inspired mostly by local traditions.

Chapter 5

1.

בצעירותי היה טבעי בעיני שתושבי קהיר מבינים זה את זה אף־על־פי שהם מדברים בשפות שונות ונקראים בשמות ממקורות שונים—מוסלמי, ערבי, נוצרי, יהודי, סורי, יווני, ארמני, איטלקי. שמות הערים בגדאד, תוניס, חַלַב, ביירות, דמשק, איסטנבול, סלוניקי, קזבלנקה, ירושלים, היו נהירים מפני שבני אדם, בעיקר קרובי משפחה, היו מתהלכים זה עם זה כמו בחדריו של בית אחד גדול. רק פריז היתה אחרת, שם רחוק המבריק באותיות של זהב על תוויות חנות הכול־בו של נונו והדוד דוד ("הציף הכחול של הקדמה", 49)

Kahanoff, "Ha-Tsa'if ha-Kahol shel ha-Qidma" 49. I am grateful to Anton Shammas for help with the translation. Part of this chapter was previously published as an article under the title "Ghostly Labor: Ethnic-Classism in the Levantine Prism of Jacqueline Kahanoff's *Jacob's Ladder*," *International Journal of Middle East Studies*, vol. 49, no. 2 (2017): 255–75.

2. In my previous writing, I used the term *ethnic-classism* to refer to that concept. See Kamal, "Ghostly Labor."

3. See the various literary and historical Arabic works recounting the history of colonial Egypt and of Egyptian Jews including Hammad; Abdel Meguid; Fetiha; Abd el-Razik; Abulghar; al-Shadhli; Ruhayyim, *Diary, Days*, and *Dreams*; Bigio, *Journey* and *Travessia*; Bowell; Cicurel; Ghali; Lagnado, *Man* and *Arrogant Years*. From Israel, see Sakal; Matalon, *The One Facing Us*. For novels from France, see Jacques, *Lumière* and *Gilda Stambouli*; Hassoun; Rossant, *Apricots, Memories*, and *Return*. From Canada see Téboul, *La lente* and *J'chuis*. For books on Cairo's and Alexandria's urban history, see Ilbert, Yannakakis, and Hassoun; Raafat, *Cairo*. For recent documentaries produced in Egypt on Egyptian Jews and foreign minorities, see *Salata Baladi*, *Jews of Egypt*, and *That Alexandria*. See the Egyptian television series *Harat el-Yahud*. From Israel see *Seret Aravit* [*An Arab Movie*].

4. See Starr, *Remembering* and "Drinking"; Hochberg, *In Spite*; Levy.

5. On the question of memory and class relation, I draw on Ann Laura Stoler's analysis of the "politics of memory" in the memoirs of elites from colonial Java, which often represent domestics in a romantic, nostalgic light. This representation contradicts the account of the actual workers who served in colonial houses. See Stoler 24.

6. See Aciman; Cialente, *The Levantines* and *Ballata Levantina*; Ghali; Jacques, *Lumière*; Téboul, *La lente*.

7. See sources in previous note.

8. On the mixed courts system in Egypt, see Hoyle.

9. Later in life, Kahanoff describes Levantinism as a prism; see chapter 6.

10. In a later writing, Kahanoff explains that "the role of an artist [is] to reflect the multiplicity of a lived and living truth, through the prism of an individual experience" (qtd. in Starr and Somekh, "Editors' Introduction" xvii).

11. See Alcalay, *After Jews* and *Keys*; Starr and Somekh, *Mongrels or Marvels*; Hochberg, *In Spite*; Matalon, *The One*; Shammas.

12. "Alice watched them go, a rowdy band of girls, dashing and sport loving. They made her think of the *Jeunes Filles en Fleurs* Proust had collectively loved on the mysterious and brilliant beach of Balbec" (*Jacob's Ladder* 201).

13. The Duc de Saint-Simon was a *mémorialiste*, not to be confused with Henri de Saint-Simon, the philosopher and utopian who initiated Saint-Simonianism.

14. "Il faisait une nuit transparente et sans souffle; j'imaginais que la Seine coule entre ses ponts circulaires, faits de leur plateau et de son reflet, devait ressembler au Bosphore. Et, symbole soit de cette invasion que prédisait le défaitisme de M. de Charlus, soit de la coopération de nos frères musulmans avec les armées de la France, la lune étroite et recourbée comme un sequin semblait mettre le ciel parisien sous le signe oriental du croissant" (Proust, *Recherche* 2218). [It was a transparent and a breathless night; I imagined that the Seine, flowing between the twin semicircles of the span and the reflection of its bridges, must look like the Bosporus. And—a symbol perhaps of the invasion foretold by the defeatism of M. de Charlus, or else of the co-operation of our Muslim brothers with the armies of France—the moon, narrow and curved like a sequin, seemed to have placed the sky of Paris beneath the oriental sign of the crescent; *In Search*, 386].

15. See Shohat, *Taboo Memories*; Alcalay, *After Jews*; Starr, *Remembering*; Raafat, *Cairo*; Ilbert, Yannakakis, and Hassoun.

16. "Puis c'etaient les batiments eux-mêmes, d'une immensité exagérée, vus à vol d'oiseau... Au delà Paris s'étendait, mais un Paris rapetissé, mangé par le monstre... L'horizon tombait en poudre" (Zola, *Au Bonheur* 468).

17. "Tout des dalles de marbre, des colonnes en style Louis XVI, avec des feuilles d'acanthe, pour cette époque là c'était un luxe innoui [sic], des vitrines... Le magasin avait été spécialement construit avec nos plans à nous, c'est à dire le magasin avait le rez-de-chaussée, et le premier étage, qui étaient très vastes, et le reste c'était... il y avait trois étages par dessus... de très très beau et très grands appartements [sic]. Au rez-de-chaussée il y avait... une mercerie d'abord, mercerie très très bien achalandée, des

tissue [sic], à droite et à gauche il y avait le rayon de bonneterie pour hommes et pour femmes, et plus loin alors des articles spéciaux pour hommes et plus à l'intérieur les articles de lingerie. Le fond du magasin était occupé par l'ameublement à gauche et le rayon de chaussures à droite, et tout ça avec des comptoirs en accajou [sic] ciré, et avec des vitrines ravissantes.... Il y avait de très grands ateliers pour la haute couture. Il y avait deux grandes premières de Paris ... On avait aussi une très très bonne modiste de Paris et une corsetière de Paris" (Shohet, "Communauté Juive," November 1964, Tape 1 40–42). Another translation of this passage was cited in Reynolds, *Commodity Communities* 137–38.

18. For more on Najib al-Rihani's Kish-Kish Bey, see "Najib al-Rihani."

19. For more on the popular culture of the era, see Z. Fahmy, *Ordinary Egyptians*; el-Ariss, *Arab Renaissance*. The image of unfitting ready-made clothes is a common trope in the department store to highlight this disconnection between culture and its performance. As discussed in chapter 2, Zola's main protagonist in *Au Bonheur des dames*, Denise, faces the derision of bourgeois clients when she fails to model a coat properly, a gesture that betrays the working-class roots she could not erase.

20. A *habbara* is a traditional fabric used by women to wrap around their bodies (refer to fig. 4.1).

21. Rachel's detailed household description, including the Ten Commandments and the Balfour Declaration, are based on Kahanoff's early memories of her grandfather's home (Kahanoff, "Childhood" 3).

22. "Jacob left Beersheba and went toward Haran. He came to the place and stayed there that night, because the sun had set. Taking one of the stones of the place, he put it under his head and lay down in that place to sleep. And he dreamed that there was a ladder set up on the earth, and the top of it reached to heaven; and behold, the angels of God were ascending and descending on it! And behold, the Lord stood above it [or "beside him"] and said, 'I am the Lord, the God of Abraham your father and the God of Isaac; the land on which you lie I will give to you and to your descendants; and your descendants shall be like the dust of the earth, and you shall spread abroad to the west and to the east and to the north and to the south; and by you and your descendants shall all the families of the earth bless themselves. Behold, I am with you and will keep you wherever you go and will bring you back to this land; for I will not leave you until I have done that of which I have spoken to you'" (Genesis 28:11–19).

23. Kahanoff could be emulating Proust's *Recherche*, in which the narrator depicts his father at the beginning of the novel as a modern, slightly comic image of Abraham wearing both a silk robe and a headscarf.

24. See Myers's introduction in *The Empire of Things*.

25. Sharia Boulac (Bulaq) and Emad el-Din, currently Sherif and 26 July Streets, where the real Chemla store is located.

26. Nancy Reynolds refers to Jeremiah Lynch's memoirs of Abbassiyeh. Lynch also divides the city into two sections but considers Abbasiyeh, occupied by Greek, Italian, and French residents, as New Cairo (Reynolds, *City Consumed* 27).

27. Compare this scene to Charles Baudelaire's "Morale de Joujou" (1853), mentioned in the introduction, which depicts a toy emporium to critique French class divides.

28. Original French text from the interview: "Nos parents tenaient à ce que mes cousines et moi soyions habillées très élégamment, d'abord parce que ça leur faisait de la réclame, on demandait 'd'où vient cette robe? Ah, naturellement c'est sûr, c'est une fille Chemla, c'est sûr qu'elle a de jolies robes avec l'atelier de couture qu'elles ont!" Aussi maman et ma tante, puis plus tard, ma tante Pia, la femme de mon oncle Clément, quand celui-ci s'est marié, s'habillait aussi au magasin" (17).

29. The novel uses the word *nursemaid* to refer to a nanny or a governess. I use these words interchangeably since in this context, the responsibility of the nursemaid is mixed. She is a governess for Rachel and a nursemaid for her young brother.

30. For a comparative situation in the British Empire, see McClintock, *Imperial Leather*, especially the nineteenth-century representation of Irish women from the working class, often featured as masculine and with a dark complexion closer to colonial subjects. In this case, the intersectional slippage takes place along class, gender, and race simultaneously. See also note 5 in this chapter.

31. As a young woman, Kahanoff and some of her friends volunteered in a clinic in Harat al-Yahud. She is aware of the neighborhood's human geography, which is different from Alice's and Miss Nutting's reductive classist and colonial perspectives (Starr and Somekh, "Editors' Introduction" xv).

32. Ronald Cicurel, the son of the founder of the Cicurel department stores, remembers his Slovenian governess in Egypt. Like Hamamsy, he provides a picture of her in his memoirs (30–34). All these accounts shed light on the impact of European governesses on the Egyptian bourgeoisie and their memories of the era, which are filtered through the eyes of the governesses.

33. For the context of al-Azbakiyya, Ezbekieh, garden, see chapter 2.

34. Du Bois describes his realization of racial difference as follows: "Then it dawned upon me with a certain suddenness that I was different from the others; or like [them perhaps] in heart and life and longing, but shut out from their world by a vast veil. I had thereafter no desire to tear down that veil, to creep through; I held all beyond it in common contempt and lived above it in a region of blue sky and great wandering shadows" (Du Bois and Edwards 8). Kahanoff's language and metaphor of the veil strongly resemble those of Du Bois. Her likely allusion to Du Bois hints at the influence of her educational experience in the United States. See Starr and Somekh, "Editors' Introduction," xvi.

35. For the history of this class tension, see Marsot, *Egypt's Liberal Experiment* 204–6.

36. Rachel's realization recalls Fanon's in *Black Skin, White Masks*, explaining the psychological divide in the colonized subject who perceives himself through the European Other. It is also a reminder of Du Bois's famous concept of double consciousness (Du Bois and Edwards 8).

37. The image of the wet nurse abandoning her baby to feed the bourgeois Levantine child recalls the image of Aleksandrinke in Slovenian cultural memory. For more on this phenomenon, see Biancani, "Gender." As Biancani argues, Slovenian domestic workers played a similar role to that described by Kahanoff in crystallizing the image of modern cosmopolitan Egyptian bourgeoisie.

38. See chapter 2 for the context of the inauguration and the memory of Yvonne Shohet Chemla of Ismail's speech.

39. The letters refer also to Kahanoff's actual childhood memories. She writes about these letters in detail in her short story "A Letter from Mama Camouna" 164–76.

40. Describing Paris during the war, Proust's narrator says: "It was not the Orient of Decamps or even Delacroix that began to haunt my imagination... but the old Orient... I thought of the Caliph Harun al-Rashid going in search of adventures in the hidden quarters of Baghdad... The rare taxis which I met, driven by Levantines and Negros did not even take the trouble to respond to my signs." *In Search* 173; see also 524–25.

41. Kahanoff alludes to the French expression "Our ancestors the Gauls" typically used in French history books and ironically included in the curricula used for Francophone colonial subjects, who obviously cannot identify with that foundational narrative.

Chapter 6

1. For *belle époque* nostalgia and reconstruction of cultural heritage across the Middle East, see Daher and Maffi.

2. See, for instance, *Mr. Selfridge* (Davies), *The Paradise* (Gallagher), *Velvet* (Campos and Neira), and *Il Paradiso delle signore* (Testa), which take the department store as backdrop to narrating their respective social histories in England, Spain, and Italy. Other TV series refer briefly to department stores to stress a key historical or social transformation; see *Haret al-yahud* [The Jewish Quarter]. The Egyptian series begins with a scene at a Cairene department store to recall the memory of the Jewish Egyptian community.

3. Dodman refers to Hartog's "regime of historicity," see Hartog.

4. The film was shot between September and November 1929 (Niogret 78). The stock market crash took place in October 1929 (S. Reynolds 111).

5. "Le 20ème siècle est la preuve que la démocratie fabriquait elle-même son ennemi et surtout qu'elle ne peut et ne veut être jugée que sur ses adversaires pas ses résultats" (28:43). "La civilisation apparait comme la condition suffisante de la rupture de la civilisation" (29:02).

6. On France's economic policies under Macron and the "yellow vests" movement, see Shultziner and Kornblit.

7. See chapters 2 and 5. For a list of various texts and documents regarding this era, see the final note in this chapter.

8. For the images from the campaign, see Goude and Mauriès.

9. "C'était à l'époque où de grands magasins venaient de s'ouvrir au Caire, et je me souviens encore de la joie que j'eus en recevant une robe de soie rouge de chez Pascal, une jaquette sport du Dé Rouge et une ombrelle... chez Omar Effendi. Je ne connaissais ces magasins que pour être passée devant eux, en voiture, aux rares occasions où l'on me conduisit dans ces quartiers du Mousky, de L'ezbekieh ou de Wagh el Birka... je n'y étais jamais entrée, non plus qu'aucune dame ou jeune fille de la société d'alors. Les vendeuses venaient à domicile... Pour une faveur particulière et contraire aux coutumes, mon père me consulta pour ces achats. Oh! Ce n'était jamais directement, mais je trouvais, comme par hasard, des catalogues, et d'un trait de crayon, je marquais ce qui me plaisait" (118). Author also known as Out-el-Kouloub al-Demerdashiyya.

10. The image of the wedding dress strikingly recalls a passage from Kahanoff's novel (discussed in chapter 5) when young Rachel visits the atelier at her grandparents' store (*Jacob's Ladder* 57). The seamstresses, who hail from different parts of the Mediterranean, playfully dress her as a bride. In that scene, Rachel symbolizes the Pygmalion fantasy of emporialism and Levantinism fashioned by the collaborative work of Levantine workers.

11. "La femme du Bey m'a demandée où j'ai acheté ma robe. Chez Cicurel, ma chère, mais le prix c'est de la braise ardente" (18).

12. "Elle nous raconte que M. Shemoul le responsable de l'Agence juive de Jérusalem, lui aurait mis les bâtons dans les roues quand elle a voulu repartir. Il lui aurait dit: 'Vous verrez Madame S., ce pays sera un paradis dans cinquante ans.' Elle lui aurait répondu: 'dans ce cas, je reviendrai dans cinquante ans!'" (42).

13. "Cicurel au Caire était la réplique des *Galeries Lafayette*, voyez un peu la destinée!" (70).

14. "Mais que veulent-ils ces maudits juifs? Ils possèdent déjà tous les grands magasins d'Égypte. Cicurel c'est eux. Chemla, c'est eux. Gattegno, c'est eux. Et Orosdi-Back, ce n'est pas eux par hasard? Encore heureux que nous ayons Sednaoui!" (216).

15. For a detailed history of the *efendiyya* class, see Ryzova.

16. See Philip Mansel's definition of Levantinism, which in contrast to Kahanoff's, places the Muslim-Christian cultural exchange and dialogue as a central aspect of the history of Levantinism ("We Are All").

17. Durrell's famous Alexandria Quartet, set in Alexandria before World War II, gives a glimpse of the city's Levantine society through a series of love stories and romantic affairs, centering on that of Darley, an Irish school teacher, and Justine, a Jewish Egyptian woman married to Nessim, an Egyptian Copt.

18. For a critique of Eurocentric view of Alexandria see K. Fahmy, "For Cavafy" and "The Essence of Alexandria" 1, 2; Halim.

19. In the title of this section, I allude to Jarrod Hayes's expression "The queer skeletons in the nation's closet" (97).

20. The original Hebrew, *Zeh 'im ha-panim elynu*, was published in 1995.

21. On Arabic language in Mizrahi literature, see Levy 189–237.

22. On "Interpellation," see Althusser 173–76.

23. On the Egyptian context, see Krämer 205–21.

24. Shohat provides a survey of Israeli films in which "ethnic/class division is presented . . . as natural and inevitable" (*Israeli Cinema* 119–20). Arab Jews are Orientalized and presented as either domestic help or humble workers, while Ashkenazi Jews are portrayed as leaders and intellectuals. See Swirski 44–55; Alcalay, *After Jews* 24–27.

25. On *Avoda Aravit*, see Rosenberg.

26. See the Facebook pages "History of Egyptian Jews," "Jews Remembering Egypt," and "Juifs d'Egypte." Members exchange memories of their parents or their souvenirs of Egypt and their experience afterward. In some cases, they try to locate a family member or a friend. See the various literary and historical works recounting the history of Egyptian Jews, including Abd al-Razik; Abdel Meguid; Abulghar; al-Shadhli; Atiya; Hammad; Fetiha; Ruhayyim, *Diary*, *Days*, and *Dreams*; Cicurel; Bowell; Lagnado, *The Man* and *Arrogant Years*; Rossant, *Apricots*, *Memories*, and *Return*. From Brazil, see Bigio, *Journey*. From Israel, see Sakal; Matalon, *The One*. For novels from France, see Jacques, *Lumière* and *Gilda*; Hassoun. From Canada, see Téboul, *La lente* and *J'chuis*. For books on Cairo's and Alexandria's urban history, see Ilbert, Yannakakis, and Hassoun; Raafat, *Cairo*; Wahba. For recent documentaries produced in Egypt on Egyptian Jews and foreign minorities, see *Salata Baladi*; *Jews of Egypt*; *That Alexandria*. See the Egyptian television series *Harat el-Yahud*. From Israel, see *Seret Aravit*.

Works Cited

Abbreviations

BF   Bibliothèque Forney
BNF   Bibliothèque Nationale de France, Paris
CEALEX   Centre d'études Alexandrines
WMF   Women and Memory Forum, Cairo

Abd al-Razik, Midhat. *Mitsrayim. Hikayat wa 'Ai'lat yahud Misr al-Malakiyya* [Mitsrayim. Tales and the Royal Families of the Jews of Egypt]. Al-Rewaq, 2022.

Abdel Meguid, Ibrahim. *No One Sleeps in Alexandria.* American University in Cairo Press, 2006.

Abi-Mershed, Osama W. *Apostles of Modernity: Saint-Simonians and the Civilizing Mission in Algeria.* Stanford University Press, 2010.

Abulafia, David. *The Great Sea: A Human History of the Mediterranean.* Oxford University Press, 2011.

Abulghar, Mohamed. *Yahud Misr fi al-Qarn al-i'shrin. Kayfa Ashu wa Limatha Kharaju?* [The Jews of Egypt in the Twentieth Century. How Did They Live and Why Did They Depart?]. Dar El Shorouk, 2021.

Abu-Lughod, Janet. *Cairo: 1001 Years of the City Victorious.* Princeton University Press, 1971.

Aciman, André. *Out of Egypt.* Farrar, Straus and Giroux, 1994.

Agamben, Giorgio. *Sovereign Power and Bare Life.* Translated by Daniel Heller-Roazen. Stanford University Press, 1998.

Agulhon, Maurice. *The French Republic 1879–1992.* Translated by Antonia Nevill. Blackwell, 1993.

———. *Marianne into Battle: Republican Imagery and Symbolism in France, 1789–1880.* Translated by Janet Lloyd. Cambridge University Press, 1981.

———. *The Republican Experiment, 1848–1852.* Translated by Janet Lloyd. Cambridge University Press, 1983.

Ahmed, Leila. *Women and Gender in Islam: Historical Roots of a Modern Debate.* Yale University Press, 1992.

Alcalay, Ammiel. *After Jews and Arabs: Remaking Levantine Culture.* University of Minnesota Press, 1993.

———. *Keys to the Garden: New Israeli Writing.* City Lights, 1996.

Alleaume, Ghislaine. *L'école polytechnique du Caire et ses élèves. La formation d'une élite technique dans l'Égypte du XIX siècle.* PhD diss., Université de Lille III, 1993.

Allen, Roger. *The Arabic Novel: An Historical and Critical Introduction.* Syracuse University Press, 2004.

Althusser, Louis. "Ideology and Ideological States Apparatuses." *Lenin and Philosophy and Other Essays.* Translated by Ben Brewster. Montly Review Press, 1971.

Amin, Ash, and Nigel Thrift. *Cities: Reimagining the Urban.* Polity Press, 2002.

Amin, Qasim. *al-'Amal al-Kamela* [The Complete Works]. Dar El Shorouk, 1989.

———. *The Liberation of Women: A Document in the History of Egyptian Feminism.* Translated by Samiha Sidhom Peterson. American University in Cairo Press, 1992.

Amireh, Amal, and Lisa Suhair Majaj, editors. *Going Global: The Transnational Reception of Third World Women Writers.* Routledge, 2000.

Anderson, Benedict. *Imagined Communities.* Verso Books, 1991.

Anderson, Elijah. *The Cosmopolitan Canopy: Race and Civility in Everyday Life.* Norton, 2011.

Andia, Béatrice de, editor. *Les cathédrales du commerce parisiens.* Action Artistique, 2006.

Anidjar, Gil. *The Jew, the Arab: A History of the Enemy.* Stanford University Press, 2003.

Annuaire: 1908–1910. Université égyptienne du Caire. Institut français d'archéologie orientale, 1910.

Appadurai, Arjun. *The Social Life of Things: Commodities in Cultural Perspective.* Cambridge University Press, 1986.

Apter, Emily. "Acting Out Orientalism: Sapphic Theatricality in Turn-of-the-Century Paris." *L'Esprit Créateur,* vol. 34, 2017, pp. 102–16.

———. *Against World Literature: On the Politics of Untranslatability.* Verso Books, 2013.

Atiya, Nayra. *Zikrayat. Eight Jewish Women Remember Egypt.* American University in Cairo Press, 2020.

Aunay, Alfred d'. *Le Louvre: Grand hôtel et grands magasins.* Morin, 1878–1908.

Auslander, Leora. "The Gendering of Consumer Practices in Nineteenth-Century France." *The Sex of Things: Gender and Consumption in Historical Perspective,* edited by Victoria De Grazia and Ellen Furlough, pp. 79–112. University of California Press, 1996.

Avenel, Paul. *Les Calicots.* Albert Delveau, 1866.

Avierino, Alexandra. "Mu'tamar al-Salam."*Anis al-Jalis,* 31 October 1900, pp. 393–94.

Bachelard, Gaston. *La Poétique de l'espace.* Presses universitaires de France, 1957.

Badel, Laurence. "Employer's Organisations in French Department Stores During the Inter-War Period: Between Conservatism and Innovation." *Cathedrals of*

Consumption: The European Department Store 1850–1939, edited by Goeffrey Crossick and Serge Jaumain, pp. 299–317. Ashgate, 1999.

Badran, Margot. *Feminists, Islam, and Nation: Gender and the Making of Modern Egypt*. Princeton University Press, 1995.

———. "Introduction." *Harem Years: The Memoirs of an Egyptian Feminist (1879–1924)*. Translated by Margot Badran. Virago Press, 1986.

Bakhtin, Mikhail. *The Dialogic Imagination. Four Essays by M.M. Bakhtin*. Translated by Caryl Emerson and Michael Holquist, edited by Michael Holquist. University of Texas Press, 1981.

———. *Rabelais and His World*. Translated by Helene Iswolsky. Indiana University Press, 1984.

Balfour, Rosa. "The Transformation of the Union for the Mediterranean: Profile." *Mediterranean Politics*, vol. 14, no. 1, 2009, pp. 99–105.

Balzac, Honoré de. "Histoire et physiologie des boulevards de *Paris de La Madeleine à la Bastille*." 1845. *Le diable à Paris: Paris et les Parisiens*, pp. 164–67. Maresque, 1853.

———. *Oeuvres complètes de H. De Balzac*. Nabu Press, 2013.

Barak, On. *On Time: Technology and Temporality in Modern Egypt*. University of Cairo Press, 2013.

Baron, Beth. *Egypt as a Woman: Nationalism, Gender, and Politics*. University of Cairo Press, 2005.

———. "Unveiling in Early Twentieth Century Egypt: Practical and Symbolic Considerations." *Middle Eastern Studies*, vol. 25, no. 3, 1989, pp. 370–86.

———. *The Women's Awakening in Egypt: Culture Society and the Press*. Yale University Press, 1994.

Barrows, Susanne. *Distorting Mirrors: Visions of the Crowd in Late Nineteenth-Century France*. Yale University Press, 1981.

Barthes, Roland. *The Fashion System*. Translated by Matthew Ward and Richard Howard. Hill and Wang, 1983.

———. *The Language of Fashion*. Edited by Andy Stafford and Michael Carter. Berg, 2006.

Batignani, Piero. *I Primi Grandi Magazzini di Firenze. Gli Antenati dello Shopping*. Angelo Pontecorboli, 2016.

Baudelaire, Charles. "Morale du joujou."*Oeuvres complètes*, vol. 1, pp. 581–87. Éditions Gallimard, 1976.

———. *The Painter of Modern Life and Other Essays*. Translated by Jonathan Mayne. Phaidon, 1964.

———. "Le Peintre de la vie moderne." *Oeuvres complètes*, vol. 2, pp. 683–724. Éditions Gallimard, 1976.

Beck, Ulrich. *The Cosmopolitan Vision*. Translated by Ciaran Cronin. Polity Books, 2006.

Beecher, Jonathan. *Charles Fourier: The Visionary and His World*. University of California Press 1990.

Beinin, Joel. *The Dispersion of Egyptian Jewry*. University of California Press, 1998.
———. *Workers and Peasants in the Middle East*. Cambridge University Press, 2001.
Beinin, Joel, and Zachary Lockman. *Workers on the Nile: Nationalism, Communism, Islam, and the Egyptian Working Class, 1882–1954*. Princeton University Press, 1987.
Benjamin, Walter. *The Arcades Project*. Translated by Howard Eiland and Kevin Mclaughlin. Belknap Press, 1999.
Bennett, Tony. *The Birth of the Museum: History, Theory, Politics*. Routledge, 1995.
Berlanstein, Lenard R., editor. *The Industrial Revolution and Work in Nineteenth Century Europe*. Routledge, 1992.
Bhabha, Homi K. *The Location of Culture*. 1994. Routledge, 2004.
———. *Nation and Narration*. Routledge, 1999.
Biancani, Francesca. "Gender, Mobility and Cosmopolitanism in a Trans-Mediterranean Perspective: Female Migration from Trieste's Littoral to Egypt, 1860–1960." *Gender & History*, vol. 31, no. 3, 2019, pp. 699–716.
———. "*Let Down the Curtains around Us*": *Sex Work in Colonial Cairo 1882–1952*. PhD diss., Oxford University, 2012.
Bigio, Alain. *The Journey: From Ismaeleya to Higienópolis—The Story of an Egyptian Jew*. Kindle, 2014.
———. *A Travessia de Ismaeleyah a Higienópolis: A História de Um Judeu Egípcio Contemporâneo*. Editora e Libraria Sêfer, 2013.
Bloom, Harold, editor. *Émile Zola, Bloom's Modern Critical Views*. Chelsea House, 2004.
Booth, Marilyn. "Between Harem and Houseboat: 'Fallenness,' Gendered Spaces, and the Female National Subject in 1920s Egypt." *Harem Histories: Envisioning Places and Living Spaces*, edited by Marlyn Booth, pp. 342–73. Duke University Press, 2010.
———. "Biography and Feminist Rhetoric in Early Twentieth-Century Egypt: May Ziyada's Studies of Three Women's Lives." *Journal of Women's History*, vol. 3 no. 1, 1991, pp. 38–64.
———. "Girlhood Translated?: Fénelon's Traité de l'éducation Des Filles (1687) as a Text of Egyptian Modernity (1901, 1909)." *Migrating Texts: Circulating Translations around the Ottoman Mediterranean*, edited by Marilyn Booth, pp. 266–99. Edinburgh University Press, 2019.
———. *May Her Likes Be Multiplied: Biography and Gender Politics in Egypt*. University of California Press, 2001.
———. *Writing Feminist History through Biography in Fin-De-Siècle Egypt*. Edinburgh University Press, 2015.
Booth, Marilyn, and Anthony Gorman. *The Long 1890s in Egypt: Colonial Quiescence, Subterranean Resistance*. Edinburgh University Press, 2014.
Bourdieu, Pierre. *Distinction: A Social Critique of Judgment of Taste*. Translated by Richard Nice. Harvard University Press, 1984.
———. *Outline of a Theory of Practice*. Translated by Richard Nice. Cambridge University Press, 2013.

Bowell, Viviane. *To Egypt with Love: Memories of a Bygone World.* UK Book Publishing, 2021.
Bracco, Carolina. "The Creation of the Femme Fatale in Egyptian Cinema." *Journal of Middle East Women's Studies,* vol. 15, no. 3, 2019, pp. 307–29.
Braudel, Fernand. *L'identité de la France.* France loisirs, 1986.
———. *La Méditerranée et le monde méditerranéen à l'époque de Philippe II: Destins collectifs et mouvements d'ensemble.* Armand Colin, 1999.
———. *La Méditerranée et le monde méditerranéen à l'époque de Philippe II: Les événements, la politique et les hommes.* Armand Colin, 1999.
———. *La Méditerranée et le monde méditerranéen à l'époque de Philippe II: La part du milieu.* Armand Colin, 1999.
———. *The Mediterranean and the Mediterranean World in the Age of Philip II: The Mediterranean as a Human Unit.* University of California Press, 2005.
Bräutigam, Isabelle. "Une phare à l'entrée du canal de Suez." *L'Épopée du Canal de Suez,* edited by Gilles Gauthier and Claude Mollard, pp. 82–85. Éditions Gallimard, 2018.
Brémontier, Jeanne. "Toutes les femmes du monde pour la paix." *La Fronde,* no. 12, 6 June 1926.
Brown, Garret Wallace, and David Held, editors. *The Cosmopolitan Reader.* Polity Books, 2010.
Brummett, Palmira. "Visions of the Mediterranean: A Classification." *Journal of Medieval and Early Modern Studies,* vol. 37, no. 1, 2007, pp. 9–55.
Burckhardt, Monica. *Le Bon Marché Rive Gauche: l'invention d'un magasin.* Assouline, 2012.
Butler, Judith. *Gender Trouble.* Routledge, 1991.
Canac, Sybil. *Passages couverts de Paris.* Charles Massin, 2011.
Caracalla, Jean-Paul. *Le Roman du Printemps. Histoire d'un grand magasin.* Éditions Denoël, 1989.
Castel-Bloom, Orly. "Ummi fi Shughl." *Sipurim bilti retsoniyim* [Involuntary Stories], pp. 8–11. Zemora-Bitan, 1993.
Certeau, Michel de. *L'invention du quotidien.* Vol. II. Éditions Gallimard, 1994.
———. *The Practice of Everyday Life.* Translated by Steven Rendall. University of California Press, 1984.
Certeau, Michel de, Luce Giard, and Pierre Mayol. *The Practice of Everyday Life. Vol. II: Living and Cooking.* Translated by Timothy J. Tomasik. University of Minnesota Press, 1998.
Chakrabarty, Dipesh. *Provincializing Europe: Postcolonial Thought and Historical Difference.* Princeton University Press, 2000.
Chandet, Henriette, editor. "Chronique étrangère." *Union nationale des femmes,* no. 82, 10 March 1935, p. 4.
———, editor. "Chronique étrangère." *Union nationale des femmes,* no. 87, 10 October 1935.

———. "L'émancipation de la femme égyptienne." *Union nationale des femmes*, no. 79, 10 December 1934, p. 2.

Charlet, Nicolas Toussaint. "Épisode de la campagne de la Russie." Musée des Beaux-Arts de Lyon, 1836.

Charley, Sébastien. *Histoire du Saint-Simonisme. 1825–1864*. 1931. Perrin, 2018.

Chaulet-Achour, Christiane. *Les 1001 nuits et l'imaginaire du xx*e *siècle*. L'Harmattan, 2004.

Chessel, Marie-Emanuelle. "Training Sales Personnel in France between the Wars." *Cathedrals of Consumption: The European Department Store 1850–1939*, edited by Goeffrey Crossick and Serge Jaumain, pp. 279–98. Ashgate, 1999.

Chevalier, Michel. "Le Globe, 31 janvier 1832." *Le Saint-Simonisme, L'Europe et la Méditerranée*, pp. 105–10. Manucius, 2008.

———. "Le Globe, 5 février 1832." *Le Saint-Simonisme, L'Europe et la Méditerranée*, pp. 111–16. Manucius, 2008.

———. "Le Globe, 12 février 1832." *Le Saint-Simonisme, L'Europe et la Méditerranée*, pp. 117–33. Manucius, 2008.

Cialente, Fausta. *Ballata Levantina*. Filtrinelli Editore, 1961.

———. *The Levantines: A Modern Novel of a Distant World*. Translated by Isabel Quigly. Riverside Press, 1963.

Cicurel, Ronald. *Mémoires du Caire. Souvenirs d'enfance d'un grand père juif*. Sarina, 2002.

Clark, Timothy J. *The Painting of Modern Life: Paris in the Art of Manet and His Followers*. Princeton University Press, 1984.

Clausen, Meredith L. "Department Stores and Zola's 'cathédrale du commerce moderne.'" *Notes in the History of Art*, vol. 3, no. 3, 1984, pp. 18–23.

———. "The Department Store: Development of the Type." *Journal of Architectural Education*, vol. 39, no. 1, 1985, pp. 20–29.

———. *Frantz Jourdain and the Samaritaine: Art Nouveau Theory and Criticism*. Brill, 1987.

Cohen, Margret. "Panoramic Literature and the Invention of Everyday Genres." *Cinema and the Invention of Modern Life*, edited by Leo Charney and Vanessa Schwartz, pp. 227–52. University of California Press, 1995.

Coilly, Nathalie, and Philippe Régnier, editors. *Le siècle des saint-simoniens: Du nouveau christianisme au canal de Suez*. BNF, 2006.

Colla, Elliott. *Conflicted Antiquities: Egyptology, Egyptomania, Egyptian Modernity*. Duke University Press, 2007.

Cordier, Henri. "The Statutory Ninth International Congress of Orientalists." *T'oung Pao*, vol. 2, no. 5, 1891, pp. 411–33.

Cosgrove, Denis C. *Geography and Vision: Seeing, Imagining and Representing the World*. I.B. Tauris, 2008.

———. *Social Formation and Symbolic Landscape*. University of Wisconsin Press, 1998.

Cosgrove, Denis C., and Stephen Daniels, editors. *The Iconography of Landscape*. Cambridge University Press, 1988.
Creed, Barbara. *The Monstrous-Feminine: Film, Feminism, Psychoanalysis*. Routledge, 1993.
Crenshaw, Kimberlé. "Demarginalizing the Intersection of Race and Sex." *Feminist Legal Theory*, edited by Katherine T. Bartlett and Rosanne Kennedy, pp. 81–94. Westview Press, 1991.
Cromer, Evelyn Baring. *Modern Egypt*. Macmillan, 1916.
Crosnier Leconte, Marie-Laure, and Mercedes Volait. *L'Égypte d'un architecte: Ambroise Baudry (1838–1906)*. Éditons d'Art, 1998.
———. *Maisons de France au Caire. Le remploi de grands décors mamelouks et ottomans dans une architecture moderne*. Institut français d'archéologie orientale, 2012.
Crossick, Geoffrey, and Serge Jaumain, editors. *Cathedrals of Consumption: The European Department Store 1850–1939*. Ashgate, 1999.
Crownshaw, Richard. "Reconsidering Postmemory: Photography, the Archive, and Post-Holocaust Memory in W.G. Sebald's 'Austerlitz.'" *Mosaic*, vol. 37, no. 4, 2004, pp. 215–36.
Da Costa Meyer, Esther. *Dividing Paris: Urban Renewal and Social Inequality, 1852–1970*. Princeton University Press, 2022.
Daher, Rami, and Irene Maffi. *The Politics and Practices of Cultural Heritage in the Middle East*. Tauris, 2014.
Dakhlia, Jocelyne. *Lingua franca: histoire d'une langue métisse en Méditerranée*. Actes Sud, 2008.
Dalachanis, Angelos. *The Greek Exodus from Egypt: Diaspora Politics and Emigration*. Berghahn, 2017.
Daly, M. W. *Imperial Sudan: The Anglo-Egyptian Condominium 1934–56*. Cambridge University Press, 1991.
Damrosch, David. *What Is World Literature?* Princeton University Press, 2003.
Danforth, Loring M. "The Ideological Context of the Search for Continuities in Greek Culture." *Journal of Modern Greek Studies*, vol. 2 no. 1, 1984, pp. 53–85.
De Grazia, Victoria. "Changing Consumption Regimes." *The Sex of Things: Gender and Consumption in Historical Perspective*, edited by Victoria De Grazia and Ellen Furlough, 11–24. University of California Press, 1996.
Delanty, Gerald, editor. *Routledge Handbook of Cosmopolitanism Studies*. Routledge, 2012.
Delbeuf, Régis. *La Turquie et l'Orient à l'exposition de 1900*. BNF, 1900.
Deleuze, Gilles, and Felix Guattari. *A Thousand Plateaus: Capitalism and Schizophrenia*. University of Minnesota Press, 2005.
Delvau, Alfred. *Dictionnaire érrotique modern. Deuxième édition*. Imprimerie de la Société, 1874.
Derrida, Jacques. *L'autre cap*. Minuit, 1991.
Derrida, Jacques, and Anne Dufourmantelle. *De l'hospitalité*. Calmann Levy, 1997.

des Cars, Jean. *Haussmann La gloire de Second Empire*. Perrin, 1985.
Devereux, Cecily. "'The Maiden Tribute' and the Rise of the White Slave in the Nineteenth Century: The Making of an Imperial Construct." *Victorian Review*, vol. 26, no. 2, 2000, pp. 1–23.
Dicharry, Elsa. "Les 96 HLM de la Samaritaine inaugurés dans le coeur de Paris." *Les Echos*, 23 September 2021.
Diyab, Hanna. *Min Halab ila Baris: Rihla ila Balat Louis al-Rabi' 'Ashar* [From Aleppo to Paris: A Journey to the Court of Louis XIV], edited by Mohamed Mustapha al-Jarush and Safa' Abu Shahla Jubran. Al-Kamel, 2017.
Dobie, Madeleine. "For and against the Mediterranean Francophone Perspectives." *Comparative Studies of South Asia, Africa, & the Middle East*, vol. 34, no. 2, 2014, pp. 389–404.
Dodman, Thomas. *What Nostalgia Was: War, Empire, and the Time of a Deadly Emotion*. University of California Press, 2019.
Domosh, Mona. *American Commodities in an Age of Empire*. Routledge, 2006.
D'Souza, Aruna, and Tom McDonough. *The Invisible Flâneuse*. Manchester University Press, 2006.
Dubech, Lucien, and Pierre d'Espezel. *Histoire de Paris*. Payot, 1926.
Du Bois, W. E. B., and Brent Hayes Edwards. *The Souls of Black Folk*. Oxford University Press, 2007.
Dubuisson, Paul. *Les voleuses des grands magasins*. Storck, 1902.
Du Camp, Maxime. *Souvenirs d'Egypte*. Hachette, 1892.
Ducaris, Yvonne. "Notes biographiques et historiques." Louli Sanua, *Figures féminines. Mil neuf cent neuf-Mil neuf cent neuf*. Siboney, 1949.
Durand, Marguerite, editor. "Autour du congrès." *La Fronde*, no. 14, 8 June 1926, p. 2.
———. "Salut des femmes de tous les pays." *La Fronde*, no. 7, 1 June 1926, p. 1.
Durrell, Lawrence. *The Alexandria Quartet: Justine, Balthazar, Mountolive, Clea*. Faber and Faber, 1968.
Ebrahim, Reza-Zia. *The Emergence of Iranian Nationalism: Race and the Politics of Dislocation*. Columbia University Press, 2016.
El-Ariss, Tarek, editor. *The Arab Renaissance: A Bilingual Anthology of the Nahda*. Modern Language Association of America, 2018.
Eldem, Edhem. "Les Ottomans, un empire en porte-à-faux." *Après L'orientalisme: L'orient créé par l'orient*, edited by François Pouillon and Jean-Claude Vatin, et al., pp. 285–302. Institut d'études de l'Islam et des sociétés du monde musulman, 2011.
———. "Plurality, Cosmopolitanism, and Integration: The Dangers of Comparing the Incomparable." *The Economies of Urban Diversity: The Ruhr Area in Istanbul*, edited by Darja Reuschke, Monika Salzbrunn, and Korinna Schonharl, pp. 47–62. Palgrave, 2013.
Eleb, Monique. "L'Appartement de l'immeuble Haussmannien." *Paris-Haussmann: "Le Pari d'Haussmann,"* edited by Jean des Cars and Pierre Pinon, pp. 284–95. Pavillon de L'Arsenal, 1991.

Elhariri, Yasser, and Edwige Tamalet, editors. *Critically Mediterranean: Temporalities, Aesthetics, and Deployments of a Sea in Crisis*. Palgrave, 2018.

Elkadi, Galila, and Dalia Elkerdani. "Belle-époque Cairo: The Politics of Refurbishing the Downtown Business District." *Cairo Cosmopolitan: Politics, Culture, and Urban Space in the New Globalized Middle East*, edited by Diane Singerman and Paul Amar, pp. 345–66. American University in Cairo Press, 2006.

Elsadda, Hoda. *Gender, Nation, and the Arabic Novel: Egypt, 1892–2008*. Edinburgh University Press, 2012.

———. "Hawwa' Idris wa Masar al-Haraka al-Nisa'yya" [Hawwa' Idris and the Course of the Women's Movement]. *Ana wa-l-Sharq*, pp. 18–21. WMF, 2016.

El Shakry, Omnia. *The Great Social Laboratory: Subjects of Knowledge in Colonial and Postcolonial Egypt*. Stanford University Press, 2007.

Elsheshtawy, Yasser. "Urban Transformations: The Great Cairo Fire and the Founding of a Modern Capital, 1952–1970." *Built Environment*, vol. 40, no. 3, 2014, pp. 408–25.

Emery, Lynne Fauley. *Black Dance: From 1619 to Today*. Princeton Book, 1988.

"Emporium." *Oxford Dictionary of English Etymology*, edited by C. T. Onions et al., Oxford University Press, 1966.

Erll, Astrid. "Remembering Across Time, Space, and Cultures: Premediation, Remediation and the 'Indian Mutiny.'" *Mediation, Remediation, and the Dynamics of Cultural Memory*, edited by Astrid Erll and Ann Rigney, pp. 109–38. De Gruyter, 2009.

Fabian, Johannes. *Time and the Other: How Anthropology Makes Its Object*. Columbia University Press, 1983.

Fahmy, Khaled. *All the Pasha's Men: Mehmed Ali, His Army, and the Making of Modern Egypt*. Cambridge University Press, 1997.

———. "For Cavafy with Love and Squalor: Some Critical Notes on the History and Historiography of Modern Alexandria." *Alexandria, Real and Imagined*, edited by Anthony Hirst and Michael Silk. Ashgate, 2004.

———. "The Essence of Alexandria," pt. 1. *Manifesta Journal*, no. 14, 2012, pp. 64–72.

———. "The Essence of Alexandria," pt. 2. *Manifesta Journal*, no. 16, December 2012, pp. 22–27.

Fahmy, Ziad. "Jurisdictional Borderlands: Extraterritoriality and 'Legal Chameleons' in Precolonial Alexandria, 1840–1870." *Comparative Studies in Society and History*, vol. 55, no. 2, 2013, pp. 305–29.

———. *Ordinary Egyptians: Creating the Modern Nation through Popular Culture*. Stanford University Press, 2011.

Fanon, Frantz. *Black Skin, White Masks*. Translated by Charles Lamm Markmann. Grove Press, 1967.

———. *The Wretched of the Earth*. Translated by Constance Farrington. Grove Press. 1963.

Fénelon, François de Salignac de la Mothe. *Éducation des filles de Fénelon*. Edited by Octave Gréard. Librairie des Bibliophiles, 1890.

Fenoglio-Abd El Al, Irène. *Défense et illustration de l'Egyptienne. Au début d'une expression féminine*. Centre d'études et de documentation économiques, juridiques et sociales, 1980.

Ferry, Jules. *Les Comptes fantastiques d'Haussmann. (Suivi de) Les finances de l'hotel de ville par J.E. horn*. Guy Durier, 1979, pp. 1–93.

Fetiha, Moataz. *Akhir Yahud al-Iskandariyya* [The last Jew of Alexandria]. Oktob, 2009.

Fleischmann, Ellen L. "'The Other Awakening': The Emergence of Women's Movements in the Modern Middle East, 1900–1940." *Globalizing Feminisms, 1789–1945*, edited by Karen Offen, pp. 170–92. Routledge, 2010.

Flinn, Margaret C. "Julien Duvivier and Inter-War 'Banlieutopia.'" *Screening the Paris Suburbs: From the Silent Era to the 1990s*, edited by Philippe Met and Derek Schilling, pp. 62–76. Manchester University Press, 2018.

Foord, Edward. *Napoleon's Russian Campaign of 1812, Illustrated with Thirty-Two Portraits and Historical Paintings and Several Maps and Plans*. Hutchinson, 1914.

Fosca, François. *Histoire des cafés de Paris*. Firmin-Didot, 1934.

Foucault, Michel. *Discipline and Punish*. Translated by Alan Sheridan. Vintage, 1995.

———. *History of Sexuality, Vol. 1: An Introduction*. Translated by Rober Hurley. Vintage, 1990.

Foucault, Michel, and Jay Miskowiec. "Of Other Spaces." *Diacritics*, vol. 16, no. 1, 1986, pp. 22–27.

Fourier, Charles. "An Architectural Innovation: The Street Gallery." *The Utopian Vision of Charles Fourier: Selected Text, on Work and Love and Passionate Attraction*, translated and edited by Jonathan Beecher and Richard Bienvenu, pp. 242–45. Beacon Press, 1971.

———. "The Phalanstery." *The Utopian Vision of Charles Fourier. Selected Text, on Work and Love and Passionate Attraction*, translated and edited by Jonathan Beecher and Richard Bienvenu, pp. 240–42. Beacon Press, 1971.

———. *Théorie de quatre mouvements et des déstinées générales. Prospectus et annonce de la découverte*. 1808. BNF.

Franckenberg, Ruth. "Introduction: Local Whiteness/Localizing Whiteness." *Displacing Whiteness*, edited by Ruth Franckenerg, pp. 1-33. Duke University Press, 1997.

Friedberg, Anne. *Window Shopping: Cinema and the Postmodern*. University of California Press, 1993.

Fureix, Emmanuel, and François Jarrige. *La Modernité désenchantée: Relire l'histoire du XIXe siècle français*. La Découverte, 2015.

Garnier, Charles. *Le Nouvel opéra de Paris. Volume 1*. Ducher, 1878.

Garrigues, Henri. *Les grands magasins de nouveauté et le petit commerce de détail*. Rousseau, 1898.

Gaston-Breton, Tristan. *Galeries Lafayette: La légende d'un siècle*. ClioMédia, 1997.

Gendzier, Irene I. *The Practical Visions of Ya'qub Sanu'*. Harvard University Press, 1966.

Gerhardt, Mia Irene. *The Art of Story-Telling: A Literary Study of the Thousand and One Nights*. Brill, 1963.

Gershoni, Israel, and James Jankowski. *Commemorating the Nation: Collective Memory, Public Commemoration, and National Identity in Twentieth Century Egypt*. Middle East Documentation Center, 2004.

Ghali, Waguih. *Beer in the Snooker Club*. Andre Deutsch, 1964.

Giacomelli, Milva, and Ezio Godoli. *Architetti e ingegneri italiani in Egitto dal diciannovesimo al ventunesimo secolo* [Italian Architects and Engineers in Egypt from the Nineteenth to the Twenty-First Century]. Aschietto, 2008.

Giedion, Siegfried. *Space, Time, and Architecture: The Growth of a New Tradition*. Harvard University Press, 1959.

Giese, Francine, Mercedes Volait, and Ariane Varela Braga. *A l'Orientale: Collecting, Displaying and Appropriating Islamic Art and Architecture in the 19th and Early 20th Centuries*. Brill, 2019.

Giffard, Pierre. *Paris sous La Troisième République*. *Les Grands Bazars*, edited by Victor Havard. 1882.

Gitre, Carmen M. K. *Acting Egyptian: Theatre Identity and Political Culture in Cairo, 1869–1930*. University of Texas Press, 2019.

Göçek, Fatma Müge. *Rise of the Bourgeoisie, Demise of Empire: Ottoman Westernization and Social Change*. Oxford University Press, 1996.

Godlewska, Anne Marie. *Geography Unbound: French Geographic Science from Cassini to Humboldt*. University of California Press, 1999.

Godlewska, Anne Marie, and Neil Smith. *Geography and Empire*. Blackwell, 1994.

Goffette, Jean-Dominique. "D'un imaginaire à l'autre: boulevards balzaciens, boulevards flaubertiens." *Les grands boulevards*, special issue of *Romantisme*, no. 134, 2006, pp. 33–42.

Goude, Jean-Paul, and Patrick Mauriès. *The Goude Touch: A Ten-Year Campaign for Galeries Lafayette*. Thames and Hudson, 2010.

Gregory, Derek. *Explorations in Critical Human Geography: Hettner Lecture 1997*. University of Heidelberg, 1998.

———. *Geographical Imaginations*. Blackwell, 1994.

Gullickson, Gay L. *Unruly Women of Paris: Images of the Commune*. Cornell University Press, 2018.

Gunn, Simon. "Between Modernity and Backwardness: The Case of the English Middle Class." *The Making of the Middle Class Toward a Transnational History*, edited by Ricardo A. Lopez and Barbara Weinstein, pp. 58–74. Duke University Press, 2012.

Gurney, Peter. *The Making of Consumer Culture in Modern Britain*. Bloomsbury, 2017.

Habermas, Jürgen. *The Structural Transformation of the Public Sphere: An Inquiry into a Category of Bourgeois Society*. MIT Press, 1999.

Hahn, H. Hazel. *Scenes of Parisian Modernity: Culture and Consumption in the Nineteenth Century*. Palgrave, 2009.

Halbwachs, Maurice. *On Collective Memory*. Edited by Lewis A. Coser. University of California Press, 1992.

Halim, Hala. *Alexandrian Cosmopolitanism: An Archive*. Modern Language Initiative, 2013.

Hallstead, Tracy M. *Pygmalion's Chisel: For Women Who Are "Never Good Enough."* Cambridge Scholars, 2013.

Hamamsy, Chafika Soliman. *Zamalek: The Changing Life of Cairo Elite, 1850–1945*. American University in Cairo Press, 2005.

Hamdi, Emad, and Walaa Gamal. "Sednawi T'atazim Tarh 9 Foru' l-il-sharaka ma' al-qita' al-Khas" [Sednawi Plans to Offer Nine Store Branches for Cooperation with the Private sector]. *Jaraditat al-Bursa*, 23 October 2014, www.alborsaanews.com/2015/09/29/743619.

Hammad, Hanan. *The Unknown Past: Layla Murad. The Jewish-Muslim Star of Egypt*. Stanford University Press, 2022.

Hammad, Hanan and Francesca Biancani. "Prostitution in Cairo." *Selling Sex in the City: A Global History of Prostitution, 1600s–2000s*, edited by Magaly Rodríguez García et al., pp. 233–60. Brill, 2017.

Hanley, Will. "When Did Egyptians Stop Being Ottomans? An Imperial Citizenship Case Study." *Multilevel Citizenship: Democracy, Citizenship and Constitutionalism*, edited by Willem Maas, pp. 89–109. University of Pennsylvania Press, 2013.

Hannoosh, Michèle. *Baudelaire and Caricature: From the Comic to an Art of Modernity*. Penn State University Press, 1992.

———. *Jules Michelet: Writing Art and History in Nineteenth Century France*. Penn State University Press, 2020.

———. *Painting and the Journal of Eugène Delacroix*. Princeton University Press, 1995.

Hartog, François. *Regimes of Historicity. Presentism and Experiences of Time*. Translated by Saskia Brown. Columbia University Press, 2015.

Harvey, David. *Marx, Capital, and the Madness of Economic Reason*. Oxford University Press, 2018.

———. *Paris: Capital of Modernity*. Routledge, 2003.

Hassoun, Jacques. *Alexandries*. La Découverte, 1985.

Hathaway, Jane. *The Chief Eunuch of the Ottoman Harem: From African Slave to Power Broker*. Cambridge University Press, 2018.

Havard, Henry. *L'Art dans la maison (grammaire de l'ameublement)*. Rouvyere et G. Blond, 1884.

Hayes, Jarrod. *Queer Nations: Marginal Sexualities in the Maghreb*. University of Chicago Press, 2000.

Haykal, Muhammad Hussayn. *Zaynab*. 1913. Hindawi, 2012.

Heath, Elizabeth. *Wine, Sugar, and the Making of Modern France: Global Economic Crisis and the Racialization of French Citizenship, 1870–1910*. Cambridge University Press, 2014.

Heidegger, Martin. *Basic Writings from Being and Time*. Edited by David Farrell Krell. HarperCollins, 1993.

———. *The Question Concerning Technology and Other Essays*. Translated by William Lovitt. Garland, 1997.

Hendrickson, Robert. *The Grand Emporiums: The Illustrated History of America's Great Department Stores*. Stein and Day, 1979.

Herzfeld, Michael. "Honour and Shame: Problems in the Comparative Analysis of Moral Systems." *Man*, vol. 15, no. 2, 1980, pp. 339–51.

———. "The Horns of the Mediterraneanist Dilemma." *American Ethnologist*, vol. 11, no. 3, 1984, pp. 439–54.

———. "Practical Mediterraneanism: Excuses for Everything from Epistemology to Eating." *Rethinking the Mediterranean*, edited by W. V. Harris, pp. 45–63. Oxford University Press, 2006.

Hetrick, Bethany. "Mannequins, Mass-Consumption and Modernity in *Au Bonheur Des Dames*: The Department Store as Ladies' Paradise?" *Equinoxes*, no. 3, spring/summer 2006. www.brown.edu/Research/Equinoxes/journal/Issue%207/eqx7_hetrick.htm.

Hifzi, Shaymaa. "Qita' al-a'mal Taftatih Moll Sednawi b-il-'Ataba ba'd Tatwiroh bi-Mosharakat al-Qita' al-Khas" [The Public Business Sector Inaugurates Sednawi Mall in Ataba after its Renovation in Cooperation with the Private Sector]. *Masrawy*, 26 September 2019, www.masrawy.com/news/news_economy/details/2019/9/26/1641703.

Hillairet, Jacques. *Dictionnaire historique des rues de Paris*. Les Éditions de Minuit, 1985.

Hille, Charlotte, and Renée Gendron. "Circassia: Remembering the Past Empowers the Future." *Iran and the Caucasus*, vol. 23, no. 2, 2019, pp. 199–215.

Hobsbawm, Eric, and Terence Ranger. *The Invention of Tradition*. Cambridge University Press, 1983.

Hochberg, Gil Z. "'Permanent Immigration': Jacqueline Kahanoff, Ronit Matalon, and the Impetus of Levantinism." *boundary 2*, vol. 31, no. 2, 2004, pp. 219–43.

———. *In Spite of Partition: Jews, Arabs, and the Limits of Separatist Imagination*. Princeton University Press, 2007.

Hoganson, Kristin. *Consumers' Imperium: The Global Production of American Domesticity*. University of North Carolina Press, 2007.

Holquist, Michael. "Introduction." *The Dialogic Imagination. Four Essays by M.M. Bakhtin*, edited by Michael Holquist, translated by Caryl Emerson and Michael Holquist, pp. xv–xxxiii. University of Toronto Press, 1981.

"Hommage à Monsieur Boucicaut—1810–1877." 1912. Microfilm, MFiche 8-LN27-56704 BNF.

Hoodfar, Homa. "Return to the Veil: Personal Strategy and Public Participation in Egypt." *Working Women: International Perspectives on Labour and Gender Ideology*, edited by Nanneke Redclift and M. Thea Sinclair, pp. 105–25. Routledge, 1991.

Horden, Peregrine, and Nicholas Purcell. *The Corrupting Sea: A Study of Mediterranean History*. Oxford University Press, 2000.

Houellebecq. Michel. *La Soumission*. J'ai lu, 2015.

Hourani, Albert. *Syria and Lebanon: A Political Essay*. Oxford University Press, 1946.

Hoyle, Mark S. W. "The Mixed Courts of Egypt 1938–1949." *Arab Law Quarterly*, vol. 3, no. 1, 1988, pp. 83–115.

Hugo, Victor. *Notre Dame de Paris*. Wentworth Press, 2017.
Humboldt, Alexander von. *Tableaux de la Nature*. Translated by M. CH. Galuski. Librairie Des Sciences Naturelles, 1865.
Huysmans, Joris-Karl. *Against the Grain (A Rebours)*. Dover, 1969.
———. *À Rebours*. Éditions Gallimard, 1977.
Idris, Ḥawwaʾ. *Ana-wa al-Sharq: Muthakkarat Ḥawwaʾ Idrīs*. WMF, 2016.
Ilbert, Robert. *Héliopolis: le Caire 1905–1922. Genèse d'une ville*. Centre national de la recherche scientifique, 1981.
Ilbert, Robert, Ilios Yannakakis, and Jacques Hassoun, eds. *Alexandria 1860–1960: A Brief life of a Cosmopolitan Community*. Translated by Colin Clement. Harpocrates, 2007.
Isabella, Maurizio, and Konstantina Zanou, editors. *Mediterranean Diasporas: Politics and Ideas in the Long 19th Century*. Bloomsbury, 2016.
Ivray, Jehan d'. *L'aventure Saint-Simonienne et les femmes*. Félix Alcan, 1928.
Jacob, William Chaco. *Working Out Egypt: Effendi Masculinities and Subject Formation on Colonial Modernity, 1870–1940*. Duke University Press, 2011.
Jacques, Paula. *Gilda Stambouli souffre et se plaint*. Mercure de France, 2002.
———. *Lumière de l'oeil*. Mercure de France, 1980.
Jameson, Fredric. *Archaeologies of the Future: The Desire Called Utopia and Other Science Fictions*. Verso, 2007.
———. *Postmodernism, or, the Cultural Logic of Late Capitalism*. Duke University Press, 1991.
Jarry, Paul. *Les magasins de nouveautés. Histoire rétrospective et anecdoctique*. André Barry & fils, 1948.
Johnson, Rebecca C. *Stranger Fictions: A History of the Novel in Arabic Translation*. Cornell University Press, 2020.
al-Jumayyil, Antun. *Al-Fatah wa-l-Bayt*. Al Maʿarif, 1916.
Kahanoff, Jacqueline Shohet. "A Culture Stillborn." 1973. *Mongrels or Marvels: The Levantine Writings of Jacqueline Shohet Kahanoff*, edited by Deborah A. Starr and Sasson Somekh, pp. 114–27. Stanford University Press, 2011.
———. "Afterword: From East the Sun." 1968. *Mongrels or Marvels: The Levantine Writings of Jacqueline Shohet Kahanoff*, edited by Deborah A. Starr and Sasson Somekh, pp. 243–59. Stanford University Press, 2011.
———. "Alexandria." *Mongrels or Marvels: The Levantine Writings of Jacqueline Shohet Kahanoff*, edited by Deborah A. Starr and Sasson Somekh, pp. 74–88. Stanford University Press, 2011.
———. "Childhood in Egypt." *The Levantine Writings of Jacqueline Shohet Kahanoff*, edited by Deborah A. Starr and Sasson Somekh, pp. 1–13. Stanford University Press, 2011.
———. "Ha-Tsaʾif ha-Kaḥol shel ha-Qidma." *Jacqueline Kahanoff: Bein Shnei ʻOlamot*, edited by David Ohana, pp. 49–61. Keter, 2005.
———. *Jacob's Ladder*. London, Harvill Press, 1951.

———. "A Letter from Mama Camouna." *Mongrels or Marvels: The Levantine Writings of Jacqueline Shohet Kahanoff*, edited by Deborah A. Starr and Sasson Somekh, pp. 164–76. Stanford University Press, 2011.

———. "To Remember Alexandria." 1976. *Mongrels or Marvels: The Levantine Writings of Jacqueline Shohet Kahanoff*, edited by Deborah A. Starr and Sasson Somekh, pp. 213–31. Stanford University Press, 2011.

———. "Such Is Rachel." 1946. *Mongrels or Marvels: The Levantine Writings of Jacqueline Shohet Kahanoff*, edited by Deborah A. Starr and Sasson Somekh, pp. 20–31. Stanford University Press, 2011.

Kahf, Mohja. "Huda Sha'rawi's 'Mudhakkirati': The Memoirs of the First Lady of Arab Modernity." *Arab Studies Quarterly*, vol. 20, no. 1, 1998, pp. 53–82.

———. "Packaging 'Huda': Sha'rawi's Memoirs in the United States Reception Environment," *Going Global: The Transnational Reception of Third World Women Writers*, edited by Amal Amrireh and Lisa Suhair Majaj, pp. 148–72. Garland, 2000.

Kamal, Amr. "Ghostly Labor: Ethnic Classism in the Levantine Prism of Jacqueline Kahanoff's *Jacob's Ladder*." *International Journal of Middle East Studies*, vol. 49, no. 2, 2017, pp. 255–75.

———. "'A Living Tableau of Queerness': The Orient at the Crossroad of Genre and Gender in Proust's *Recherche*." *Queer Jews, Queer Muslims: Race, Religion and Representations*, edited by Adi Bharat, 75–101. Wayne State University Press, 2024.

———. "Reflections on Art and Nation Building: The Museum of Islamic Art in Doha, Qatar." *Islamic Ecumene: Comparing Muslim Societies*, edited by David S. Powers and Eric Tagliacozzo, pp. 238–51. Cornell University Press, 2023.

Kermel, Amédée. "Les passages de Paris." *Paris ou le livre des cent-et-un. Tome X*, pp. 49–72. Ladvocat, 1833.

Kesrounay, Maya I. *Prophetic Translation. The Making of Modern Egyptian Literature*. Edinburgh University Press, 2019.

Klein, Ernest. *A Comprehensive Etymological Dictionary of the Hebrew Language for Readers of English*. Carta Jerusalem, 1987.

Kozma, Liat. *Global Women. Colonial Ports: Prostitution in the Interwar Middle East*. State University of New York Press, 2017.

———. *Policing Egyptian Women. Sex, Law, and Medicine in Khedival Egypt*. Syracuse University Press, 2011.

Kozma, Liat, Cyrus Schayegh, and Avner Wishnitzer. "Introduction." *A Global Middle East, Mobility, Materiality and Culture in the Modern Age (1880–1940)*, edited by Liat Kozma, Cyrus Schayegh, and Avner Wishnitzer, pp. 1–15. Tauris, 2015.

Krakauer, Siegfried. *The Mass Ornament. Weimar Essays*. Translated and edited by Thomas Y. Levine. Harvard University Press, 1995.

Krämer, Gudrun. *The Jews in Modern Egypt: 1914–1952*. University of Washington Press, 1989.

Kristeva, Julia. *Pouvoirs de l'horreur: Essai sur l'abjection*. Editions Seuil, 1977.

Kupferschmidt, Uri M. *European Department Stores and Middle Eastern Consumers: The Orosdi-Back Saga*. Ottoman Bank Archives and Research Centre, 2007.

———. "Who Needed Department Stores in Egypt? From Orosdi-Back to Omar Effendi." *Middle Eastern Studies*, vol. 43, no. 2, 2007, pp. 175–92.

La Blache, Paul Vidal de. *Principes de géographie humaine*. Edited by Emmanuel de Martonne. Armand Colin, 1922.

———. *Principles of Human Geography*. 1903. Translated by Millicent Todd Bingham, edited by Emmanuel de Martonne. Constable, 1926.

———. *Tableau de la géographie de la France*. 1903. Paris, La table ronde, 1994.

Laertius, Diogenes. *Lives of Eminent Philosophers II*. Translated by R. D. Hicks, edited by E. Capps, T. E. Page, and D. H. Rouse. William Heinemann, 1925.

Lagnado, Lucette. *The Arrogant Years: One Girl's Search for Her Lost Youth, from Cairo to Brooklyn*. Ecco, 2012.

———. *The Man in the White Sharkskin Suit: A Jewish Family's Exodus from Old Cairo to the New World*. Ecco, 2008.

Lagrange Frédéric. *Musiciens et poètes en Egypte au temps de la Nahda. Vol. 3. Annexes*. PhD diss., Université de Paris VIII à Saint Denis, 2004.

———. "Women in the Singing Business, Women in Songs." *History Compass*, vol. 7, no. 1, 2009, pp. 226–50.

"La Mission de Mlle Sanua en Orient et les femmes en Egypte." *Bulletin de l'AID, Organe de l'association d'institurices diplomées*, no. 60, November 1924, pp. 3–4.

Langle, Henri-Melchior de. *Le petit monde des cafés et debits parisiens aux XIX siècle: évolution de la sociabilité citadine*. Presses Universitaires de France, 1990.

Lasc, Anca I. *Interior Decorating in Nineteenth-Century France: The Visual Culture of a New Profession*. Manchester University Press, 2018.

Latour, Bruno. *We Have Never Been Modern*. Translated by Catherine Porter. Harvester, 1991.

Le Blond, Maurice. "Notes et commentaires." *Au Bonheur de dames*. F. Bernouard, 1928.

Le Bon, Gustave. *Psychologie des foules*. Félix Alcan, 1895.

Le Brun, Eugénie. (Niya Salima). *Harems et musulmanes d'Egypte*. Société d'éditions et de publications, 1909.

Lefebvre, Henri. *The Production of Space*. Translated by Donald Nicholson-Smith. Blackwell, 1991.

Les Mille et une nuits. Translated by Antoine Galland. Lehuby, 1843.

LeTailleur, Gérard. *Histoire insolite des cafés de Paris*. Perrin, 2011.

Levallois, Michel, and Philippe Régnier. "A la rencontre de l'orient musulman." *Le siècle des saint-simoniens: Du nouveau christianisme au canal de Suez*, edited by Nathalie Coilly and Philippe Régnier, pp. 102–45. BNF, 2006.

Levy, Lital. *Poetic Trespass: Writing between Hebrew and Arabic in Israel/Palestine*. Princeton University Press, 2014.

Lockman, Zachary. *Contending Visions of the Middle East: The History and Politics of Orientalism*. Cambridge University Press, 2010.

Lopez, Ricardo A., and Barbara Weinstein. *The Making of the Middle Class toward a Transnational History.* Duke University Press, 2012.

Lumbroso, Olivier. *Zola: La plume et le compas. La Construction de l'espace dans les Rougon-Macquart d'Émile Zola.* Honoré Champion, 2004.

Mabro, Robert. "Nostalgic Literature on Alexandria." *Historians in Cairo: Essays in Honor of George Scanlon*, edited by Jill Edwards, pp. 237–66. American University in Cairo Press, 2002.

Mack, Mehammed. *Sexagon: Muslims, France, and the Sexualization of National Culture.* Fordham University Press, 2017.

MacPherson, Kerrie L., editor. *Asian Department Stores.* Curzon, 1998.

"Magasin." *Larousse Dictionnaire étymologique*, edited by Jean Dubois, et al. Larousse, 2014.

"Magasin." *Le Robert: Dictionnaire culturel en langue française*, edited by Alan Ray, pp. 242–45. Dictionnaires Le Robert, 2005.

MagShamhráin, Rachel. "The Ambivalence of the Department Store Kleptomaniac: On the Juridico-Medical Treatment of Cases of Middle-Class Female Theft around 1900." *Das Berliner Warenhaus: Geschichte und Diskurse. The Berlin Department Store: History and Discourse*, edited by Godela Weiss-Sussex and Ulrike Zitzlsperger, pp. 63–91. Peter Lang, 2013.

Makdisi, Saree. *Romantic Imperialism: Universal Empire and the Culture of Modernity.* Cambridge University Press, 1998.

Mangold-Will, Sabine. "Ahmad Zaki et la culture allemande." Ahmad Zaki et al., *L'univers à Paris, 1900: Un Lettré Égyptien À L'exposition Universelle De 1900*, translated by Randa Sabry, edited by Mercedes Volait, pp. 239–47. Norma Éditions, 2015.

Mansel, Philip. *Paris between Empires, 1814–1852.* Saint Martin's Press, 2003.

———. "We Are All Levantine Now." *Le Monde Diplomatique*, April 2012, mondediplo.com/2012/04/16levant.

Mansfield, Peter. *The British in Egypt.* Holt, Rinehart and Winston, 1972.

Marbach, Christian. "Peindre la campagne de Russie: la place des X." *Bulletin de la Sabix*, no. 62, 2018, pp. 83–90.

Marques Jeanne. "L'Égypte musulmane et les fondateurs de ses monuments par Mme R. L. Devonshire." *L'Egyptienne*, no. 26, May 1927, pp. 8–15.

Marrey, Bernard. *Les Grands magasins des origines à 1939.* A. Picard et fils, 1979.

Marsot, Afaf Lutfi al-Sayyid. *Egypt in the Reign of Muhammad Ali.* Cambridge University Press, 1984.

———. *Egypt's Liberal Experiment, 1922–1936.* University of California Press, 1977.

———. *A Short History of Modern Egypt.* Cambridge University Press, 1985.

Marx, Karl. *Capital. A Critical Analysis of Capitalist Production.* Vol. 1. Edited by Frederich Engels. International Publishers, 1972.

Marx, Karl, and Friedrich Engels. *The Communist Manifesto.* Edited by Frederic L. Bender. Norton, 2013.

Matalon, Ronit. *The One Facing Us*. Translated by Marsha Weinstein. Metropolitan Books, 1998.

———. *Zeh 'im ha-panim elenu*. 'Am 'Oved, 1995.

Mathur, Saloni. *India by Design: Colonial History and Cultural Display*. University of California Press, 2007.

Mayeur, Jean-Marie, and Madeleine Reberioux. *The Third Republic from Its Origins to the Great War, 1871–1914*. Translated by J. R. Foster. Cambridge University Press, 1973.

McBride, Theresa M. "A Woman's World: Department Stores and the Evolution of Women's Employment, 1870–1920." *French Historical Studies*, vol. 10, no. 4, 1978, pp. 664–83.

McCann, Carol R., and Seung-Kyung Kim. "Introduction." *Feminist Theory Reader: Local and Global Perspectives*, edited by Carol R. McCann and Seung-Kyung Kim, pp. 11–27. Routledge, 2013.

McCann, Carol R., and Seung-Kyung Kim, editors. *Feminist Theory Reader: Local and Global Perspectives*. Routledge, 2013.

McClintock, Ann. *Imperial Leather: Race, Gender and Sexuality in the Colonial Context*. Routledge, 1995.

———. "Maidens, Maps, and Mines: The Reinvention of Patriarchy in Colonial South Africa." *South Atlantic Quarterly*, vol. 87, no. 1, 1988, pp. 147–92.

McDowell, Linda. *Gender, Identity and Place: Understanding Feminist Geography*. University of Minnesota Press, 1999.

———. *Redundant Masculinities: Employment Change and White Working Class Youth*. Blackwell, 2003.

———. *Working Bodies: Interactive Service Employment and Workplace Identities*. Blackwell, 2009.

McGrath, Caitlin. "'Crippled by Sight': Detail in Au bonheur des dames." *Modernism/Modernity*, vol. 21, no. 3, 2014, pp. 641–64.

Mead, Christopher Curtis. *Charles Garnier's Paris Opéra: Architectural Empathy and the Renaissance of French Classicism*. MIT Press, 1991.

———. *Making Modern Paris: Victor Baltard's Central Markets and the Urban Practice of Architecture*. Penn State University Press, 2012.

Miccoli, Dario. *Histories of the Jews of Egypt: An Imagined Bourgeoisie, 1880s–1950s*. Routledge, 2015.

Michelet, Jules. *Histoire de la France. Tome 1*. J Hetzel, 1869.

———. *Introduction à l'histoire universelle*. Hachette, 1831.

Mikhail, Francis. *Al-Tadbir al-Manzili al-Hadith*. Al-Ma'arif, 1910.

Milhaud, Jean. *Retrouver le temps vécu 1. "Louli Sanua vivante."* Imprimerie Nationale, 1969.

Miller, Michael B. *The Bon Marché: Bourgeois Culture and the Department Store 1869–1920*. Princeton University Press, 1981.

Mitchell, Timothy. *Colonising Egypt*. University of California Press, 1991.

———. *Rule of Experts: Egypt, Techno-Politics, Modernity*. University of California Press, 2002.
Moeran, Brian. "The Birth of the Japanese Department Store." *Asian Department Stores*, edited by Kerrie L. MacPherson, pp. 141–76. Routledge, 1998.
Moncan, Patrice de. *Les Passages couverts de Paris: Histoire des passages couverts de Paris*. Mécène, 1996.
———. *Les Passages en Europe*. Mécène, 1993.
Morris, Ian. "Mediterraneanization." *Mediterranean Historical Review*, vol. 18, no. 2, 2003, pp. 30–55.
Moses, Claire Goldberg. *French Feminism in the 19th Century*. State University of New York Press, 1984.
Moses, Claire Goldberg, and Leslie W. Rabine. *Feminism, Socialism, and French Romanticism*. Indiana University Press, 1993.
Moussa, Sarga. *La Relation orientale: Enquête sur la communciation dans les récits de voyage en Orient 1811–1861*. Klincksieck, 1995.
Moustapha, Ebtissam. "The Rehabilitation of Sednaoui Al Khazendar and the Khazendar Square: An Attempt to Revive Egypt's Belle Époque." *Design Principles and Practices*, vol. 5, no. 3, 2011, pp. 125–48.
Mukhtar, Mahmud. "Nahdat Masr" [cover page]. *al-Kashkul*, no. 185, 28 November 1924.
———. "Nahdat Masr" [cover page]. *al-Musawwar*, no. 16, 6 February 1925.
Musa, Nabawiyya. *Tarikhi biqalami*. WMF, 1999.
al-Musawi, Muhsin J. *The Arabian Nights in Contemporary World Cultures: Global Commodification, Translation, and the Culture Industry*. Cambridge University Press, 2021.
Musset, Alfred de. "Un boulevard parisien." *Alfred de Musset: Oeuvres complètes illustrées*, pp. 281–84. Librairie de France, 1929.
Musso, Pierre. *Critique des réseaux*. Presses Universitaires de France, 2003.
———. *Saint-Simon et le Saint-Simonisme*. Presses Universitaires de France, 1999.
———, editor. *Le Saint-Simonisme L'Europe et la Méditerranée*. Paris, Manucius, 2008.
Myers, Fred R. "Introduction: The Empire of Things." *The Empire of Things: Regimes of Value and Material Culture*, edited by Fred R. Myers, pp. 3–61, School of American Research Press, 2001.
Myntti, Cynthia. *Paris along the Nile: Architecture in Cairo from the Belle Epoque*. American University in Cairo Press, 2003.
Nabaraoui, Céza. "La grande pitié des maisons arabes." *L'Égyptienne*, January 1927, no. 22, pp. 5–12.
———. "Une kermesse orientale de l'U.F.E." *L'Egyptienne*, March 1927, no. 24, pp. 49–55.
"Najib Al-Rihani: From Buffoonery to Social Comedy." *Journal of Arabic Literature*, vol. 4, 1973, pp. 1–17.
Nasser, Tahia Abdel. *Literary Autobiography and Arab National Struggles*. Edinburgh University Press, 2017.
Nelson, Brian. *Émile Zola: A Selective Analytical Bibliography*. Grant & Cutler, 1982.

Nelson, Cynthia. *Doria Shafik: Egyptian Feminist. A Woman Apart*. American University in Cairo Press, 1996.
Niogret, Hubert. "La fin d'une époque avant le passage au parlant." *Positif*, no. 572, vol. 10, 2008, pp. 78–80.
Noorani, Yaseen. "Normative Notions of Public and Private in Early Islamic Culture." *Harem Histories: Envisioning Places and Living Spaces*, edited by Marilyn Booth, pp. 49–68, Duke University Press, 2010.
Nora, Pierre. "Between Memory and History: Les Lieux de Mémoire." *Representations*, no. 26, 1989, pp. 7–24.
Nord, Philip G. *The Politics of Resentment: Shopkeeper Protest in Nineteen-Century Paris*. Routledge, 2017.
Nussbaum, Martha C. *The Cosmopolitan Tradition. A Nobel but Flawed Ideal*. Belknap Press, 2019.
———. "Kant and Stoic Cosmopolitanism." *Journal of Political Philosophy*, vol. 5, no. 1, 1997, pp. 1–25.
Oulebsir, Nabila, and Mercedes Volait. *L'Orientalisme architectural: entre imaginaires et savoirs*. A. Picard et fils, 2009.
Out-el-Kouloub. *Ramza*. Éditions Gallimard, 1958.
Owens Scott, Craig. "Posing." *Beyond Recognition: Representation, Power and Culture*, edited by Scott Bryson et al., pp. 201–17. University of California Press, 1992.
Paletschek, Sylvia, and Bianka Pietrow-Ennker. *Women's Emancipation Movements in the Nineteenth Century: A European Perspective*. Stanford University Press, 2004.
Pao, Angela Chia-yi. *The Orient of the Boulevards: Exoticism, Empire, and Nineteenth-Century French Theater*. University of Pennsylvania Press, 1998.
Papadia, Elena. *La Rinascente*. Il mulino, 2005.
Papayanis, Nicholas. *Planning Paris before Haussmann*. Johns Hopkins University Press, 2004.
Parmentier, Marie. *Paris ou le livre des cent-et-un: Anthologie*. Honoré Champion, 2015.
Pasdermadjian, Hrandt. *The Department Store: Its Origins, Evolution and Economics*. Newman Books, 1954.
Paul, Jean Dean. *Journal d'un voyage à Paris au mois d'août 1802*. A. Picard et fils, 1913.
Peled, Shimrit. "Photography, Home, Language: Ronit Matalon Facing Joseph Conrad's Colonial Journeys in the Heart of Darkness." *Prooftexts*, vol. 30, no. 3, 2010, pp. 340–67.
Petricioli, Marta. *Oltre il mito: l'Egitto degli italiani (1917–1947)*. B. Mondadori, 2007.
Picon, Antoine. *Les Saint-Simoniens: Raison, Imaginaires et utopie*. Belin, 2012.
———. "L'utopie-spectacle d'Enfantin. De la retraite de Ménilmontant au procès et à l'année de la Mère.'" *Le siècle des saint-simoniens: Du nouveau christianisme au canal de Suez*, edited by Nathalie Coilly and Philippe Régnier, pp. 68–76. BNF, 2006.
Pierson, Ruth Roach. "Nations: Gendered, Racialized, Crossed with Empire." *Gendered Nations: Nationalism and Gender Order in the Long Nineteenth Century*, edited by Ida Blom et al., pp. 41–61. Berg, 2000.

Piketty, Thomas. *Capital in the Twenty-First Century*. Translated by Arthur Goldhammer. Belknap Press, 2014.
Pilbeam, Pamela. *Saint-Simonians in Nineteenth Century France: From Free Love to Algeria*. Palgrave Macmillan, 2014.
Pinon, Pierre. "Percée, tracée, la ville reformée." *Paris-Haussmann: "Le Pari d'Haussmann,"* edited by Jean des Cars and Pierre Pinon, pp. 88–93. Pavillon de L'Arsenal, 1991.
———. "Le Projet de Napoléon III et d'Haussmann. La 'Transformation de Paris.'" *Paris-Haussmann: "Le Pari d'Haussmann,"* edited by Jean des Cars and Pierre Pinon, pp. 73–80. Pavillon de L'Arsenal, 1991.
———. "Une nouvelle géométrie pour la ville." *Paris-Haussmann: "Le Pari d'Haussmann,"* edited by Jean des Cars and Pierre Pinon, pp. 81–87. Pavillon de L'Arsenal, 1991.
Plessis, Alain. *The Rise and Fall of the Second Empire, 1852–1871*. Translated by Jonathan Mandelbaum. Cambridge University Press, 1985.
Pollard, Lisa. *Nurturing the Nation: The Family Politics of Modernizing, Colonizing and Liberating Egypt, 1805–1923*. University of California Press, 2005.
Pollock, Griselda. "The Politics of Theory: Generations and Geographies in Feminist Theory and the Histories of Art Histories." *Generations and Geographies in the Visual Arts: Feminist Readings*, edited by Griselda Pollock, pp. 2–27. Routledge, 1996.
Poovey, Mary. *Uneven Development: The Ideological Work of Gender in Mid-Victorian Britain*. University of Chicago Press, 1988.
Pratt, Mary Louise. *Imperial Eyes: Travel Writing and Transculturation*. Routledge, 1992.
———. "Scratches on the Face of the Country; or, What Mr. Barrow Saw in the Land of the Bushmen." *Critical Inquiry*, vol. 12, no. 1, 1985, pp. 119–43.
Priest, Robert D. "Ernest Renan's Race Problem." *Historical Journal*, vol. 58, no. 1, 2015, pp. 309–30.
Proust, Marcel. *In Search of Lost Time. Volume Six. The Fugitive. Time Regained*. Translated by C. K. Scott Moncrieff, Andreas Mayor, and Terence Kilmartin., Folio Society, 1992.
———. *À la recherche du temps perdu*. Quarto Gallimard, 1999.
Raafat, Samir. *Cairo, the Glory Years: Who Built What, When, Why and for Whom*. Harpocrates, 2005.
———. "The House of Cicurel." *Al Ahram Weekly*, 15 December 1994. egy.com/judaica/ (unedited version).
———. *Maadi 1904–1962: Society and History in a Cairo Suburb*. Palm Press, 1995.
———. "Murder at the Villa Cicurel." *Cairo Times*, 20 April 2000. www.egy.com/giza/00-04-20.php.
———. "Sednaoui." *Cairo Times*, 29 May 1997. www.egy.com/landmarks.
Rabinow, Paul. *French Modern: Norms and Forms of the Social Environment*. University of Chicago Press, 1995.
Rachline, Sonia. *Printemps un modèle de mode*. La Martinière. 2015.

Rafik, Farah. "Sednaoui El-Khazendar: Egypt's Galeries Lafayette." *Egyptianstreets.com*, 16 June 2022, egyptianstreets.com/2022/06/16/sednaoui-el-khazendar-egypts-galeries-lafayette/.

Ramazani, Vaheed. "Gender, War, and the Department Store: Zola's *Au Bonheur des Dames*." *Substance*, vol. 36, no. 2, 2007, pp. 126–46.

Rambuteau, Claude-Philibert Barthelot. *Mémoires du comte de Rambuteau publiés par son petit-fils*. Calmann-Levy, 1905.

Rappaport, Erika Diane. *Shopping for Pleasure. Women in the Making of London's West End*. Princeton University Press, 2000.

Ray, Marcie. "*My Fair Lady*: A Voice for Change." *American Music*, vol. 32, no. 3, 2014, pp. 292–316.

Raymond, André. *Le Caire*. Fayard, 1993.

Redclift, Nanneke, and M. Thea Sinclair, editors. *International Perspectives on Labour and Gender Ideology*. Routledge, 1991.

Remus, Emily. *A Shoppers' Paradise: How the Ladies of Chicago Claimed Power and Pleasure in the New Downtown*. Harvard University Press, 2019.

Reuschke, Daria, Monika Salzbrunn, and Korinna Schonharl, editors. *The Economies of Urban Diversity: The Ruhr Area in Istanbul*. Palgrave, 2013.

Reynolds, Nancy. *A City Consumed: Urban Commerce, the Cairo Fire, and the Politics of Decolonization in Egypt*. Stanford University Press, 2012.

———. *Commodity Communities. Interweavings of Market Cultures, Consumption Practices, and Social Power in Egypt, 1907–1961*. PhD diss., Stanford University, 2003.

———. "Entangled Communities: Interethnic Relationships among Urban Salesclerks and Domestic Workers in Egypt, 1927–61." *European Review of History*, vol. 19, no. 1, 2012, pp. 113–39.

Reynolds, Sian. *France Between the Wars: Gender and Politics*. Taylor and Francis, 1996.

Ribeill, Georges. "Les chemins de fer: de la doctrine aux réalisations." *Le siècle des saint-simoniens: Du nouveau christianisme au canal de Suez*, edited by Nathalie Coilly and Philippe Régnier, pp. 130–35. BNF, 2006.

Richer, Léon. *La femme libre*. E. Dentu, 1877.

Richmond, Walter. *The Circassian Genocide*. Rutgers University Press, 2013.

Rigney, A. "Plenitude, Scarcity and the Circulation of Cultural Memory." *Journal of European Studies*, vol. 35, 2005, pp. 11–28.

al-Rihani, Najib. *Mudhakkarat Najib-al-Rihani*. Kalimat Arabiyyah, 2011.

Riot-Sarcey, Michèle. "L'affirmation d'une doctrine et l'organisation d'une religion alternative." *Le siècle des saint-simoniens: Du nouveau christianisme au canal de Suez*, edited by Nathalie Coilly and Philippe Régnier, pp. 42–49. BNF, 2006.

Ritivoi, Andreea Deciu. *Yesterday's Self: Nostalgia and the Immigrant Self*. Rowman and Littlefield, 2002.

Roberts, Mary. *Intimate Outsiders: The Harem in Ottoman and Orientalist Art and Literature*. Duke University Press, 2007.

Robida. Albert. "Au bonheur des dames. Coupe du roman de M. Émile Zola." *La Caricature*,. no. 170, 3 March 1883. pp. 100–101.

———. *Le Vingtième siècle. Roman d'une Parisienne d'après demain*. E. Dentu, 1883.

Rochefort, Florence. "The French Feminist Movement and Republicanism, 1868–1914." Translated by Amy Jacobs. *Women's Emancipation Movements in the Nineteenth Century: A European Perspective*, edited by Sylvia Paletschek and Bianka Pietrow-Ennker, pp. 77–101. Stanford University Press, 2004.

Rodinson, Maxime. *Europe and the Mystique of Islam*. Translated by Roger Veinus. Tauris, 2002.

Rosenberg, Anat. "'Avoda Aravit' - Breaking TV Barriers. Milestone Show Is the First Sitcom Featuring Mainly Arab Characters Speaking Arabic on Prime Time." *Jerusalem Post*, 28 January 2008.

Ross, Kristin. *Communal Luxury: The Political Imaginary of the Paris Commune*. Verso, 2015.

———. *The Emergence of Social Space: Rimbaud and the Paris Commune*. University of Minnesota Press, 2008.

———. "Introduction: Shopping." Émile Zola, *The Ladies Paradise*, pp. v–xxiii. University of California Press, 1991.

Ross, Robert. *Clothing: A Global History*. Polity Press, 2008.

Rossant, Colette. *Apricots on the Nile: A Memoir with Recipes*. Bloomsbury, 2001.

———. *Memories of a Lost Egypt: A Memoir with Recipes*. Clarkson Potter, 1999.

———. *Return to Paris: A Memoir*. Atria Books, 2003.

Rothberg, Michael. "Introduction: Between Memory and Memory: From Lieux de mémoire to Noeuds de mémoire." *Yale French Studies*, vols. 118–19, 2010, pp. 3–12.

Rothermund, Dietmar. *The Global Impact of the Great Depression 1929–1939*. Taylor and Francis, 1996.

Roy, Ananya, and Aihwa Ong. "Introduction: Worlding Cities, or the Art of Being Global." *Worlding Cities: Asian Experiments and the Art of Being Global*, edited by Ananya Roy and Aihwa Ong, pp. 1–26. Blackwell, 2011.

Rubin, Gayle. "The Traffic in Women: Notes on the 'Political Economy' of Sex." *Toward an Anthropology of Women*, edited by Rayna R. Reiter, pp. 157–210. Monthly Review Press, 1975.

Ruhayyim, Kamal. *Days in the Diaspora: A Trilogy, Volume II*. Elain, 2021.

———. *Diary of a Jewish Muslim: A Trilogy, Volume 1*. Elain, 2021.

———. *Dreams of Coming Home: A Trilogy, Volume III*. Elain, 2021

Russell, Mona. *Creating the New Egyptian Woman: Consumerism, Education, and National Identity 1863–1922*. Palgrave, 2004.

Russell Pasha, Thomas. *Egyptian Service: 1902–1946*. Murray, 1949.

Ryzova, Lucie. *The Age of the Efendiyya: Passages to Modernity in National Colonial Egypt*. Oxford University Press, 2018.

Said, Edward. *Culture and Imperialism*. Vintage Books, 1994.

———. *Orientalism*. Vintage Books, 1978.

Saint-Simon, Claude Henri. *Oeuvres complètes*, 4 vols. Presses Universitaires de France, 2012.
Sakal, Moshe. *Yolanda*. Translated by Valérie Zenatti. Stock, 2012.
Saleh, Sahar. "Iftitah Moll Sednaoui al-'Ataba ba'd Tatwiroh bi-Taklifat 80 Milion Junayh." *CCESR*, 26 September 2019, ccsr-eg.com/news/news.aspx?id=7483.
Sanu', Ya'qub. *Abu Rida wa Ka'b al-Khayr*. Hindawi, 2017.
———. *Al-Amirah al-Iskandaraniyya*. Hindawi, 2017.
Savile, Anthony. "Naturalism and the Aesthetic." *Émile Zola: Bloom's Modern Critical Views*, edited by Harold Bloom and Janyce Marson, pp. 221–41. Chelsea House, 2004.
Schmitt, Éric-Emmanuel. *Monsieur Ibrahim et les fleurs du Coran*. Albin Michel, 2001.
Schneider, Donald David. *The Works and Doctrine of Jacques Ignace Hittorff 1792–1967*, 2 vols. Garland, 1997.
Schwartz, Vanessa R. *Spectacular Realities: Early Mass Culture in Fin-de-Siècle Paris*. University of California Press, 1998.
Scott, Joan Wallach. *The Politics of the Veil*. Princeton University Press, 2009.
Selim, Samah, editor. *The Translator: Studies in Intercultural Communication*. Vol. 15 No. 1. *Nation and Translation in the Middle East*. Routledge, 2009.
Sermain, Jean-Paul. *Les mille et une nuits entre Orient et Occident*. Desjonquères, 2009.
Sewell, William, Jr. *Work and Revolution in France: The Language of Labor from the Old Regime to 1848*. Cambridge University Press, 1980.
Sibalis, M. "The Palais-Royal and the Homosexual Subculture of Nineteenth-Century Paris." *Journal of Homosexuality*, vol. 41, nos. 3–4, 2001, pp. 117–29.
Shaarawi, Huda. *Harem Years: The Memoirs of an Egyptian Feminist (1879–1924)*. Translated by Margot Badran. Virago Press, 1986.
———. *Mudhakkarat R a'idat al-Mar'ah al-'Arabiyya Huda Sha'rawi*. al-Hilal, 1981.
al-Shadhli, Osama Abd el-Raouf. *Awraq Sham'un al-Masry*. al-Rewaq, 2022.
Shakespeare, William. "The Merchant of Venice." *The Complete Works of William Shakespeare*. Shakespeare Head Press, 1996.
Shammas, Anton. *Arabesques*. Translated by Vivian Eden. University of California Press, 2001.
Sharawi Lanfranchi, Sania. *Casting off the Veil: The Life of Hoda Shaarawi*. Tauris, 2012.
Shaya, Gregory. "The Flâneur, the Badaud, and the Making of a Mass Public in France, circa 1860–1910." *American Historical Review*, no. 109, 2004, pp. 41–77.
Shepard, Todd, editor. *French Mediterraneans: Transnational and Imperial Histories*. University of Nebraska Press, 2016.
———. *Sex, France, and Arab Men, 1962–1979*. University of Chicago Press, 2017.
Shohat, Ella. "Dislocated Identities: Reflections of an Arab Jew." *On the Arab-Jew, Palestine, and Other Displacements: Selected Writings of Ella Shohat*, pp. 77–82. Pluto Press, 2017.
———. *Israeli Cinema: East/West and the Politics of Representations*. Tauris, 2010.

———. "Rupture and Return: Zionist Discourse and the Study of Arab Jews." *Social Text*, vol. 21, no. 2, 2003, pp. 49–74.

———. *Taboo Memories, Diasporic Voices*. Duke University Press, 2007.

Shultziner, Doron, and Irit S. Kornblit. "French Yellow Vests (Gilets Jaunes): Similarities and Differences with Occupy Movements." *Sociological Forum*, vol. 35, no. 2, 2020, pp. 535–42.

Siegfried, Anne. *Window Shopping: Cinema and the Postmodern*. University of California Press, 1993.

Silverman, Kaja. "Liberty, Maternity, Commodification." *Point of Theory*, 1994, pp. 18–31.

Simonsen, Kirsten. "Bodies, Sensations, Space and Time: The Contribution from Henri Lefebvre." *Geografiska Annaler*, no. 87, 2005, pp. 1–14.

Smail Salhi, Zahia. *Occidentalism: Literary Representations of the Maghrebi Experience of the East-West Encounter*. Edinburgh University Press, 2022.

Smith, Bonnie G. *Ladies of the Leisure Class: The Bourgeoises of the Northern France in the Nineteenth Century*. Princeton University Press, 1981

Smith, Neil. "Homeless/Global: Scaling Places." *Mapping the Futures: Local Cultures, Global Changes*, edited by Jon Bird et al., pp. 87–120. Routledge, 1993.

———. *Uneven Development. Nature, Capital, and the Production of Space*. Blackwell, 1984.

Smith, Paul. *Feminism and the Third Republic: Women's Political Civil Rights in France 1918–1945*. Clarendon Press, 1996.

Solé, Robert. *Le Tarbouche*. Editions Seuil, 1992.

———. "L'inauguration." *L'Épopée du Canal de Suez*, edited by Gilles Gauthier and Claude Mollard, pp. 52–61. Éditions Gallimard, 2018.

Spiekermann, Uwe. "Theft and Thieves in German Department Stores, 1895–1930: A Discourse on Morality, Crime, and Gender." *Cathedrals of Consumption: The European Department Store 1850–1939*, edited by Goeffrey Crossick and Serge Jaumain, pp. 135–59. Ashgate, 1999.

Spivak, Gayatri Chakravorty. *A Critique of Postcolonial Reason: Toward a History of the Vanishing Present*. Harvard University Press, 1999.

———. "Three Women's Texts and a Critique of Imperialism." *Critical Inquiry*, vol. 12, no. 1, 1985, pp. 243–61

St-Fulchrand, Monsieur le Chevalier de. *Soirée de Frascati ou memoirs de feu le Cher. de St-Fulchrand*. Rabier et Batignot, 1824.

Starr, Deborah A. "Drinking, Gambling, and Making Merry: Waguih Ghali's Search for Cosmopolitan Agency." *Middle Eastern Literature*, vol. 9, no. 3, 2006, pp. 271–85.

———. *Remembering Cosmopolitan Egypt: Literature, Culture, and Empire*. Routledge, 2009.

Starr, Deborah A., and Sasson Somekh, "Editors' Introduction: Jacqueline Shohet Kahanoff—A Cosmopolitan Levantine." *Mongrels or Marvels: The Levantine Writings of Jacqueline Shohet Kahanoff*, edited by Deborah A. Starr and Sasson Somekh, pp. xi–xxiv. Stanford University Press, 2011.

———, editors. *Mongrels or Marvels: The Levantine Writings of Jacqueline Shohet Kahanoff.* Stanford University Press, 2011.

Stein, Sarah Abrevaya. *Extraterritorial Dreams: European Citizenship, Sephardi Jews, and the Ottoman Twentieth Century.* Chicago University Press, 2016.

Stewart, Susan. *On Longing: Narratives of the Miniature, the Gigantic, the Miniature, the Souvenir, the Collection.* Duke University Press, 1993.

Stoler, Ann Laura. *Carnal Knowledge and Imperial Power: Race and the Intimate in Colonial Rule.* University of California Press, 2002.

Stoler, Ann Laura, and Frederick Cooper. "Between Metropole and Colony: Rethinking a Research Agenda." *Tensions of Empire: Colonial Cultures in a Bourgeois World*, edited by Ann Laura Stoler and Frederick Cooper, pp. 1–56. University of California Press, 1997.

Stoler, Ann Laura, Carole McGranahan, and Peter C. Perdue, editors. *Imperial Formations.* Santa Fe, School of Advanced Research Press, 2007.

Swebach, Bernard Édouard. *La retraite de Russie.* 1832. Musée des Beaux-Arts et d'Archéologie.

Swirski, Shlomo. *Israel: The Oriental Majority.* Translated by Barbara Swirski. Zed Books, 1989.

Szendy, Peter. *The Supermarket of the Visible: Toward a General Economy of Images.* Translated by Jan Plug. Fordham University Press, 2019.

Szurek, Emmanuel. "Go West: Variations sur le cas kémaliste." *Après L'orientalisme: L'orient créé par l'orient*, edited by François Pouillon and Jean-Claude Vatin, et al., pp. 303–23. Institut d'études de l'Islam et des sociétés du monde musulman, 2011.

Tageldin, Shaden M. *Disarming Words: Empire and the Seductions of Translation in Egypt.* University of California Press, 2011.

al-Tahtawi, Rifa'a Rafi'. *Al-Murshid al-amin lil-banat wa-l-banin.* 1872. Dar al-kitab al-misri, 2012.

Taine, Hippolyte. *Les Origines de la France Contemporaine III.* Hachette, 1904.

———. *Philospohie de l'art.* Vol. 1, 18th ed. Hachette, 1921.

Téboul, Victor. *J'chuis un gars d'Alex: de mon désir fou d'être québécois.* Autofiction. Tolerance.ca Éditeur, 2018.

———. *La lente decouverte de l'étrangeté.* Les intouchables, 2002.

Tiersten, Lisa. "Marianne in the Department Store: Gender and Politics of Consumption in Turn-of-the-Century Paris." *Cathedrals of Consumption: The European Department Store 1850–1939*, edited by Goeffrey Crossick and Serge Jaumain, pp. 116–34. Ashgate, 1999.

———. *Marianne in the Market. Envisioning Society in Fin-de-Siècle France.* University of California Press, 2001.

Tignor, Robert L. *Egypt: A Short History.* Princeton University Press, 2010.

———. *Modernization and British Colonial Rule in Egypt, 1882–1914.* Princeton University Press, 1966.

Todd, David. *A Velvet Empire: French Informal Imperialism in the Nineteenth Century.* Princeton University Press, 2021.
Trevor-Roper, H. R. "Fernand Braudel, the Annales, and the Mediterranean." *Journal of Modern History*, vol. 44, no. 4, 1972, pp. 468–79.
Troutt Powell, Eve M. *A Different Shade of Colonialism. Egypt, Great Britain, and the Mastery of the Sudan.* University of California Press, 2003.
———. *Tell This in My Memory: Stories of Enslavement from Egypt, Sudan and the Ottoman Empire.* Stanford University Press, 2012.
Tucker, Judith E., editor. *The Making of the Modern Mediterranean: Views from the South.* University of California Press, 2019.
———. *Women in Nineteenth-Century Egypt.* Cambridge University Press, 2002.
Turnaoğlu, Banu. *The Formation of Turkish Republicanism.* Princeton University Press, 2014.
Uslu, Seza Sinanlar. "Un critique français à Constantinople: Régis Delbeuf (1854–1911)." *Synergie Turquies*, no. 6, 2014, pp. 141–50.
Van Loo, Anne, and Marie-Cécile Bruwier, editors. *Héliopolis.* Fond Mercator, 2010.
Van Zanten, David. *Building Paris: Architectural Institutions and the Transformation of the French Capital, 1830–1870.* Cambridge University Press, 1994.
———. *Designing Paris: The Architecture of Duban, Labrouste, Duc and Vaudoyer.* MIT Press, 1987.
Venuti, Lawrence, "Translation, Community, Utopia." *The Translation Studies Reader*, edited by Lawrence Venuti, pp. 468–88. Routledge, 2000.
Viollet-le-Duc, Eugène-Emmanuel. *Dictionnaire raisonné du mobilier français: de l'époque carlovingienne à la Renaissance.* A. Morel, 1868.
———. *Entretiens sur L'architecture. Tome II.* A. Morel, 1863–1872.
Voilquin, Suzanne. *Souvenirs d'une fille du peuple, ou La Saint-Simonienne en Égypte, 1834–1836.* E. Sauzet. 1866.
Volait, Mercedes, "Ahmad Zaki: une vie à la croisée de plusieurs mondes." Ahmad Zaki et al., *L'univers à Paris, 1900: Un Lettré Égyptien À L'exposition Universelle De 1900*, translated by Randa Sabry, edited by Mercedes Volait, pp. 21–27. Norma Éditions, 2015.
———. *Antique Dealing and Creative Reuse in Cairo and Damascus 1850–1890: Intercultural Engagements with Architecture and Craft in the Age of Travel and Reform.* Brill, 2021.
———. *Architectes et architectures de l'Égypte moderne (1830–1950). Genèse et essor d'une expertise locale.* Maisonnneuve et Larose, 2015.
———, editor. *Le Caire-Alexandrie: Architectures européenes, 1850–1950.* Institut français d'archeologie orientale, 2001.
———, editor. *Émile Prisse D'avennes: Un artiste-antiquaire en Égypte au xixe siècle.* Institut français d'archéologie orientale, 2013.
———. *Fous du Caire: excentriques, architectes et amateurs d'arts en Égypte, 1863–1914.* L'Archange Minotaure, 2009.

———. "The Reclaiming of 'Belle Époque' Architecture in Egypt (1989–2010): On the Power of Rhetorics in Heritage-Making." *Abe Journal*, vol. 3, 2013. doi.org/10.4000/abe.371.

Volait, Mercedes, and Blas Gimeno Ribelles. *Maisons de France au Caire: Le Remploi de grands décors mamelouks et ottomans dans une architecture moderne*. Institut français d'archéologie orientale, 2012.

Wahba, Magdi. "East and West: Cairo Memories." *Encounter*, vol. 62, no. 5, May 1984, pp. 74–79.

Walsh, Claire. "The Newness of the Department Store: A View from the Eighteenth Century." *Cathedrals of Consumption: The European Department Store 1850–1939*, edited by Goeffrey Crossick and Serge Jaumain, pp. 46–71. Ashgate, 1999.

Walter, Peter Klaus. "'La rançon du progrès.' Le discours naturaliste et sa transposition à l'écran entre le muet et le sonore: les adaptations de Au Bonheur des Dames par J. Duvivier (1929) et A. Cayatte (1943)." *Excavatio*, vol. 14, 2001, pp. 127–39.

Watenpaugh, Keith David. *Being Modern in the Middle East*. Princeton University Press, 2006.

Weber, Eugene. *Peasants into Frenchmen: The Modernization of Rural France, 1870–1914*. Stanford University Press, 1976.

Weber, Samuel. *Unwrapping Balzac: A Reading of La Peau de Chagrin*. University of Toronto Press, 1979.

Werbner, Pnina. "Vernacular Cosmopolitanism." *Theory, Culture & Society*, vol. 23, nos. 2–3, 2006, pp. 496–98.

Weiss-Sussex, Godela, and Ulrike Zitzlsperger, editors. *Das Berliner Warenhaus: Geschichte und Diskurse. The Berlin Department Store: History and Discourse*. Peter Lang, 2013.

Weitz, Eric D. *Weimar Germany: Promise and Tragedy*. Princeton University Press, 2007.

Werner, Michael, and Bénédicte Zimmerman, editors. *De la comparaison à l'histoire croisée*. Editions Seuil, 2004.

Wertsch, James V. *Voices of Collective Remembering*. Cambridge University Press, 2002.

Whitaker, Jan. *The World of Department Stores*. Vendome Press, 2011.

Wild, Jonathan. *Literature of the 1900s: The Great Edwardian Emporium. The Edinburgh History of Twentieth-Century Literature in Britain. Volume 1*. Edinburgh University Press, 2017.

Wolter, Jennifer. "Viewing 'Au Bonheur des Dames' in the Context of Occupied France." *Excavatio*, vol. 14, 2001, pp. 140–53.

Woolf, Penelope. "Symbol of the Second Empire: Cultural Politics and the Paris Opera House." *The Iconography of Landscape: Essays on the Symbolic Representation, Design, and Use of Past Environments*, edited by Denis E. Cosgrove and Stephen Daniels, pp. 214–35. Cambridge University Press, 1988.

Yannakakis, Ilios. "The Death of Cosmopolitanism." *Alexandria 1860–1960: A Brief Life of a Cosmopolitan Community*, translated by Colin Clement, edited by Robert Ilbert, et al. pp. 190–94. Harpocrates, 2007.

———. "Farewell Alexandria." *Alexandria 1860–1960: A Brief Life of a Cosmopolitan Community*, translated by Colin Clement, edited by Robert Ilbert et al., pp. 106–26. Harpocrates, 2007.
Young, Iris Marion. *Justice and the Politics of Difference*. Princeton University Press, 1990.
Zaki, Ahmad. *Al-Dunya fi Baris. 1900*. Hindawi, 2012.
———. *al-Safar ila-l-Mu'tamar*. Al-Amiryya Press, 1893.
———. *Qamus al-Joghrafia al-Qadima b-il-'Arabi wa-l-Fransawi*. Al-Amiryya Press, 1899.
Zaki, Ahmad, et al. *L'univers à Paris, 1900: Un Lettré Égyptien À L'exposition Universelle De 1900*. Translated by Randa Sabry, edited by Mercedes Volait. Norma Éditions, 2015.
al-Zayyat, Latifah. *Al-Bab al-Maftuh*. Maktabat al-Osra, 2003.
Zerubavel, Yael. "The 'Mythological Sabra' and Jewish Past: Trauma, Memory, and Contested Identities." *Israel Studies*, vol. 7, no. 2, 2002, pp. 115–44.
Zola, Émile. *L'argent*. Éditions Gallimard, 1978.
———. *Au Bonheur des dames*. Librairie Générale Française, 1998.
———. *The Dreyfus Affair: "J'accuse"and Other Writings*. Translated by Eleanor Levieux, edited by Alain Pagès. Yale University Press, 1996.
———. *Émile Zola: Correspondance. Tome IV. Juin 1880-décembre 1883*. Edited by B. H. Barker. Presse de l'université de Montréal, 1983.
———. *Émile Zola: écrits sur l'art*. Éditions Gallimard, 1991.
———. *The Ladies' Paradise*. Translated by Brian Nelson. Oxford University Press, 2008.

Select Archival Documents and Illustrations

Abdel Hay, Saleh. "Lissah Ṭali' min el-Bayda." Catalogue Polyphone, 1929, private collection of Frédéric Lagrange.
A la Place Clichy. La première maison du monde pour ses importations orientales. Eugène Grasset. 1898. Atelier Chéret. Poster. IFN-9015850. BNF.
Adam, Juliette. La grande Amie d'Egypte." *L'Egyptienne*, no. 29, August 1927. WMF.
———. Portrait of Juliette Adam. *L'Egyptienne* February 1925, no. 1, p. 22. WMF.
"A Play at a Kermess." *L'Egyptienne*, no. 24, March 1927. CEALEX. bdd.cealex.org/bibliotheque/periodiques_rep_liste.php.
"A Play at a Kermess. Performers in Costumes." *L'Egyptienne*, no. 24. March 1927. CEALEX. bdd.cealex.org/bibliotheque/periodiques_rep_liste.php.
"Cairo the Gay City on the Nile as It Is Today." *al-Lata'if al-Musawwara*, 13 October 1919, p. 5. Dar al-Kutub.
Carjat, Etienne. Caricature de Ferdinand de Lesseps par Etienne Carjat [Ferdinand de Lesseps parting the Isthmus of Suez. Caricature]. *Le Boulevard*, no. 26, 29 June 1862, p. 5. BNF, FOL-LC13-66.

Chemla Frères. Advertisement. *L'Egyptienne*, no. 23, February 1927. CEALEX. bdd .cealex.org/bibliotheque/periodiques_rep_liste.php.

Couvreur, A. "Les Femmes aux différentes époques de l'histoire." Conférences faites au dames égyptiennes. Fasicule 1. L'université du Caire 1910. Dupuy, 1910. BNF, MFICHE 8-R-23690.

"Egypt's Awakening," by Mahmud Mukhtar. *L'Egyptienne*, no. 38, June 1928. CEALEX. bdd.cealex.org/bibliotheque/periodiques_rep_liste.php.

Fourier, Charles, and Victor Considérant. *L'avenir: perspective d'un phalanstère ou palais sociétaire dédié à l'humanité* [d'après le plan de Ch. Fourier] / [signé Victor Considérant]. BNF, NUMM-850954.

Galeries Lafayette. *Déliberation du conseil d'administration*. 1936–1937. Archives Galeries Lafayette.

———. "Galeries Lafayette Tapis. Agrandissements considérables des nouveaux rayons tapis ameublements." Jacques Debut, graveur V. Michel, ca 1910. Recueil. Grands magasins. Annonces de presse et documents publicitaires de très grand format: Au Bon Marché, Galeries Lafayette, Grands magasins du Louvre, Printemps, Samaritaine. BF, Cote: RES ICO 7491.

———. Photograph of Interior Hall, Galeries Lafayette. 1914. Archives Galeries Lafayette.

Grands magasins de nouveautés Paschal & Cie. CG Meïmarachi & Cie, successeurs au Caire: [calender]. Imp. F. Champenois, 1895. BF.

Ivray, Jehan d'. *Les Porteuses de Torches*. Albert Méricant, 1923. BNF, S89/10582.

———. Portrait of Jehan d'Ivray. *L'Egyptienne*, no. 36, March 1928. CEALEX.

al-Koussi, Ehsan Ahmed. "Les grandes figues féminines d'Egypte. Mme. Ehsan Ahmed." *L'Eyptienne*, no. 26, May 1927. CEALEX. bdd.cealex.org/bibliotheque /periodiques_rep_liste.php.

La Samaritaine. "Deux créateurs, Ernest Cognacq, Louise Cognacq, une oeuvre." Samaritaine en progrès constants [poster], illustrated by Emilio Vila, 1929. Private collection, Amr Kamal.

———. Jouets, étrennes, 1914, lundi 1er décembre et pendant tout le mois, [Noël 1913–étrennes 1914] : [catalogue commercial] Monnaie . . . , Paris; [illustration de couverture], O. Andrein. BF RES CC 275"1913"déc.

———. Jouets, étrennes, 1932, Noël 1931–étrennes 1932, catalogue commercial. Illustration de couverture, Jean Chaperon. BF, RES CC 275"1931"déc.

———. Jouets, étrennes, 1938, mardi 23 novembre et jours suivants, Noël 1937–étrennes 1938: catalogue commercial, illustration de couverture, Jean Chaperon. BF, RES CC 275"1937"déc.

Le Bon Marché. Advertisement. *L'Egyptienne*, no. 49, May 1929. CEALEX. bdd.cealex .org/bibliotheque/periodiques_rep_liste.php.

———. Advertisement. *L'Egyptienne*, no. 76, January 1932. CEALEX. bdd.cealex.org /bibliotheque/periodiques_rep_liste.php.

———. Agenda-buvard. *Carte des colonies françaises dressée spécialement pour les magasins du Bon Marché*. 1897. BNF, IFN-53029338. .

———. "Arménienne." Maison du Bon Marché, principaux modèles de confections pour dames, saison d'été, 1869, catalogue commercial, Recueil de catalogues Au Bon Marché (FOL-WZ-211) (1865–1877). BNF.

———. "Desert Caravans." Maison Aristide Boucicaut, catalogue, *A Partir de Lundi 23 Septembre. Éxposition spéciale et grande mise en vente des tapis de l'Orient*. 187? BNF, FOL-WZ-211 (1873) Recueil de catalogues Au Bon Marché [FOL-WZ-211 (1869–)]. BNF.

———. Étrennes, jouets, 1913, lundi 2 décembre et pendant tout le mois, Noël 1912-étrennes 1913, catalogue commercial, illustration de couverture, Marcellin Auzolle. BF, RES CC 182"1912"déc A.

———. "Exterior of Au Bon Marché." Au Bon Marché, nouveautés, modèles des confections, hiver 1879–80 [catalogue commercial]. BF, CC 182"1879"déc3.

———. "Harem Scene." Maison Aristide Boucicaut, catalogue, *A Partir de Lundi 23 Septembre. Éxposition spéciale et grande mise en vente des tapis de l'Orient*. 187? BNF, FOL-WZ-211 (1873) Au Bon Marché [FOL-WZ-211 (1869–)]. BNF.

———. Historique des magasins du Bon Marché, Paris, 1904. Catalogue commercial. BF, CC 182"1904"juil.

———. Interior Hall, Le Bon Marché. Historique des magasins du Bon Marché, catalogue commercial, 1904, p. 20. BF, CC 182"1904"juil.

———. Jouets, étrennes. 1929–1930 [Toy advertisement Cairo]. *Images*, 22 December 1929, pp. 28–29. CEALEX. bdd.cealex.org/bibliotheque/periodiques_rep_liste.php.

———. "Musulmane." Maison du Bon Marché, principaux modèles de confections pour dames, saison d'été, 1869: commercial catalogue, Recueil de catalogues Au Bon Marché (FOL-WZ-211) (1865–1877).

———. *L'Orient: offert par les grands magasins du Bon Marché aux visiteurs du salon des artistes français*. Au Bon Marché catalogue, 1911. BNF, Folio 4-WZ-13721.

———. L'Orient par J. L. Gérome. Offert par les grands magasins du Bon Marché, Paris, aux visiteurs du Salon des artistes français 1910, catalogue commercial, texte par Frédéric Masson, suivi de L'ameublement au XVIIIe siècle. BF, CC 182"1910"mai A.

———. Plan de l'Exposition universelle de 1900, dressé spécialement pour l'agenda-buvard des magasins du Bon-Marché. Dessin à la plume de A. Guibal, Gallica. BNF, IFN-53029452. .

———. Plan de Paris des magasins du Bon Marché Maison Aristide Boucicaut Paris. Ca 1908. BNF, IFN-8444584.

———. Le Salon de 1914, offert par les grands magasins du Bon Marché, catalogue commercial, suivi de L'ameublement du Bon Marché. BF, CC 182"1914"A.

———. Souvenir of the Bon Marché, Paris. 1889. Promotional Booklet. D. H. Ramsey Library, special collections, University of North Carolina at Asheville. oto.lib.unca.edu/booklets/bon_marche/default_bon_marche.htm.

———. *Succurscale d'Algerie et du Caire*. Dépliant [leaflet]. Ca. 1925? Annonces de presse et documents publicitaires de très grand format: Au Bon Marché, Galeries

Lafayette, Grands magasins du Louvre, Printemps, Samaritaine. BF, Cote: RES ICO 7491.

———. *Succursale Vichy*. Ca. 1925. Recueil. Grands magasins. Annonces de presse et documents publicitaires de très grand format: Au Bon Marché, Galeries Lafayette, Grands magasins du Louvre, Printemps, Samaritaine. BF, Cote: RES ICO 7491.

———. Workshop for the preparation of mail samples. *Historique des magasins du Bon Marché*, catalogue, 1904, p. 32. BF, CC 182"1904"juil.

———. "Aux visiteurs du salon des artistes français 1913." L'Orient par Edouard Detaille, offert par les grands magasins du Bon Marché [catalogue commercial]. BF, CC 182"1913"B.

L'Egyptienne. [magazine cover], no. 76, January 1932. CEALEX. bdd.cealex.org/bibliotheque/periodiques_rep_liste.php.

"L'Humour égyptien." *Images*, 22 December 1929, p. 30. CEALEX. bdd.cealex.org/bibliotheque/periodiques_rep_liste.php

Map of Alexandria. Charles E. Goad, *Insurance plan of Alexandria Egypt* 1898–1905. Harvard Map Collection, Harvard University. nrs.lib.harvard.edu/urn-3:fhcl:3746612.

Martel, Edouard. "35 photos des différents pavillons de l'exposition universelle de Paris en 1900." BNF, IFN-8470091.

Napoléon at Wanamaker's. "A dramatic history in realistic tableaux of the most interesting events in the career of the famous emperor" [poster]. BF, AF 82730 MF.

Nehru, Kamala. Portrait of Kamala Nehru. *L'Egyptienne*, no. 83, September 1932. CEALEX. bdd.cealex.org/bibliotheque/periodiques_rep_liste.php

Printemps. Un étage entier au Printemps, exposition jeudi 2 février et jours suivants, plus de 100.000 tapis garantis de matière et d'origine [c. 1939] [catalogue commercial]. BF, CC 274"1939"févr A.

———. Paris, le blanc, toile, trousseaux, lingerie, mouchoirs, collection illustrée de la petite bibliothèque Printemps, le lin & la toile, notre exposition annuelle de blanc est fixée au lundi 24 janvier, articles exposés et vendus à partir du lundi 17 janvier [1910], [catalogue commercial]. BF, CC 274"1910"janv.

———. Au Printemps, tapis & ameublements, un bazar oriental au Printemps, lundi 8 septembre, 1913 [catalogue commercial]. BF, CC 274"1913"sept A.

———. Souvenir de l'inauguration des nouveaux magasins du Printemps, Paris, avril 1910 [catalogue commercial]. BF, CC 274"1910"avr A.

Rouchdi Pacha, Eugénie (Niyya Salima). Portrait of Madame Rouchdi Pacha. *L'Egyptienne*, no. 14, March 1926. CEALEX. bdd.cealex.org/bibliotheque/periodiques_rep_liste.php.

Sainte Croix, Eugénie Avril de. Portraits d'Eugénie Avril de Sainte-Croix. IFN-10336378.

Sednaoui. "L'Été chez Sednaoui." Advertisement. *La femme nouvelle*, été 1950. CEALEX. bdd.cealex.org/bibliotheque/periodiques_rep_liste.php.

———. Le Caire, Alexandrie, Mansourah, Hiver 1928–29 [catalogue commercial]. BF.

———. Nouveautés d'hiver 1927–28, S.S. Sednaoui et Co Ltd, Le Caire, Alexandrie, Mansourah [catalogue commercial]. BF.

Shaarawi, Huda. "Les grandes figures féminines d'Egypte. Madame Hoda Charaoui Pacha." Portrait of Huda Shaarawi. *L'Egyptienne*, no. 17, June 1926. WMF.
———. "Mushkilat al-Usra al-Masriyya." Private collection of Hawwa' Idris. Rare Books and Special Collections. American University in Cairo.
———. Photograph of Hoda Shaarawi at her Desk, ca 1930. WMF.
Sanua, Louli. *Figures féminines. Mil neuf cent neuf-Mil neuf cent neuf*. Siboney, 1949. BNF, MFICHE 16-G-978.
Siegfried, Jules. Madame Jules Siegfried, debout, la main sur le dossier d'un fauteuil, photographie. Bibliothèque Marguerite Durand, 099 B 317.
"The progress of fashion over a half a century." *Rose al-Yusef*, 13 January 1927, p. 11. WMF.
"This dress is incomplete." Cartoon, *al-Lata'if al-Musawwara*, 23 April 1922, p. 16. Dar al-Kutub.
"Women in Public Spaces." *al-Lata'if al-Musawwara*, 19 March, 1917, p. 8. Dar al-Kutub.
"Yesterday and Tomorrow." *al-Lata'if al-Musawwara*, 21 July 1919, p. 13. Harvard University.
Zola, Émile. *Œuvres. Manuscrits et dossiers préparatoires. Les Rougon-Macquart. Au Bonheur des dames. Dossier préparatoire*. 1881. NAF 10277 and 10278, BNF.
———. Map of internal setting of *Au Bonheur des dames*. Émile Zola, dossier préparatoire. NAF Mss 10278, BNF.
———. Street map for the location of *Au Bonheur des dames*. Émile Zola, dossier Préparatoire. NAF Mss. 10278, BNF.

Unpublished Interviews

Shohet, Yvonne. "Communauté Juive d'Egypte." Tape 1. Interview by Jaqueline Kahanoff, 20 November 1964. Déreh Hachalom. Oral History Department, Institute of Contemporary Jewry, Hebrew University, Jerusalem.
———. "Communauté Juive d'Egypte." Tape 2. Interview by Jaqueline Kahanoff, 20 November 1964. Déreh Hachalom. Oral History Department, Institute of Contemporary Jewry, Hebrew University, Jerusalem.
———. "Communauté Juive d'Egypte après la guerre." Interview by Jaqueline Kahanoff, 16 December 1964. Part I, Bande 536. Oral History Department, Institute of Contemporary Jewry, Hebrew University, Jerusalem.

Films and Television Productions

Au Bonheur des dames. Directed by Julien Duvivier, Le Film d'Art, 1930.
Au Bonheur des dames. Directed by André Cayatte, Continental Films, 1943.
Banat Hawwa. Directed by Niazi Mustafa, 1954.

Campos, Ramón, and Gema R. Neira, creators. *Velvet*. Bambú Producciones, 2013–2016.
Davies, Andrew, creator. Mr. *Selfridge*. ITV Studios, 2013–2016.
Gallagher, Bill, creator. *The Paradise*. BBC, 2012.
Harat al-Yahud. Directed by Mohamed Gamal el-Adl and Mahmoud Zahran, El-Adl Group, 2015.
Jews of Egypt. Direted by Amir Ramsis, Session, 2012.
La'bit al-sit. Directed by Wali al-Din Samih, 1946.
Monsieur Ibrahim et les Fleurs du Coran. Directed by François Dupeyron, Sony Pictures Classics, 2004.
Nashala Hanim. Directed by Hassan al-Saifi, 1953.
Nocturama. Directed by Bertrand Bonello, Rectangle Productions, 2016.
Salata Baladi. Directed by Nadia Kamel, WomenMakeMovies, 2007.
Seret 'Aravit. Directed by Eyal Saguee Bizawie and Sarah Tsifrono, Go2films, 2015.
Testa, Crisitano creator. *Il Paradiso delle Signore*. Rai Ficton, 2015.
That Alexandria. Directed by Sherif Fathi Salem, Spot1tv and Aljazeera Documentary Channel, 2013.

French Magazines

Bulletin de l'AID
Images
La Femme nouvelle
La Fronde
Le boulevard
L'Egyptienne
L'Egypte nouvelle
L'Union nationale des femmes

Arabic Magazines and Journals

Anis al-Jalis
al-Fukaha
al-Kashkul
al-Kashkul al-Musawwar
al-Lata'if al-Musawwara
al-Muqtataf
al-Musawar
al-Nil
al-Sufur

Fatat al-Sharq
Kawkab al-Sharq
Kul Shay' wa-l-Dunya
Masr al-Haditha al-Musawwara
Rose al-Yusef

Index

Abbasiyya (Abbasieh, Abbasiyeh), 205, 208, 218; 298n26
Abdel Hay, Saleh, 96–97, 283n29
Abdel Nasser, Gamal, 179, 242; Pan-Arabism, 189, 262
Abolitionism, 166, 177–78, 252. *See also* prostitution; sex work; slavery
Aboukir (street), 50
Aciman, André, 284n34, 297n6
Adam, Juliette, 169, 175, 178
Agha, Said, 160–62, 164–66
agora-cosmopolitanism, 5, 35, 44, 68, 150
Ahmed, Leila, 165
Aida, opera, 79
Alcalay, Ammiel, 189, 198, 297n11
Aleksandrinke, 219, 300n37
Aleppo, 33, 55, 83, 187
Alexandria, 2, 14, 30, 33, 50, 55, 80, 92, 105, 152, 153, 159–68, 175, 194, 199, 231, 240–43, 247, 253, 259–70, 293n4, 296n3, 301n17&18
Alexandrie (street), 50
Algeria, 41, 55, 126, 132, 179, 281
Ali, Mehmet, 76, 256, 282n11. *See also* Mohamed Ali
Ali, Mohamed (Mohammed), 155; 240; Place, 242, 282n6
alignment, philosophy of, 32
Alliance Israelite, 193, 201
allotopic, 10; geography, 244, 249
Alsace-Lorraine, 31, 55, 62, 110, 114, 243, 247

Amin, Qasim, 155, 167, 176–77, 293n11, 295n30
Anis al-Jalis (journal), 89, 157
année de la Mère, 76
Anti-Semitism 118, 131
Appadurai, Arjun, 3
Apter, Emily, 18, 180
Arabe du coin, 11, 249, 250
Arab-Israeli conflict, 105, 264
À Rebours, 111, 285n11
Aryanization, 242–43, 247
Ashby, Margery Corbett, 179
Ashkenazi (people), 81, 181, 194–95, 218, 263, 266–68, 302n24
Atatürk, Kemal, 153, 179, 258
Au bonheur des dames (novel). *See* Zola, Émile
Auclert, Hubertine, 176
Austrian (people), 80, 86
Avierino, Alexandra, 89, 157, 293n14
Avoda Aravit (tv show), 268
Azbakiyya (garden), 97–99, 219, 253, 299n33

Bader, Théophile, 54, 104, 247
Baghdad, 33, 83, 187, 215–16, 228–29, 300n40
Bahithat al-Badiya, 156. *See also* Malak Hifni Nassif
Bakhtin, Mikhail, 16, 19, 32, 41, 112
Balfour Declaration, 206, 230, 298n21
Baltard, Victor, 45, 121
de Balzac, Honoré, 66, 112–13, 116, 285n13
Bank Misr, 83

Baring, Evelyn (earl of Cromer), 84, 154–55, 258
Baron, Beth, 92–93, 154, 156–57, 167, 181–82
Barrault, Émile, 77, 281n2
Bartholdi, Frédéric Auguste, 77–78, 181
Baudelaire, Charles, 1, 66, 277n5, 299n27
bayt al-Maṣriyya (the household of the Egyptian woman), 183
bayt al-ṭāʿa (obedience house), 160
bazaar, 8, 11, 35, 44–45, 48, 55, 80, 83, 107–9, 111, 120, 128, 133, 144–45, 150, 167, 200–1, 230, 243, 249, 287n29
Bazar de l'Hôtel de Ville (department store), 2, 52, 54, 244
Beirut, 33, 80, 83, 187
belle époque, 60, 117, 199, 237–38, 240–43, 249, 269, 282n13, 300n1
Ben-Gurion, David, 194
Benjamin, Walter, 31, 48, 51, 59, 65, 66, 110, 118, 143, 277n12, 279n30&31, 280n39, 292n77
Benzion (department store), 75, 105
Berlin, 33, 80–81, 84
Biancani, Francesca, 97–99, 219, 284n30, 300n37
bint el-balad, 88
biopower, 28, 156, 161, 277n6, 293n12
Blondel, Jacques François, 121
Boileau, Louis Charles, 53
Au Bon Marché (department store), 2, 8–12, 28, 32, 33, 42, 52, 56, 63, 75, 83, 88, 97, 143, 152, 279n36; and French colonialism, 32, 53, 55; and the "Oriental Salon," 57–59, 107–8, 125–30, 136–37, 142, 144, 244, 289n45; and the Paris cityscape, 53, 109–16
Bonaparte, Napoleon, 50–52, 76, 137; in Egypt, 30, 50, 115, 256, 279n31, 282n11&13; in Italy, 279n30
Bonello, Bertrand, 248
Booth, Marilyn, 158, 162, 178, 293n15
Boucicaut, Aristide, 52–53, 56, 59, 116, 279n35, 280n43
Boulac, street, 81, 202, 208, 269, 298n25
Bourdieu, Pierre, 4, 35, 40, 91, 140, 191, 220, 291n70

bourgeoisie, 4, 34–47, 53; and Egyptian nationalism, 103–4, 162; and furniture, 60; and Orientalist material culture, 59, 183–84; and shoplifting, 64–65
Bowell, Vivian, 296n3, 302n6
boycott, British products, 103, 162, 175
Braudel, Fernand, 262, 264, 276n19, 286n17
Brummett, Palmira, 144, 263

Cairo, 2, 14, 33, 80–84, 90, 93, 94, 97–98, 104–5, 152–53, 163, 167, 177, 181, 187–88, 193–97, 200–231, 237, 253, 254–57, 262–64, 266–67, 269–70, 279n34, 282n11, 293n5, 296n3, 298n26; Abbasiyya [Abbasieh] Quarter of, 205, 208, 218, 298n26; American University in, 102, 169, 294n27; fire, 104, 254–56, Harat al-Yahud in, 204, 218, 299n31; Haussmannized area of, 80, 174, 184
calicot, 54, 67
campagnonnage, 56, 280n42
capital; economic, 164, 191, 214, 221. *See also* cultural capital
capitulation, 81, 276n17, 282n10, 284n30
carnival grotesque, 40, 41
carpet seller, 10, 34, 35, 44. See also *marchand de tapis*
cartographic anxiety, 110–11, 134
Casta, Laetitia, 251–52
Castel-Bloom, Orly, 264, 266–69
Cayatte, André, 246
celestial globe, 32
Certeau, Michel de, 119, 238, 276n12
Chalon (department store), 75, 152, 240, 293n16
Chanut, Ferdinand, 54
Charaoui, Houda. *See* Shaarawi
Charleston (dance), 97, 102
Chauchard, Auguste, 54
Chemla (department store), 2, 75, 80, 81–83, 85, 89, 97, 104–5, 187, 193, 197, 199, 202–4, 209, 214–16, 252, 256, 258, 269, 271, 298n25, 299n28
Chevalier, Michel, 33, 77, 117, 277n12, 280n47
Chicago World's Fair, 157
chronotope, 32, 112; multichronotopic 17

cialente, Fausta, 190, 297n6
Cicurel (department store), 2, 10, 75, 80, 82–83, 85, 93, 103, 104–5, 162, 254–58, 265, 269–70, 299n3
Cicurel, Ronald,104–5, 299n32
Cicurel, Slavator, 83, 105
Circassian (people), 153, 166, 172, 182, 293n7
citizenship; multilevel 14. *See also* extraterritoriality. *See* sovereignty
civilizing mission, 3, 18, 37, 38, 41, 43, 51, 57, 63, 78, 87, 99, 135, 140, 142, 143, 155, 171, 182, 217, 218, 220–22, 227, 230, 233, 264, 268, 273, 278n18
Clausen, Meredith, 44
Clément, Marguerite, 174, 175
Crane, Charles, 183
Cognacq, Ernest, 53, 56–57, 248
Commune (of 1871), 41, 64, 110, 132–33, 176
comparative literature. *See* world literature
consumerism, 4, 8, 9, 12, 13, 37–38, 49, 50–52, 57, 60, 85, 88, 108, 123–24, 129, 130, 133, 151, 218, 248, 278n18; and gender, 95, 163; topographies of consumption, 10
cosmography, 3, 9, 187, 241, 243
cosmology, 1, 9, 150; cosmological, 3
cosmopolitanism, 4–6, 9, 11, 13–14, 35, 38, 44, 68, 85, 168, 188, 193, 200, 203, 218–19, 233, 241–43, 259, 264, 273, 275n10. *See also* agora-cosmopolitanism
cour de miracles, 50
Coutan, Jules, 181
Couvreur, A., 51, 174, 294n24, 295n33
Crane, Charles, 183
Creed, Barbara, 39–40
cult of domesticity, 38
cultural capital, 4, 9, 13, 40, 57, 113, 132, 139, 140, 141, 189, 191, 192, 204, 205, 213, 216, 218, 220, 222, 243, 266, 271
Cynic, 5; tradition 5
Czechoslovakia, 242–43

dallala, 167–68, 294n23. *See also* ambulant seller; peddler
Damiette (street), 50
Darwinism, 108, 150, 168, 185, 249
déclassement, 64, 141, 159

Delacroix, Eugène, 107, 117, 118, 129, 300n40
department stores: definition of, 13, 45–47. *See also grands magasins*
Deraismes, Marie, 176
Détaille, Édouard, 60, 129
Diogenes, 5–6
Dodman, Thomas, 239, 300n3
Domestic Workers, 65, 99, 100–2, 166–67, 190–92, 197, 205, 207–9, 218, 221–28, 231–33, 256, 281n53. *See also* Aleksandrinke; nanny; governess; nursemaid; eunuch
Dreyfus affair, 118
Du Bois, W.E.B., 224, 299n34&36
Durand, Marguerite, 175, 177
Durrell, Lawrence, 190, 260, 263, 301n17
Duvivier, Julien, 246
Dyab, Hanna, 49

Eberhardt, Isabelle, 179
Eclecticism, 60, 61, 182–84, 280n48; empire, 48, 52, 80; emporialism, 52, 79; utopianism, 55, 143
Edib, Halidé, 179
efendiyya, 86–87, 89, 103–4, 258, 283n15, 301n15. *See effendi*
effendi, 86–89, 103–4, 181, 258; *effendification*, 229. *See also efendiyya*
Egypt, 2–3, 9–10, 12, 14, 15, 30, 33, 46, 48, 50–52, 58, 62, 75–105, 115, 138, 152–86, 187–234, 237–43, 251–73, 276n16, 279n31, 281n1, 282n11&13, 284n30&34, 286n19; independence of 7–8, 104–5, 253
Egypt Carrying Light to Asia. See Bartholdi
Egyptian Feminist Union (EFU), 98, 153, 154, 178–80
Egyptomania, 50, 62
Eiffel, Gustave, 53; Eiffel tower image, 251
Empathy (architecture), 60, 122
empire: British, 2, 8, 14, 37–38, 81, 90, 100, 152, 153, 193, 217–18, 276n17, 299n30; French, 2, 8, 14, 32, 50, 62, 78, 86–89, 97, 100, 111, 152, 153, 193, 281n1 (*See also* Second Empire); German, 31, 44, 62, 110, 114, 143, 243, 246–47, 287n22; Greek, 62, 263; Italian, 14; Ottoman, 2, 8, 14, 27–28,

empire (*continued*)
30, 48–49, 75, 79, 80–88, 94, 97, 100, 111, 150, 152, 153–57, 159, 161–62, 165–68, 180, 188, 192, 193–94, 224–25, 242–43, 252, 257–58, 276n17, 277n3, 283n14, 294n22; Roman, 62, 263

emporialism: definition, 2–8; and history, 9–13, 28; and the ideal bourgeois woman 36–40; and the Mediterranean, 16; and Orientalist aesthetics, 33–36; in Zola's novel, 110

emporium: origin of the word, 47

Enfantin, Barthélemy-Prosper, 76, 277n12

Engels, Friedrich, 4, 17, 112

Enlightenment, 78

Erll, Astrid, 12, 245

ethnic-classism, 296n1. *See* ethno-class; ethno-classism

ethno-class, 86, 111, 204, 21–198, 229, 232–33, 266; ethno-classism, 11, 37, 38, 189, 196, 218, 249, 278; gendered 36, 38, 86, 99

Eugène, Charles, 54

eunuch, 100, 160–61, 164–66, 168, 175, 185, 219, 294n22

Exodus (book of), 195–97, 231–32

extraterritoriality, 14, 81, 276n17, 280n10

Fabian, Johannes, 275n9

family of man, 37, 44

Fanon, Frantz, 134, 220, 223, 299n36

fellah, 77–78, 182; *fellaha*, 137

feminism, 15–16, 76–77, 98–99, 102, 150–59, 168–86, 252–54, 293n3

feminist convention, Rome, 154, 157, 173

Femme nouvelle (magazine), 102–3

fez (headdress), 42, 83, 86, 257–58. *See also* tarbouche

Filles-Dieu, couvent, 50

flânerie, flâneur, 65–66, 277n5, 281n56

Foucault, Michel, 28, 172, 221–22, 244

Fourier, Charles, 56, 143, 176, 280n39&40. *See also* phalanstery, phalanx

four movements (theory), 176

France Bearing the Torch of Civilization, 181

Franco-Egyptian, 2, 9, 15, 30, 94, 177, 256, 257. *See* Francophone, Francophonie

Francophilia, 86

Francophone, 8, 30, 83, 85, 88, 90, 99, 102, 173, 176, 179, 180, 188, 189, 190, 197, 199, 201, 202, 203, 204, 215, 226, 227, 241, 242, 251, 252, 257, 258, 264, 266, 300n41

Francophonie, 241. *See* Franco-Egyptian, Francophone

Franco-Prussian war, 41, 247. *See also* German: annexation; empire: German

Free Officers, 104, 253

Galeries de Bois, 65

Galeries Lafayette (department store), 2, 8, 10, 52, 54–55, 75, 80, 82, 83, 104, 237, 238, 246–47, 251, 257, 283n26

Garden City (neighborhood), 206, 218

Garnier, Charles, 116, 121–22, 282n11, 292n78

Gattegno (department store), 75, 258

genesis amnesia, 191

German (people), 54, 83–84, 99, 114, 180, 181, 277n8; annexation, 110, 114, 247. *See also* empire: German

Gérome, Jean-Léon, 129

Ghali Pasha, Wasif, 173

Ghali, Waguih, 296n3, 297n6

Giedion, Siegfried, 66, 281n55

Gitre, Carmen, 181

Godlewska, Anne, 115

Goude, Jean-Paul, 251

governess, 98, 99, 158, 191–92, 196, 219–22, 224, 226, 228, 233, 269, 299n32. *See also* nanny; nursemaid

grand magasin: in Egypt, 8, 80–83, 97, 152, 160, 187, 202–5, 207, 219, 253; in France, 11, 37, 46, 52–56, 64, 75, 109, 116, 117, 119, 149–50, 170, 243, 249, 279n35, 284n2; origin of the term, 48, 276n2

grands boulevards, 49, 50, 54, 65, 66, 116, 119

Grasset, Eugène-Samuel, 34

Greek (people), 8, 14, 27, 82, 98–99, 180, 181–82, 187, 190, 197, 204, 218, 225, 240–42, 260–63, 277n3, 298n26

Greek Orthodox faith, 82, 157

Gregory, Derek, 77–79, 110, 271, 286n18
Guérin, Marguerite, 56
Gunn, Simon, 7, 185, 186

Habermas, Jürgen; public sphere 35, 96
habitus, 40, 57, 91, 140, 141, 191, 219, 232, 256, 291n70
Halles, 45, 121, 278n22
Hamamsy, Chafika, 184, 219, 222, 224, 299n32
Hannaux (department store), 75, 82, 240
Hannoosh, Michèle, 66, 114
Harat-al-yahud, 204, 218, 296n3, 299n31, 302n26
harem: as description of department stores, 108, 109, 111, 120, 123–25, 127, 140, 142, 144, 150, 243, 289n45; as Orientalist imagery, 42, 57–58, 90, 118, 135, 154–55, 158, 162, 164, 173
harmony, interior design, 60, 280n46
Hartog, François, 239–40
Harvey, David, 3, 40
Hassoun, Jacques, 302n26
Haussmann, Baron Georges-Eugène, 7, 33, 61, 62, 66, 76, 77, 108–11, 116, 118–20, 126, 130, 135, 143–44, 280n48, 281n55, 282n8; influence on parts of Cairo, 80, 82
Havard, Victor, 60–62, 280n46
Haykal, Muhammad Hussayn, 182
Hegemony, 188, hegemonic 18
Heidegger, Martin, 18, 276n20
Héliopolis: construction of by Baron Empain, 184
Helmi II, Abbas (Sultan), 88
Hériot, Auguste, 54
Herzfeld, Michael, 17
heteroglossia, 16, heteroglossic, 85, 257, 166
heterotopia, 2, 50, 244–45, 264, 271–73
hexis, 40
histoire croisée, 15
historicity: regime of 240, 300n3; of nostalgia, 239–40
Hittorff, Jacques Ignace, 62
Hobsbawm, Eric, 240
Hochberg, Gil, 194, 198, 264–67
homo islamicus, 35, 42, 249

Hourani, Albert, 198
Hugo, Victor, 112, 200, 285n12
von Humboldt, Alexander, 115, 286n19
Huysmans, Joris-Karl, 111, 250
Hysteria, 67, 133–34

iconography, 3, 28, 33, 39, 42, 44, 49, 50, 53, 61, 62, 75, 78, 80, 81, 86, 87, 91, 94, 109, 116, 133, 150, 151, 170, 173, 178, 181, 182, 202, 245, 247, 251, 254, 259, 272, 276n12
iconomic, 115, 272
ideological work of gender, 155–56
Idris, Hawwa', 153, 179, 252
Idris, Huriyya, 153, 179
industrialism, 37, 137, 273, 277n12
Ingres, Jean-Auguste-Dominique, 107, 117
Intercolonial, 100, 189
Interimperial, 8, 38, 100, 189, 193tra
Intersectional 8, 9, 10, 11, 13, 14, 15, 19, 41, 67, 86, 93, 99, 100, 103, 151, 156, 166, 168, 182, 185, 189, 190, 192, 196, 218, 219, 249, 272, 299n30. *See* intersectionality
Intersectionality, 16. *See* intersectional
Invalides, 109, 112, 285n6
Invented traditions, 240
Iron Palace, 52
Ismail (khedive of Egypt), 78, 79, 88, 153, 227, 282n8
Israel, 3, 105, 187–206, 234, 254, 256–57, 259, 260–61, 263–64, 266–68, 302n24
Istanbul, 14, 33, 80–81, 111, 152, 187, 282n8
Italian (people), 8, 82, 85, 217, 263, 282n11
Italy, 261, 300n2
d'Ivray, Jehan, 83, 169, 179, 294n26

Jacob's Ladder (novel). *See* Kahanoff
Jacques, Paula, 3, 255–57
Jaluzot, Jules, 54
Jay, Louise, 53, 248
Jeanne d'Arc, 172
Jerusalem, 187, 230–31, 256, 261, 264, 301n12
Josephine, empress of France, 51, 279n34
Jourdain, Frantz, 52–54, 120–22, 125, 248–49, 287n29
July Monarchy, 32–33

344 | Index

Kahanoff, Jacqueline, 3, 105, 187–234, 259–65, 268, 297n10, 298n23, 299n31, 299n34, 300n37, 300n39, 301n10, 301n16
Kahf, Mohja, 151, 165
Kahn, Alphonse, 54
Kant, Emmanuel, 5, 6
Kasr-al-Nil (street), 174, 270
Kermel, Amédëe, 51, 279n33
Kish-Kish Bey, 203–4, 298n18. *See also* Vaudeville; al-Rihani
Kleptomania, 64, 65, 67, 133–35

L'Egyptienne (magazine), 168–69, 173–75, 178–79, 182, 184, 202
de La Blache, Paul Vidal, 114–16, 286n17,18,21
La'bit al-sit (film), 103–4
Lagnado, Lucette, 284n34, 296n3, 302n26
La Maison du chat qui pelote, 113
Lanfranchi, Sania Sharawi, 158, 175, 183–84, 293n16
La Peau de chagrin, 113, 285n13
Lasciac, Antonio, 183–84
al-Lata'if al-Musawwara (journal), 89–91, 93–95
Latour, Bruno, 7, 198
Le Bon, Gustave, 168–69, 184, 294n24
Le Brun, Eugénie, 164, 179
Lebanese (people), 8, 95, 181, 190, 226, 227, 251
Lebanon, 153
de Lesseps, Ferdinand, 76–79, 255
Levantinism, 144, 187–234, 259–66, 273, 297n9, 301n10&16
lieu de mémoire, 239–40, 244, 270
London, 14, 28–29, 33, 46, 84, 86, 94, 151, 217, 283n26
Louis Philippe (king of France), 62, 65
Louis XIV (king of France), 48–49
Lyon, 170

Macron, Emmanuel, 248–49, 300n6
Maghreb, 30, 55, 82, 174, 182, 248
MagShamhráin, Rachel, 65
makhzan, 48, 276n2; makhāzin (plural), 28, 80, 276n2

Manshiyya (square), 242. *See also* Place de Consuls; Place Mohammed Ali
marchand de tapis, 10
Marianne, 77, 78, 88
Mariette, Auguste, 79
Marseille, 98, 170, 278n25
Marx, Karl, 3, 4, 17, 112
Marxism, 8,16, 17
Mashriq, 55, 82
Matalon, Ronit, 3, 198, 264–69
McClintock, Ann, 37, 38, 110, 133, 220–21, 224–25, 278n18
McDowell, Linda, 15–16, 40, 96, 99–100
Mead, Christopher, 122, 287n31
Mediterranean, 2, 7–9, 13–20, 33, 98, 105; aesthetics, 54, 60–61, 82; as unifier of East and West; 61, 68, 75–80, 83, 94
Mediterraneanism, 17
Mediterraneanization, 17
Merchant of Venice, 131
Mère, la (Saint-Simonianism), 76
Michelet, Jules, 114, 116, 286n18
Milner, Lord Alfred, 84
Miniature 2, 31, 36, 43, 77, 89, 94, 95, 96, 119, 143, 211, 215, 216, 275n1, 275n2, 277n5, 283n26
Mitchell, Timothy, 67
Mitsukoshi (department store), 33, 46, 283n26
Mixed courts, 178, 193, 297n8
Mizrahi (people), 82, 189, 194–95, 198, 200, 206, 209, 218, 234, 259–64, 266–68, 302n24
Mizrahi, Togo, 203–4
Monsieur Ibrahim et les fleurs du Coran (film), 250–51, 268
Morris, Ian, 17
Mousky, 301n9. *See also* Muski
Moyal, Esther Azhari, 157
Mukhtar, Mahmoud, 180, 181–82
Multiplanar, 8, 15–20, 99, 271. *See also* plane
Multiscalar, 6, 15, 16, 18, 99. *See also* scale
Musa, Nabawiyya, 157, 173, 295n30
Muski (neighborhood), 80–82, 253. *See also* Mousky
de Musset, Alfred, 65–66

Nabaraoui, Céza, 154, 173–75, 184
al-Nadi, Lotfia, 179
Naguib, Mohamed, 252
Nahdat Misr. See Mukhtar
nanny, 191, 197, 217, 219–33, 299. See also nursemaid; governess
Naples, 170
Napoleon I (emperor of France). See Bonaparte
Napoleon III (emperor of France), 32, 33, 52–53, 110, 117. See also Second Empire
Nashala Hanim (film), 103
Nasser, Gamal Abdel, 179, 189, 242, 262
Nassif, Malak Hifni, 156
National Council for French Women, 175, 178
Nationalization, 7–8, 104–5, 242, 270. See also sequestration
naturalism, 60, 111–13, 116, 120, 122, 132, 158, 285n12
Nebi Daniel (street), 261–62, fig. 6.3
Nehru, Kamala, 179
New York, 10, 33, 46, 152, 193
Nil (street), 50
Nocturama (film), 248
noeud de mémoire, 245
Noorani, Yaseen, 162, 294n20
Nora, Pierre, 239–40, 244
Nord, Philip, 119
Nostalgia, 9, 30, 199, 200, 201, 206–7, 237, 238–41, 249, 269–70, 272, 297n5, 300n1; emporial 238, 240, 242; historicity of, 239
Notre Dame, 109, 112, 285n6
nuptial bed (Saint-Simonian Mediterranean), 33, 117, 137
nursemaid, 217–22, 299. See also nanny; governess
Nussbaum, Martha, 5

Occidentalism, 30, 277n7
odalisque, 58, 125, 137, 140
Omar Effendi (department store), 3, 10, 83, 86, 253, 258, 301
"Oriental Salon." See Bon Marché
Orientalism, 13, 28, 29–31, 48, 57–67, 84, 107, 125–36, 151, 159, 180, 182, 190, 196, 218–19, 225, 251, 268, 279n32; aesthetics of, 34, 49–51, 183–84, 187, 279n34, 280n48, 296n43; and consumerist fantasy. 2, 10, 80, 108, 118, 123–32, 142, 200; and Saint-Simonianism, 33, 76–78, 117, 122, 170, 273
Orosdi-Back (department store), 75, 83, 258. See also Omar Effendi
Ottoman Empire. See under empire
Out-el-Kouloub, 3, 97, 252–54

Paix, rue de la, 46, 116
Palestine, 3, 153, 177, 195–96, 230–32
Palestinian (people), 196, 266, 268
Pan-Arabism, 189, 262, 267
panorama, 44, 47, 51, 57–58, 65–66, 112, 126, 128, 132, 180, 246, 281n54, 289n48; panoramania 281n54
Panthéon, 109, 112, 285n6
Parcq, George, 82, 94
Paris, 2, 8, 11, 14, 27–55, 62–66, 75, 88, 93–95, 104, 107–25, 133–43, 149–53, 157, 168–81, 183, 187–88, 194, 199, 200, 202–3, 229, 237, 243–51, 255–57, 278n25, 279n26, 280n40, 281n56, 283n26, 292n78, 293n4, 297n14, 300n40; Haussmannization of, 7, 76, 77, 111, 119–20, 143–44, 280n48
Paschal & Cie (department store), 88, fig. 2.7
Pasini, Alberto, 58
Passage du Caire (Paris), 50–51, 62, 111, 279n30-31
Peddler, 28, 47, 167, 185, 209–10, 218–19. See also ambulant seller, *dallala*
percement, 32; philosophy of; ideology of 77, 281n2
Père, le, 56 (department store patriarchal culture); 76 (Saint Simonianism). See also Enfantin; Cognacq
phalanstery, 55–57, 119, 142–44
Phalanx, 55, 56, 142
Piaf, Edith, 247, 251
Place de Consuls, 242
Planchet, Jean-Alexandre, 53
Plane, 14, 15, 16, 18, 20, 42, 271. See also multiplanar
Plessis, Alain, 53
Pollard, Lisa, 174, 182

346 | Index

Polyglossia, 16, 85, 95, 226, 257
Poovey, Mary, 155, 278n17
Postcolonialism, 17, 238–39
Postmodernism, 238–39
Pratt, Mary Louise, 263, 282n7
Printemps (department store), 2, 8, 36–44, 52, 54, 55, 75, 83, 89, 290n58
Prism (Levantine), 205, 260, 296n1, 297n9&10
Prostitution, 65, 67, 97, 98, 133, 135, 139, 177, 284n30. *See also* sex work; abolitionism
Proust, Marcel, 199, 205, 229, 297n12–14, 298n22, 300n40
Pygmalion, 89, 278n16; dream, 89; fantasy, 36, 93, 301n10

Raafat, Samir, 269–70
Raca, Soliman Moustapha (emissary of Sultan Mehmed IV), 48–49
Rambuteau, Claude-Philibert Barthelot, 62, 281n49
Reynolds, Nancy, 85, 203, 255, 298n26
rhetoric of exemplarity, 178
Richer, Léon, 176
al-Rihani, Najib, 203–5
Rivoli (street), 84
Robida, Albert, 111, 124, 285n10
Roman Catholicism, 61, 63, 112
Rome, 33, 154, 157, 260
Ross, Kristin, 41
Rothberg, Michael, 245
Rougon-Macquart, 108–9, 114, 116, 144
Rubin, Gayle, 135–36
Ruel, Xavier, 54
Russell, Mona, 87–89, 91, 93, 162, 283n16&23, 293n4, 294
Russell (Pacha), 98
Russia, 55, 195, 293n7

Sabra, 260–61
Sadat, Anwar, 105, 293n6
Said, Edward, 51, 127, 221, 250
de Saint Croix, Avril, 175, 178
de Saint Point, Valentine, 175
de Saint-Simon, Claude Henri, 7, 32, 76, 144, 228, 297n13

Saint-Simonianism, 32–33, 41, 53, 55–57, 61, 75–79, 83, 89, 94, 108, 115, 116, 117–20, 122, 125, 136–44, 150, 168–70, 176, 179, 181, 241, 255, 272–73, 277n12, 280n40, 281n1, 292n79, 294n26. *See also* Orientalism, phalanstery, phalanx, utopianism
Sakal, Moshe, 296n3, 302n26
Salata Baladi (documentary), 296n3, 302n26
Salima, Niyya, 179
Samaritaine (department store), 2, 42–43, 52, 53–54, 56–57, 121, 143, 237, 246, 248–49
Sanu', Ya'qub, 175, 283n16
Sanua, Louli (Louise), 175–77, 295n35
Seller (ambulant), 87, 167–68, 170. *See also* peddler
Sex work, 65, 97, 284n30. See prostitution; abolitionism
Scale, 6, 7, 31, 33, 34, 36, 37–40, 44, 47, 48, 52, 66, 80, 87–91, 95, 96, 109, 110, 152, 184, 202, 243, 273. *See also* multiscalar
Scheherazade, 49, 124, 142, 144, 199, 228–29
Schema, 12, 245, iconographic 259, 272, narrative 245, 254, spatial 272, urban 12
Schemata, 9, 12, 13, 161, 276n12, 245; narrative 254, urban, 9, 13. *See also* schema
Schwartz, Vanessa, 65, 238
Second Empire (in France), 7, 31, 32, 41, 52–53, 55, 57, 61, 66, 76, 110, 113, 116–17, 130, 143–44, 176, 237, 243, 246, 248, 277n12, 279n35, 281n55, 286n18, 287n31
Seder, 231, 265
Sédille, Paul, 54
Sednaoui (department store), 2, 75, 80, 82, 93–99, 102–3, 105, 237, 240, 251, 258–59, 271
Sednaoui, Sam'ān, 82
Sedanoui, Salim, 82
Sephardi (people), 181, 194, 260
Sequestration 104, 242. *See also* nationalization
Seret Aravit, 302n26
Shaarawi, Huda, 3, 92, 102, 149–86, 201, 202, 253, 254, 293n2, 293n16, 294n24&27, 295n30, 296n45
Shafik, Doria, 102, 252
Shahryar, 123, 144

Shakespeare, 131
Sha'rawi. *See* Shaarawi
shari'a, 160
Sharif, Omar, 251
Shelley, Percy, 29
Shohat, Ella, 17, 267–68
Shohet, Yvonne (née Chemla), 81–82, 202–3, 214
Shoplifting, 64, 133–35. *See also* kleptomania
Shylock, 131
Siegfried, Julie, 175, 178
Sikourel, 265. *See also* Cicurel
slavery, 42, 48, 98, 101–2, 109, 123, 129, 135, 153, 165–66, 252, 284n33, 294n22. *See also* eunuch
Solé, Robert, 3, 180, 257–59
Sovereignty, 172; overlapping, 6, 14
Spain, 30, 54, 300n2
Spivak, Gayatri Chakravorty,16, 18, 276n20
Statue of Liberty, 77, 78, 282n4
Stein Oriental Goods Store, 80, 86
Stewart, A.T., 52
Stewart, Susan, 40, 61, 95–96
Stoler, Ann Laura, 207, 297n5, 299n30; and Frederick Cooper, 14, 221
Sudan, 30, 79, 80, 100, 153, 175
Sudanese (people), 101, 165, 190, 222, 226–28, 265
Suez Canal, 2, 7, 30, 33, 52, 63, 75–79, 80, 82, 101, 104–5, 144, 153, 169, 188, 204, 227, 242, 254–55, 270, 281n2, 282n13, 292n79
Sultan, Mohamed Pasha (Huda Shaarawi's father), 153–55, 163
Sultan, Umar Pacha (Huda Saarawi's brother), 184
Swirski, Shlomo, 268
Syria, 48, 82, 126, 153, 177
Syrian (people), 8, 49, 82, 85, 95, 157, 180, 181, 187, 190, 197, 225, 226–27, 257–58, 260
Szendy, Peter, 20, 31, 115

tableau, 27, 47, 50, 59,63, 66, 68, 84, 111, 113–18, 128–30, 180–81, 216, 241, 263, 285n14, 286n16, 286n2

Taine, Hippolyte, 41, 116, 121–22, 125, 128, 289–90n50
taqtūqa (Egyptian song form), 96–97, 99, 283n27
tarbouche, 257–58. *See also* fez
taxonomy; social, 14; of race and class, 268; of relations 150
Téboul, Victor, 296n3, 297n6, 302n6
Third Republic (in France), 62–66, 116–17, 171, 176, 179, 237, 246, 293n15
Tietz (department store), 80–81
Tiring (department store), 80–81, 86
Tokyo, 33, 46, 94
topographies of consumption, 10
translation, 6, 12–13; of Huda Shaarawi's memoirs, 151; of *The Thousand and One Nights*, 49
translocal, 8
transnational, 7, 8, 28, 149, 150, 151, 159, 173, 175, 177, 178, 185, 201, 275n6, 279n36, 293n15
transparency (architecture), 121–22
transregional, 8
Tunis, 33, 55, 81–82, 83, 187, 210, 212
Tunisia, 14, 81, 85, 193, 197, 215, 226, 228
Turkey, 14, 27, 48, 55, 85, 86, 107, 127, 153, 293n9
Turkish (people), 37, 44, 78, 111, 153, 179, 180, 182, 250, 258

Universal Exhibitions, 7, 18, 27–28, 29, 31–32, 42, 45, 53, 63, 67, 75–76, 115, 131, 157, 181, 184, 241, 244, 277n11&12, 279n31; Orientalist fantasies at, 48–49
utopianism, 1–7, 29, 32, 36, 39–43, 53, 55–57, 60, 66–67, 75–80, 94, 96, 115–17, 129, 136–38, 143–44, 169–70, 176, 183, 194, 196, 200, 211, 230–33, 241–42, 244, 248–49, 252, 271–72, 277n12, 280n42; utopian gesture, 271–72

value regimes, 3, 5, 6, 9, 15, 18–20
Van Zanten, David, 130
vaudeville theater, 51, 67; plays 204
Verdi, Giuseppe, 79
Vichy, 55, 83

Viollet-le-Duc, Eugène, 60, 280n48
Voilquin, Suzanne, 77–78
Volait, Mercedes, 15, 277n7, 296n45

al-Wafd, 154, 173
Wagh al-Birka, 97–98, 253, 301n9
Wanamaker (department store), 46, 52
Wertsch, James, 244–45
Whitely (department store), 28, 29
White Sale, 142, 144–45
Worlding, 18, 276n20; literature, 18
world literature, 4, 17–18
World War I, 42, 65, 86, 117, 179, 199, 229, 284n30
World War II, 43, 103, 152, 176, 179, 194, 195, 234, 237, 243, 247, 301n17

xenophobia, 111, 250

Yannakakis, Ilios, 3, 240–47, 259

Zaghloul, Safiyya, 173
Zaki Pacha, Ahmad, 27–34, 44, 68, 75, 76, 184, 276n1–2, 277n3–8
Zananiry, Nelly, 179–81
Zaynab, 182
al-Zayyat, Latifa, 3, 254–56
Zionism, 189, 190, 194–95, 230–31, 234, 257, 260–61, 264, 266–68
Zola, Émile, 3, 46, 55, 107–45, 150, 158, 171, 187, 200, 202, 207, 243–44, 246, 248, 249, 254

www.ingramcontent.com/pod-product-compliance
Ingram Content Group UK Ltd.
Pitfield, Milton Keynes, MK11 3LW, UK
UKHW021843140426
5217IPUK00022B/1568